THE PUBLIC
INTERNATIONAL
LAW OF MONEY

THE PUBLIC
INTERNATIONAL
LAW OF MONEY

BY

M. R. SHUSTER

LL.B; LL.M; D. PHIL. (OXON.)

OXFORD
AT THE CLARENDON PRESS
1973

Oxford University Press, Ely House, London W. 1

GLASGOW NEW YORK TORONTO MELBOURNE WELLINGTON
CAPE TOWN IBADAN NAIROBI DAR ES SALAAM LUSAKA ADDIS ABABA
DELHI BOMBAY CALCUTTA MADRAS KARACHI LAHORE DACCA
KUALA LUMPUR SINGAPORE HONG KONG TOKYO

*Printed in Great Britain
at the University Press, Oxford
by Vivian Ridler
Printer to the University*

PREFACE

THE preparation and completion of this work was only possible due to the kind assistance of many persons, including J. E. S. Fawcett, E. Patenia, G. Schwarzenberger and P. Shuster. A number of institutions also made contributions of varying kinds: Canada Council, Brasenose College, the Bodleian Law Library and the Clarendon Press.

The author expresses his gratitude and appreciation to them all.

CONTENTS

PART THREE

POST-FUND PERIOD: (B) REGIONAL AND BILATERAL MONETARY ARRANGEMENTS

ABBREVIATIONS

A.J.I.L.	*American Journal of International Law*
B.L.E.U.	Belgium, Luxembourg Economic Union
B.O.L.S.A.	*Bank of London and South America Review*
B.Y.I.L.	*British Year Book of International Law*
C.A.C.M.	Central American Common Market
CARIFTA	Caribbean Free Trade Association
C.F.A.	Communauté financière africaine
D.I.L.	*Digest of International Law*
E.M.A.	European Monetary Agreement
E.P.U.	European Payments Union
E.Y.	*European Yearbook*
F.C.N.	Treaties of Friendship, Commerce, and Navigation
F.C.S.C.	United States Foreign Claims Settlement Commission
F.D.	*Finance and Development*
G.A.B.	General Arrangements to Borrow
G.A.T.T.	General Agreement on Tariffs and Trade
I.B.R.D.	International Bank for Reconstruction and Development
I.C.J.	International Court of Justice
I.C.L.Q.	*International and Comparative Law Quarterly*
I.D.A.	International Development Association
I.E.T.	Interest Equalization Tax
I.F.C.	International Finance Corporation
I.L.M.	*International Legal Materials*
I.L.R.	*International Law Reports*
I.M.F.	International Monetary Fund
J.O.	*Journal officiel de la République française*
J.O.C.E.	*Journal officiel des Communautés européennes*
J.W.T.L.	*Journal of World Trade Law*
L.A.F.T.A.	Latin American Free Trade Association
L.N.T.S.	League of Nations Treaty Series
O.E.C.D.	Organization for Economic Co-operation and Development
O.E.E.C.	Organization for European Economic Co-operation
P.C.I.J.	Permanent Court of International Justice
R.C.	*Recueil des cours*, Académie de droit international de la Haye
U.N.C.T.A.D.	United Nations Conference on Trade and Development
U.N.T.S.	*United Nations Treaty Series*
W.L.R.	*Weekly Law Reports*
Y.L.J.	*Yale Law Journal*

The legal profession has generally treated international monetary policy as off limits. Although lawyers have now staked out a role in space development, computer technology, and other fields of yesterday's science fiction, the veil of monetary mystery still mutes even the blatant in other areas of public policy. Some may occasionally ask whether it makes much sense to take gold out of holes in South Africa and put it into holes in Fort Knox. Some may wonder if a few so-called central bankers really 'hold the balance of the world'—and if so, why. Some may even question whether the dollar should be 'as good as gold', rather than the reverse. But most appear to believe they can't possibly understand the international monetary system. As a result, lawyers rarely seem involved in the real issues of conflict that arise when the system constrains public policy objectives.

But 'international financial policy is too important to leave to financiers'. Institutional arrangements for ordering affairs are traditionally lawyers' business; it is time that lawyers became more involved in the arrangements for international monetary affairs.

'Legal Problems of International Monetary Reform',
20 *Stanford Law Review* (1968-2) p. 870.

INTRODUCTION

I

THE TERMS OF REFERENCE

1. *Definition*

FOR the purposes of this study the public international law of money can be defined as that set of rules established by international law which effects some degree of regulation and control over certain areas of a State's monetary affairs.[1] This definition can be further elucidated by (*a*) delimiting specifically some of the particular facets of a State's monetary affairs which are so regulated and (*b*) delimiting the sources of international law through which these rules are established. Turning our attention first to (*a*), that is, the delimitation of the facets of a State's monetary affairs which are the object of international legal regulation, the following, *inter alia*, can be listed as falling into this category: (i) currency valuation (exchange rates); (ii) exchange restrictions; (iii) correction of balance of payments disequilibria; and (iv) international liquidity.

(i) *Currency valuation.*[2] It is a well-established principle in both municipal and international law[3] that *jus cudendae monetae*[4] is one of the fundamental attributes of State sovereignty, which, as is pointed out by Fawcett, 'enables the State to issue money in defined units of account; to regulate its use as currency in the territory of the State, and in particular the conditions,

---

[1] Cf. Lazar Focsaneanu, 'Les aspects juridiques du système monétaire international', 95 *Journal du droit international* (1968) pp. 239–47.

[2] Below, pp. 24–7.

[3] F. A. Mann, *The Legal Aspect of Money* (2nd ed., 1953) pp. 13–16, 419.

[4] See *The Emperor of Austria* v. *Day and Kossuth* (1861), I *British International Law Cases*, p. 22 at 52: "The right of issuing notes for payment of money, as part of the circulating medium in Hungary, seems to follow from the *jus cudendae monetae* belonging to the supreme power in every state."

including rates, of its exchange there for foreign currencies . . .'[1]
This right of each State to determine unilaterally the value of
its basic monetary unit for the purposes of both the international
and the national money markets was in the period before the
end of the Second World War only marginally affected by
international law. In the post-war period, however, it will
be seen that States have significantly limited their freedom of
action in this sector of their international affairs through their
participation both in international arrangements of a global
nature, such as the International Monetary Fund (I.M.F.),[2]
one of whose stated purposes is 'To promote exchange stability,
to maintain orderly exchange arrangements among members,
and to avoid competitive exchange depreciation',[3] and in
various regional arrangements, such as the European Economic
Community (E.E.C.),[4] which prescribes in Article 107 (1) of the
Treaty of Rome that: 'Each Member State shall treat its policy
with regard to exchange rates as a matter of common interest.'

(ii) *Exchange restrictions.*[5] These have been defined as 'all
enactments which control the movement of currency, property
and services for the purpose of protecting the financial resources of a country'.[6] As such, they prima facie constitute an
integral part of a State's internal monetary policy and are
therefore considered to be matters of an essentially domestic
nature, beyond the pale of international regulation. During
the depression years of the 1930s and the war years of the 1940s,
however, when such restrictions were utilized by a large sector
of the community of nations with the resultant adverse impact
on international trade and payments, the need for some form
of international regulation of exchange restrictions became

[1] J. E. S. Fawcett, 'The International Monetary Fund and International
Law', 40 B.Y.I.L. (1964) p. 49.
[2] For text of this treaty in its original version, see *United Nations Monetary and
Financial Conference, Final Act, August 1944*, Cmd. 6546 or 2 U.N.T.S. 39. For the
text in its amended version, see *Special Drawing Rights in the International Monetary
Fund, June 1968*, Cmnd. 3662 or *Proposed Amendment of Articles of Agreement. A
Report by the Executive Directors to the Board of Governors* (I.M.F., Apr. 1968). This
Report is hereinafter simply referred to as *The Report* (1968).
[3] Art. 1, para. (iii).
[4] For text of this agreement see 298 U.N.T.S. 11.
[5] Below, pp. 27–37.
[6] F. A. Mann, 'Money in Public International Law', 96 R.C. (1959–I) p. 56.
For a more detailed discussion on the nature of exchange restrictions, see below,
pp. 30–4.

apparent. Consequently, since the early 1930s the regulation of exchange restrictions has been of major concern to the international community, and, indeed, it can be safely stated that it is in this area of a State's monetary sovereignty that international law, particularly in the past two decades, has made the greatest impact.

(iii) *Balance of payments*.[1] It will be shown that under the present regime as it is evolving, the correction of a disequilibrium in a country's balance of payments cannot be undertaken unilaterally and indiscriminately by the affected State, but must rather be undertaken within the framework of certain established rules.

(iv) *International liquidity*.[2] Liquidity is inextricably bound up with the adjustment process, its function being to ensure that the central monetary authority has sufficient reserve assets to enable temporary imbalances in foreign payments to be accommodated without undue strain while corrective adjustment measures are applied. Here again, however, before the end of the Second World War no attempt was made to regulate either the quantum or the nature of international reserve assets through the instrumentality of international law. Today, however, such regulation has, at both the global[3] and the regional (E.M.A.)[4] levels, become commonplace.

Examining next (*b*), that is, the sources of international law[5] through which these rules are established, one finds that of the three principal sources, international conventions, international customary law, and general principles of law recognized by civilized nations, the first, international conventions, is by far the most important. A careful examination reveals that an extensive network of international agreements has been concluded by States establishing monetary rules of varying scope and impact. From the I.M.F., which is at least potentially global in membership, through regional arrangements of a more limited scope such as the E.E.C., down to bilateral treaties such as those which fall under the general head of 'Treaties of Friendship, Commerce and Navigation', one finds

---

[1] Below, pp. 21–3. [2] Below, pp. 39–42.
[3] Below, pp. 198–226. [4] Below, pp. 261–3.
[5] For a general discussion of the sources of international law, see G. Schwarzenberger, *A Manual of International Law* (5th ed., 1967) pp. 26–35. See also J. G. Starke, *An Introduction to International Law* (6th ed., 1967) pp. 30–53.

that provisions prescribing a particular mode of behaviour for member States in their monetary affairs are more far-reaching and elaborate than is generally realized.[1]

The remaining two sources, international customary law and the general principles of law recognized by civilized nations, also provide rules of conduct, although to a much more limited extent. In this respect, the efficacy will be considered of principles such as *'abus de droit'*, 'non-discrimination', and 'the illegal interference with property rights of aliens', in providing a measure of protection against the arbitrary and indiscriminate manipulation of exchange rates and exchange restrictions.

It might be suggested that the above definition is incomplete in that it omits the consideration of certain relevant issues—for example, counterfeiting of a foreign State's currency, or duties of a belligerent occupant towards the occupied territory's monetary system. In the study of a discipline, however, which has only recently emerged and which is constantly and rapidly evolving, changes due to the emphasis and importance placed on one aspect of the subject-matter, often to the detriment of another, are bound to occur. Concerning the developments which had taken place in the short span of ten years from 1949 to 1959, Dr. F. A. Mann makes the following comment:

> The views expressed in these earlier publications sometimes differ from the suggestions made in the present lectures. The author confesses freely and without embarrassment that in so novel, ever-changing and rapidly developing a branch of the law a constant and critical re-examination of views is necessary and bound to lead to variations in opinion and emphasis.[2]

Consequently, while there is no doubt of the existence of a rule in international law forbidding the counterfeiting of a foreign State's currency[3] as well as of rules governing the mone-

---

[1] See, e.g., D. G. Carreau, 'The U.S. Balance of Payments Programs', 2 *Journal of World Trade Law* (1968) p. 642. For other sources, such as the rules evolved by the International Chamber of Commerce, see Fawcett, 'Trade and Finance in International Law', 123 R.C. (1968–I) pp. 219–23.

[2] F. A. Mann, 'Money in Public International Law', 96 R.C. (1959–I) p. 8 n. 2. See also I. S. Friedman, 'The International Monetary System', 10 *IMF Staff Papers* (1963) p. 219.

[3] In support of this rule see, *inter alia*, Vattel, 3 *The Law of Nations or the Principles of Natural Law*, translation of the edition of 1758 by C. G. Fenwick (1916) p. 46; L. Oppenheim, I *International Law* (8th ed., by Lauterpacht, 1955) p. 333; F. A. Mann, *The Legal Aspect of Money* (2nd ed., 1953) pp. 436–7; *The Emperor of*

tary conduct of a belligerent occupant power in the occupied territory,[1] these rules are of only tangential interest to the contemporary international monetary lawyer who is concerned with monetary problems of a far more fundamental nature. The problem today, as is suggested by the above definition, and substantiated by Article I of the International Monetary Fund Agreement, which sets out the 'purposes' of that organization, is 'to facilitate the expansion and balanced growth of international trade, and to contribute thereby to the promotion and maintenance of high levels of employment and real income'; 'to promote exchange stability, to maintain orderly exchange arrangements among members, and to avoid competitive exchange depreciation'; 'to assist in the establishment of a multilateral system of payments and in the elimination of foreign exchange restrictions which hamper the growth of world trade'; and 'to shorten the duration and lessen the degree of disequilibrium in the international balance of payments of members'.

Finally, inasmuch as this study is mainly concerned with the former, a distinction must be made between the public and the private international law of money. Only those rules which emanate from one of the three sources of international law enumerated above will be the subject of review. The relevant rules of private international law will not be considered. This distinction, however, is not a completely valid one, since States have by international agreement (Article VIII, Section 2 (*b*) of the Fund Agreement;[2] European Convention on

---

Austria v. *Day and Kossuth* (1861), I *British International Law Cases*, p. 22; *U.S.* v. *Arjona*, 120 U.S. 479 at 483 (1887); *International Convention for the Suppression of Counterfeiting Currency (with Protocols)*, 5 United Kingdom Treaty Series (1960), Cmnd. 932 or Hudson, IV *International Legislation* (1931) pp. 2692–709.

[1] For a discussion of this aspect of international monetary law, see L. Oppenheim, II *International Law* (7th ed., by Lauterpacht, 1952) pp. 437–8; A. Nussbaum, *Money in the Law National and International* (2nd ed., 1950) pp. 492–501; F. A. Mann, *The Legal Aspect of Money* (2nd ed., 1953) pp. 437–44.

[2] Material on this Article is particularly voluminous and the following references are, therefore, by no means exhaustive: A. Nussbaum, 'Exchange Control and the International Monetary Fund', 59 Y.L.J. (1949–50) pp. 421–30; B. S. Meyer, 'Recognition of Exchange Controls after the International Monetary Fund Agreement', 62 Y.L.J. (1952–3) pp. 867–910; F. A. Mann, 'The Private International Law of Exchange Control under the International Monetary Fund Agreement', 2 I.C.L.Q. (1953) pp. 97–107; P. R. Lachman, 'The Articles of Agreement of the International Monetary Fund and the Unenforceability of

Foreign Money Liabilities)[1] affected the substance of private international law as it pertains to money. To this extent, therefore, the private international law of money is determined by public international law and the two disciplines are not distinguishable. Even in these cases, however, although such international provisions will be noted, the changes in the private international law of money to which they give rise will not be examined, this being more properly the concern of the private rather than the public international lawyer.

2. Problems of Economic Terminology, Theory, and Sovereignty[2]

Unlike other branches of international law, the public international law of money, as it has been defined above, has as its primary objective the regulation of a very esoteric and elusive facet of international relations. It can readily be appreciated, for example, that the objects of regulation of the law of the sea which include the continental shelf, the territorial sea, etc., being legal concepts, that is, created and defined by and for the use of lawyers, are more readily accessible to the un-initiated international lawyer than are concepts such as, *inter alia*, exchange rates, exchange restrictions, balance of payments, international liquidity (conditional and unconditional), fundamental disequilibrium, etc., which constitute the objects of regulation of international monetary law but are economic rather than legal concepts, designed for the use not of lawyers but of economists.[3] Consequently, the international monetary

Certain Exchange Contracts', 2 *Nederlands tijdschrift voor internationaal recht* (1955) pp. 148–66; C. H. Alexandrowicz, *World Economic Agencies: Law and Practice* (1962) pp. 189–202; J. Gold, *The Fund Agreement in the Courts* (1962); F. D. Trickey, 'The Extraterritorial Effect of Foreign Control Laws', 62 *Michigan Law Review* (1964) pp. 1232–41.

[1] No. 60 in the European Treaty Series. See also I *Information Bulletin of the Directorate of Legal Affairs*, Council of Europe (Mar. 1969) p. 5.

[2] For a discussion of the interrelationship between international law and international economics, see W. Röpke, 'Economic Order and International Law', 86 R.C. (1954–II) pp. 207 ff.

[3] This point is succinctly stated by J. Gold, with respect to the Fund Agreement: 'It is not possible to understand or interpret the articles unless it is constantly kept in the mind that they are a legal document that regulates the activities of States in monetary and economic affairs ... Lawyers would be able to say with assurance what is meant by "libel", or "contingent remainders", or "consideration", but it is much less likely that they would be able to give confident definitions of "fundamental disequilibrium", or "competitive exchange alteration", or even

lawyer (unlike his counterpart concerned with the law of the sea, or the law of international institutions, etc.) is confronted with certain additional obstacles of a non-legal character which he must first surmount before he can even begin to grapple with the legal problems which are his immediate concern.

The first obstacle which must be overcome is that of becoming familiar with the meaning of certain economic concepts which, as mentioned above, lie at the very heart of the discipline with which he is concerned. Having satisfied, at least superficially, this requirement by referring to the texts of certain prominent economists,[1] the second obstacle which he must face at the outset is the realization and acceptance of the fact that his role in this area of international relations is a limited one. It is the function of the economist to deal with disputed economic policies (for example, fixed rates versus floating rates versus periodically adjustable par values), while the function of the lawyer is limited to providing the legal framework within which those economic policies can be most successfully implemented. In this respect, therefore, legal discipline must take second place to economic theory. Indeed, to adopt the opposite approach and to make economic policies the object of legal obligation without first ensuring that such obligations are economically viable would be to invite failure. So it has been asserted with regard to the international legal regulation of exchange rates that:

It would be a mistake to imagine that it would be sufficient to declare the parity relationships within the Union immutable by a legal act. If no action is taken to safeguard the actual economic basis for this measure, circumstances could well render it inapplicable, since decisions and developments in the national economies might affect the market in such a way as to make nonsense of legal undertakings.[2]

"discriminatory currency arrangements" or "multiple currency practices".' J. Gold, 'Interpretation by the International Monetary Fund of its Articles of Agreement II', 16 I.C.L.Q. (1967) pp. 293-4.

[1] In this respect the following general texts, *inter alia*, should be instructive: W. M. Scammell, *International Monetary Policy* (2nd ed., 1965); F. Hirsch, *Money International* (1967); B. Tew, *International Monetary Co-operation 1945-1965* (1965); R. Triffen, *Our International Monetary System Yesterday, Today, and Tomorrow* (1968).

[2] Dr. Hans von der Groeben, *European Monetary Policy—Towards the Gradual Establishment of a European Monetary System*, Commission of the European Communities (1968) p. 12.

and with regard to exchange controls that:

Law and treaty clauses can only try to be helpful in the step-by-step efforts to eliminate the economic conditions forcing countries to introduce and to hold on to exchange control and to keep the idea of equality in international trade relations alive meanwhile. Until these efforts are successful, all attempts to introduce a legal prohibition on discrimination in the form of a treaty clause which is too wide in scope and too strict in its application necessarily lead to a disregard of the law, and thus achieve results contrary to those intended.[1]

The relevance of these observations can be extended to all the other economic concepts under discussion in this study, and although it may be advantageous periodically to question the economist's approach in dealing with certain problems from the viewpoint of which is most susceptible to regulation by international law, the basic position stated above is not open to challenge.

Finally, there can be no doubt that the notion of economic sovereignty[2] (the monetary matters under discussion are an integral part of a State's economic sovereignty) constitutes the greatest single obstacle to the advance of any rules of law into the monetary sector of a State's activities. This is a difficulty which cannot be easily resolved:

One obvious fundamental aspect of the present system, like many other obvious fundamental facts, tends to be neglected: any system today must be based on the existence of national governments and national sovereignty . . . and any evaluation of a given system must make some assumption as to how far national governments are willing to go in creating supranational institutions and being regulated by supranational policies in the financial field, and, on the other hand, how far they wish to insist that their own financial policies and practices dominate the actions of others.[3]

This fundamental conflict between a State choosing to follow its own 'financial policies' on the one hand and 'being regulated by supranational policies' on the other stems directly from the

[1] W. A. Kewenig, 'Exchange Control, the Principle of Nondiscrimination and International Trade', 16 *Buffalo Law Review* (1967) p. 413.

[2] For a general discussion of economic sovereignty, see W. Röpke, op. cit., pp. 246–50; J. Fawcett, 'Trade and Finance in International Law', 123 R.C. (1968–I) pp. 242 ff. See also *Customs Regime Between Germany and Austria* (Advisory Opinion, 1931), P.C.I.J., ser. A/B, no. 41.

[3] I. S. Friedman, op. cit., pp. 220–1.

fact that (subject to express agreements to the contrary and to certain other rules of international customary law such as *abus de droit* and non-discrimination) a State possesses exclusive jurisdiction over its currency. In the often quoted words of the Permanent Court of International Justice: 'It is indeed a generally accepted principle that a State is entitled to regulate its own currency.'[1] Consequently, a State, as part of this right to regulate its own currency, is free to define unilaterally the value of its basic monetary unit for the purpose of foreign exchange transactions; moreover, it is free to vary that value either by devaluation or by revaluation, and if it finds it advantageous or necessary to do so, it is free either partially or completely to curtail foreign exchange transactions by the use of the exchange control mechanism. In support of this principle that a State possesses sovereignty over its currency and monetary affairs, ample evidence is available, and it is not necessary to expand upon this point at any great length.[2] What must be borne in mind, however, is the serious limitation which the operation of this principle places upon any attempts which purport to establish a supranational authority which has as its primary objective the regulation of some of those currency matters which now fall within a State's exclusive domestic jurisdiction. The general failure of the League of Nations to achieve, at various conferences convened under its auspices, any agreement on inter-State monetary and economic matters in the post-First World War period is evidence of the disruptive nature of this principle.[3] The reason for and the magnitude of this problem is forcefully set out by a noted international economist:

It is inevitable that individual nations in their approach to

[1] *The Serbian and Brazilian Loans Cases*, P.C.I.J., ser. A, nos. 20/21, p. 44. But this statement is subject to an important qualification (a point often overlooked by publicists), for the Court went on to say: 'The application of the laws of such State involves no difficulty so long as it does not affect the substance of the debt to be paid and does not conflict with the law governing such debt.'

[2] The literature confirming this principle is abundant. See, *inter alia*, I *Blackstone's Commentaries* (16th ed., 1825) p. 277; Vattel, op. cit., p. 45; Jean Bodin, *Six Books of the Commonwealth* (16th Century), abridged and translated by M. J. Tooley (Oxford, 1967) p. 47.

[3] For a discussion of the activities of the League of Nations in the area of international economic relations in the post-First World War period, see Hill, *The Economic and Financial Organization of the League of Nations* (1946).

international monetary planning should be influenced by their own economic aspirations. It is best to be realistic and to admit that unless a satisfactory answer can be given to the question 'what is there in this for us?' co-operation will be, at best, ephemeral. In any international gathering, be it *ad hoc* committee, conference, or permanent body, some means must be found of sinking divergent national policies in the general aims of the group. In an international institution for currency stabilisation the views of new countries, old countries, self-supporting and importing countries, primary producers and industrial producers, debtors and creditors, great powers and tiny states must all be fused. This is not an easy task. It is certain from time to time to involve sacrifice on somebody's part and an infinite genius for compromise.[1]

Although the task is not an easy one, and although States are not quick to submit their sovereign rights to the scrutiny of the international community, it is no exaggeration to say that some not unremarkable progress has been achieved in this volatile area of international relations since the end of the Second World War. Although, in terms of numbers, the rules of international law which have emerged in this period may be few, they are nevertheless of fundamental importance, in that they represent the first systematic and conscious attempt at regulating an increasingly important sphere of inter-State activity in which hitherto States had virtually complete free-dom of action. Moreover, the following observations, made by prominent international monetary lawyers, that 'it would be wrong to regard the present as more than the opening phase of a new era',[2] and that 'they [referring to the monetary rules of law established by the Fund Agreement] are perhaps only the first great move toward the development of international law in this field',[3] indicate that the role of international law as a regulatory force in this area of inter-State activity has only just begun to emerge. However, although this process has just begun, advances are being made and new areas of importance are continuously being subjected to legal regulation (the Special Drawing Rights Facility and the Basle facility for dealing with the sterling balances being the most recent),[4]

[1] Scammell, op. cit., pp. 8–9.

[2] F. A. Mann, 'Money in Public International Law', 96 R.C. (1959–I) p. 8.

[3] J. Gold, 'The International Monetary Fund and International Law: An Introduction', *I.M.F. Pamphlet Series* (1965) p. 11.

[4] Below, pp. 198–226 and 238–40 respectively.

so that the observation made twenty-five years ago by Sir John Fischer Williams, that legally, international economic relations were 'a sort of no-man's-land in which every side is free to do what it pleases',[1] has no validity today.

3. The International Legal Regulation of Money in Historical Perspective

(i) *Standardizing agreements*. Historically, the study of money, as an object of regulation by international law, reveals that international agreements of a monetary nature have existed since the days of the early Greek city-states *c.* 500 B.C. and perhaps earlier.[2] These early agreements, which have been referred to as 'standardizing agreements',[3] were primarily concerned with coins, that is, with metallic circulating media, and sought, as the term 'standardizing' would suggest, to establish a common standard of coinage with respect to metal, fineness, weight, form, impress, etc. among the signatories of the particular treaty regime in question.

In the monetary convention concluded about 400 B.C. between Phocaea and Mytilene,[4] for example, the two contracting parties agreed to issue electrum coins identical in weight and fineness, to accept the convention coins minted by each other as legal tender within their respective communities, and each city agreed to close its mint in each alternate year, allowing the other to supply all the required coins for that particular year (this was to ensure an equal division of profits). In fact, it is further mentioned by Burns that the issue of electrum coins assumed such great proportions that they 'developed into the international currency of the Western part of Asia Minor during the latter part of the 5th and throughout the 4th century B.C.'[4] The Scandinavian Monetary Union,

---

[1] As cited in Alexander Elkin, 'The European Monetary Agreement: its Structure and Working', 7 E. Y., p. 149.

[2] See A. R. Burns, *Money and Monetary Policy in Early Times* (1927) p. 95.

[3] This is an expression which seems to have been coined by A. Nussbaum. For an extensive and more detailed survey of these standardizing agreements, see the following three studies, all by Nussbaum: (i) *Money in the Law* (1939) pp. 153–7; (ii) 'International Monetary Agreements', 38 A.J.I.L. (1944) pp. 242–8; (iii) *Money in the Law National and International* (2nd ed., 1950) pp. 502–8. See also A. Nielsen, 'Monetary Unions', X *Encyclopedia of the Social Sciences* (London) pp. 595–601.

[4] Burns, op. cit., p. 92.

established on 27 May 1873 between Denmark and Sweden and later joined by Norway in 1875, which survived, although in modified form, until 1931, and the Latin Monetary Union (Union latine) established in 1865 between France, Belgium, Switzerland, and Italy, are illustrative of more recent standardizing agreements concluded between sovereign States.[1]

In the latter agreement, the standard coins of the union (which were modelled after domestic French coins in so far as weight, form, metal, tolerance, and diameter were concerned) were the gold 100, 50, 20, and 5 franc coins and the silver 5 franc coin, all of fineness of 9/10. Other smaller, subsidiary coins made of baser materials and paper money remained national, independent of the treaty. In order to assure circulation of the union currency, the Treasury of each member State was obliged to accept the convention coins in payment of debts. This obligation of receivability did not extend to the general public as a whole. In other words, the union moneys were legal tender only against the Treasury of each country, but not as between the nationals of the member countries. The union was to remain in force until 1900 and was automatically renewable for another fifteen-year period unless renounced at a year's notice. Although the founders of the union envisaged it as being the corner-stone of a future world-wide monetary union and correspondingly made provision in the agreement which allowed other States to join, the only country to do so was Greece, which joined in 1868. Other countries—the Papal State, Spain, the Balkan countries, and some of the Central American States—adopted the franc standard but did not formally adhere to the agreement. Difficulties soon arose for the union (as early as 1870, due to the depreciation of silver), and it finally succumbed to the aftermath of the First World War.

Since the demise of the Latin and Scandinavian monetary unions, no new standardizing agreements have been concluded. In any event, it is submitted that had such agreements been concluded, they would have been doomed to failure, or at best relegated to a position of only marginal importance,

---

[1] For a more detailed analysis of these two arrangements with extensive references, see A. Nussbaum, 'International Monetary Agreements', 38 A.J.I.L. (1944) pp. 242–57.

since monetary problems, as they have existed since the demise of the gold standard—that is, the arbitrary use of exchange restrictions and the random fluctuation of rates of exchange—required a new form of international co-operation for their solution. This is not to suggest, however, that the notion of a monetary union with common metallic coins circulating freely among the union's member States has been completely abandoned. Recent events in the European Economic Community would appear to suggest the opposite. At its session of 28 November to 2 December 1966, the European Parliament held a debate[1] on the Community's future activities in the field of monetary policy and on the possible creation of a European monetary union. During the debate it was suggested by the Parliamentary Committee that as one step towards the creation of a monetary union, coins of one and five 'Eurofrancs' be struck. It was further maintained that 'the exchange difficulties that might result did not appear insurmountable', and that such a move 'would certainly have a considerable psychological impact'. In support of this proposal the following Resolution was adopted by the European Parliament:

Résolution sur l'activité future de la Communauté dans le domaine de la politique monétaire et la création d'une union monétaire européenne.[2]

which includes, *inter alia*, the following provisions:

. . . vu les dispositions des articles 104 à 109 du traité instituant la Communauté économique européenne,

.   .   .

5. Recommande, comme premier pas vers une union monétaire européenne, de frapper des pièces de monnaie européennes ayant cours dans tous les pays de la Communauté;
6. Propose que ces pièces de monnaie européennes soient frappées par les États membres, auxquels le bénéfice de frappe serait réservé.[3]

---

[1] For a précis of this debate in English, see *EEC Bulletin* (Jan. 1967) p. 37. The desire to create a European currency unit was again reiterated on 13 May 1968, see *EEC Bulletin* (May 1968) p. 31.
[2] 9 *Journal officiel des Communautés européennes* (1966) p. 3911. For an English translation of this Resolution, see *EEC Bulletin* (Jan. 1967) p. 74.
[3] Ibid.

The similarity between the proposed Community monetary union and the convention concluded between the two Greek city-states, Phocaea and Mytilene, discussed above is of particular interest, if only as evidence of the age-old maxim that history repeats itself. In both instances the currency concerned is a metallic coin, which is to be struck in the mints of the respective member States, and which is to be accepted by all union members as legal tender in their respective territories. It would be a mistake, however, to conclude from the above similarity that monetary unions or convention metallic coins constitute by themselves some sort of panacea for contemporary monetary problems; indeed, a careful examination of the European Parliament's debate would indicate that the proposed minting of 'Eurofrancs' is regarded as being primarily of psychological value designed to strengthen the sense of unity within the community rather than being a monetary cure-all. Moreover, the opening sentence in the preamble to the Resolution—'vu les dispositions des articles 104 à 109 du traité instituant la Communauté économique européenne'— indicates the Parliament's awareness that the satisfactory resolution of the issues raised in those Articles is a necessary pre-condition for the development of a viable Community monetary policy, regardless of the form it ultimately assumes.

As has already been suggested, a detailed survey of standardizing agreements (monetary unions) is only of limited relevance to this study. It is, therefore, to the historical and economical evolution of the issues raised in Articles 104 to 109 of the Community Treaty, that is, the inter-State regulation of exchange rates and exchange restrictions, which it is submitted constitute the core of contemporary international monetary law, that we now direct our attention.

(ii) *The gold standard.* It is an established economic fact that 'the money flows of which a payments system consists are but the result of flows of goods and services which reflect the international specialisation which is the motivating force of all international trade'.[1] Conversely, one may deduce from this that the flow of goods and services across national frontiers is dependent upon the unfettered flow of payments for such goods and services. Consequently, if the free transfer of international

---

[1] Scammell, op. cit., p. 14.

payments is tampered with (that is, blocked or subjected to administrative technicalities which are in themselves restrictive), the flow of international trade is threatened and will be proportionately decreased or redirected according to the nature and severity of the restrictions so imposed. Similarly, if the means of payment—that is, currency—is subject to arbitrary fluctuations in value on the international money market, the resultant impact on international trade is very often detrimental.[1]

In the period before the outbreak of the First World War in 1914, and in a modified form in the period 1925–31, the unfettered flow of international payments and currency stability were maintained under the auspices of the gold standard regime[2] which, it has been suggested, represented 'the first clear instance of an organized international monetary and financial system'.[3] The gold standard regime rested on two basic legal undertakings. (It should be noted, however, that both these undertakings emanated from municipal rather than from international rules of law.) First, the national currency unit of each gold standard country was defined by law in terms of a specified quantity of gold. Exchange rates of gold standard countries were thus defined through the medium of gold. Secondly, the monetary authorities of all countries on the gold standard were legally obliged to give on demand unlimited amounts of gold of a defined quality in exchange for paper currency and vice versa at the fixed exchange rate. For example, before 1914, and from 1925 to 1931, when the United Kingdom was on the gold standard, the Bank of England was under statutory obligation to sell to any person, against payment in legal tender, gold bullion at the price of £3. 17s. 10½d. per standard oz. of gold, 11/12 fine.[4] Similarly, the United

---

[1] For a discussion of the negative impact which currency instability has had and continues to have on international trade and investment, see A. M. Strong, 'Minimizing Monetary Risks in Foreign Trade', *University of Illinois Law Forum* (1959) pp. 355–63.

[2] For a more detailed survey of the gold standard, see, *inter alia*, R. G. Hawtry, *The Gold Standard in Theory and Practice* (1927). See also G. N. Halm, *International Monetary Cooperation* (1945) pp. 11–24.

[3] S. Horie, *The International Monetary Fund Retrospect and Prospect* (1964) p. 1.

[4] Sect. 6 of the Bank of England Act, 1833 (3 & 4 Will. IV, ch. 98). Under Subsect. 2 of Sect. 1 of the Gold Standard Act, 1925 (15 & 16 Geo. V, ch. 29) the Bank was obliged to sell only gold bars of approximately 400 oz. of fine gold to any purchaser who tendered £3. 17s. 10½d. per standard ounce of gold. Subsect. 2 of

States Treasury bought and sold gold at $20.67 per fine oz.[1] Accordingly, the 'mint rate' of exchange between the dollar and sterling was determined by comparing the gold value of the dollar with the gold value of the pound sterling. The market rates of exchange tended to fluctuate narrowly around this figure. They were determined by the supply of and demand for the two currencies on the exchange markets. If the demand for dollars increased relatively to that for sterling, the value of sterling in terms of dollars tended to fall, that is, the price of dollars in terms of sterling tended to rise. At some point it would pay British merchants, with debts to settle in the United States, to buy gold at the Bank of England at the fixed rate and send it to the United States instead of sending the now more expensive dollars. The costs of transporting gold (freight, insurance, etc.) were borne by the debtor, so that the exchange rate in London would never rise above the mint parity exchange rate plus the cost of exporting gold. At this upper rate of exchange further pressure would simply cause more gold to move out of the country. The exchange rate at which it became more profitable to export gold rather than paper currency came to be known as the 'gold export point', while the 'gold import point' was the exchange rate at which it became profitable to import gold. Accordingly, under the gold standard regime, the rates of exchange between any two currencies did not fluctuate outside the gold points—that is, the rates at which it became profitable to import or export gold bullion. Moreover, from the viewpoint of balance of payments disequilibrium, the gold standard system operated in such a way that the movement of gold between countries tended automatically to set in motion a series of correctives, thus making it unnecessary for the country suffering from the deficit to take other less desirable steps— for example, altering its rate of exchange or resorting to direct controls.[2] Briefly, the supply of money in a gold standard

Sect. 1 of the Gold Standard Act, 1925 was repealed by Subsect. 2 of Sect. 1 of the Gold Standard Amendment Act, 1931 (21 & 22 Geo. V, ch. 46), and so the Bank was relieved of its duty to sell gold for the notes issued by it.

[1] For a more detailed analysis of the legal aspects of the dollar, see A. Nussbaum, 'The Law of the Dollar', 37 *Columbia Law Review* (1937) pp. 1057–91.

[2] Consequently, as pointed out by R. N. Cooper, 'National Economic Policy in an Interdependent World Economy', 76 Y.L.J. (1967–2) p. 1276: 'In the four decades before World War I most of the major countries were on the gold standard

country was linked to the supply of gold.[1] Since an increase in a country's gold holdings (surplus country) exerted an expansionary influence on the money supply, and a decrease in a country's gold holdings (deficit country) exerted a restrictive influence, gold movements tended to harmonize price and cost relationships among the various countries and thus tended to restore equilibrium in the balance of payments.[2]

Consequently, the gold standard served three important functions in international monetary relations: (i) it assured the stability of exchange rates, often to the detriment of internal economic stability—that is, through high domestic unemployment; (ii) it provided the mechanism through which balance of payments disequilibrium would be adjusted; and (iii) it made possible an unrestricted multilateral interchange of payments, since under the gold standard the currencies of all member countries were freely convertible into one another and into gold. If, for example, a trader in country X had to make a payment to a creditor in country Y, he could pay either in his own currency, in the currency of the creditor, or in the currency of a third country. The creditor in country Y would have no hesitation in accepting the currency of country X, or that of any third country in the settlement of the debt since, all currencies being freely interchangeable either for gold or for other currencies, he could in turn utilize the currency so acquired as he saw fit.

Under such a system, all that was required of any country was that its balance of payments in the aggregate, that is, its total payments to and from all other countries, be equalized. Such a system enabled all States to import goods and services on the basis of commercial considerations, that is, on the basis of price, quality, availability, marketability, and other conditions of purchase and sale, and similarly it enabled all States to export their goods and services to those markets which

---

(implying fixed exchange rates) most of the time, capital was free to move into or out of most countries, trade was impeded only by comparatively moderate tariffs and quotas were generally absent.' See also W. A. Kewenig, op. cit., p. 389.

[1] In the United States the statutory link between gold and the domestic money supply was finally abolished in 1968. See 12 U.S.C. § 413 (Supp. II, 1965–6), *repealed*, Act of 18 Mar. 1968, Pub. L. no. 90–269.

[2] For a more detailed explanation of the automatic adjustment process, see G. N. Halm, op. cit., p. 12.

offered the best conditions. In both cases, importing and exporting, the issue of the means of payment presented no difficulty.

During the latter part of the nineteenth century and the early part of the twentieth, the above international economic mechanism functioned satisfactorily. The First World War, however, produced a disruptive change in the world economic order in that the gold standard from that period onwards, apart from a brief interlude in the late twenties (1925–31), lost its control in regulating the international economy. The death-blow was struck in 1931, when the United Kingdom abandoned the gold standard, thereby allowing the true external sterling exchange rate to be determined by the free interplay of market forces. This resulted in a devaluation of the pound sterling (which had been previously over-valued in relation to gold and other currencies) and in turn triggered off a world-wide chain reaction of competitive currency depreciations and various other protectionist devices such as multiple rates, fluctuating exchange rates, and direct controls. By 1933, except for the final stubborn effort of the European 'gold bloc',[1] nothing resembling the gold standard remained.

Historically, therefore, it is from the beginning of 1914 and in particular since the early 1930s that international law began to assume a place of importance in this area of international relations. Before that period there was little or no incentive for it to develop (this is subject to a few exceptions which will be discussed in the following two chapters), since the international monetary system, as illustrated above, operated quite satisfactorily under the gold standard regime which, it should be pointed out, was based on an 'economic ideology rather than on an international legal set-up'.[2] Rules of international law,

---

[1] The 'gold bloc' was established in 1933 by France, Belgium, Switzerland, Italy, Poland, and the Netherlands. These countries declared their intention of continuing to adhere to the operation of the gold standard at the existing parities and within the framework of the existing laws. Poland, Italy, and Belgium abandoned the 'bloc' in 1934. France, the Netherlands, and Switzerland followed suit in 1936. See A. Nussbaum, *Money in the Law National and International* (2nd ed., 1950) p. 511.

[2] Opinion on the point, however, is divided. See C. H. Alexandrowicz, *World Economic Agencies* (1962) p. 168; W. Röpke, op. cit., pp. 225, 259; A. Elkin, op. cit., p. 150; F. Hirsch, op. cit., pp. 27–8, and E. P. Hexner, 'Worldwide International Economic Institutions', 61 *Columbia Law Review* (1961–I) p. 355. On the

like rules of municipal law, evolve in response to those social and environmental conditions which are prevalent in a community at any given point in time, and the development of international monetary law is no exception. Consequently, in tracing the growth of international monetary law, one is able to trace simultaneously with this growth a parallel and opposite occurrence, that is, the demise of the gold standard regime. It is for this reason that a knowledge of the gold standard and the mechanism which it generated is of fundamental importance for a proper understanding of the development of international law in this sector of inter-State economic affairs. Moreover, it is submitted that this development from international comity[1] to international treaty law will continue and ultimately culminate in the establishment of some general principles of international customary law.[2] This possibility will be explored more fully in the concluding chapter of this book.

other hand, see Fawcett, 'Trade and Finance in International Law', 123 R.C. (1968–I) pp. 245–6; Scammell, op. cit., p. 11, and R. A. Mundell, 'The International Monetary Fund', 3 J.W.T.L. (1969) p. 457.

[1] Schwarzenberger, *A Manual of International Law* (5th ed., 1967) p. 4.

[2] The notion that such a development is in fact taking place has been put forward by Fawcett, 'The International Monetary Fund and International Law', 40 B.Y.I.L. (1964) p. 54. See similarly Starke, *An Introduction to International Law* (6th ed., 1967) pp. 319–24.

II

THE OBJECTS OF REGULATION

> In the modern age of economic and political inter-
> dependence most questions which, on the face of it,
> appear to be essentially domestic are, in fact, essentially
> international.
>
> H. LAUTERPACHT, 'The International Protection
> of Human Rights', 70 R.C. (1947) p. 25.

1. *Introduction*

IN Chapter I were enumerated, together with a brief description thereof, the principal economic concepts which constitute the international monetary system. In this chapter these
concepts will be examined in greater detail with the intention of defining them more positively and so making them
more comprehensible to the uninitiated lawyer. In doing so,
it will be necessary to draw upon economic as well as legal
sources.

Since many of these concepts have been incorporated into
contemporary commercial and economic treaties, it is possible
to arrive at a fairly comprehensive, legally orientated definition.
However, where it is either advantageous (for the sake of clarity)
or necessary (owing to the lack of legal documentation) to do so,
reference will be made to economic texts. In all instances,
however, preference where possible will be given to legal
definition.

Finally, it should be reiterated that no attempt will be made
at theoretical economic analysis, this being more properly
the concern of the economist. Rather the approach will be
mainly a descriptive one. In turn, the concepts to be described
are: (i) balance of payments; (ii) monetary unit of account;
(iii) direct controls; (iv) domestic economic policies; and (v)
international liquidity.

2. The Balance of Payments[1]

The general economic framework. The various factors of production—that is, labour, natural resources, and capital—differ among the world's several national economies with the result that one country A, due to its particular type of climate or capital resources, or the special talents of its population, will be a more appropriate producer of one type of commodity X, while another country B will, for similar reasons, excel in the production of commodity Y. Under such conditions, it is more advantageous for country A to specialize in the production of commodity X (at the expense of not producing commodity Y), to export any excess production thereof, and with the proceeds to import commodity Y from country B.[2] In actual practice, such an international exchange of goods and services is carried out on a multilateral level and in respect of a multitude of commodities; that is to say, A exports to and imports from not only B, but a large number of other countries, and in respect of a wide range of products.

Such an interchange, however, necessitates an international payments system and is only possible to the extent that payments in respect of such transactions can be freely made from country to country. Transactions which are not paid for have little chance of being repeated. Governments will not normally interfere with these payments so long as the country's balance of payments (a country's balance of payments being defined as 'a systematic record of the economic transactions during a given period between its residents and residents of the rest of the world')[3] is, over a certain selected period, in equilibrium. This does not mean, however, that every country

[1] For a more detailed examination of a country's balance of payments, together with a breakdown of the various items of which a balance of payments statement is composed and an explanation thereof, see F. Hirsch, op. cit. pp. 47 ff.; B. J. Cohen, *Balance of Payments Policy* (1969); P. Høst-Madsen, 'What Does it Really Mean?—Balance of Payments', F.D. (Mar. 1966) pp. 31–40; id., 'What Does it Really Mean?—A Deficit in the Balance of Payments', 3 F.D. (Sept. 1966) pp. 171–8.

[2] The theoretical economic basis upon which international trade rests is known as the 'Theory of Comparative Costs'. For a succinct explanation of this theory, see Hirsch, op. cit. pp. 44–6.

[3] *Balance of Payments Manual* (3rd ed., 1961) p. 2. For other definitions, see James K. Weeks, 'The Cross of Gold: United States Trade and Travel Restrictions and Monetary Crisis', 19 *Syracuse Law Review* (1967–8) p. 871, and Robert A. Mundell, 'The International Monetary Fund', 3 J.W.T.L. (1969) p. 466.

must be in payments equilibrium with every other country on a bilateral basis, or that material equilibrium must be achieved in each accounting period. Country A may, for example, have a payments deficit with country B, but so long as A is in 'over-all' payments equilibrium, it will have a payments surplus with some other country C, which surplus (assuming currency convertibility and multilateral payments settlement) it will be able to utilize in offsetting its deficit with B. If, on the other hand, A does, in fact, suffer from an over-all payments deficit in any period, it can meet this deficit (assuming that the deficit is not persistent or, in the terminology of the Fund Agreement, the disequilibrium is not 'fundamental',[1] in which case more permanent corrective measures are required) by resorting to its gold and foreign currency reserves or by being granted credit facilities by countries in surplus. For the system to operate satisfactorily, all that is required is that A's balance of payments be in material equilibrium over a certain selected period.

If the condition of material equilibrium described above prevails not only in respect of A's international transactions, but also in respect of all other nations, so that there is equality between the total payments which every country makes to and receives from all other countries, a regime of multilateral payments and currency convertibility will be maintainable. Under such ideal conditions international trade will flourish, traders will buy and sell on the basis of commercial considerations only, and State intervention will be at a minimum. Payments being no obstacle, exporters from country A or any other country will accept payment from an importer of country B in the currency of B or in any other currency since the importer will, on his part, be able to transfer those funds freely, and the exporter will, on his part, be able to convert those earnings freely into any other currency of which he may have need at any future date.

The above regime of multilateral payments and currency convertibility will function satisfactorily, however, only as long as multilateral payments equilibrium is maintained, and it comes into jeopardy if that equilibrium is disrupted. If,

---

[1] Art. IV, Sect. 5 (a) of the Fund Agreement reads: 'A member shall not propose a change in the par value of its currency except to correct a fundamental disequilibrium.'

for example, country A should suffer from a deficit in its material balance and if the deficit is of such a persistent nature that the gap cannot be met by means of accommodation financing, then A, in order to restore the situation—according to current economic theory—will have to resort to one of the following corrective mechanisms or a combination thereof: (*a*) Exchange rate alteration—that is, by reducing the value of the domestic currency in terms of foreign currencies, exports will become cheaper and therefore increase while imports will become more expensive and tend to decrease. The result will be an improvement in the balance of payments. (*b*) Introduce direct controls—that is, by regulating foreign currency transactions through the imposition of exchange controls or by directly regulating the flow of goods by the imposition of commercial controls, such as quantitative restrictions, it is possible to eliminate a payments deficit by limiting the quantity of goods which are allowed to enter the restricting country to a quantity equal in value to the proceeds arising out of current export sales. In this way, current expenditure on imports will equate current earnings from exports and equilibrium will be maintained. (*c*) Introduce internal economic measures designed to change the domestic price and income structure— that is, by—*inter alia*—reduction of the internal income level, total demand for imports would be reduced, and by the reduction of internal prices, exports would increase, thereby tending to produce a favourable balance. (*d*) A fourth device, although not corrective in nature, but complementary to the others, is the official financing by the State of the deficit from its store of international reserve assets. These reserve assets which are normally in the form of gold, United States dollars, special drawing rights, and other currencies will be made available to the foreign exchange market by the Central Bank, Treasury, or other appropriate body whenever there is an imbalance between the supply and demand of its currency *vis-à-vis* other currencies which threatens to disrupt the established rate of exchange.

It is with the regulation of the use by States of these devices (which, as is apparent from the brief description given above, have an extraterritorial effect when resorted to) that international monetary law is in the main concerned.

3. *Monetary Unit of Account*[1]

(i) *Definition.* The sovereignty of the State in monetary affairs implies the competence to fix the unit which constitutes the basis of its monetary system—for example, the dollar, mark, franc, pound, peso, rouble, etc. This basic unit is commonly referred to as the monetary unit of account and is designated as such either by municipal legislation as with the Canadian dollar:

3 (1) The monetary unit of Canada is the dollar.

(2) The denominations of money in the currency of Canada are dollars, cents and mills, the cent being one one-hundredth of a dollar and the mill one-tenth of a cent.[2]

by international law as with the CFA franc:

Article 5. L'unité monétaire légale des États signataires est le franc de la Communauté financière africaine.[3]

by custom and usage as with the pound sterling:

It appears that the 'pound' or 'pound sterling' has been accepted by usage as the monetary unit of the United Kingdom, but that the 'pound' has not been designated by statute as the monetary unit.[4]

Moreover, having designated for example, the 'dollar' as the basic unit of account and determined the multiples and fractions of such unit, for example cents and mills, the unit is then further defined either in terms of gold, in terms of another monetary unit, or in terms of a previous basic monetary unit. More particularly, from the viewpoint of international law, all States which are members of the International Monetary Fund are obliged by the terms of Article IV, Section 1 of the Fund Agreement to define their basic monetary unit either 'in terms of gold as a common denominator or in terms of the United States dollar of the weight and fineness in effect on July 1, 1944'. In Fund parlance, this relationship between the member's currency and gold is known as the par value and

[1] For a more detailed discussion of this fundamental aspect of all municipal monetary systems, see H. Aufricht, 'The Fund Agreement and the Legal Theory of Money', 10 *Österreichische Zeitschrift für öffentliches Recht* (1959–60) pp. 26–45; H. Aufricht, *Comparative Survey of Central Bank Law* (1965) pp. 53–64; F. A. Mann, *The Legal Aspect of Money* (2nd ed., 1953) pp. 3–57.

[2] Sect. 3 of Currency, Mint and Exchange Fund Act (R.S., 1952, c. 315).

[3] Traité instituant une Union Monétaire Ouest-Africaine. The text of this treaty in French is reproduced in *La Zone franc en 1961*, pp. 445–7. For the text in English, see 90 *Journal du droit international* (1963) pp. 871–3.

[4] H. Aufricht, *Comparative Survey of Central Bank Law* (1965) p. 54.

is the basis for determining the rates of exchange for transactions among member States.

(ii) *The monetary unit and rates of exchange.* Since the international monetary system lacks a monetary unit of its own, payments between States for goods, services, and capital movements must be made in national monetary units (normally in U.S. dollars or pounds sterling). It is necessary, therefore, to bring the various monetary units into relationship with one another through a system of exchange rates. Thus, where the price of the monetary unit of account of country A is defined in terms of the monetary unit of account of country B, the resultant price is known as the 'rate of exchange' or the 'foreign exchange rate'. For Fund members, it will be seen that the rate of exchange is allowed to fluctuate within very narrow margins (Article IV, Section 3) of the established par value (Article IV, Section 1). For other than Fund members, assuming the absence of other regional or bilateral treaty arrangements, the rate is generally determined by the interplay of governmental policy and normal market forces.

(iii) *Depreciation, devaluation, appreciation, revaluation.* Exchange rates are not immutable. Indeed, when viewed in their historical perspective, fluctuations in the rates of exchange of certain currencies have been particularly violent.[1] According to its nature, a change in a currency's rate of exchange can be classified as resulting from a depreciation, devaluation, appreciation, or revaluation. Although the first two and the last two concepts are often interchangeably used by economists, from the viewpoint of international monetary law[2] and therefore for the purposes of this book, the four concepts are considered as representing four distinct forms of exchange rate alteration.

---

[1] '. . . currency devaluation is not a stranger to the world—debased currencies have been known since the time of Nero (A.D. 54–68) and 112 currencies since World War II have undergone one or more devaluations', James K. Weeks, 'The Cross of Gold: United States Trade and Travel Restrictions and Monetary Crisis', 19 *Syracuse Law Review* (1967–8) p. 872.

[2] The distinction adopted for the purposes of this paper is also adopted by the International Monetary Fund. See J. Gold, 'Maintenance of the Gold Value of the Fund's Assets', *I.M.F. Pamphlet Series* (1965) p. 2. A similar distinction is made by Fawcett, 'Trade and Finance in International Law', 123 R.C. (1968–I) p. 248; Aufricht, 'The Fund Agreement and the Legal Theory of Money', 10 *Österreichische Zeitschrift für öffentliches Recht* (1959–60) p. 42 n. 52; B. A. Wortley, *Expropriation in Public International Law* (1959) pp. 47–50. See also Tabar Claim (No. 1) (1953), I.L.R., p. 211 at 212, where the United States International Claims Commission makes a similar distinction.

Depreciation is primarily an economic phenomenon characterized by 'loss of purchasing power in the market of exchange or goods or both'[1] and is 'a continuous and ever changing process'[1] fashioned by economic forces. Devaluation is a legislative phenomenon characterized by 'the fixation of the ratio between gold and the monetary unit on a lower level, designed to create a lasting situation'.[1] In this respect, therefore, it can be said that the pound sterling, before 18 November 1967, was depreciating (although only to the lower limits permitted by Article IV, Section 3 (1) of the Fund Agreement) due to pressures created by speculation, and that this continuous and ever-changing process ultimately culminated in devaluation, whereby the value of the pound sterling was officially reduced in terms of gold and the United States dollar by the British Government. Devaluation in this sense is but the end-result of depreciation.

On the other hand, appreciation is the increase, under economic forces, in the purchasing power of the currency, or in its exchange for other currencies, while revaluation is the increase by legislative act of the parity rate. Examples of appreciation and revaluation are rare, one of the most recent being that of the Federal Republic of Germany which for a short period in September–October 1969 allowed the D-mark to appreciate in response to normal market forces—that is, to float. On 26 October 1969 the West German Government officially reduced the dollar parity of the German mark from 4·00 to 3·66 marks per 1 U.S. dollar, which is tantamount to a revaluation of approximately 9·3 per cent. In this case, the revaluation was but the end-result of the previous appreciation.[2]

(iv) *Gold clauses*.[3] To protect against the adverse effects of

[1] A. Nussbaum, *Money in the Law* (1950) p. 172.

[2] See the *Financial Times*, 25 Oct. 1969, p. 1. In March 1961, the Federal Republic of Germany reduced the dollar parity of the German mark from 4·20 to 4·00, which is tantamount to a revaluation of approximately 5 per cent; the Netherlands similarly reduced the dollar parity of the Dutch guilder from 3·800 to 3·620. See *I.M.F. Schedule of Par Values*, thirtieth and thirty-first issues, and *European Economic Community Bulletin* (Mar. 1961) p. 32. As a result of the 18 Dec. 1971 currency realignment, certain major currencies including the mark and yen will be revalued.

[3] For a more detailed discussion of the juridical and economic aspects of gold and other protective clauses, see G. R. Delaume, *Legal Aspects of International Lending and Economic Development Financing* (1967) pp. 257–89; Nussbaum, *Money in the Law* (2nd ed., 1950) pp. 223–309, 414–45; Mann, *Legal Aspect of Money* (2nd ed., 1953) pp. 103–34, 256–70.

currency fluctuations, it was, before 1931, common practice to incorporate gold and other protective clauses into long-term contracts (both of a domestic and of an international nature) such as mortgage deeds, life insurance policies, and loan bonds. By tying the substance of the debt to the relatively stable value of gold, creditors are afforded a measure of protection against currency fluctuation, because the debtor when making repayment has to provide gold of the same weight or currencies whose value is approximately equal to the amount of wealth, measured in terms of its gold value, which he originally received from, or owed to, his creditor. For example, the government of a country which has in the past frequently devalued its currency may find it difficult to borrow on the capital markets of the world unless the loan contains a 'gold clause', which offers lenders the security of repayment in terms of the gold equivalent of the currency at the time the loan was floated. Thus in such cases, if by the date of redemption the currency has fallen to only half as much in terms of gold as when the loan was issued, repayment will be made at double the amount of the currency that was borrowed.[1] As mentioned, before 1931 such clauses were frequently inserted into both national and international contracts. Following the economic disturbances generated by the First World War and by the 1931 depression, the use of such clauses was prohibited in most countries by abrogating legislation.[2] Inasmuch as such legislation abolishes the protection afforded to foreign nationals and other States, in private and public international law contracts respectively, the legality of such action from the viewpoint of international law comes into question. This issue will accordingly be considered in Chapter III of this study.

4. Direct Controls

(i) *General nature.* Direct controls, as the term itself suggests, are governmental legislative or administrative acts which interfere with the free international flow of goods, services, or

---

[1] In this respect see a study by the U.N.C.T.A.D. Secretariat entitled *International Monetary System—Issues Relating to Development Finance and Trade of Developing Countries*, TD/3/198, 23 Oct. 1968, p. 8.

[2] For a complete list of the countries which abrogated gold clauses in the post-First World War and post-1931 periods with references to the abrogating legislation, see A. Nussbaum, *Money in the Law* (2nd ed., 1950) pp. 280–3.

capital. They are normally imposed by a State for one of three reasons: (a) to correct a balance of payments disequilibrium by allowing only that amount of imports of goods and services and outflows of capital as can be financed by earnings from exports of goods and services and inflows of capital; (b) to protect national production by prohibiting the free entry into the domestic market of like foreign products; and (c) to prohibit nationals from trading with certain States for politically motivated reasons.

Owing to the multiplicity of such controls—virtually every country imposes some form of direct control—it is impossible to describe, country by country, all the various systems currently in force.[1] In any event, various studies of this nature have been undertaken, and it is to these that anyone requiring more specific information is referred.[2] Nevertheless, for a proper understanding of the current international legal regulation with respect to the introduction, use, and administration of direct controls, certain basic distinctions have to be made— for example, trade versus financial controls, capital versus current transactions, exchange control versus exchange restriction, etc. These and other related matters will now be briefly considered.

(ii) *Trade and financial controls.* Direct controls fall into two basic categories, financial or trade, and are classified as financial controls if they affect the means of payment for an international transaction, and as trade controls if they affect the underlying transaction itself. From an economic viewpoint the distinction is not an important one, since

In its effects exchange control on payments may correspond closely to quotas or prohibitions on the import of goods, since foreign currencies are bought *inter alia* as a preliminary to buying foreign goods. Hence restrictions on the purchase of foreign currencies can be made to reduce imports of goods just as effectively as import restrictions, while conversely restrictions on imports are an effective device for curtailing the demand for foreign currencies. Thus it is

---

[1] But note the observation made by F. A. Mann, *Legal Aspect of Money* (2nd ed., 1953) p. 335: 'In their kernel the exchange control regulations of the world are identical, though they may differ in detail . . .'

[2] See, *inter alia*, H. S. Ellis, *Exchange Control in Central Europe* (1941). For an account on a country-by-country basis of past and existing controls, see the various Reports on Exchange Restrictions published by the I.M.F. (1950 to date).

frequently only a matter of administrative convenience whether a given aim is attained by exchange control or by import quotas or prohibition.[1]

From the legal viewpoint, however, the distinction is of some significance. Indeed, in the *Case Concerning Rights of Nationals of the United States of America in Morocco*,[2] the International Court of Justice 'confirmed that exchange controls and import controls, even though from the economic point of view they may be complementary measures, remain juridically distinct.'[3] And although this aspect of the Court's decision has—rightly—been criticized[4] on the basis that the Court failed to take cognizance of the fact that in their economic effect exchange and import controls are identical, the distinction is nevertheless a fundamental one when one views money as the object of international organization. The approach has, in the main, been to treat trade and financial controls as separate issues requiring separate regulation. Thus, the International Monetary Fund is concerned only with the regulation of financial restrictions on trade, while the G.A.T.T. is concerned with the regulation of commercial restrictions on trade. But even here the distinctions are not watertight. So it is provided in Article XV, paragraph 4 of the G.A.T.T. that the 'Contracting parties shall not, by exchange action, frustrate the intent of the provisions of this Agreement, nor, by trade action, the intent of the provisions of the Articles of Agreement of the International Monetary Fund'. Moreover, the G.A.T.T.,[5] as do the E.F.T.A.[6] and several other regional economic arrangements,[7] permits the imposition of quantitative restrictions as a temporary corrective device whenever a member State is faced with sudden balance of payments difficulties. In keeping with the approach adopted

---

[1] B. Tew, op. cit., p. 27.   [2] I.C.J. Reports (1952) p. 176.

[3] D. H. N. Johnson, 'The Case Concerning Rights of Nationals of the United States of America in Morocco', 29 B.Y.I.L. (1952) p. 422.

[4] See Johnson, op. cit., pp. 401–23; F. A. Mann, 'Money in Public International Law', 96 R.C. (1959–I) pp. 56-62; J. E. S. Fawcett, 'The International Monetary Fund and International Law', 40 B.Y.I.L. (1964) pp. 60–3; A. De Laubadère, 'Le statut international du Maroc et l'arrêt de la Cour internationale de justice du 27 août 1952', 6 *Revue juridique et politique de l'Union française* (1952) pp. 429 ff.

[5] Art. XII.

[6] Art. 19 of the Convention establishing the E.F.T.A.; 370 U.N.T.S. 18.

[7] See, *inter alia*, Art. 5 of the Australia–New Zealand Trade Agreement, 5 I.L.M. (1966) p. 307; Art. 18 of the Convention establishing a free trade area between the United Kingdom and the Republic of Ireland, Cmnd. 2858.

by international organizations, this study will concentrate on an analysis of the international legal regulation of financial controls. To the extent, however, that commercial controls are utilized for balance of payments reasons or are otherwise inextricably bound up with the international monetary system, they too will be the object of analysis.

(iii) *Exchange control.* The principal form of direct financial intervention is the exchange control mechanism. Under a system of free exchange, residents of a country are free to buy and sell currencies on the foreign exchange markets for any purpose—that is, trade, travel, speculation, etc.—and in any amount. In practice, however, such a completely *laissez-faire* system is non-existent because all countries, for some reason or other, and to a greater or lesser extent, engage in, and therefore control, market operations. The control may be limited—for example, traders may, for statistical purposes, simply be required to notify all exchange transactions to the designated governmental body. (In almost all countries the official agency charged with intervening in the foreign exchange markets is either the central bank or an off-shoot of the Treasury or Finance Ministry. For convenience, in this study, the competent authority will be referred to as 'official agency'.) Or the official agency may itself periodically buy and sell currencies or gold on the foreign exchange markets whenever it is necessary to maintain the exchange rate within the permitted margins. Or the control may be comprehensive, so that all purchases and sales of foreign exchange—that is, in respect of both current and capital transactions (this distinction will be examined further below)—are handled by the official agency. Under such a regime, any resident wishing to purchase foreign currency for any purpose can do so only through the official agency, and any resident who wishes to exchange any foreign currency earned as a result of export sales for the currency of the State in which he is resident can only do so by selling it to the official agency. In this way, a government, having established for itself a monopoly over all foreign exchange transactions is not only able to maintain a balance of payments equilibrium (usually at an artificially high rate of exchange), by rationing the available foreign currency so that total supply equals total allocation, but is also able to discriminate against a particular currency or against particular commodities through the imposition of a system of multiple exchange rates.

Finally, under a comprehensive system of exchange control, payments for imports may be credited to blocked accounts[1] in the name of the foreign exporter, who may be prohibited—at least for a time—from freely drawing on such accounts. For example, when Germany introduced exchange controls on leaving the gold standard in 1931, payments at the time due to foreign merchants were transferred to blocked accounts, some of which were released later at a rate of exchange disadvantageous to the foreign holders.[2] Similarly, accounts blocked in Britain would be those which the Treasury would not allow to be disposed of under the usual regulations applying to external accounts. These blocked accounts could only be withdrawn under certain conditions: for example, they could be sold at a discount to non-residents who wished to invest in Britain.[3] The United States has likewise blocked certain annuity payments (the annuities involved are social security, railway retirement, and veterans' benefits) to residents of a number of communist countries on the ground that there was no reasonable assurance that the money would actually be received or that it could be converted into local currency at a fair rate of exchange.[4]

(iv) *The nature of exchange restrictions.* The term 'exchange control', in the comprehensive manner in which it has been discussed above, must, however, be clearly distinguished from the narrower concept of exchange restrictions because, as Fawcett points out: 'All exchange restrictions are a form of control; but not all exchange control is restrictive of international payments.'[5] Fawcett gives the following reasons for making this distinction;

. . . under a régime of convertibility and free exchange markets,

---

[1] Art. 21 of the O.E.C.D.'s Code of Liberalisation of Capital Movements (Jan. 1969) provides: 'In this Code: (1) "Blocked Funds" shall mean funds owned by residents of other Member States in accordance with the laws and regulations of the Member where the funds are held and blocked for balance of payments reasons.'

[2] J. L. Hanson, *A Dictionary of Economics and Commerce* (1965) p. 42.

[3] P. A. S. Taylor, *A New Dictionary of Economics* (1966) p. 17.

[4] M. M. Whiteman, 8 D.I.L. (1967) pp. 944–5, 949–50; 952.

[5] J. E. S. Fawcett, 'The International Monetary Fund and International Law' 40 B.Y.I.L. (1964) p. 42.

parity margins will be maintained by intervention of the monetary
authorities in the market, a form of exchange control which is not
restrictive; again the requirement that exchange transactions be
carried out through authorized dealers, or the checking of the
purposes for which foreign currency is needed, or the requirement
that foreign currency obtained from export sales be surrendered
for local currency, are all forms of exchange control which are
not in themselves restrictions upon the payments made.[1]

It is apparent from these observations that the various national
exchange control regimes consist of many rules and regulations,
only some of which are directly restrictive of international payments. It is primarily with the abolition of exchange restrictions
—that is, those aspects of an exchange control regime which
prohibit or limit the making and transferring of international
payments rather than with the abolition *in toto* of the exchange
control mechanism—that international law is concerned. This
is a distinction which is made not only by the International
Monetary Fund:

> Hence, notwithstanding the wording, it is not the '*abandonment*'
> or *abolition* of restrictions of payments for current transactions, which
> the Articles of Agreement contemplate. They are not, and cannot
> be, concerned with lifting the burdens of domestic controls which
> are imposed upon residents and involve the completion of applica-
> tion forms, licences to be granted by Exchange Control Authorities,
> penalties for non-disclosure and so forth. They are concerned with
> the *administration* of a continuing system of exchange control in
> such a manner as to ensure that transfers for current transactions
> will in fact be granted, though the mere necessity for an application
> is a restriction. The restriction which the Articles of Agreement
> wish to abolish is, not the resident trader's inability to make pay-
> ments at his discretion, but the Exchange Control Authorities'
> power to withhold licences for payments for current transactions
> to non-residents.[2]

but also by the O.E.C.D.'s two Codes on the liberalization of
Capital and Current Invisible transactions:

> (*a*) The measures of liberalisation provided for in this Codeshall
> not limit the powers of Members to verify the authenticity of

---

[1] Fawcett, p. 42.
[2] F. A. Mann, 'Money in Public International Law', 96 R.C. (1959–I) p. 64.

transactions or transfers nor to take any measures required to prevent evasion of their laws or regulations.[1]

Although the above distinction is generally applied in most international agreements concerned with the regulation of exchange controls, certain arrangements between States are more rigorous in that they provide for the abolition not only of 'restrictions' but of other 'controls' as well. This is evidenced by the definition of exchange restrictions to be found in certain of the treaties of Friendship, Commerce, and Navigation recently concluded and ratified by the United States of America. For example, Article XII, paragraph (5) of the treaty concluded with Japan on 2 April 1953[2] defines exchange restrictions as follows:

The term 'exchange restrictions' as used in the present article includes all restrictions, regulations, charges, taxes, or other requirements imposed by either Party which burden or interfere with payments, remittances, or transfers of funds or of financial instruments between the territories of the two Parties.

A similar, but more detailed, provision is to be found in the treaty concluded with Israel on 23 August 1951[3] which provides in Article XII, paragraph (1) that:

The treatment prescribed in the present Article shall apply to all forms of control of financial transactions, including (a) Limitations upon the availability of media necessary to effect such transactions, (b) rates of exchange, and (c) prohibitions, restrictions, delays, taxes, charges and penalties on such transactions; and shall apply whether a transaction takes place directly, or through an intermediary in another country. As used in the present Article, the term 'financial transactions' means all international payments and transfers of funds effected through the medium of currencies, securities, bank deposits, dealings in foreign exchange or other financial arrangements, regardless of the purpose or nature of such payments and transfers.

Although the latter provision is more comprehensive than the former, it can be seen that in both the Articles it is not only 'exchange restrictions' which the parties seek to abolish

---

[1] Art. 5 (a) of the Jan. 1969 version of the O.E.C.D.'s Capital Code. Similarly see Art. 5 (a) of the Nov. 1967 version of the O.E.C.D.'s Current Invisible Code.
[2] 206 U.N.T.S. 143. [3] 219 U.N.T.S. 237.

but other forms of 'control' as well. More particularly the words 'burden' and 'delays' seem to be sufficiently broad to include within their meaning a regulation such as one which necessitates 'the checking of the purposes for which foreign currency is needed', a requirement which in itself is not directly restrictive of the means of international payment and is therefore more properly considered a control rather than a restriction. Clearly then, in determining what forms of conduct are to be prohibited, each treaty provision must be examined separately and judged on its own merits. Nevertheless, as a general rule and for the purposes of this study it is in the narrower sense that exchange controls will be considered.

(v) *Current and capital transactions.* Another distinction which is almost invariably made in the international organization of money is that between current (visible and invisible)[1] and capital transactions. The International Monetary Fund, for example, is concerned with the regulation of restrictions on current transactions only. Similarly, while both the O.E.C.D. and E.E.C. seek to abolish restrictions on both current and capital transactions, in discharging these obligations they treat the two types of transactions separately. Thus the O.E.C.D. has one legal code dealing with the liberalization of capital movements and another separate code dealing with the liberalization of current invisible transactions. A similar approach has been adopted by the E.E.C. The distinction is clearly a fundamental one in the international organization of money. It thus becomes necessary for the lawyer to be able to identify and distinguish a capital from a current transaction. This distinction can be made either on an economic or on a legally orientated basis.

(a) Economic definition. From an economic viewpoint, a payment is a payment for a current transaction if it gives rise to the immediate return of goods or services, while a payment is a payment for a capital transaction if it gives rise to a future return. In other words, a capital transfer is one that has as its counterpart a claim to a future return, while the counterpart

---

[1] In most current invisible operations a service, instead of goods, is supplied against payment. Transport, insurance, repairs, professional or technical services, and the exhibition of films are examples. On the other hand, in current visible operations goods, instead of a service, are supplied against payment.

to a payment for a current transaction is the receipt of goods and services.

(*b*) Legal–institutional definition. Article XIX (i) of the Fund Agreement introduces the following formula for distinguishing payments for current transactions from capital transfers:

Payments for current transactions means payments which are not for the purpose of transferring capital, and includes, without limitation:

(1) All payments due in connection with foreign trade, other current business, including services, and normal short-term banking and credit facilities;

(2) Payments due as interest on loans and as net income from other investments;

(3) Payments of moderate amount for amortization of loans or for depreciation of direct investments;

(4) Moderate remittances for family living expenses.

The Fund may, after consultation with the members concerned, determine whether certain specific transactions are to be considered current transactions or capital transactions.

This definition, which is considered in some detail in Chapter VII, apart from deeming certain payments, which would by the above-mentioned economic definition clearly be capital transfers, to be current payments, does not in itself add much to a clarification of this vital distinction.

Annex A to the O.E.C.D.'s Code of Liberalisation of Capital Movements,[1] which enumerates item by item those transactions which are deemed to be capital in nature, and Annex VII to the 'Treaty for East African Co-operation',[2] which enumerates item by item those payments which are deemed to be current in nature, are more helpful in this respect. Similar enumerations appear in other international legal instruments.[3] However, it is not intended to examine here the various items

[1] Since this Code is periodically revised and brought up to date, for the purposes of this study all references will be to the Jan. 1969 version.

[2] The text of this treaty, together with all annexes, is reproduced in 6 I.L.M. (1967) pp. 932–1057, and without annexes in 7 *Journal of Common Market Studies* (1968) pp. 129–91.

[3] For a list of the capital transactions which are to be liberated under the auspices of the Treaty of Rome, see 1960 J.O. 921 and 1963 J.O. 63. For a list of the invisible transactions which are to be liberated under the auspices of the Treaty of Rome, see Annex III to the Treaty establishing the E.E.C., 298 U.N.T.S. 116.

enumerated in the above-mentioned documents. A reader requiring more detailed information is referred directly to the Annexes and related studies.[1] Suffice it to say that by examining these various lists, the lawyer will be able to ascertain fairly quickly and specifically what is a capital and what is a current transaction.

(vi) *Other forms of financial and commercial control*. Finally, it is important to note that with the exchange control mechanism being made more and more the object of international regulation, it has become common practice for States to interfere with the free flow of international trade through the use of other more sophisticated financial controls. A similar pattern has developed with respect to direct commercial controls. These more sophisticated forms of State interference are now commonly referred to as 'Non-Tariff Distortions of Trade', and include such practices as:

(*a*) Retention quotas:

This cryptic phrase denotes a practice, very widespread in Europe after World War II, whereby exporters—generally to the dollar area—were not bound to surrender the whole of their export earnings, but could use part of them either directly for transactions not normally permitted—for example, to import goods subject to quota in excess of the established quotas for local use or re-export— or indirectly for sale at free market prices to other nationals who in their turn, with the aid of this exchange, carried out transactions not normally permitted. Such a practice has many features in common with multiple exchange rates, and if it became widespread it would have the effect of entirely distorting the system of international payments.[2]

(*b*) Advance deposits:

. . . importers are required to deposit in local currency a certain proportion of the cost of the import before the item is imported, and this deposit is released sometime later, usually after the import has arrived. From the point of view of the importer, this amounts to a requirement that some part or all of the bill for imports be paid in

[1] Etienne-Sadi Kirschen, *Financial Integration in Western Europe* (1969); *The Development of a European Capital Market*, Report of a group of experts appointed by the E.E.C. Commission (Brussels, 1966); *Liberalisation of Current Invisibles and Capital Movements* (O.E.E.C., C/60/98, Mar. 1961).

[2] Jean van der Mensbrugghe, 'Consultations with the Fund', 2 F.D. (June 1965) p. 91.

advance, and thus it clearly has some inhibiting effect upon imports and the consequent flow of import payments.[1]

(c) Import surcharge:

This refers to the imposition of a temporary tariff on all or a majority of goods imported.[2]

Other less-known distortions to trade include customs classification and valuation, public procurement policies, antidumping regulations, border tax adjustments, export credit subsidies, domestic subsidies and taxation, technical and health regulations. The regulation of these and other measures is increasingly becoming the concern of international organization and will be briefly considered in Chapter VII.

5. *Domestic Economic Policies*

The third corrective device to which States may resort in order to correct a fundamental payments disequilibrium is the manipulation of internal economic policies. Before 1931 and the demise of the gold standard, this constituted the principal corrective mechanism. Under that standard, which in its classical sense implied fixed exchange rates and the absence of direct controls, external adjustment was necessarily realized through alterations in the domestic economy—that is, through the restriction of the money supply in the gold-losing, 'deficit country', and the increase of the money supply in the gold-gaining, 'surplus country' which set into motion a train of corrective influences, such as the lowering of prices and wages and the increase of unemployment. Following the demise of that standard the maintenance of full employment became one of the most important responsibilities of national governments, and countries became increasingly less willing to make domestic price and income adjustments for the sake of external equilibrium. However, under the present system as it has evolved—that is, with the remaining two corrective devices, exchange rate alteration and direct control subject to legal regulation—it may well be that the wheel has come round full circle. Indeed, it has been suggested in a recent United Nations

[1] S. Makdisi, 'Restrictions on the Movement of Funds within Latin America', 10 *I.M.F. Staff Papers* (1963) p. 197.
[2] J. H. Jackson, 'The Puzzle of GATT', 1 J.W.T.L. (1967) p. 156.

report[1] on the international monetary system that as a result of these developments 'the manipulation of domestic demand through fiscal and monetary policy has become the most important instrument for adjustment of imbalances in international payments'.[2]

These internal economic adjustments, which, as mentioned, may be either of a fiscal or of a monetary nature, will be so orientated as: (a) in the case of a persistent surplus to raise domestic wages and prices in relation to other countries, thereby making foreign goods more attractive on the domestic market and thus raising the nation's propensity to import, while making domestic goods less attractive on foreign markets and thus decreasing the nation's propensity to export; and (b) in the case of a persistent deficit, to lower domestic wages and prices in relation to other countries, thereby making foreign goods less attractive on the domestic market and thus lowering the nation's propensity to import, while making domestic goods more attractive on foreign markets and thus increasing the nation's propensity to export.

Clearly, therefore, 'The choice of national adjustment policies has obvious international ramifications.'[3] In response to this situation the Fund at the global level, and the E.E.C. and other such arrangements at the regional level, have become increasingly involved with the regulation of domestic policies to the extent that such policies have international repercussions. In its annual consultation with member States as well as in many of the letters of intent concluded with member States in connection with stand-by arrangements, the Fund has increasingly concerned itself with this question.[4] Indeed, a senior official of the Fund's legal department has suggested

[1] International Monetary System—Issues Relating to Development Finance and Trade of Developing Countries, study by the U.N.C.T.A.D. Secretariat, TD/B/198, 23 Oct. 1968.
[2] Ibid. p. 17, para. 36.
[3] R. A. Mundell, 'The International Monetary Fund', 3 J.W.T.L. (1969) p. 469. For a further illuminating discussion in which the author suggests that certain national economic policies should be subjected to international scrutiny or co-ordination on an international level, see J. J. Polak, 'International Coordination of Economic Policy', 9 I.M.F. Staff Papers (1962) pp. 149–81.
[4] This aspect of the Fund's activities, with practical illustrations, is discussed by S. Silard, 'The Impact of the International Monetary Fund on International Trade', 2 J.W.T.L. (1968) pp. 148–56.

that the Fund's policies in this regard have been and are being so rigorously applied that they may well develop into rules of customary international law:

Study of the general economic policies which the Fund would support by making its resources available is thus instructive for the assessment of the impact of the Fund's activities on international trade generally, and on various categories of economic policies in particular. When a member wishes to make use of the resources of the Fund, favourable action by the Fund is required. The processes of co-operation and quiet 'technical diplomacy' whereby the Fund and its members agree on the terms for the use of the Fund's resources are at the same time the most intricate and the most delicate, and represent a most significant aspect of international monetary co-operation as it is practised today. As will be seen in the discussion of the specific areas of impact, these processes provide for an important form of interaction between the pursuit of national trade policies and the evolving international consensus relating to them. This international consensus represents, through the gradual accretion of precedents, a growing body of practices which may well be recognized some day as rules of customary international economic law.[1]

As will be seen in the discussion on regional monetary arrangements, similar efforts have been made by the E.E.C. and other regional economic groupings[2] to subject internal fiscal and monetary policies to a measure of supranational regulation.

6. *International Liquidity*

International liquidity has been defined as

the resources available to national monetary authorities to finance potential balance of payments deficits—that is, in their command over compensatory official financing. It may consist in the possession of assets or in the ability to borrow internationally. Typical items entering into international liquidity are holdings of gold and convertible foreign exchange; but claims on international institutions or entitlements to borrow from international institutions, from foreign governments, or even from private sources abroad, may be included in the concept.[3]

---

[1] Ibid. pp. 130–2. A similar suggestion is made by I. S. Friedman, 'The Fund Agreement as a Code of Conduct', 1 F.D. (Sept. 1964) p. 101.

[2] Below, Ch. X.

[3] J. Marcus Fleming, 'The Fund and International Liquidity', 11 *I.M.F. Staff Papers* (1964) p. 177. Studies on international liquidity are voluminous. The

More particularly, the concept may be considered in terms of its nature and its function.

As regards the former—that is, its nature—a nation's monetary reserve assets consist primarily of gold, foreign exchange (mainly in the form of United States dollars, pounds sterling, and to a very limited extent French francs), and its reserve position in the Fund. Respectively, in terms of billions of U.S. dollars, these comprise: gold, 38·9; foreign exchange, 27·5; reserve position in Fund, 6·5 of the total value of 72·9 of unconditionally available liquidity.[1] Moreover, during the period 1970–2 an additional $9·5 billion of unconditional liquidity will become available through the allocation of Special Drawing Rights. In addition to these, drawings under member's credit tranche positions in the Fund are conditionally available to members. On 30 November 1968 these amounted in value to U.S. $17·2 billion.[1] Finally, if necessary, unlimited amounts of drawing facilities can be made available through the conclusion of swap arrangements and related credit arrangements between central banks and Treasuries. This latter device has become increasingly important in recent years. For example, the 1968 Basle Credit Arrangement, which made U.S. $2·0 billion available to Britain to meet any fall in the sterling balances of overseas sterling areas, falls into this category.[2]

In its functional capacity international liquidity is closely related to the adjustment process. This is the case because balance of payments deficits, rather than being eliminated by the use of one or a combination of the three corrective measures enumerated above, may be financed by a nation from its store of monetary reserves. However, since no nation has access to an unlimited supply of such reserves, the adjustment process will, sooner or later, depending on the quantum of available reserves, have to be activated. In other words, the more ample is the provision of liquidity, the less rapidly need the chosen instruments for permanent adjustment operate.

International law affects both the nature and the function of liquidity. As regards the former, it has already been mentioned

uninitiated lawyer, however, might find the following two studies, owing to their less technical approach, particularly helpful: J. K. Horsefield, 'International Liquidity', 1 F.D. (Dec. 1964) pp. 170–7, and P.-P. Schweitzer, 'International Liquidity and the Fund', 3 F.D. (June 1966) pp. 99–106.

[1] *Annual Report I.M.F.* (1969) pp. 14–25.　　　　　　　　[2] Ibid. p. 64.

that gold tranche drawing rights on the Fund are treated as part of a nation's store of international liquid assets. Moreover, with the coming into force on 28 July 1969 of the amendments to the Fund's Articles of Agreement, a new reserve asset, special drawing rights (S.D.R.s)—commonly referred to as paper gold—was created. This new asset, unlike the existing assets, is the creation of an international legal instrument, and therefore possesses qualities which the other assets lack, perhaps the most significant being that member States who opt to participate in the scheme will be under a legal obligation to accept, subject to certain limitations, S.D.R.s in the settlement of international debts. S.D.R.s are therefore akin to money by fiat, as that term is understood in municipal monetary systems,[1] and in this respect they constitute international legal tender. It will be remembered, on the other hand, that gold, dollars, and pounds, although currently accepted as means of international settlement, derive their acceptability from the holder's confidence that they will maintain their value and will be willingly accepted by others in payment of future debts. Once confidence is eroded—as was the case with the pound sterling immediately before and after the devaluation in November 1967—States, being uninhibited by legal obligation, will switch out of the suspect currency. If this occurs on a sufficiently large scale, the entire international monetary system can be placed in jeopardy. Indeed, to prevent sterling area countries from running down their sterling reserve assets too quickly, the United Kingdom entered into bilateral treaty arrangements with all sterling area countries whereby the latter, in exchange for a dollar value guarantee, agreed not to run down their sterling balances beyond an agreed minimum. What was previously a matter of confidence is now a matter of legal obligation.[2]

As regards the latter—that is, the functional aspect of international liquidity—it will be seen[3] that under the Fund's amended provisions, the quantum of international liquidity will be the object of international scrutiny and regulation. Since the adjustment process is intimately bound up with the availability of liquidity, any system which seeks to regulate the latter will by implication affect the former. Moreover, institutional

[1] See F. A. Mann, *The Legal Aspect of Money*, p. 38.
[2] Below, pp. 238–40.   [3] Below, pp. 198–200.

credit facilities—for example, the International Monetary Fund's credit tranche facilities[1] and the European Fund's drawing rights[2]—are invariably made available to member States subject to the condition that the drawing members simultaneously undertake corrective measures of a fundamental and permanent nature.

[1] Below, pp. 190–2.   [2] Below, pp. 261–3.

Part One

PRE-FUND PERIOD

INTRODUCTION

PART One of this study examines in some detail the customary international law of money as it pertains in particular to exchange rates and exchange controls. It also alludes very briefly to certain pre-1945 treaty provisions which were concerned with these two issues. In Chapter III, entitled 'Currency Valuation', the following issues are examined: (i) whether States, from the point of view of customary international law, are entitled unilaterally to define the value of their basic monetary unit for purposes of the international money market or otherwise to manipulate the value of their currency (for example, abrogate gold clauses or resort to inflationary economic policies resulting in currency depreciation) without being held internationally responsible for injuries thereby inflicted upon foreign nationals or States; (ii) having established that the answer to question (i) is in the affirmative, whether there exist any rules of customary international law, or general principles of international law, limiting the exercise of this right. In Chapter IV, entitled 'Exchange Restrictions', the following issues are examined: (i) whether States, from the viewpoint of customary international law, are entitled unilaterally to introduce exchange controls; (ii) again, having shown that the answer to question (i) is in the affirmative, whether there exist any rules of customary international law, or general principles of international law, limiting the exercise of this right. In both Chapters III and IV the absence of treaty obligations—global, regional, bilateral—is assumed. Such obligations as were contracted in the context of international agreement during the inter-war period are examined in Chapter V.

Finally, it remains to be explained why the writer chooses to examine the customary law of money under the general head of 'Pre-Fund Period'. The reason for treating the customary law of money as a pre-Fund phenomenon (when, in fact, such customary law is still, in certain circumstances, applicable in the post-1945 period) is to make a clear distinction between it and the more dynamic developments which have been taking place in international monetary law in the post-Second World War period. These post-war developments have taken place almost exclusively within the framework of treaties, and have been so far-reaching that not only have they relegated the customary law of money to a position of relatively minor importance, but they may also prove to be responsible for bringing about a change in the very substance and content of customary monetary law as it at present exists. For example, it will be shown in the following two chapters of this study that under contemporary international customary law (assuming the complete absence of treaties, a situation which by and large prevailed in the period before 1945), a State is uninhibited in its capacity to alter the rate of exchange of its currency and to impose exchange controls (subject to certain largely ineffective limitations), without thereby giving rise to an international wrong, even though foreign creditors and international trade will almost invariably be adversely affected by such measures. The period since 1945, however, has witnessed the emergence of several multilateral, regional, and bilateral treaty regimes concerned with international monetary relations, with the result that the prerogatives which States enjoy regarding exchange rates and exchange controls under international customary law have been drastically curtailed. Indeed, if the present trend continues, it may well be the case that the post-war years will be viewed by monetary historians as representing the embryonic stage in the development of a new customary law of money. Whether the present trend will continue, thereby further strengthening the case for evolving new rules of international customary law from rules of international conventional law, remains to be seen. Nevertheless, it is safe to suggest that, at the very least, traces of such a development are already clearly discernible.

III

CURRENCY VALUATION

1. *International Law and Currency Valuation: the General Principle*

THE answer to the question 'Are States, under customary international law, free to alter the value of their currency without being held internationally responsible for injuries thereby inflicted on foreign parties?' was, as early as the sixteenth century, thought to be in the negative. Bodin, in his treatise, *Les Six Livres de la République* (1576), put forward the contention that a prince was not free to prejudice foreigners by debasing his coins, as such measures would be contrary to the law of nature.[1] A similar opinion was expressed by Mr. Justice Holt in an early English case (1688).[2] He held that a bill of exchange, drawn in Portuguese currency (1000 Mille Rees), which currency was subsequently devalued before the date of maturity of the bill, 'ought to be paid according to the ancient value for the King of Portugal may not alter the property of a subject of England'. The above position was also subscribed to by Wharton, who in a treatise on the conflict of laws states that

> when a currency at the place of payment has depreciated between the time of contract and the period when payment is claimed, then, viewing the matter according to the principles of international law, the plaintiff . . . is entitled to recover that which would give him an equivalent in currency to that which he would have been entitled to had no such depreciation taken place.[3]

Apart from the few authorities cited above,[4] however, the

---

[1] J. Bodin, *Les Six Livres de la République* (1576) Book Six, Ch. 3, p. 957.

[2] *DuCosta* v. *Cole* (1688), 90 E.R.; Skinner 272.

[3] Wharton, 2 *A Treatise on the Conflict of Laws* (1905) Sect. 517, p. 1231.

[4] See also J. M. Pardessus, V *Cours de droit commercial* (5th ed., 1841) pp. 271 ff.; J. B. Moore, VI D.I.L. (1906) pp. 753–4; Whiteman, 8 D.I.L. (1967) pp. 1152–3; *Damascus (Municipality of)* v. *Liquidator of X Company* (1931–2) I.L.R. p. 286.

bulk of the available evidence discernible from (i) international and national tribunals, (ii) State practice, and (iii) publicists would suggest that the question under consideration must be answered in the affirmative.

(i) *Tribunals.* In the *Adams* case,[1] brought before the American British Claims Commission, the claimant, William Adams, a British subject domiciled in England, alleged that he was in 1862 the owner of certain bonds of a railway company in the United States; that in the year 1862 the Congress of the United States passed a law making paper money legal tender, and that as a result of that law, paper money of the United States had depreciated in value. As he was obliged to receive payment of his interest in such depreciated currency and as the face value of the bonds had themselves similarly depreciated, he claimed damages for these losses from the Government of the United States. The Commission unanimously dismissed his claim holding that: 'The commissioners are of the opinion that the matters alleged in the memorial do not constitute the basis of any valid claim against the United States . . .'

The American Mexican Claims Commission has similarly held on several occasions[2] that 'it is elementary law that states are not responsible for losses caused by currency fluctuations'.[3] Indeed, the position of the law was so succinctly stated by the American Commissioner in his appraisal of the claim of Quimichis Colony against the Mexican Government for losses suffered due to currency depreciation that it merits citation in full:

Now, coming to the matter of the General Claim, I may say that there is no precedent in international law cited by the present American Agent for holding a government responsible for the depreciation of its currency. However, in these currency claims the present American Agent does not make any such contention, so we do not have that issue here; but I am merely calling attention to the circumstance that there does not seem to be a single precedent

---

[1] J. B. Moore, 3 *International Arbitrations Digest* (1898) pp. 3066–7.

[2] All the relevant decisions are reproduced in *American Mexican Claims Commission, Report to the Secretary of State*, Department of State Publication 2859 (1948), Arbitration Series 9. See in particular the following cases: *Scott and Bowne, Inc.,* pp. 147–50; *Borden Covel, Administrator, Estate of Leo Sigmund Kuhn, Deceased,* pp. 168–70; *Will and Baumer Candle Company,* pp. 229–31.

[3] *Borden Covel, Administrator, Estate of Leo Sigmund Kuhn, Deceased,* p. 169.

in the long history of currency debacles which would support such
a view, so I take the position that under international law, unless
the claim is modified by circumstances which give it the support of
some other principle, no government is responsible for the mere
depreciation of its currency. Such a calamity is a general one
affecting nationals and foreigners alike. No government desires that
its currency be depreciated to the point of extinction in value or
nearly so. It is unquestionably to a government's interest to strive
as vigorously as it can to preserve the value of its money and the
national credit; but unhappily it has sometimes happened that
entire series of issues have become worthless, or nearly so; but never,
so far as I know, has any claim been made and sustained in an
international arbitration on such account.[1]

A series of decisions[2] recently delivered by the United States
Foreign Claims Settlement Commission[3] likewise support this
general principle. In the *Zuk Claim*,[4] for example, the claimant,
an American national, brought an action against the Soviet
Government under Section 305 (*a*) of the United States International Claims Settlement Act, 1949, as amended, which
states in part that:

(*a*) The Commission shall receive and determine in accordance with
   applicable substantive law, including international law, the
   validity and amounts of . . .

[1] *The Claim of Quimichis Colony*, Docket no. 688. Reported in *American Mexican
Claims Commission, Report to the Secretary of State*, Department of State Publication
2859 (1948), Arbitration Series 9, p. 336.
[2] In addition to the leading decisions discussed in the text, the Foreign Claims
Settlement Commission awarded similar judgments in a large number of other
claims. These are available in the various Semiannual Reports of the Foreign
Claims Settlement Commission to the United States Congress. For the Pilot
Decision in the Polish Claims Series, see *In the Matter of the Claim of Herbert S. Hale*,
F.C.S.C., *Fifteenth Semiannual Report, December 31 1961*, pp. 32–3. This decision also
appears in Whiteman, 8 D.I.L. (1967) pp. 984–5. Decisions to the same effect
against Czechoslovakia are reported in *F.C.S.C.*, *Fourteenth Semiannual Report,
June 30, 1961*, p. 8.
[3] For a discussion of the Foreign Claims Settlement Commission, see Edward
D. Re, 'The Foreign Claims Settlement Commission: Completed Claims Pro-
grams', 3 *Virginia Journal of International Law* (1963) pp. 101–20; 'The Foreign
Claims Settlement Commission and the Cuban Claims Program', I *International
Lawyer* (1966) pp. 81–5; Ernest Schein, 'Settlement of World War II Claims',
I *International Lawyer* (1967) pp. 444–56; Whiteman, D.I.L. 8 (1967) pp. 1111–29;
Z. R. Rode, 'The 1968 Amendments to the International Claims Settlement Act
of 1949', 63 A.J.I.L. (1969) pp. 296–304.
[4] (1958–II) I.L.R. p. 284. Also reported in *F.C.S.C.*, *Tenth Semiannual Report,
June 30, 1959*, pp. 172–3. This decision is also discussed in Whiteman, 8 D.I.L.
(1967) pp. 982–3.

(2) claims, arising prior to November 16, 1933, of nationals of the
United States against the Soviet Government.[1]

His claim was based upon losses sustained as the owner of
500,000 Imperial Russian roubles issued in 1912 by a predecessor to the present Soviet Government. By a decree of 7 March
1924, the Soviet Government fixed a ratio of equivalence
between the newly created State Treasury Notes of 1924 and
the currencies which were previously in circulation, whereby
one new rouble was equivalent to (a) 50,000 roubles of the issue
of 1923, (b) 5,000,000 roubles of the issue of 1922, and (c)
50,000,000,000 roubles of all issues before 1922. As a result of
this decree the 500,000 roubles belonging to the claimant had,
for all practical purposes, become valueless. In answering the
issue before it, that is, 'whether losses sustained as a result of
the devaluation of the Russian rouble give rise to a valid claim
against the Soviet Government under international law',[2] the
Commission had no difficulty in arriving at a negative answer
and stated quite categorically that 'Under international law,
such a claim cannot be recognized'.[3] In the *Malan Claim*,[4]
also before the United States Foreign Claims Settlement Commission, the claimant brought a claim against the Italian
Government under Section 304 of the United States International Claims Settlement Act, 1949, as amended.[5] The claim
in this case was for the sum of U.S. $23,074 in respect of losses
due to devaluation of a lira account with the Banca d'Italia.
The sum claimed was the difference between the value of
the account as it existed on 3 September 1939, the date of the
deposit, at which time the rate of exchange was 19·50 lira to
1·00 dollar, and the value of the account at the time of the
filing of the claim, when the rate of exchange between the lira
and dollar had fallen to 625 to 1. The Commission again held
that: 'It is well established in international law that a currency
reform resulting in the devaluation of a nation's currency is
an exercise of sovereign authority which does not give rise to
a claim against that nation.'[6] Finally, from the viewpoint of
national law and national judicial pronouncements, the above

---

[1] (1958–II) I.L.R. p. 737.   [2] Ibid. p. 285.
[3] Ibid. p. 286.   [4] Ibid. pp. 290–1.
[5] Ibid. p. 736.   [6] Ibid. p. 291.

position is supported by the near-universal adoption of the nominalistic principle.[1]

(ii) *State practice*. In considering the diplomatic protection accorded by States to their injured nationals owing to debtor States defaulting (where default is defined as including both currency depreciation or devaluation and gold clause abrogation)[2] in their bond obligations to foreign nationals, the following observation has been made on the nature of State practice in such circumstances:

> For these several reasons the governments of the creditors have in principle declined to consider a default a breach of international law or a matter of concern to the nation as a whole. They have maintained that they would not make the mere losses of their citizens the basis of an international claim and interpose diplomatically for their vindication or collection.[3]

Even in those few instances where States have utilized their diplomatic channels to assist their injured nationals, such claims were not based on the violation of any rule of international law but rather on the basis of equity. The 'British Holders of Rentes'[4] incident and the recent diplomatic activity arising out of the devaluation of the Argentine currency[5] are two signal illustrations of such an approach being adopted by the Government of the United Kingdom.[6] In the latter incident, the Argentine peso was devalued in October 1955, with the

[1] Nussbaum, *Money in the Law* (2nd ed., 1950) p. 175. For a more detailed discussion of this principle as it applies in municipal and private international law, see Nussbaum, ibid. pp. 172 ff., 348–52; Mann, *The Legal Aspect of Money* (2nd ed., 1953) pp. 58 ff., 229 ff.

[2] E. Borchard, *State Insolvency and Foreign Bondholders, Volume I, General Principles* (1951) pp. 127–8, and in particular n. 11 at p. 128 where Borchard gives historical examples of 'depreciation', 'devaluation', and 'gold clause abrogation'.

[3] Ibid. p. 232.

[4] Cmd. 3779; 33 *United Kingdom State Papers* (1930–1) pp. 375–86.

[5] E. Lauterpacht, 'The Contemporary Practice of the United Kingdom in the Field of International Law—Survey and Comment', 5 I.C.L.Q. (1956) pp. 426–7.

[6] A similar approach was adopted by the United States Government in a diplomatic note sent to the Spanish Government in 1800: Moore, VI D.I.L. (1906) p. 754. The Advisory Commission on War Claims of Canada was also of the opinion that claims for losses in the value of money due to inflation should not be allowed, *Report of the Advisory Commission on War Claims* (1952) p. 63.

result that pensions remitted to British pensioners of Argentine companies were no longer calculated at the old rate of exchange of about 39 pesos to the pound sterling but at the new rate of 106 pesos to the pound sterling, so that pensions transferred by the Argentine Government to British pensioners were reduced by approximately 60 per cent in terms of the pound sterling. Her Majesty's Government accordingly made representations to the Argentine Government requesting the Government to provide an equitable solution to this problem. As is pointed out by Lauterpacht: 'The reference . . . to an "equitable solution" of the problem suggests that Her Majesty's Government do not regard the particular measure of devaluation as giving rise in the circumstances to any claim at law in respect of detriment suffered by British interests.'[1]

(iii) *Publicists*. Most contemporary writers, when dealing with the issue of international law and currency valuation, also adopt the position that as a general rule currency valuation is essentially a matter which falls within a State's domestic jurisdiction. Nussbaum states quite emphatically and seemingly without qualification: 'Nor does public international law offer a remedy to injured creditors. In the absence of a treaty to the contrary the right of a government to resort to inflationary emission of paper money and eventually to currency devaluation is uncontested.'[2] Other writers, although adopting in general a similar attitude, often add certain qualifications to the exercise of this prerogative (for example, that the measures must be undertaken for bona fide economic reasons).[3] O'Connell, for example, after first stating that 'In principle a State is uninhibited in law in its capacity to alter the rate of exchange or otherwise manipulate its money', then adds the restricting qualification that such measures must be 'in the interests of monetary stabilisation and solvency'.[4]

Finally, as has already been suggested, the abrogation of gold clauses can also result in the depreciation of foreign currency obligations, and therefore the question of whether the general

---

[1] However, see J. E. S. Fawcett, 'The International Monetary Fund and International Law', 40 B.Y.I.L. (1964) p. 56.

[2] Nussbaum, *Money in the Law*, p. 352.

[3] B. A. Wortley, *Expropriation in Public International Law* (1959) p. 49.

[4] O'Connell, op. cit. p. 1098. See similarly F. A. Mann, 'Money', 96 R.C. (1959–I) p. 95.

principle enunciated above extends to cover this type of State conduct must also be considered. A survey of the available evidence would seem to suggest that, as a general principle, States are free in international customary law to abrogate such clauses.[1] Bindschedler summarizes the situation as follows:

Du reste, la pratique internationale n'offre, à part deux exceptions, pas d'exemple où des Etats auraient obtenu ou même demandé d'un autre Etat le maintien de la clause-or (ou une indemnité pour sa suppression). Et pourtant nombreux sont les Etats qui ont supprimé la clause-or ou qui en ont limité l'usage.

On ne saurait donc prétendre que la suppression de la clause-or donne naissance à la responsabilité internationale de l'Etat qui y procède.[2]

On the authority of the above evidence it can be concluded that a State is not liable under customary international law for losses stemming from fluctuations in the value of its currency —or to put it in a positive sense: a State is free to manipulate the value of its currency without thereby engaging international responsibility. From the economic, political viewpoint the legal position could not be otherwise. States do not, as a rule, knowingly resort to economic policies which will result in currency depreciation or devaluation. Rather it is more frequently the case that depreciation or devaluation is dictated to the State by factors over which it has little or no control.[3] Accordingly, were the law to make actionable conduct which is determined by uncontrollable economic forces, it would only be encouraging its own disregard and demise.

This rule, however, does have an important corollary that gives rise to interesting legal ramifications, in that it will only be applicable if such currency measures (depreciation, devaluation, gold clause abrogation) can be shown to be legitimate acts undertaken as a result of economic difficulties and for the purpose of ensuring economic stability within the legislating country (as, for example, was the case in the November 1967

[1] In this respect see Nussbaum, *Money in the Law*, pp. 443–4, and Mann, 'Money', 96 R.C. (1959–I) p. 95.

[2] R. L. Bindschedler, 'La protection de la propriété privée en droit international public', 90 R.C. (1956–II) p. 227.

[3] In this respect see Fawcett, 'Trade and Finance in International Law', 123 R.C. (1968–I) p. 246.

devaluation of the pound sterling and other currencies closely linked thereto). The United States Foreign Claims Settlement Commission, for example, in dismissing a claim for losses suffered due to depreciation of the Hungarian pengö currency, did so on the basis of the above distinction, finding that the depreciation was not a deliberate act of the Hungarian Government, but rather the result of serious economic difficulties beyond its control:

> While the currency devaluation caused economic loss to a great many individuals holding such currency, in or out of banks, it was not a nationalization, compulsory liquidation, or other taking of property by the Government of Hungary. Such loss was the result of tremendous damage inflicted upon the Hungarian economy, principally by the war and post-war conditions, and not of any action by the Government of Hungary giving rise to a compensable claim under the Act.[1]

It therefore follows that if such measures are undertaken not for bona fide economic reasons but for the express purpose of eliminating foreign indebtedness or otherwise maliciously prejudicing foreign nationals—in short, for reasons which cannot be justified on legitimate economic grounds (as has been suggested with regard to the ruinous German mark inflation of 1918–23)[2]—then international law may well object. As is pointed out by Wortley,[3] however, the real difficulty in applying the economic test for determining liability lies in ascertaining exactly where the legitimate use of economic defence ends, and where the deliberate taking of property (by changing the rate of exchange) begins. This, as is further pointed out, 'is a difficult question, and the answer to it in any given case may well depend upon whether there has been an abuse of the power to legislate which entails responsibility in international law'. Whether, and if so in what circumstances, such measures will amount to an illegal interference with property rights, or to an *abus de droit*, or to any other international tort will now be examined.

---

[1] *Chobady Claim* (1958–II) I.L.R. pp. 292–4. See similarly the *Muresan Claim* (1958–II) I.L.R. pp. 294–5.
[2] F. A. Mann, *The Legal Aspect of Money*, p. 423.
[3] B. A. Wortley, op. cit. pp. 48–9.

2. *Exceptions to the General Principle within Customary International Law and General Principles of Law*

(i) *Illegal interference with property rights of aliens.* The argument that monetary measures which are prejudicial to foreign creditors and for which adequate compensation is not paid will amount to an illegal interference with property rights of aliens had been put forward over 100 years ago in 1864 by de Martens, who maintained that

when a state has recourse to violent financial operations tending to do away with inherent obligations to satisfy indebtedness, the violation of property rights which results is sufficient to authorize other nations to take up in this respect the cause of their subjects, and to employ for their protection every means authorized by the law of nations.[1]

A similar attitude is expressed by some contemporary publicists. Borchard, for example, is of the opinion that the practice of many ex-belligerent countries after the First World War of repaying in inflated paper currencies obligations which had originally been contracted in metal currencies amounted to a 'form of confiscation'.[2] Judge Lauterpacht, in his separate judgment in the *Norwegian Loans* case, similarly expressed the opinion that 'The question of the treatment by a State of property rights of aliens—including property rights arising out of international loans—is a question of international law'.[3] Similarly, Schwarzenberger, after first stating that 'interference with foreign property by taxation or measures of monetary policy such as devaluation of the national currency, on a footing of *de jure* and *de facto* equality, does not normally constitute an interference amounting to expropriation and calling for compensation', goes on to suggest: 'Yet, in particular circumstances, such action, as well as other forms of interference, may amount to creeping nationalisation.'[4]

In practice, however, tribunals, both national and international, have almost invariably held that currency depreciation or devaluation does not constitute an illegal taking of property. In the judicial practice of the United States this rule

[1] Moore, VI *International Law Digest* (1906) p. 754.
[2] Borchard, op. cit. p. 128 n. 11.
[3] (1957) I.C.J. Reports, p. 38.
[4] G. Schwarzenberger, *Foreign Investments and International Law* (1969) p. 4.

was firmly established in the famous *Legal Tender Cases*[1] where Mr. Justice Strong, in considering whether the Legal Tender Acts were prohibited by the spirit of the Fifth Amendment to the United States Constitution, which prohibits the taking of private property for public use without just compensation or due process of law, stated:

But was it ever imagined this was taking private property without compensation or without due process of law? Was the idea ever advanced that the new regulation of gold coin was against the spirit of the Fifth Amendment? And had anyone, in good faith, avowed his belief that even a law debasing the current coin by increasing the alloy would be taking private property?

A similar position has been adopted in international judicial practice.[2] The United States Foreign Claims Settlement Commission recently dismissed a series of claims for losses arising out of currency depreciation on the basis that:

It is well established that a currency reform resulting in devaluation of a nation's currency is an exercise of sovereign authority which does not give rise to a cause of action against the nation in question. Accordingly, such loss as claimant may have sustained by reason of devaluation of the crown currency on which her claim is based in part cannot be considered a nationalization, compulsory liquidation or other taking of property within the meaning of Section 303 (2).[3]

For example, in the *Claim of Zofia Walag*,[4] the claimant was the owner of a bank account with the Postal Savings Bank in Warsaw to the amount of 1,815 złotys. After the Second World War this account was consolidated with the bank accounts of other members of the claimant's family, making a total balance of 5,285 złotys. Pursuant to a law of 30 October 1950, on Monetary Reform, the consolidated account was converted into so-called 'new złotys' at the rate of 3 new złotys for 100 'old złotys', resulting in a balance of 158·58 new złotys. On 1

---

[1] *Knox* v. *Lee*; *Parker* v. *Davis* (1870), 12 Wall., 457. For the judicial practice of other national Courts in this respect, see F. A. Mann, 'State Contracts and State Responsibility', 54 A.J.I.L. (1960) pp. 584–5.

[2] But note the following two decisions of the United States Foreign Claims Settlement Commission: *Claim of B. Dworetsky* and *Claim of A. Bigot*, in F.C.S.C., *Twentieth Semiannual Report, June 30, 1964*, at pp. 30–1 and 21–2 respectively.

[3] *Mascotte Claim* (1958–II) I.L.R. p. 275.

[4] F.C.S.C., *Twentieth Semiannual Report, June 30, 1964*, pp. 22–3.

September 1960 the bank sent the claimant $4·68 in full pay-
ment thereof. In dismissing her claim for compensation for the
loss sustained as a result of depreciation or devaluation of the
Polish złoty, the Commission found that 'Under international
law a state is generally entitled to regulate its own currency,
and losses resulting by reason of such depreciation or devaluation cannot be construed as a nationalization, appropriation
or other taking of property'. Similarly in the *Tabar Claim
(No. I)*,[1] the claimants contended that a Yugoslav law on the
Settlement of Pre-War Obligations, which came into force
on 13 November 1945, and which provided that obligations
incurred prior to 18 April 1941 should be settled at the rate
of ten old Yugoslav dinars to one new dinar of the Yugoslav
Democratic Federative Republic, constituted a taking of their
property in that a sum of dinars which they had deposited in a
Yugoslav bank before the war had, due to the above law,
depreciated by 90 per cent of its original value. The Commission, after finding that the claim must fail, went on to say:

> From what has been said it is evident that Yugoslavia violated
> no principle of international law in providing, as part of the re-
> establishment of its monetary system, for the payment of obligations
> incurred prior to military occupation at a rate of ten old dinars to
> one new dinar, and that the operations of the Yugoslav law on the
> Settlement of Pre-War Obligations did not constitute a 'nationali-
> zation' or 'taking' of property . . .[2]

Similarly, Article 10, paragraph 5 of the Harvard Draft
Convention on the International Responsibility of States for
Injuries to Aliens[3] provides in part that 'An uncompensated
taking of property of an alien or a deprivation of the use or
enjoyment of property of an alien which results . . . from a
general change in the value of currency . . . shall not be considered wrongful',[4] provided that it is not, *inter alia*, (*a*) a
clear and discriminatory violation of the law of the State concerned, (*b*) an unreasonable departure from the principles of
justice recognized by the principal legal systems of the world,

---

[1] *Tabar Claim (No. 1)* (1953) I.L.R. p. 211.
[2] Ibid. p. 213.
[3] L. B. Sohn and R. R. Baxter, 'Responsibility of States for Injuries to the
Economic Interests of Aliens', 55 A.J.I.L. (1961) pp. 545–84.
[4] Ibid. p. 554.

and (c) it is not tantamount to an abuse of rights.[1] It is further provided in an explanatory note to this Article that:

A revaluation of the currency of a particular State, if not adopted in a manner which discriminates against aliens individually or collectively, may deprive an alien of a portion of his economic wealth, but the measure is not on that account wrongful.[2]

Clearly then, devaluation or depreciation will not constitute an illegal interference with the property rights of aliens. Rather it is when this device is deliberately utilized in a discriminatory, abusive, or arbitrary fashion that a State exceeds the permitted limits of action.

Moreover, this principle of non-liability enunciated in the cases discussed above has also been extended to apply in circumstances other than those in which the losses suffered by foreign nationals arose out of their holding of bank deposits which had become valueless owing to devaluing legislation. For example, in the *Endreny Claim*[3] it was held that a loss sustained in connection with the claimant's ownership of a mortgage which had become worthless owing to the fact that it was expressed in a currency which had subsequently been devalued did not constitute a nationalization, compulsory liquidation, or other taking of the claimant's property.

However, should a State expropriate property and offer compensation to the deprived foreign national in a depreciated currency, then such conduct may well come into conflict with certain established rules of international law. So when the Japanese Government, in furtherance of a land reform programme, enacted laws providing for the purchase by the Japanese Government of certain types of agricultural land and tendered payment in depreciated yen currency which at that time had no foreign exchange value, the Legal Section of the Supreme Command for the Allied Powers intervened on behalf of the absentee American landowners, maintaining that:

10a. Compensation in a depreciated yen currency is not the fiscal equivalent of 'adequate effective and prompt' compensation or 'just compensation' in accordance with the requirements

---

[1] Sohn and Baxter, loc. cit.

[2] Ibid. p. 561. See also Art. 12, para. (4), ibid. p. 567; and the Explanatory Note, ibid. p. 574.

[3] (1958–II) I.L.R. p. 278.

set by international law to counterbalance the full loss suffered by the absentee owner. Payments in a debased currency, as in the present case, would act to the discrimination of, and financial loss to an American owner.

11. It is the opinion of the Legal Section that the proposed expropriation by the Imperial Japanese Government of agrarian property owned by American Citizens which was legally acquired prior to the enactment of the agrarian land reform laws, by payment in yen, would be confiscatory and illegal.[1]

Here again, however, it is important to note that it was not depreciation *per se* which constituted a wrongful taking. Rather it was the Japanese Government's failure to satisfy the well-established international legal norm that compensation in respect of expropriated property must be adequate, prompt, and effective that was wrongful and constituted the basis of the complaint. Clearly, payment to foreign nationals in a currency that has no established foreign exchange value is neither adequate nor effective.[2]

(ii) *Non-discrimination and* abus de droit. In considering the efficacy of notions such as non-discrimination and *abus de droit* in providing a measure of protection against the arbitrary manipulation of exchange rates, it would seem that, in practice at least, their value is limited, inasmuch as international claims based on such notions would not meet with a large degree of success. Judge Read, in his dissenting opinion in the *Norwegian Loans* case, expressed the opinion: 'Further, I should be disinclined to bring notions of "good faith" and *abus de droit* into the question. Practically speaking, it is, I think, impossible for an international tribunal to examine a dispute between two sovereign States on the basis of either good or bad faith or of abuse of law.'[3] This state of affairs can primarily be attributed to the theoretical vagueness of these notions, which in turn stems,

---

[1] Whiteman, 8 D.I.L. (1967) pp. 1152-3.

[2] In this respect, Article 39 of the *Harvard Draft Convention on the International Responsibility of States for Injuries to Aliens*, 55 A.J.I.L. (1961) pp. 583-4 is relevant. Its purpose is to ensure the payment of effective compensation, i.e. compensation in a currency which the claimant can freely use and at a favourable exchange rate. See also Fawcett, 'Trade and Finance in International Law', 123 R.C. (1968-I) pp. 240-1.

[3] (1957) I.C.J. Reports, p. 94. Similarly see Starke, *Introduction to International Law* (6th ed. 1967) p. 106, and W. E. Friedmann, *Legal Aspects of Foreign Investment* (1959) pp. 723-4.

at least partially, from the limited amount of research which has been carried out into the nature of State practice in relation to these two concepts.[1]

Nevertheless, in spite of the many difficulties inherent in these notions (from both the practical and the theoretical points of view), it is interesting to note just how frequently contemporary publicists and in some cases international tribunals, when considering the problem of international law and exchange rate manipulation, refer to these concepts and attribute to them—often *carte blanche*—the capacity to restrict the prerogative which States enjoy in respect of currency matters. Statements such as 'abuse of this right, and perhaps in some cases unfair discrimination, is thought to engage international responsibility'[2] and 'loss caused by discriminatory action will engage State responsibility'[3] are almost invariably to be found in any exposition on the international law of money. Statements of a similar nature are sometimes to be found in the judgments of international tribunals. In the *Zuk Claim*,[4] the United States Foreign Claim Settlement Commission, after finding that currency depreciation *per se* was not contrary to international law, went on to say: 'International law recognizes two exceptions to this general rule. The first exception is founded on the theory of denial of justice. Thus, where a state pursues a deliberate course of injuring or discriminating against foreigners, a violation of international law results.'[5]

The above remarks would seem to suggest that municipal currency legislation, if it can be shown to be either discriminatory or abusive *vis-à-vis* other States or their nationals, will give rise to an international cause of action. A closer examination of these two actions, however, will indicate that such sweeping statements (although prima facie correct) are not only a gross over-simplification of the law as it exists, but are in fact 'begging the question' in the sense that it is one thing to say that

[1] A criticism as to the unsettled nature of these concepts in international law and others of a similar nature is made by Fawcett, 'The Fund and International Law', 40 B.Y.I.L. (1964) p. 57. See also similar comments made by Mann in relation to the notion of *abus de droit*, 'Money in Public International Law', 96 R.C. (1959–I) pp. 93–4 n. 5, and P. C. Jessup, *A Modern Law of Nations* (1968) p. 35 with respect to the notion of discrimination.

[2] O'Connell, op. cit. p. 1098.

[3] Wortley, op. cit. p. 107.

[4] (1958–II) I.L.R. pp. 284–6.   [5] Ibid. p. 285.

discrimination or abuse of rights will give rise to international responsibility, but quite another matter (and indeed much more difficult) to ascertain the circumstances in which this will be the case.

(*a*) Discrimination. It has been established that a State is, as a general rule, free to alter the rate of exchange or to otherwise manipulate the value of its currency without thereby suffering any redress from international law so long as such measures are undertaken for bona fide economic reasons. It has also been suggested that a State which indulges in currency practices which are discriminatory either as between its own nationals and aliens or as between various foreign nationals will engage international responsibility. The following question then arises: does a State which, for example, utilizes multiple rates of exchange (which by their very nature are discriminatory),[1] but which does so as part of a bona fide commercial policy, commit an international wrong? Or the problem may be posed otherwise: is the right of the State to alter the value of its currency paramount, or is it subordinate to the duty of the State not to engage in discriminatory currency practices? Both legal theory and State practice lend support to the view that the right is paramount, subject to the important proviso that the right is exercised for bona fide economic reasons. In practice, many countries,[2] particularly those in the early stages of economic development or suffering from a weak balance of payments position, have resorted to multiple currency practices. Yet such arrangements, although contrary to certain treaty provisions—for example, Article VIII, Section 3 of the Fund Agreement—have not, from the viewpoint of customary international law, been challenged on the basis that they constituted a breach of the principle of non-discrimination. Legal theory is in harmony with the adopted practice. It could not be otherwise, for if this were the case, then multiple exchange rates, even though applied for bona fide economic reasons, would *ipso facto*, owing to their inherent discriminatory nature, be contrary to international law, and would give rise to State responsibility.

Clearly then, when viewed against the background of both

---

[1] Such practices have frequently been resorted to by certain Latin American countries. See in particular the exchange system of Brazil, *20th Annual Report on Exchange Restrictions*, *I.M.F.* (1969) p. 50.   [2] Ibid.

State practice and legal theory, the blanket proposition that currency valuation, if it can be shown to be discriminatory pure and simple, will give rise to an international tort is incorrect. But if discrimination *per se* is not actionable, what criterion is applicable for determining liability, it being equally clear that some forms of currency valuation may well be without the bounds permitted by international law? It is submitted that the test is essentially an economic one. Accordingly, if, for example, a State does not utilize multiple rates of exchange for bona fide economic reasons, but does so merely pursuant to a plan designed to cause economic harm to a particular State or a particular group of foreign nationals, then such practice might well give rise to an international tort. In this respect, it can be seen that the test for determining whether or not discrimination is actionable is based not on legal but on economic criteria, in the sense that it is not the discriminatory nature of multiple exchange rates which gives rise to international responsibility, but rather the use of economic mechanisms for uneconomic objectives. It is therefore submitted that currency legislation which is discriminatory *per se* will not in itself give rise to State responsibility. But if it can be shown that the discriminatory currency practices complained of are not the indirect result of bona fide economic policies but rather the direct result of action undertaken with the express intention of causing harm to another State or its nationals, then it may well come into conflict with international law. In these circumstances, the line between actionable discrimination and abuse of rights is not clear, and it may be the case that discrimination becomes actionable only when it is arbitrary, unjust, odious, in short—abusive.[1]

(b) *Abus de droit.* It has been suggested that 'the very *raison d'être* of the doctrine of abuse of rights lies precisely in the idea of defining, to the extent that it is possible in each particular

---

[1] E. Borchard, op. cit. pp. 260–1, makes the following observation: 'Discrimination against nationals is one of the customary grounds of diplomatic intervention. Yet there is some question whether a country is bound by international law not to discriminate among nationals of different countries, where there is some justification therefor, such as, under a régime of clearing agreements, the existence with some creditor countries, but not with others, of an unfavourable balance of trade. The real ground justifying intervention is an unfair or unjustified discrimination among nationals'. See similarly Mann, 'Money in Public International Law', 96 R.C. (1959–I) p. 93.

case, . . . the "limitations" to which every right is subject when there is no concrete and precise prohibitory rule directly applicable to the case.'[1] As States enjoy the right of altering or otherwise manipulating their currency, and as limitations to the exercise of this right are not subject to any concrete and precise prohibitory rules, the applicability of this notion to the problem under discussion is apparent. The difficulty with the concept of *abus de droit*, however, lies in its practical application, that is to say, in determining the point at which the exercise of a right (in this case the right of currency debasement) exceeds the acceptable 'limitation' to which it is subject, thereby becoming abusive and giving rise to State responsibility. Several criteria for the reconciliation of this dilemma have been postulated, perhaps the most common being that if the right in question is exercised in an 'anti-social',[2] 'unfair',[3] or 'unreasonable'[4] manner, thereby causing injury to another State, an *abus de droit* will occur. But on the whole, such a criterion is unsatisfactory inasmuch as it leaves unanswered the further question of determining exactly what constitutes an anti-social, unfair, or unreasonable exercise of the abusive variety. In this respect some publicists are of the opinion that the exercise of a right becomes anti-social (or in other words exceeds its limit of acceptability and becomes abusive) at the point at which the right is 'used in such a manner that its anti-social effects outweigh the legitimate interests of the owner of the right',[5] or when 'the general interest of the community is injuriously affected as the result of the sacrifice of an important social or individual interest to a less important, though hitherto legally recognised, individual right.'[6] The task of balancing the

[1] P. V. Garcia Amador, 'State Responsibility. Some New Problems', 94 R.C. (1958–II) p. 380. For a further discussion of this notion see Politis, 'Le problème des limitations de la souveraineté et la théorie de l'abus des droits dans les rapports internationaux', 6 R.C. (1925–I) pp. 5–121; H. Lauterpacht, *The Function of Law in the International Community* (1933) pp. 286–306; B. Cheng, *General Principles of Law as Applied by International Courts and Tribunals* (1953) pp. 121–36; Alexandre Kiss, *L'Abus de droit en droit international* (1952); G. Schwarzenberger, 'The Fundamental Principles of International Law', 87 R.C. (1955–I) pp. 305 ff.; I. Brownlie *Principles of Public International Law* (1966) pp. 365–7.
[2] W. Friedmann, *The Changing Structure of International Law* (1964) p. 198.
[3] H. Lauterpacht, op. cit. p. 286.
[4] P. V. Garcia Amador, loc. cit. p. 382.
[5] W. Friedmann, *The Changing Structure of International Law* (1964) p. 198.
[6] H. Lauterpacht, cit., p. 286. Particular attention should also be given to

interests of the owner of the right with the general interest of the community is, particularly from the point of view of exchange rate alterations, a very difficult one, since of necessity it must be based not on objectively definable legal criteria, but rather on subjective[1] social, political, and economic factors which by their very nature are in a constant state of flux. Consequently, what may appear to be reprehensible economic behaviour to one party may to the other be a legitimate expression of a sovereign right. It is only in a very few exceptional instances— where a State pursues a particular economic policy with the malicious intent of causing harm to another State or to its nationals—that such a dualistic interpretation of State economic policies would not be plausible. Although judicial pronouncements in this respect are rare,[2] it was held in the *Claim of Alois Szpunar*[3] that the Polish Government was guilty of such abusive conduct. At the close of the Second world War, three currencies were in circulation within Poland: German marks, złotys issued by the Bank Emisyjny in Poland and roubles of the U.S.S.R. On 31 August 1944 the then provisional government of Poland introduced a new złoty, having par value with the złoty of the Bank Emisyjny in Poland and the rouble of the U.S.S.R. Subsequently, both the 'old' Polish złoty and the German mark ceased to be legal tender. By a decree of 6 January 1945, each individual was allowed to exchange 500 'old' złotys at par and 500 marks at the rate of two marks for one złoty into 'new' złotys; and any remaining 'old' złotys and mark bank-notes had to be deposited in certain appointed financial institutions. Rouble bank-notes, however, were exchanged with 'new' złoty bank-notes at par and in unlimited amounts. The claimant, after making the permitted

pp. 304–5 where Lauterpacht suggests that economic affairs which 'are regarded as the most cherished objects of exclusive jurisdiction of the State' are also susceptible to the restricting effects of this notion.

[1] The subjectivity of this notion is, in relation to the *Fisheries Case* (1951), I.C.J Reports, p. 115, pointed out by G. Schwarzenberger in *International Law as Applied by International Courts and Tribunals* (3rd ed., 1957) p. 48.

[2] See Mann, 'International Delinquencies before Municipal Courts', 70 *Law Quarterly Review* (1954) p. 187, and D. O'Connell, op. cit. p. 1098. See also the *Lighthouses Arbitration between France and Greece: Claim No. 26* (1956) I.L.R. pp. 342–9, where the Permanent Court of Arbitration considered the issue of currency depreciation from the point of view of good faith.

[3] F.C.S.C., *Eighteenth Semiannual Report, June 30, 1963*, pp. 18–19.

transfer of 500 'old' złotys into 500 'new' złotys, deposited 29,500 'old' złotys with the Narodowy Bank Polski as required by law, but was unable thereafter to convert this sum into 'new' złotys or to make any use thereof. The tribunal, after first stating that 'A State's undeniable sovereignty over its currency is traditionally recognized by public international law', and that the Polish monetary reform 'had as its purpose the reduction of the amount of currency in circulation and for that reason was in line with sound fiscal policy as well as with international law', nevertheless found that in the claimant's case the Polish decree of 6 January 1945 'amounted to an abuse of rights, and a taking of his 29,500 złotys'.

(iii) *State as a debtor (a greater liability?)*. The issues to be examined in this section are concerned only with those cases in which the State (as opposed to the nationals of that State) becomes a debtor having entered into contractual obligations with either (*a*) foreign nationals or (*b*) other subjects of international law, that is, States or international organizations.

(*a*) Foreign nationals. It has been suggested by some publicists that if in such cases a State, by resorting to its municipal legislation (that is, by introducing legislation which has the effect of either abrogating gold clauses or devaluing the national currency), reduces the amount of debt contracted with alien creditors, such unilateral modifications will automatically be contrary to international law even in the absence of unfair discrimination or *abus de droit*. In other words, the contention is that State responsibility is greater in those cases where the injury suffered by an alien creditor as a result of some form of currency debasement arises out of a contract in which a State (as opposed to a private individual) is the debtor or where a contractual nexus does not exist.

Borchard, in theory at least,[1] in considering this issue from the point of view of foreign bondholders holding bonds issued in the national currency of the debtor government (as opposed to the currency of another State),[2] subscribes to the above view

[1] In practice, however, Borchard asserts that the situation is quite different, as governments will take up the case of their injured nationals only in exceptional cases. See Borchard, op. cit. pp. 65, 231–2, 236, 350.

[2] Ibid. pp. 136–7: 'By choosing a foreign currency as the standard of their respective rights and duties, both debtor and creditor submit to the vicissitudes

and submits that, in the absence of the plea of *force majeure* (that is, where the debtor government's currency loses its original value due to economic circumstances beyond the government's control):

> . . . if the monetary devaluation and, consequently, the injury to the bondholders' rights arises from a deliberate act on the part of the debtor government, foreign creditors would be justified in further examining the situation with a view to determining whether or not the debtor has thereby incurred an international liability . . . The partial confiscation of his rights, together with the discrimination which may result from currency devaluation between internal and external holders of a debt couched in the national currency of the debtor government, may well form the basis of a claim against the defaulting government.[1]

Wortley adopts a similar attitude and suggests that 'deliberate devaluation of a spoliatory character by a debtor Government may be a ground for international responsibility to foreigners even without discrimination against them'.[2] Opinions of a similar nature have been expressed by other authorities as well.[3]

A diametrically opposite position is taken by Fischer Williams, who states that:

> . . . where the loan is issued in the national currency . . . it is no doubt within the power of the issuing government, and it is difficult to say that it is not within its right, to regulate its own coinage in such a fashion as to diminish, and even to destroy the value of, the rights of its creditors . . . If for domestic reasons the borrowing government depreciates its currency . . . I see no foundations for any legal complaint by the bondholder, though as a matter of morality he may have a case. What the bondholder has a legal right to, is so much of the state currency. If he gets that, he has his legal due.[4]

of the international rate of exchange and are subject to the law of the state which creates that currency and determines its value.'

[1] Ibid. pp. 137–8.
[2] B. A. Wortley, op. cit. p. 107.
[3] E. H. Feilchenfield, in S. E. Quindry, II *Bonds and Bondholders' Rights and Remedies* (1934) pp. 650–2; F. S. Dunn, *The Protection of Nationals* (1932) pp. 167–8; C. E. Hyde, II *International Law* (2nd ed., 1947) pp. 991–2, 1004–7; *Damascus (Municipality of)* v. *Liquidator of X Company* (1931–2), I.L.R. pp. 286–7; *Lighthouses Arbitration between France and Greece* (1956) I.L.R. pp. 342–9; *In the Matter of the Claim of Sophia Predka*, F.C.S.C., *Twenty-first Semiannual Report, December 31, 1964*, pp. 23–5; *Perry* v. *U.S.*, 294 U.S. 330 (1935).
[4] Fischer Williams, *Chapters on Current International Law and The League of Nations* (1929) p. 291.

O'Connell[1] is of a similar opinion and suggests that in the absence of a stable unit of value being utilized in the original loan contract, as was the position in the *Serbian and Brazilian Loans Cases*,[2] repayment of government debts in devalued money will not invite sanction from international law. *The Tripartite Claims Commission*,[3] in adjudicating certain claims by the United States against both Austria and Hungary arising out of the First World War, likewise considered the public debts of the Austro-Hungarian State to be subject to no greater obligation than private debts:

In the absence of a treaty so stipulating, there is no warrant for requiring the payment in American currency at the pre-war rate of exchange of Austrian [Hungarian] public debts or debts of Austrian [Hungarian] nationals owing to American nationals which by their terms are payable in Austro-Hungarian or other non-American currency. A contract obligation of the Austrian [Hungarian] Government or of an Austrian [Hungarian] national to pay Austro-Hungarian krone is exclusively a krone obligation and is unaffected either by the purchasing power of the krone in Austria [Hungary] or by the exchange value of the krone as measured by other currencies.[4]

Finally, with the exception of France (and even here her practice, as evidenced by the following case, is not consistent) and those States influenced by her legal doctrines,[5] the practice of States has been not to treat acts by debtor States which are prejudicial to their creditor nationals as constituting international wrongs. So when the French Government had issued bonds in the United Kingdom during and immediately after the First World War, which resulted in a cash subscription of

---

[1] O'Connell, op. cit. pp. 1089–90. See also K. Strupp, 'L'intervention en matière financière', 8 R.C. (1925–III) pp. 67–8; F. A. Mann, 'Money in Public International Law', 96 R.C. (1959–I) pp. 84–5.

[2] *Serbian and Brazilian Loans Cases*, P.C.I.J. Series A, nos. 20/21, and in particular pp. 32–4 where the Court dealt with the issue of the 'gold franc' which they found had an international character; it was therefore the weight and fineness of this unit which constituted the standard according to which repayment of the bond was to be made.

[3] For details concerning the functions and jurisdiction of the Commission, see 21 A.J.I.L. (1927) pp. 599 ff.

[4] Ibid. p. 621.

[5] For a discussion of the French position, see F. A. Mann, 'State Contracts and State Responsibility', 54 A.J.I.L. (1960) pp. 577–9, and 'Money in Public International Law', 96 R.C. (1959–I) pp. 84–5.

£50 million sterling and which, owing to the depreciation of the French franc, had by 1930 fallen to a value of only £13½ million, the British Government, in taking up the case on behalf of its injured nationals, sent a diplomatic note[1] to the French Government, not complaining of an international tort but rather asking the French Government 'to grant an equitable measure of compensation to the holders of these Rentes'. In its reply the French Government noted that at no point in their memorandum did the British Government 'contest the correctness, from the juridical point of view', of the French position of repaying only the nominal amount of the debt. In a subsequent note the British Government suggested that the matter be referred 'to an arbitrator of high international standing, who should be asked to decide the equitable and just basis upon which, having regard to all circumstances', a settlement should be made. In reply, the French Government again emphasized that in law their obligation towards the British bondholders was limited to the payment of the amount promised in French francs at their present value, and that a request for an arbitration which sought to increase, on grounds of equity, an amount which a country was bound to pay in law constituted a real innovation.

Similarly, the Government of the United States of America has, on the whole, been reluctant to take up, at the diplomatic level, the cases of its aggrieved nationals and has done so only in exceptional circumstances.[2] What will constitute an exceptional circumstance is illustrated by the following dispute arising out of certain Tobacco Monopoly bonds issued by the Government of Portugal[3]. By a decree of 3 June 1924, the Portuguese Government provided that the interest on certain gold bonds issued by it (Tobacco Monopoly bonds) should be paid in depreciated currency. An exception was made, however, in the case of British holders of those bonds who were to be paid in sterling. The Government of the United States protested on behalf of American holders of the bonds to the Portu-

---

[1] Cmd. 3779 or 33 *United Kingdom State Papers* (1930–1) pp. 375–86.

[2] J. R. Clark, Jr., 'Foreign Bondholdings in the United States', 32 A.J.I.L. (1938) p. 443; O'Connell, op. cit. p. 1081; Hackworth, V D.I.L. (1943) pp. 624–6; W. D. Scroggs, 'Foreign Treatment of American Creditors', XIV *Foreign Affairs* (1935–6) pp. 345–7.

[3] II *Foreign Relations* (1926) p. 880; Hackworth, V D.I.L. (1943) pp. 627–8.

guese authorities against the 'unwarranted discrimination' in favour of British holders. As a result of these protestations, Portugal agreed to pay principal and interest on the American-held bonds in pounds sterling. The point to be noted here is that the exceptional circumstance upon which the United States based its complaint was not that the accused debtor was the State of Portugal and therefore guilty *ipso facto* of an international tort when it unilaterally altered the terms of the bond agreement, but rather that the alteration *per se* was tortious since it took the form of an 'unwarranted discrimination'. In a more recent case, the United States reiterated its position:

> The applicable principles of international law do not give this claimant any better standing. The view consistently followed by the United States is that a loan contract between a state and a foreign bondholder is not an international contract nor controlled by international law. Bond holders who purchase such obligations do so upon their own responsibility and at their own risk. An intervention will not be made by the United States Government unless there has been a denial of justice, or unless the breach of contract is considered confiscatory.[1]

The bulk of the above evidence clearly leads to the conclusion that even in cases where a State is a contractual debtor, the international responsibility for currency devaluation is no greater than that which attaches to a State in similar circumstances outside the contractual nexus. In short, liability will arise, as in those cases where the State is not a party to the contract, only when the cause of action is based and sustained upon one of the traditional grounds already discussed—namely *abus de droit*, illegal interference with the property rights of aliens, denial of justice, etc.

From the point of view of legal theory, the above position could not be otherwise. A contrary position could be maintained only if it could be established that a contractual arrangement entered into between a State and a private alien is not governed by some system of municipal law (normally that of the contracting State), but rather comes under the control of international law. If this were the case, then the degree of State responsibility

---

[1] *In the Matter of the Claim of Owen Nash*, Whiteman, 8 D.I.L. (1967) pp. 945–6.

would indeed be greater in that it would encompass all the rules of treaty law, including that well-established principle that a State cannot reduce its obligations under international law by resorting to its own municipal legislation.[1] But such an agreement is untenable, as it is generally agreed[2] that contracts of this nature are subject to a municipal legal system determined by the conflict of laws.

(b) Other subjects of international law—that is, States and international organizations. With an ever-increasing number of international financial agreements being concluded either between two or more States or between international financial organizations, for example, the International Bank for Reconstruction and Development (I.B.R.D.), the International Development Association (I.D.A.), the International Financial Corporation (I.F.C.), the Asian Development Bank (A.D.B.), etc., and States, the question of the effect of currency fluctuations on the monetary provisions contained in such agreements has acquired considerable importance. The following hypothetical example raises the relevant issues. Assume that State A lends to State B, either in A's currency, B's currency, or the currency of a third State, an amount of money equivalent to $U.S.1,000,000. Assume further the absence of any maintenance of value clauses in the loan agreement and also the absence of any other international tort such as *abus de droit*,

---

[1] *Case of the Free Zones of Upper Savoy and the District of Gex*, P.C.I.J., Series A, no. 24, p. 12: '... it is certain that France cannot rely on her own legislation to limit the scope of her international obligations ...'

[2] The question of which law governs a contract between a State on the one hand and a foreign private party on the other hand is not entirely clear. On the one hand, the following publicists *inter alia* support the view that such contracts are governed in the main by municipal law. Jessup, 'Responsibility of States for Injuries to Individuals', 46 *Columbia Law Review* (1946) pp. 903–28; Lipstein, 'The Place of the Calvo Clause in International Law', 22 B.Y.I.L. (1945) p. 134; Mann, 'State Contracts and State Responsibility', 54 A.J.I.L. (1960) pp. 572–91; Whiteman, 8 D.I.L. (1967) p. 911. On the other hand, the following publicists, *inter alia*, tend to support the opposite view: Jennings, 'State Contracts in International Law', *Selected Readings on Protection by Law of Private Foreign Investments* (1964) pp. 175–214, and L. C. Wadmond, 'The Sanctity of Contract between a Sovereign and a Foreign National', ibid., pp. 139–74. Perhaps the only point that can be made with certainty in this area is that made by Jean-Flavien Lalive, 'Unilateral Alteration or Abrogation by Either Party to a Contract between a State and a Foreign National', *Symposium: Rights and Duties of Private Investors Abroad* (1965) pp. 265–79, at 271: 'The proper law of an international contract is a controversial and difficult question.'

etc., and that at the date of repayment (owing to the devaluation of the currency in which the loan was denominated) the capital value of the loan was reduced by 50 per cent to $U.S. 500,000. The question then arises, is State B liable to repay more than the now nominal value of $500,000? In answering this question a distinction, on the basis of the currency in which the loan was denominated, must be made. If the loan was denominated in the currency of the creditor State (State A) or the currency of any third country, the legal position is clear. It obliges State B to repay only that amount of currency—regardless of the now depreciated capital value—which represents the nominal value, the legal theory being that 'By contracting with reference to a specific national currency States incorporate into their treaties the monetary legislation of the country concerned and provide for a *renvoi* to the *lex monetae*'.[1] Once so seized, the well-established principle applicable in most municipal legal systems of nominalism applies equally to monetary obligations found in public international agreements as it does to monetary obligations found in private agreements. The legal position, however, is less clear if the loan is denominated in the currency of the debtor State (State B). Here the legal position is complicated by the applicability of the equally well-established rule of international law 'that no state can free itself from an obligation imposed by international law by changing its internal law'.[2] If State B, therefore, between the date of the making of the loan and its repayment, devalues its currency by municipal legislation, it comes into conflict with this rule. Dr. Mann, however, considers that even in such cases, the principle of nominalism is paramount to the international rule:

But this rule has no bearing upon a case in which the content and scope of the international obligation is, at the outset, determined and measured by national law. The quality and extent of the protection which public international law affords to a treaty are necessarily impaired if and in so far as the treaty incorporates or refers to municipal law, even though it may be the municipal law of the debtor State.[3]

[1] F. A. Mann, 'Money in Public International Law', 96 R.C. (1959-I) p. 106.
[2] Nussbaum, *Money in the Law* (2nd ed., 1950) p. 442.
[3] Mann, loc. cit. pp. 107-8.

On the other hand, both Nussbaum[1] and M. René Cassin[2] tend to support the opposite view.

In summary, subject to the uncertainty with respect to monetary obligations denominated in the debtor State's currency, the current legal position appears to be that in the absence of protective clauses and other traditional international torts, losses due to currency devaluation will be borne by the creditor State.

It has accordingly become increasingly commonplace for international financial agreements containing monetary obligations expressed in a particular national currency, and therefore subject to fluctuation, to include in the agreements maintenance of value clauses (that is, gold clauses or option of currency clauses).[3] Unlike monetary obligations expressed in the currency of the debtor State, gold clauses cannot be unilaterally altered or abrogated without falling foul of international law,[4] and they, therefore, provide a guaranteed measure of protection against exchange rate losses. The Treaty between the United States and Panama (Isthmian Canal Convention) over payment for the use of the canal is a case in point. In 1933, Congress declared that any treaty of the United States Government that required payment in gold was against public policy; that all previous obligations of this type were void; and that the Government was forbidden to enter into such obligations in the future. The resolution abrogated several American treaties. For example, under the Isthmian Canal Convention, the U.S. had agreed to pay $250,000 in gold annually for the use of the canal zone. The U.S. refused to make these payments in gold after 1933. The treaty was then renegotiated to provide for annual payments of $430,000 in dollars, a sum which took into account the depreciated value of the dollar.

---

[1] Nussbaum, *Money in the Law*, p. 442.

[2] *In the Matter of the Diverted Cargoes (Greece v. Great Britain)* (1955) I.L.R. pp. 820 ff. at 836.

[3] For a discussion of the current use of such clauses with extensive practical examples, see G. R. Delaume, *Legal Aspects of International Lending and Economic Development Financing* (1967) pp. 257–89.

[4] Nussbaum, loc. cit.; Borchard, op. cit. pp. 138–9; Mann, 'Money in Public International Law', 96 R.C. (1959–I) pp. 117–18.

IV

EXCHANGE RESTRICTIONS

1. *International Law and Exchange Restrictions: the General Principle*

As a matter of customary international law, there can be no doubt that States are, within certain limitations, free unilaterally to introduce and administer exchange restrictions without being held internationally responsible for any resultant adverse international repercussions.

(i) *Tribunals.* This principle was clearly enunciated in a decision rendered by the United States International Claims Commission in the *Tabar Claim (No. 3)*.[1] The facts which gave rise to the dispute can be summarized briefly as follows. The claimants had, before the outbreak of the Second World War, deposited a sum of 357,000 dinars in a Yugoslav bank. Subsequently, owing to certain Yugoslav exchange control regulations, they were refused the necessary permission by the Yugoslav authorities to have these funds transferred to the United States. In considering the claimant's contention that this refusal constituted a ground for compensation on the part of the Yugoslav Government, the Commission stated that:

Exchange controls usually follow a general pattern whereby residents, nationals as well as non-nationals, must surrender their foreign exchange, gold and foreign securities; foreign currency must not be exported, and domestic currency must not be exported or imported; nonresident creditors cannot have the sum owed transferred, irrespective of the currency involved; and rates for foreign exchange and gold are fixed by government decree.

International law and the usual commercial treaties are no bar to exchange restrictions. So long as the control measures are not discriminatory, no principle of international law is violated.[2]

Similarly, *In the Matter of the Claim of Mitzi Schoo*,[3] the

---

[1] (1953) I.L.R. pp. 242–3.   [2] Ibid. p. 242.
[3] F.C.S.C., *Seventeenth Semiannual Report, December 31, 1962*, p. 194.

claimant brought a claim against the Government of Czecho-slovakia, based on the refusal by that Government to allow the claimant's brother in Czechoslovakia to forward money from Czechoslovakia to the claimant in the United States in pay-ment of the purchase price of a house. In dismissing the claim, the tribunal gave the following reasons:

It appears from the record that the sole act of which the claimant complains is the refusal of the Government of Czechoslovakia to allow her brother in that country to forward money to her in the United States in payment of a debt. It is a well established principle of international law that a State has an absolute right to regulate its own currency. In the exercise of this right, a State may properly prohibit the export of currency.[1]

Finally, it was held *In the Matter of the Claim of Erna Spielberg*[2] that the above principle applied not only to the regulation of money *per se*, but also to the regulation of money in kind. In that claim, the claimant had sought to import jewellery into the United States from Czechoslovakia, but was prevented from doing so because she had been refused the necessary export licence as required under the foreign exchange regulations then in effect in Czechoslovakia. It was held that the enactment of such regulations and the refusal to grant an export licence did not constitute a taking of property 'since it is generally accepted that a state also has the sovereign right to impose such restric-tions'.[3]

The War Claims Commission, in adjudicating on certain claims arising out of the Second World War, adopted a similar position with respect to exchange control measures, holding that, with the exception of such measures which were clearly tantamount to confiscation or sequestration, 'It is universally recognized that any country has the right, in the protection of its economy, to pass currency regulations and to prevent the flow of capital beyond its borders', and, therefore, that such restraints 'cannot furnish the basis for a compensable claim'.[4]

(ii) *State practice.* The approach adopted by the Governments of both the United States and the United Kingdom *vis-à-vis* the imposition by other States of exchange restrictions is in

[1] F.C.S.C., *Seventeenth Semiannual Report, December 31, 1962*, p. 194.
[2] F.C.S.C., *Fourteenth Semiannual Report, June 30, 1961*, pp. 146–7.
[3] Ibid. p. 147.   [4] Whiteman, 8 D.I.L. (1967) p. 981.

accordance with this general principle. Replying to a request that it protest against Chilean foreign exchange regulations, the United States Department of State said that 'Such legislation does not ordinarily afford grounds for protest by foreign governments in the absence of discrimination against their respective nationals'.[1] In reviewing the over-all practice of the United States in this respect, Hyde concludes that 'As a witness of numerous measures for the control of foreign exchange which have been taken by certain foreign States within recent years, the United States has acknowledged the right of a territorial sovereign to have recourse to such procedure'.[2] The Government of the United Kingdom has similarly adopted the position that the imposition of exchange restrictions is a matter which lies within a State's domestic jurisdiction. This was evidenced by the reply of the Minister of State for Foreign Affairs who stated that the release of blocked funds in Israel, belonging to British subjects, 'is a matter for a foreign Government, and we are not in a position to dictate to them what their currency regulations should be'.[3]

(iii) *Publicists.* As regards academic opinion, leading authorities such as Fawcett,[4] Hug,[5] Hyde,[6] Mann,[7] Metzger,[8] Nussbaum,[9] etc.,[10] all agree that, in the absence of restrictions which are abusive, discriminatory, etc., States are at liberty to introduce and administer such measures without thereby committing an international tort. Wortley neatly sums up the legal position: 'when currency control is a defensive measure to

[1] Hackworth, II D.I.L. (1941) p. 68. For further similar pronouncements by the United States Department of State in respect of the introduction of exchange controls by other countries, see ibid., pp. 68–78.

[2] Hyde, I *International Law* (1947) p. 690. See also J. W. Gantenbein, *Financial Questions in United States Foreign Policy* (1939) p. 99.

[3] *House of Commons Parliamentary Debates*, 25 Apr. 1956, vol. 551, col. 1753.

[4] Fawcett, 'The International Monetary Fund and International Law', 40 B.Y.I.L. (1964) pp. 58–9.

[5] W. Hug, 'The Law of International Payments', 79 R.C. (1951–II) pp. 591–2.

[6] Hyde, op. cit. pp. 690–2.

[7] Mann, *The Legal Aspect of Money* (2nd ed., 1953) p. 419, and 'Money in Public International Law', 96 R.C. (1959–I) p. 97.

[8] Metzger, 'Exchange Controls and International Law', *University of Illinois Law Forum* (1959) p. 312.

[9] Nussbaum, *Money in the Law*, p. 475.

[10] A. A. Fatourus, *Government Guarantees to Foreign Investors* (1962) p. 49; W. A. Kewenig, loc. cit. pp. 387–9; F. K. Nielsen, *American–Turkish Claims Settlement* (1937) pp. 603–21 and in particular at 611–12.

protect the national currency, it operates like taxation and may be treated as such, and though it may cause considerable indirect loss it will not, if made bona fide, be unlawful in international law.'[1]

This is not to suggest, however, that the prerogative which States enjoy *vis-à-vis* exchange restrictions is an unlimited one. Limitations, as suggested by Mr. Justice Upjohn in the *In re Claim by Helbert Wagg & Co. Ltd.*,[2] do exist:

> In my judgement these courts must recognize the right of every foreign state to protect its economy by measures of foreign exchange control and by altering the value of its currency . . . That, however, is subject to the qualifications that this court is entitled to be satisfied that the foreign law is a genuine foreign exchange law, that is, a law passed with the genuine intention of protecting its economy in times of national stress and for that purpose regulating (inter alia) the rights of foreign creditors, and is not a law passed ostensibly with that object, but in reality with some object not in accordance with the usage of nations.[3]

Exchange restrictions which are not in accordance with the usage of nations may come into conflict with the notions of *abus de droit* or the illegal interference with the property rights of aliens. These notions, as the following examples will illustrate, ensure that in extreme cases aggrieved parties—even in the absence of specific treaty obligations—will not be without a remedy.

2. *Exceptions to the General Principle within Customary International Law and General Principles of Law*

(i) *Illegal interference with the property rights of aliens.* It has not infrequently been suggested that certain forms of exchange control will constitute a taking of property for which adequate, prompt, and effective compensation becomes payable. So it has been asserted in a Report of the Committee on Nationalization of Property of the American Branch of the International Law Association that:

> . . . A taking need not be total; title need not pass. To fall within the ambit of our analysis, a taking may well involve lesser measures

---

[1] Wortley, op. cit. p. 49.   [2] (1956) 2 W.L.R. 183.
[3] Ibid. p. 199.

which have the effect, in whole or in part, of an appropriation or destruction by the State of alien interests in property and contract. Among such measures may be sequestration, custodianship, breach by a State of a contract with an alien, arbitrary measures of taxation and exchange control . . . These examples are but illustrative of the fact that the opportunities of the State either to regulate or to abuse the rights of foreigners are manifold. We use the word 'taking' with the potential of such abuse in mind.[1]

Similarly, following the wholesale nationalization of property belonging to nationals of the Netherlands by the Indonesian Government in the late 1950s (the measures included exchange controls in respect of the transfer of company profits and other remittances to the Netherlands),[2] it was maintained that:

. . . There can be said to be confiscation, not only when the entire property is 'taken' by a Government, so that *all* rights of ownership are lost to the owners, but also in the event of 'seizure or denial of interests less than full legal ownership'. Thus the taking over of the *rights of control* over the property from the owners of the enterprises in itself constitutes confiscation, while we have seen that, in consequence of the refusal in advance to grant permission for the transfer of operating profits to the owners, the latter have also been deprived of all *enjoyment* of their property. What is left to them is no more than bare ownership, without, however, any rights of *disposition*. They remain the owners in name only.[3]

Academic opinion also favours this position: for example, Fawcett,[4] Mann,[5] and Wortley[6] are all of the opinion that exchange restrictions will, in certain circumstances, constitute a taking of property. However, the particular circumstances in which such measures give rise to an internationally compensable claim have, to date, been somewhat uncertain. In this respect a series of claims recently considered by the United States Foreign Claims Settlement Commission are of great value because they go a considerable distance towards filling the gap, and will, for this reason, be examined in detail in this study.

---

[1] Whiteman, 8 D.I.L. (1967) p. 1007.
[2] 5 *Nederlands tijdschrift voor internationaal recht* (1958) p. 236.
[3] Ibid. p. 242.
[4] Fawcett, 'Trade and Finance in International Law', 123 R.C. (1968–I) p. 289.
[5] Mann, 'Money in Public International Law', 96 R.C. (1959–I) p. 91.
[6] Wortley, op. cit. pp. 46–50.

It will be remembered[1] that the Commission was charged with the responsibility of determining, in accordance with applicable substantive law including international law, the validity of claims brought by nationals of the United States against specified foreign governments for failure to pay effective compensation for the nationalization, compulsory liquidation, or other taking of property of the nationals of the United States. Several of the claims brought before the Commission were concerned with the issue of whether the introduction of exchange restrictions by certain of these States was tantamount to the taking of property. They are therefore of direct and immediate relevance.

In considering this question, the Commission found that prima facie the introduction of exchange restrictions is a legitimate exercise of a State's economic sovereignty and does not therefore constitute a taking of property. It went on to suggest, however, that the position would be otherwise if it were shown either (i) that such measures were not justifiable on bona fide economic grounds, but were in fact undertaken for other more spurious motives, or (ii) that the exchange restrictions were so severe that they did not merely limit or restrict the foreign national's enjoyment and use of his currency, but, in fact, extinguished or terminated his ownership thereof, that is, the restrictions were, in fact, a disguised form of confiscation. The following claims illustrate the Commission's approach.

(a) The economic test. In the *Chobady Claim*,[2] the claimant had, before 1925, deposited a sum of 102,000 korona in a savings account with the Hungarian–Italian Bank Limited. Subsequently, owing to Hungarian currency reforms, the claimant's korona deposit had not only depreciated in value (by 1946, due to devaluation of the Hungarian currency, the deposit had become completely worthless), but was also not transferable out of Hungary. The claimant brought a claim against the Hungarian Government in respect of the loss of his deposit. The Commission, after holding that that part of the Hungarian currency reform legislation which had the effect of reducing the value of its currency did not constitute a taking of claimant's property, went on to say in respect of the exchange

---

[1] Above, pp. 49–50.   [2] (1958–II) I.L.R. pp. 292–4.

restrictions: 'Likewise, a prohibition against transfer of funds outside of a country is an exercise of sovereign authority which, though causing hardship to nonresidents having currency on deposit within the country, may not be deemed a "taking" of their property . . .'[1] In setting out the reasons in support of this decision, the Commission relied heavily upon the disrupted nature of the Hungarian economy at the time when these currency measures were introduced, and found that 'the grievance of the claimant is the consequence of severe currency devaluation and restrictions on the transfer of currency out of Hungary brought about by general economic conditions'[1]— that is as a result of the damage inflicted upon the Hungarian economy owing to the unfavourable war and post-war conditions, 'rather than by any specific action of the Hungarian Government which may be characterized as a "nationalization, compulsory liquidation, or other taking" of claimant's property'.[1] Clearly the implication of these remarks is that exchange restrictions will not constitute a taking of property if they are economically necessary, and that the position may well be otherwise where the proper economic basis is lacking.

Two further claims, the *Evanoff Claim*[2] and the *Muresan Claim*,[3] brought against the Bulgarian and Romanian Governments respectively, were similarly disposed of by the Commission, which again held, on the basis of the attendant economic circumstances, that the imposition of exchange restrictions, coupled with currency devaluation resulting in loss of claimants' funds, constituted an exercise of sovereign authority and did not amount to a nationalization, compulsory liquidation, or other taking of claimants' property. Moreover, the Commission made it clear in the latter claim that the severity of the restrictions, as well as the economic conditions giving rise thereto, was also an important element in determining liability. It found in this respect that 'there still exists in Rumania in some institution of credit, an account in favour of the claimant, however small in value, and however restricted may be his use and enjoyment thereof'.[4] In the Commission's opinion, exchange restrictions may limit or reduce the owner's enjoyment and use of his funds, but so long as they do not eliminate or

---

[1] (1958–II) I.L.R. p. 293.
[2] Ibid. pp. 301–2.
[3] Ibid. pp. 294–5.
[4] Ibid. p. 295.

extinguish his ownership thereof, they will not be considered as confiscatory.

(*b*) Severity test. This latter test for determining liability—that is, the severity of the restrictions—was also applied by the Commission in the adjudication of a series of claims which were brought against the Soviet and Czechoslovak Governments. The Commission found that the restrictions imposed by the Czechoslovak Government did not constitute a 'taking', while the restrictions imposed by the Soviet Government were, on the basis of this test, of a confiscatory nature. The facts giving rise to the Czechoslovak claims were as follows.[1] On 1 November 1945 the Government of Czechoslovakia replaced, by Presidential Decree No. 91/45 Sb, all old pre-war koruna currency at the ratio of 1:1. Incidental to this monetary reform, all old koruna deposits with financial institutions were blocked, effective 1 November 1945. The blocking provision, Section 7 (1) of the Presidential Decree, provided in part that:

> All deposits of whatever nature (deposit books, deposit certificates, current accounts and so on) with Post Office Savings Bank, financial institutions and financial enterprises in the Czechoslovak Republic, insofar as they have not been made in the new media of payment, are blocked as from 1st November, 1945. On the same day the payment of interest upon them shall also cease.[2]

The Commission was of the opinion that the blocking of funds by Section 7 (1) of the Presidential Decree did not (in so far as prejudiced American creditors were concerned) constitute, from the point of view of international law, a nationalization or other taking of their property. It went on to say that in the present circumstances this contention of no liability was further strengthened by virtue of the fact that the blockings were not complete—that is, even though all old koruna deposits were blocked, some withdrawals from the blocked accounts were nevertheless permitted. The position reached by the Commission was stated as follows:

> The recognized rule of international law that blocking in and of

[1] For a more detailed survey of the post-war course of events in Czechoslovakia with respect to that Government's treatment of bank deposits and savings accounts and the prevailing rate of exchange between the United States dollar and the Czechoslovak crown, see *F.C.S.C., Seventeenth Semiannual Report, December 31, 1962*, Exhibit XXVII, pp. 167–70.

[2] Ibid. p. 167.

itself does not amount to a nationalization or other taking of property, in the present case is also supported by the fact that by blocking the deposits the Government of Czechoslovakia did not deprive the owner of such deposits entirely because withdrawal was possible within limitations.[1]

In the period 1945–53 the above-mentioned blocked accounts were the subject of several other legislative provisions;[2] however, during this period depositors still retained their ownership of the blocked funds and withdrawals within prescribed limits were still permitted.[3] However, in 1953, by Law 41/53 Sb, all deposits in the blocked accounts were annulled, effective June 1953. As a result of this annulment a series of claims were brought against the Czechoslovak Government by United States nationals who had been deprived of their funds by the annulment legislation. It was held by the Commission *In the Matter of the Claim of John Stipkala*[4] and other similar claims[5] that the funds in blocked accounts were 'taken' by the Government of Czechoslovakia on 1 June 1953. It is important to note that in all these claims the operative date of 'taking' was deemed by the Commission to have been 1 June 1953, the date of the annulment, rather than 1 November 1945, the date at which the deposits were blocked. Although the restrictions of 1 November 1945 had the effect of limiting claimant's enjoyment and use of his funds, they did not eliminate or extinguish his ownership thereof, since withdrawals, albeit only to a limited extent, were still permitted.[6]

On the other hand, if it can be established that the exchange restrictions are in fact merely a disguised form of confiscation,

---

[1] Ibid.

[2] See ibid., where these subsequent legislative provisions are enumerated.

[3] See *In the Matter of the Claim of John H. Lusdyk, F.C.S.C., Seventeenth Semiannual Report, December 31, 1962*, pp. 223–6.

[4] This was the leading claim, see ibid., p. 191.

[5] The Commission decided several similar claims. See, *inter alia*, the following: *Claim of Barney Capek*, ibid. p. 193; *Claim of Louise Hrubes et al.*, ibid. pp. 204–6; *Claim of Otto Mlnarik et al.*, ibid. pp. 211–12; *Claim of Alexander Feigler*, ibid. pp. 226–9; *Claim of Frantiska Gasparovic et al.*, ibid. pp. 249–50; *Claim of Ann Unger et al.*, ibid. pp. 262–72; *Claim of Frank Dvorak*, ibid. pp. 198–9; *Claim of L. R. Thiel, F.C.S.C., Twentieth Semiannual Report, June 30, 1964*, pp. 33–5.

[6] Certain claims were also brought before the Commission based on bank deposits made after 1 Nov. 1945 in new koruna currency. See, *inter alia*, the following claims: *Claim of Karolin Furst, F.C.S.C., Seventeenth Semiannual Report, December 31, 1962*, pp. 199–200; *Claim of John H. Lusdyk*, ibid. pp. 223–6.

then the position, as is evidenced by the decisions rendered by the Commission in the *Tanglefoot Company Claim*[1] and other similar claims[2] brought by United States nationals against the Soviet Government, will be quite different. In the Tanglefoot claim, the claimant company had on deposit on 30 June 1917 the sum of 156,124 roubles with the Petrograd branch of the National City Bank of New York, a foreign-owned private bank. On 27 December 1917 the Soviet Government nationalized by Decree all Russian-owned private banks. Although foreign-owned banks were not liquidated until a later date, they were nevertheless affected by the restrictions imposed by the Soviet Government in implementing the 27 December 1917 Decree. United States nationals who had deposits in foreign-owned as well as Russian-owned banks were also affected by these restrictions. The following were some of the conditions and restrictions implemented by the Soviet Bank Commission in administering the decree of 27 December:

(1) A depositor was required to first secure permission in writing from the local Soviet authorities to withdraw funds.
(2) Such permission would not be granted unless the depositor applied for same in person and could establish that he had no other means of subsistence.
(3) Withdrawals, upon permission, were limited to small monthly allotments.
(4) Withdrawals, upon permission, of "pre-revolution" accounts of Soviet business enterprises were authorized if the money was needed for the payment of wages.[3]

The National City Bank of New York was affected by these restrictions because it was unable to withdraw at will, after the December Decree, deposits which it had with the Russian State Bank and other private Russian-owned banks, and was therefore unable in turn to honour requests for withdrawals by its own depositors, of which the claimant company was one. The Tanglefoot Company brought a claim against the Soviet Government to recover the dollar value of a rouble account which it had on 28 December 1917 with the Petrograd branch of the National City Bank of New York.

[1] 30 I.L.R. pp. 120–2.
[2] For references to similar claims, see *F.C.S.C.*, *Index—Digest of Decisions*, p. 17.
[3] *F.C.S.C.*, *Tenth Semiannual Report, June 30. 1959*, p. 210.

The Commissioners allowed the claim on the grounds that the restrictions imposed by the Soviet Government in implementing the 27 December 1917 Decree constituted a confiscation of claimant's deposit. The Commission therefore awarded claimant the sum of $20,296.12 (plus interest), which sum represented the dollar value of the 156,124 rouble deposit on 28 December 1917, the date at which the restrictions came into effect. A similar claim[1] was brought by the Guaranty Trust Company of New York against the Soviet Government in respect of certain securities and bank deposits which were also adversely affected by the December Decree. The Commission, in allowing the claim, stated:

By Decree dated December 27, 1917, the Soviet Government nationalized Russian-owned banks. Russian Branches of foreign-owned banks were not covered by said Decree but were subsequently liquidated by the Soviet Government. However, the Commission finds that as the result of restrictions and regulations promulgated to implement the nationalization, deposits standing to the credit of United States nationals in foreign-owned banks as well as Russian-owned banks were taken by the Soviet Government on December 28, 1917.[2]

The test which the Commission applied in determining whether the Soviet restrictions were of a confiscatory nature was based primarily on the severity of the restrictions—that is, whether the effect of the restrictions was merely to limit a claimant's enjoyment and use of his funds or to extinguish, *de facto*, his ownership thereof. It found on the basis of this formula that the restrictions were of the latter variety, and therefore held that the taking of deposits belonging to the United States nationals occurred on 28 December 1917, the date on which the 'confiscatory restrictions'[3] came into effect.

In conclusion, on the basis of the above evidence, it is possible to make the following general observations on the nature of the relationship between the introduction and implementation of exchange restrictions and the notion 'illegal interference with the property rights of aliens': (1) Prima facie the use of exchange restrictions will not be tantamount to a

---

[1] *Guaranty Trust Company of New York Claim*, 30 I.L.R. pp. 134–5.
[2] Ibid. p. 135.
[3] This terminology is used by the Commission, *F.C.S.C.*, *Tenth Semiannual Report*, *June 30, 1959*, p. 209.

'taking' of property. As the Commission pointed out, restrictions are by and large employed during times of economic stress, and although they will invariably restrict the accessibility of currency, they do not in normal conditions sever the legal bond of ownership; (2) The above presumption can be rebutted, however, if it is established (a) that the restrictions do not merely limit the foreign national's enjoyment and use of his currency, but do in fact extinguish his ownership thereof, or (b) that the restrictions are not introduced for reasons of economic necessity, but for other, more spurious motives. In so far as this latter exception is concerned, however, it is probably correct to suggest that an international cause of action arising out of such circumstances would be more appropriately based on the notion *abus de droit*.

However, before considering the efficacy of the notion *abus de droit* in providing a measure of protection against the arbitrary use of exchange restrictions, a further problem relating to currency convertibility and the taking of property requires examination. The issue to be considered is one in which alien-owned property—for example, land, factories, etc. —has been expropriated by the host State and compensation becomes payable. It will be remembered that according to a well-established norm of international law, such compensation must be 'adequate, prompt and effective'.[1] The question then arises: does payment, if made in the local currency of the nationalizing State and if neither freely convertible nor freely transferable, satisfy the criterion of 'effectiveness'?

An affirmative answer is suggested by Metzger: 'There is no international law rule requiring that any other than the local currency of the taking state, whether it is convertible into foreign exchange or not, be paid for taken property.'[2] Moreover, he further contends with enumerated reasons[3] 'that it would be undesirable to attempt to create such a rule of customary, or indeed of treaty, law'.[4]

On the other hand, it is suggested by Higgins that ' "Effectiveness" means that the payment must not be illusory; the alien must be able to withdraw it from the country concerned

---

[1] See Schwarzenberger, *Foreign Investments and International Law* (1969) pp. 4–11.
[2] Metzger, 'Property in International Law', 50 *Virginia Law Review* (1964–I) p. 603.   [3] Ibid. pp. 604–5.   [4] Ibid. p. 604.

and use it to his benefit. The particular currency in which payment is made, for example, would often be of relevance here'.[1] It would appear that American practice tends to support the latter rather than the former view.[2] In the absence of rigid legal criteria, perhaps the approach adopted by the American Law Institute Restatement on 'Responsibility of States for Injuries to Aliens' is the most appropriate. Paragraph 190, entitled 'Effectiveness of Compensation', provides:

(1) Compensation, to be in effectively realizable form, within the meaning of §187 [defining 'just compensation'], must be in the form of cash or property readily convertible into cash. If not in the currency of the state of which the alien was a national at the time of the taking, the cash paid must be convertible into such currency and withdrawable, either before or after conversion, to the territory of the state of the alien's nationality, except as indicated in Subsection (2).

(2) Such conversion and withdrawal may be delayed to the minimum extent necessary to assure the availability of foreign exchange for goods and services essential to the health and welfare of the people of the taking state.[3]

While sub-paragraph (1) provides that compensation, when made, must be made in freely convertible and transferable currency, sub-paragraph (2) ensures that such payments may be temporarily postponed should they endanger the economic well-being of the taking nation. Priority is given to the taking nation's internal economic stability, thereby ensuring its survival, without which all external economic relations would become meaningless.

(ii) *Non-discrimination and* abus de droit. Exchange restrictions are by their very nature discriminatory,[4] the reason being that in its allocation of scarce foreign exchange, a State will necessarily discriminate in favour of certain trading partners and against others because of—*inter alia*—(a) the trading partner's ability or inability to supply essential imports, (b) the nature and composition of the restricting State's foreign exchange,

---

[1] R. Higgins, *Conflict of Interests* (1965) p. 57.
[2] Whiteman, 8 D.I.L. (1967) p. 1183.
[3] Ibid. pp. 1184–5.
[4] For a discussion of the discriminatory nature of exchange controls, see H. S. Ellis, 'Exchange Control and Discrimination', 37 *American Economic Review* (1947) pp. 877–88.

and (c) the existence of special monetary links such as those which obtain in the franc and sterling areas.

So in the post-Second World War period, owing to the scarcity of dollars, European countries found it necessary to discriminate against imports from the United States and other countries demanding payment in dollars.[1] More recently the United Kingdom travel restrictions discriminated between sterling and non-sterling area countries. Whereas travellers to non-sterling area countries were restricted to a £50 allowance, travellers to sterling area countries were not subject to any restrictions.[2] Similarly, following the introduction by the United States of America, on 1 January 1968, of the Foreign Direct Investment Program,[3] blanket prohibitions were placed on the export of investment capital (as that term was defined in the Act) by American investors. Only by general authorization or specific exception are certain types of capital transfer permitted. In general, the amount of capital which American investors may invest in any particular country is subject to an annual limit. These annual limits are not equal but vary from country to country. For this purpose every country has been classified as a Schedule A, B, or C country. Investments into Schedule A countries—that is, underdeveloped or developing countries such as most African, Asian, and Latin American countries—are the least restricted. Investments into Schedule B countries—that is, developed countries which are heavily dependent upon United States capital, such as Australia and New Zealand—are also permitted, but to a lesser extent. Investments into Schedule C countries—that is, all continental O.E.C.D. countries (excluding Greece and Turkey) plus South Africa—are totally prohibited, although some reinvestment of earned income is permitted. Finally, the Program provides that in certain exceptional cases—that is, where strict enforcement of the Program would result in severe economic injury to a country—that country may be exempted by Presidential Decree from the operation of the Program. Canada, and to a

---

[1] M. G. de Vries, 'Exchange Restrictions: Progress toward Liberalization', 6 F.D. (1969) pp. 40–1.

[2] *The Economist*, 10 Jan. 1970, pp. 56–7.

[3] The following brief review of the United States Foreign Direct Investment Program is based on an article by D. G. Carreau, 'The U.S. Balance of Payments Programs', 2 J.W.T.L. (1968) pp. 601–55.

lesser extent Japan, were granted special concessions under this provision.

The discrimination which arises in the administration of an exchange control regime is apparent and the question then arises: is such discriminatory conduct reprehensible to, and therefore subject to redress under, customary international law?

Although it is sometimes suggested that exchange discrimination of this sort is contrary to international law,[1] such a contention, so long as the inequality of treatment stems from restrictions which are introduced in response to 'the economic needs of a country',[2] is not maintainable. So in justifying the introduction of controls, it was argued by France in the *Case Concerning Rights of Nationals of the United States in Morocco (France v. United States of America)*[3] that:

The prohibition of imports sans devises, except from France and the French Union, is not a discrimination against the United States which is contrary to public international law. To hold otherwise would be to condemn exchange control as a whole, because it never applies uniformly but is always exercised in relation to the availability of each currency. France intends to reduce exchange control as much as possible, but the dollar is scarce in Morocco whereas the means of making payments to France are not. Inasmuch as adoption of the Decree was dictated by financial necessities, and not by discriminatory or protectionist policies, it did not constitute an unjust discrimination against the United States.[4]

Indeed, an argument contrary to the one put forward by France would be plausible only if it were shown that there existed in customary international law a rule expressly prohibiting all forms of discrimination in international economic affairs. Such a rule does not exist. Moreover, it has been asserted by no less an authority than Nussbaum that not only is the contention 'that control measures must not be "discriminatory"' a tenuous one, but exchange restrictions which

---

[1] *Tabar Claim (No. 3) (1953) I.L.R.* p. 242; Hyde, I *International Law* (1947) p. 691; Fawcett, 'International Monetary Fund and International Law', 40 B.Y.I.L. (1964) p. 57. See similar pronouncements by the United States Department of State in Hackworth, II D.I.L. (1941) pp. 68–70; D. G. Carreau, loc. cit. p. 646.

[2] Hug, 'The Law of International Payments', 79 R.C. (1951–II) p. 592.

[3] (1952) I.C.J. Reports pp. 176–233.

[4] J. Gold, *The Fund Agreement in the Courts* (1962) p. 41.

are introduced for the purpose of safeguarding a country's balance of payments 'constitute acts of "self-preservation" legitimate even in the teeth of a most-favoured-nation clause'.[1]

But as Nussbaum further points out: 'The situation is otherwise where the differentiation is not justified by economic necessity, and takes on an arbitrary or offensive character . . .'[2] From this observation it is apparent that it is not the discriminatory nature of exchange restrictions *per se* which is objectionable, but rather the offensive reasons for which they may be introduced—that is, where they are introduced not for reasons of economic necessity but, for example, as weapons in waging international economic warfare or as measures preparatory to war.[3] In this latter respect it has been suggested that 'the Nazi technique of using exchange control to cheat other countries in the interests of war economy was a clear case of economic aggression of the kind that ought not to be permitted among the nations'.[4]

A more recent example of the arbitrary use of exchange control, that is, as an instrument of economic warfare, is provided by the *Indonesian Corporation P.T. Escomptobank* v. *N. V. Assurantie Maatschappij der Nederlanden van 1845* case.[5] Although this case was argued before Netherlands Municipal Courts, it is nevertheless of great importance to international economic lawyers since both the District Court of The Hague and the Court of Appeal of The Hague[6] considered the dispute,

---

[1] Nussbaum, *Money in the Law*, pp. 475–6. Other leading publicists are in agreement with Nussbaum's position. See Mann, *The Legal Aspect of Money*, pp. 424–5: 'It must, however, be admitted that a measure of discrimination is inherent in exchange restrictions and that in any event it will usually be difficult to prove any impropriety in their application'; Hug, op. cit. p. 592; Kewenig, op. cit. pp. 380–2.

[2] Nussbaum, op. cit. p. 476.

[3] Hug, op. cit., p. 592; Mann, 'Money in Public International Law', 96 R.C. (1959–I) p. 98.

[4] G. Crowther, *An Outline of Money* (1948) p. 275. Similarly See W. A. Brown, Jr., *The United States and the Restoration of World Trade* (1950) p. 45: 'Under German leadership and example trade in a large part of Europe had been made an instrument of increasing war potential and a weapon to achieve political ends.'

[5] 13 *Nederlands tijdschrift voor internationaal recht* (Netherlands International Law Review) (1966) pp. 58–70.

[6] The case was also heard by the Supreme Court of the Netherlands which reached a decision similar to that of the two lower courts; however, unlike the lower courts which based their decision on the fact that the Indonesian decrees

that is, the legality of certain Indonesian nationalization and exchange control legislation, from the point of view of international law. The facts giving rise to the dispute, although somewhat complicated, can be summarized as follows. A Netherlands insurance company, de Nederlanden van 1845 (hereinafter: the Company of 1845), owned all the shares in five Indonesian insurance companies. The five Indonesian companies were, in fact, subsidiaries of the Company of 1845. One of the subsidiaries, the Maritime and Fire Insurance Company of 1851 (hereinafter: the Company of 1851) had a number of accounts, in which the other subsidiaries also had rights, in foreign currencies, that is, United States dollars, Malayan dollars, pounds sterling, and Netherlands guilders, with an Indonesian bank (hereinafter: Escomptobank). On 26 November 1959, the Company of 1851, acting on behalf of itself as well as the other four subsidiaries, assigned its claim against Escomptobank to the Company of 1845 for the purpose of collection. The deed of assignment was executed in the Netherlands by the managing director of the five subsidiaries. The Company of 1845, having attached the assets of Escomptobank in the Netherlands, brought an action against Escomptobank for payment of the foreign currency balances and for validation of the attachment.

The subsidiaries had been brought under State control by order of the Military Command in Djakarta on 20 December 1957, and were subsequently nationalized on 16 January 1960 with retroactive effect as from 3 December 1957. The establishment of state control over the subsidiaries as well as their nationalization was directed solely against Netherlands-owned enterprises, was without compensation, and was politically motivated—that is, to force the recognition by the Netherlands of Indonesian claims to Western New Guinea.

In conjunction with the nationalization, the Indonesian Minister of Finance, by an order of 24 May 1958, prohibited all transfers of money or disposals of existing balances. The effect of this order was to subject the Company of 1851 to the Foreign Exchange Control Ordinance of 1940 which prohibited

were contrary to international law, the Supreme Court based its decision on the grounds that the Indonesian decrees were repugnant to Netherlands public policy. However, as it pointed out (ibid. p. 69 n. 1), 'both methods lead to the same result'.

all residents of Indonesia from disposing of foreign currency and foreign claims in favour of non-residents. Before the 24 May 1958 order, the Company of 1851 had possessed a general foreign exchange control licence which allowed it to dispose of the foreign currencies in question.

Escomptobank argued: (a) that as a result of the above-mentioned Indonesian nationalization decrees, the managing director had been divested of any power to make the assignment; (b) that the assignment was null and void since the required foreign exchange control licence had not been granted; and (c) that the foreign currency balance could not be collected since, again as in (b), the Indonesian exchange control authorities had not granted the necessary licence.

The District Court gave judgment for the Company of 1845. The Court dismissed Escomptobank's first defence and refused to give legal effect to the Indonesian nationalization decrees, in spite of the act of state doctrine, because the decrees, being discriminatory, without compensation, and politically motivated, were clearly contrary to international law. In respect of the latter two arguments the Court similarly held that the termination of the general foreign exchange control licence and the control of balances were also effected by the Indonesian violation of international law, and therefore no legal effect would be attached to them. The Court went on to say:

> For this reason it is objectionable to accord in regard to the assignment any legal effects to foreign exchange control provisions enacted by the Indonesian State after the establishment of the control, which provisions terminated the originally existing general licence. In so far as these provisions were enacted with the purpose of regulating the exploitation of the enterprises subsequent to control and nationalization, they are under international law as illegal as is the very control and nationalization.[1]

Escomptobank appealed to the Court of Appeal, which upheld the decision of the District Court. The Court of Appeal refused, as did the District Court, to give legal effect to the nationalization and financial decrees on the grounds that they were 'discriminatory and confiscatory and, therefore, clearly a breach of international law'.[2] It went on to say that the act of state doctrine did not apply to those state acts which were clearly

---

[1] 13 *Netherlands International Law Review* (1966) p. 61.   [2] Ibid. p. 63.

not in accordance with international law. As to Escompto-bank's contention that it could not pay balances in foreign currency on the accounts of its clients without a licence having been granted by the Indonesian exchange control authorities, which licence was in fact not forthcoming, the Court replied:

In good faith Escomptobank cannot *vis-à-vis de Nederlanden Van 1845*, as an assignee of her client, invoke her general conditions which were intended for normal business transactions in Indonesia. Performance of these conditions cannot be demanded with respect to a holder of an account who was dispossessed by Indonesia under violation of international law, who, after assignment of her claim to her mother company, identifies in the Netherlands an opportunity to attach assets in order to obtain payment and who would remain spoliated if the Indonesian foreign exchange control law which Escomptobank desires to be enforced, were to be abused to that end.[1]

The importance of the above case to the issue of exchange controls and international law is evident. It illustrates categorically and without qualification that exchange measures which are introduced not for reasons of economic necessity but rather as instruments for waging international economic warfare, and which seek to deprive foreign nationals of their deposits, will be considered as abusive and contrary to international law.[2]

---

[1] 13 *Netherlands International Law Review* (1966) p. 64.

[2] For reference to other municipal judicial decisions, see Mann, 'Money in Public International Law', 96 R.C. (1959-I) pp. 96–8.

V

PRE-FUND CONVENTIONAL
MONETARY ARRANGEMENTS

1. *Introduction*

No attempt at an exhaustive review of the treaty practice developed by States in the inter-war period with respect to international monetary affairs will be undertaken here. Such a study would be largely of historical interest only since the bulk of the contemporary conventional law of money has developed since the emergence of the International Monetary Fund in 1945. Nevertheless, a brief review of such State practice is of some importance to this study, primarily for the following two reasons: (*a*) the complete failure of the many international economic conferences convened during the inter-war period to conclude any multilateral monetary conventions illustrates the fact that although States were not yet prepared to submit their international monetary relations to the rule of international law, they were nevertheless aware of the gravity of the problem and saw the necessity of dealing with it on a multilateral level;[1] (*b*) although States were not yet willing to co-operate on a multilateral level, it will be shown that some progress was made in this direction on the bilateral treaty level. In this respect the inter-war years, viewed from the point of view of international conventional law, can be seen as constituting a transitional era, bridging the gap between the nineteenth-century gold standard regime based on international comity and the just emerging post-1945 regime based on international conventional law. It was in this period, therefore, that the seeds which ultimately culminated in the growth of post-1945 conventional monetary law, were planted.

---

[1] Cf. 'Introduction to the Fund', 1 F.D. (June 1964) p. 3. See also F. A. Southard, Jr., 'International Financial Policy, 1920–44,' 2 F.D. (Sept. 1965) p. 137.

2. Bilateral Treaty Arrangements

(i) *Exchange rates.* Provisions in some of the earlier bilateral commercial treaty agreements concluded in the inter-war period and concerned with the issue of currency depreciation were of a protectionist character, that is to say, they did not seek to prevent currency fluctuations or even to regulate them, but rather sought to provide a measure of protection against the adverse effects of any such occurrences. Article 3, paragraph 1 of the Treaty of Commerce concluded between the United Kingdom and the Czechoslovak Republic on 14 July 1923[1] illustrates such a provision:

Nothing in this Treaty shall be held to prohibit the imposition in His Britannic Majesty's territories of special rates of Customs duty on specified articles of Czechoslovak origin, other or higher than those levied on similar articles the produce or manufacture of any other foreign country, in cases where such special rates of Customs duty are levied in pursuance of legislation of general application enabling the imposition of such duties on articles the produce or manufacture of any country, where such articles are being sold or offered for sale in the part of His Britannic Majesty's territories concerned at prices which, by reason of depreciation in the value in relation to sterling of the currency of the country in which the articles are produced or manufactured, are below the prices at which similar articles can be profitably produced or manufactured in the part of His Britannic Majesty's territories concerned, and that by reason thereof employment in that part of His Britannic Majesty's territories is being, or is likely to be, seriously affected.

Under the terms of this Article the United Kingdom was entitled, in spite of the general most-favoured-nation clause provided for in Article 2 of the treaty, to impose additional rates of customs duties on such goods entering the territories of the United Kingdom, the price of which had been greatly reduced owing to the depreciation of the Czechoslovak crown in relation to the value of the pound sterling. Czechoslovakia was, in turn, entitled to renounce the treaty if the United Kingdom did decide to impose such additional duties on goods of Czechoslovak origin.[2] Under such a provision the sovereignty

---

[1] 29 L.N.T.S. 378. See similarly Art. 12 of the Treaty of Commerce and Navigation between Austria and Great Britain, 22 May 1924, 35 L.N.T.S. 175.

[2] See Para. 2 of Art. 3 of the Treaty between the United Kingdom and the

that a State possessed over its currency remained intact, and the objective of such a clause was to accord a State with a relatively stable currency (in this case the pound sterling) an effective method of counteracting any adverse effects that might arise as a result of the depreciation of the weak currency of a co-contracting State (in this case the Czechoslovak crown).

A similar but even more far-reaching provision was included in several of the first treaty arrangements concluded by the United States of America under the auspices of the 1934 Reciprocal Trade Agreement Act.[1] The first treaty to be concluded under that Act was the Commercial Agreement between the United States and the Republic of Honduras on 18 December 1935.[2] Article XI of that Agreement dealt with the issue of possible fluctuations occurring in the rate of exchange between the two currencies as follows:

> In the event that a wide variation occurs in the rate of exchange between the currencies of the United States of America and the Republic of Honduras, the Government of either country, if it considers the variation so substantial as to prejudice the industries or commerce of the country, shall be free to propose negotiations for the modification of this Agreement or to terminate this Agreement in its entirety on thirty days' written notice.

Under the terms of this Article, the two signatories were entitled, in case wide variations occurred in the rate of exchange between the two currencies, to request negotiations with the intention of modifying the agreement or, without prior negotiation, to terminate the agreement unilaterally on thirty days' notice, the only condition precedent being that the State seeking either to modify or to terminate the agreement had to establish that the variation in the exchange rate was so

Czechoslovak Republic. See also para. 2 of Art. 12 of the Treaty of Commerce and Navigation between Austria and Great Britain.

[1] 48 United States Statutes at Large (1933–4) p. 943.
[2] 167 L.N.T.S. 313. Similar provisions are to be found in the following agreements concluded by the United States: Sweden, 25 May 1935, 161 L.N.T.S. 109, Art. X; Canada, 15 Nov. 1935, 168 L.N.T.S. 355, Art. X; Guatemala, 24 Apr. 1936, 170 L.N.T.S. 345, Art. XII; Nicaragua, 11 Mar. 1936, 73 L.N.T.S. 141, Art. XII; Finland, 18 May 1936, 172 L.N.T.S. 97, Art. XIII; El Salvador, 19 Feb. 1937, 179 L.N.T.S. 219, Art. XII; Costa Rica, 28 Nov. 1936, 181 L.N.T.S. 183, Art. XII; Ecuador, 6 Aug. 1938, 193 L.N.T.S. 85; Turkey, 1 Apr. 1939, 202 L.N.T.S. 129, Art. XIV.

substantial that it was prejudicial to its industries and commerce.

In subsequent treaties concluded in the early 1940s under the Reciprocal Trade Agreement Act, however, the policy of the United States in respect to fluctuations in rates of exchange was substantially altered (foreshadowing things to come) in that the above-mentioned Article which provided for modification or termination of the treaty in case of wide fluctuations was abandoned. The new provisions were no longer protective in nature but rather sought to regulate rates of exchange on a most-favoured-nation basis. The Article[1] in question provided that:

> . . . With respect to rates of exchange and with respect to taxes or charges on exchange transactions, articles the growth, produce or manufacture of the other country shall be accorded unconditionally treatment no less favorable than that accorded to the like articles the growth, produce or manufacture of any third country . . .[2]

Moreover, this change in emphasis from a protectionist policy to a more regulatory policy *vis-à-vis* rates of exchange was further reflected in those provisions dealing with quantitative restrictions. Although the use of quantitative restrictions was to be generally prohibited, it was nevertheless provided that such restrictions could be applied, *inter alia*, in order to maintain the exchange value of the currency of the country introducing them.[3] In these latter agreements, priority was given to the maintenance of currency stability, and when exchange rates did vary, they were to be applied in such a manner that the trade of the partner State would not thereby be in a less favourable position than the trade of any other third State.

---

[1] Art. IV (2): Trade Agreement between the United States of America and the Oriental Republic of Uruguay, 21 July 1942, 120 U.N.T.S. 211.

[2] Provisions of a similar nature are to be found in the following agreements concluded by the United States: Argentina, 14 Oct. 1941, 119 U.N.T.S. 193, Art. IV (2); Mexico, 23 Dec. 1942, 13 U.N.T.S. 231, Art. IV (2); Iceland, 27 Aug. 1943, 29 U.N.T.S. 317, Art. IV (2); Iran, 8 Apr. 1943, 106 U.N.T.S. 155, Art. IV (2); Ecuador, 2 Mar. 1942, 105 U.N.T.S. 195; Cuba, 23 Dec. 1941, 119 U.N.T.S. 313, Art. VI (2).

[3] See Article XI, Trade Agreement between the United States of America and Uruguay, ibid., n. 1. Similar provisions are to be found in agreements concluded with Argentina, Article XI; Mexico, Article X; Iceland, Article XI; Cuba, Article III. For references, see ibid., n. 1.

(ii) *Exchange restrictions.*[1] (a) Period before 1931.[2] The relatively limited use which States made of exchange restrictions in the period following the First World War and prior to 1931 is reflected by the fact that only a few of the commercial agreements concluded in this period make any reference to such restrictive practices. A few isolated instances can nevertheless be found.

In the Treaty of Commerce concluded between France and Hungary on 13 October 1925,[3] the Contracting Parties agreed that they would not 'impede the importation of the products referred to in the preceding Articles by means of a control exercised over foreign exchange'.[4] Such a provision, however, expressly prohibiting the use of exchange restrictions as a means of regulating the flow of international trade was rare, and States more commonly sought to mitigate the harmful effects of exchange restrictions on international trade by the use of other less demanding provisions. For example, in the Treaty of Commerce and Navigation concluded between Austria and Great Britain on 22 May 1924,[5] it was agreed that should the Austrian Government find it necessary to introduce a temporary system of exchange control owing to exceptional economic conditions affecting the Republic, the control was to be so 'devised and worked as to cause the least possible inconvenience to British trade'.[6] It would seem to be almost impossible, however, to attribute the above provision any practical value, since it would be extremely difficult to establish an objective criterion for the purpose of determining whether or not the administration of an Austrian exchange control system was in fact causing British trade more than the 'least possible

[1] For a more detailed analysis of these provisions as applied by the United States in certain trade agreements concluded in the inter-war period, see S. D. Metzger, 'Exchange Controls and International Law', *University of Illinois Law Forum* (1959) pp. 313–18; W. A. Kewenig, 'Exchange Control', 16 *Buffalo Law Review* (1966–7) pp. 389–92.

[2] 1931 represents an important landmark in the history of exchange control. Before 1931 such controls were applied only sporadically. After 1931 their application became near-universal. Even the United States of America subjected foreign exchange transactions to restrictions from Mar. 1933 to Nov. 1934. See League of Nations, *Report on Exchange Control submitted by a Committee composed of Members of the Economic and Financial Committees*, II. Economic and Financial (1938. II. A. 10) pp. 10–11, para. 9.

[3] 48 L.N.T.S. 9.   [4] Ibid. Art. 12.
[5] 35 L.N.T.S. 175.   [6] Ibid. Art. 10.

inconvenience'.[1] Finally, a provision which was to prove very popular in both the post-1931 and post-1945 periods was one in which the contracting parties agreed to administer exchange restrictions on the basis of the most-favoured-nation standard (although here again it will be seen that this clause was only of marginal significance in guarding against the discriminatory effects of exchange restrictions). In this respect Article II of the Declarations regarding the Commercial Agreement of 4 May 1921, concluded between Austria and Czechoslovakia on 27 November 1924, may be cited:

As regards the purchase and sale of currency, both national and foreign, the Contracting Parties undertake not to accord to nationals or firms of the other Party more unfavourable treatment than that accorded to nationals and firms of the State which is granted most-favoured-nation treatment in this respect.[2]

(b) Period after 1931. Following the onset of the world economic crisis in the early 1930s, the use of exchange restrictions as a means of protecting a country's balance of payments became more widespread. To counteract the adverse effects of these restrictions on commercial transactions and to keep the channels of international trade open to at least a limited degree, many States entered into various bilateral payment, compensation, and clearing arrangements,[3] aimed at 'facilitating the transfer of funds from one country to another in such a manner as to maintain the balance of payments between the two countries in a state of reasonable equilibrium'.[4] For

---

[1] A more specific criterion was, in fact, provided in the last sentence of Art. 10: 'The conditions under which foreign currency shall be made available to pay for imports of goods . . . shall not be less favourable in any respect than those applicable to imports the produce or manufacture of any other foreign country.'

[2] 42 L.N.T.S. 201 at 441. For a similar provision, see Greece and United Kingdom Treaty of Commerce and Navigation, 16 July 1926, 61 L.N.T.S. 15, Art. 11.

[3] No detailed examination of these various bilateral arrangements, i.e. payment, compensation, and clearing agreements, will be undertaken in this study. Such agreements did not seek to regulate either the introduction or the administration of exchange restrictions (which alone is of interest to this study), but rather sought to circumvent them. As is pointed out by Mann, 'Money in Public International Law', 96 R.C. (1959-I) pp. 33-4, such arrangements are more properly considered separately. For a more detailed analysis of such agreements, see Hug, op. cit. pp. 569-74; Nussbaum, Money in the Law, pp. 515-25; League of Nations, Enquiry into Clearing Agreements, II. Economic and Financial (1935. II. B. 6).

[4] Mann, 'Money in Public International Law', 96 R.C. (1959-I) p. 32.

example, it was provided in Article I, paragraph (i) of the Payments Agreement concluded between Canada and Germany on 22 October 1936 that 'The German Government shall make available for the purchase of Canadian goods the foreign exchange accruing from German exports to Canada'.[1] In this way, by limiting the volume of imports allowed to enter country A from country B to a quantity equal in value to the proceeds arising out of exports to country B from country A, a bilateral payments balance between A and B would be realized. Although such arrangements ensured that the flow of international commerce would not become completely stagnant owing to payments restrictions, they were not entirely satisfactory, because international trade began to be increasingly conducted on a bilateral basis and therefore necessarily became distorted and discriminatory.[2]

More satisfactory in this respect, therefore, were those provisions which sought to alleviate the adverse effects of exchange restrictions through the application of other less rigid formulas which, unlike the bilateral agreements discussed above, tended towards promoting elements of non-discrimination and multilateralism in international trade. Although the United States, in keeping with its long tradition of championing the cause of non-discrimination in international commerce,[3] was in the forefront of this movement, several other States, albeit to a much more limited extent, adopted a similar approach. The provisions most commonly employed can be separated into the following three categories,[4] two of which had already appeared in the pre-1931 period: (a) those which provided that should

[1] 173 L.N.T.S. 311.
[2] League of Nations, Monetary and Economic Conference, *Draft Annotated Agenda, submitted by the Preparatory Commission of Experts*, II. Economic and Financial (1933. II. Spec. 1) p. 25, para. 2.
[3] For a historical review of United States policy with respect to foreign trade, see S. D. Metzger, 'American Foreign Policy and American Foreign Trade', 47 *Texas Law Review* (1969–II) pp. 1075–84.
[4] Several treaties also contained a provision which stated that exchange restrictions were to be administered on a non-discriminatory basis. See, for example, Art. 6 of the Exchange of Notes constituting a Temporary Agreement regarding Commercial Relations between Brazil and Great Britain and Northern Ireland, 10 Aug. 1936, 172 L.N.T.S. 273. See also the following commercial agreements concluded by the United States with Liberia, 8 Aug. 1938, 201 L.N.T.S. 163, Art. X; Guatemala, 24 Apr. 1936, 170 L.N.T.S. 345, Art. IX; Costa Rica, 28 Nov. 1936, 181 L.N.T.S. 183, Art. IX. Although these provisions could possibly be

exchange restrictions be introduced by either of the contracting parties, the available foreign exchange was to be allotted to the other contracting party on a fair and equitable basis; (*b*) those which provided that the available foreign exchange was to be allotted on a most-favoured-nation basis; (*c*) those which provided for the outright prohibition of exchange restrictions as a means of regulating the flow of international trade.

(*a*) The fair and equitable basis. The most rudimentary application of this provision is to be found in two commercial agreements concluded by Czechoslovakia with the United States of America on 29 March 1935[1] and with the Union of South Africa on 27 January 1937.[2] It was provided in the latter agreement that 'should either country establish or maintain any form of control of foreign exchange it shall administer such control so as to ensure that the commerce of the other country will be granted a fair and equitable share in the allotment of exchange'.[3] The difficulty in the practical application of this provision is manifest, since the criterion for the determination of what constitutes a 'fair and equitable' share of the available foreign exchange was nowhere defined in the treaty.

More satisfactory in this respect, therefore, were those provisions written into the trade agreements concluded by Canada with the United States of America,[4] Haiti,[5] and Guatemala,[6] and by the United States with several of her trading partners.[7] These provisions, as did the Czechoslovak ones, provided that the available foreign exchange was to be allotted on a fair and equitable basis, but, unlike the Czechoslovak provisions, went on to establish, at least in skeletal form, a formula which

classified as a fourth category, it will be seen that in practice they achieved non-discriminatory treatment similar to that achieved by those clauses embodying the most-favoured-nation standard.

[1] 159 L.N.T.S. 155.   [2] 189 L.N.T.S. 97.
[3] Ibid. Art. III.
[4] Trade Agreement, 15 Nov. 1935, 168 L.N.T.S. 355, Art. IX.
[5] Trade Agreement, 23 Apr. 1937, 194 L.N.T.S. 59, Art. V.
[6] Trade Agreement, 28 Sept. 1937, 194 L.N.T.S. 65, Art. V.
[7] See the following agreements concluded by the United States: with Honduras, 18 Dec. 1935, 167 L.N.T.S. 313, Art. VIII; Sweden, 25 May 1935, 161 L.N.T.S. 109, Art. IX; Nicaragua, 11 Mar. 1936, 173 L.N.T.S. 141, Art. IX; Guatemala 24 Apr. 1936, 170 L.N.T.S. 345, Art. IX; Finland, 18 May 1936, 172 L.N.T.S. 97, Art. X; Costa Rica, 28 Nov. 1936, 181 L.N.T.S. 183, Art. IX; El Salvador, 19 Feb. 1937, 179 L.N.T.S. 219, Art. IX.

was to be applied by the contracting parties in their determination of what constituted a 'fair and equitable allotment of the total available foreign exchange'. Article V of the Trade Agreement concluded between Canada and Haiti is illustrative of this type of provision:

If the Government of either country shall establish or maintain, directly or indirectly, any form of control of foreign exchange, it shall administer such control so as to insure that the nationals and commerce of the other country will be granted a fair and equitable share in the allotment of exchange.

With respect to the exchange made available for commercial transactions, it is agreed that the Government of each country shall be guided in the administration of any form of control of foreign exchange by the principle that, as nearly as may be determined, the share of the total available exchange which is allotted to the other country shall not be less than the share employed in a previous representative period prior to the establishment of any exchange control for the settlement of commercial obligations to the nationals of such other country.

The Government of each country shall give sympathetic consideration to any representations which the other Government may make in respect of the application of the provisions of this Article.[1]

(b) The most-favoured-nation basis.[2] Of the three types of provisions mentioned above, those which dealt with exchange restrictions on the most-favoured-nation basis were the most numerous. Although the various clauses, when examined in detail, often differed—for example, compare the relatively simple and straightforward provision contained in the Treaty of Friendship, Commerce and Navigation concluded between the Economic Union of Belgium and Luxemburg and Siam on 5 November 1937,[3] which provided in Article XII that:

Should either of the High Contracting Parties introduce exchange or payment restrictions, it shall in such questions grant most-favoured-nation treatment to the other Party.

to the more complex provision in the Treaty of Commerce and

[1] 194 L.N.T.S. 59.

[2] For a brief discussion of the most-favoured-nation standard, see G. Schwarzenberger, I *International Law as Applied by International Courts and Tribunals* (3rd ed., 1957) pp. 240–5. For a more detailed discussion, see R. C. Synder, *The Most-Favored Nation Clause* (1948).

[3] 190 L.N.T.S. 151.

Navigation concluded between Norway and El Salvador on 21 November 1939,[1] which provided in Article 7 that:

Each of the High Contracting Parties undertakes, in the absence of foreign exchange control or restrictions on foreign exchange transactions in the other country, not to apply, in relation to that country, any such control or restriction which, under the same conditions, would not likewise be applicable to any third country.

—in their objective they were identical, that is, they sought to ensure that the treatment in respect of exchange matters conferred upon the nationals of either of the contracting parties was at least as favourable as the treatment conferred by either of the contracting parties on the nationals of any third State.[2]

In practice, however, the efficacy of such provisions in mitigating the discriminatory effects of exchange restrictions on international trade was only of marginal value. In its standard form, the most-favoured-nation clause only prohibits discrimination which is based on nationality[3]—that is, in the context of the administration of exchange restrictions, it simply requires that the nationality of the prospective recipient of the available foreign exchange will be considered by the restricting State to be an irrelevant factor in its determination of who will

---

[1] 198 L.N.T.S. 157.

[2] See also the following agreements which contain similar provisions: The Netherlands and Uruguay, Convention of Commerce and Navigation, 29 Jan. 1934, 166 L.N.T.S. 43, Final Protocol, p. 49; Union of South Africa and the Netherlands, Exchange of Notes re Commerce and Navigation, 20 Feb. 1935, 160 L.N.T.S. 143; Norway and Uruguay, Convention of Commerce and Navigation, 4 Apr. 1936, 176 L.N.T.S. 115, Final Protocol, p. 121; El Salvador and Sweden, Exchange of Notes re Commercial Relations, 23 June 1936, 171 L.N.T.S. 291; Guatemala and Sweden, Exchange of Notes re Commercial Relations, 11 July 1936, 171 L.N.T.S. 299; United States of Brazil and the Netherlands, Exchange of Notes re Commercial Relations, 15 Mar. 1937, 179 L.N.T.S. 395; Brazil and Lithuania, Exchange of Notes re Commercial Relations, 28 Sept. 1937, 186 L.N.T.S. 403; Dominican Republic and Newfoundland, Exchange of Notes re Commercial Relations, 16 Mar. 1940, 203 L.N.T.S. 141, Art. 3; United States of America and Argentina, Trade Agreement, 14 Oct. 1941, 119 U.N.T.S. 193, Art. IV; United States of America and Mexico, Trade Agreement, 23 Dec. 1942, 13 U.N.T.S. 231, Art. IV; United States of America and Iran, Trade Agreement, 8 Apr. 1943, 106 U.N.T.S. 155, Art. IV; United States of America and Iceland, Trade Agreement, 27 Aug. 1943, 29 U.N.T.S. 317, Art. IV.

[3] See S. D. Metzger, 'Exchange Controls and International Law', *University of Illinois Law Forum* (1959) pp. 315–16; F. A. Mann, 'Money in Public International Law', 96 R.C. (1959–I) pp. 70–1; cf. W. A. Kewenig, op. cit., who submits that most-favoured-nation treatment goes beyond the prohibition of discrimination on the basis of nationality.

receive the allotted foreign exchange. Since, as is pointed out by Mann,[1] and substantiated by State practice,[2] discrimination in the administration of exchange control turns not on the nationality of the prospective recipient but rather on his residence, or more particularly the currency area with which, through his residence, he is associated, the most-favoured-nation clause is of little practical value.[3]

(c) Prohibition of exchange restrictions. Finally, a provision which explicitly prohibited the use of exchange restrictions as a means of regulating the flow of international trade was introduced into several of the trade agreements concluded by the United States of America in the late 1930s:

In the event that the United States of America or the Czechoslovak Republic establishes or maintains, directly or indirectly, any form of control of the means of international payment, it shall, in the administration of such control:

(a) Impose no prohibition, condition, restriction, or delay on the transfer of payment for imported articles the growth, produce or manufacture of the other country, or on the transfer of payments necessary for and incidental to the importation of such articles;

(b) Accord unconditionally, with respect to rates of exchange and taxes or surcharges on exchange transactions in connection with payments for or payments necessary and incidental to the importation of articles the growth, produce or manufacture of the other country, treatment no less favorable than that accorded in connection with the importation of any article whatsoever the growth, produce or manufacture of any third country; and

(c) Accord unconditionally, with respect to all rules and formalities applying to exchange transactions in connection with payments for or payments necessary and incidental to the importation of articles the growth, produce or manufacture of the other country, treatment

---

[1] 96 R.C. (1959–I) pp. 70–1.

[2] In this respect, see M. G. de Vries, 'Exchange Restrictions: Progress towards Liberalization', 6 F.D. (1969–3) pp. 40–1.

[3] It was perhaps owing to the realization of this fact that certain of the trade agreements concluded in this period had grafted on to the most-favoured-nation clause additional clauses which provided for more stringent obligations concerning the allocation of foreign exchange. See in this respect the following commercial agreements concluded by the United States of America with: Brazil, 2 Feb, 1935, 166 L.N.T.S. 211, Art. VI, and Exchange of Notes, pp. 238–9; Siam, 13 Nov. 1937, 192 L.N.T.S. 247, Art. 3, last paragraph and Final Protocol, p. 264, Art. 5; Turkey, 1 Apr. 1939, 202 L.N.T.S. 129, Arts. 8, 9, and Exchange of Notes, p. 146.

no less favorable than that accorded in connection with the importation of the like articles the growth, produce or manufacture of any third country.[1]

It should be noted that this provision did not prohibit the introduction by either contracting party of an exchange control regime. Rather it provided that the control was to be administered in such a way as not to interfere in any manner whatsoever with the transfer of payments in respect of current trade transactions between the contracting parties. In short, only those aspects of the exchange control mechanism that were tantamount to exchange restrictions (as that term has been defined for the purposes of this study)[2] were prohibited. Consequently, while both the 'fair and equitable' and 'most-favoured-nation' clauses sought only to mitigate the adverse effects of exchange restrictions on international trade, this latter provision went considerably further and sought the outright prohibition of all restrictions in respect of payments for current trade transactions. In this respect, therefore, this latter provision foreshadowed the provisions set out in Article VIII of the International Monetary Fund Agreement.

3. Multilateral Treaties

In spite of the many international economic conferences held during the inter-war period,[3] no multilateral treaties dealing with international monetary affairs were forthcoming, even though it was specifically declared at the 1933 London Conference that 'the common aim of all delegations was to find solutions of the problems which would constitute the basis of international conventions and agreements'.[4] Nations, although

[1] United States of America and Czechoslovakia, Trade Agreement, 7 Mar. 1938, 200 L.N.T.S. 87, Art. X. See also the following agreements concluded by the United States containing a similar provision: Ecuador, 6 Aug. 1938, 193 L.N.T.S. 85, Art. X; Liberia, 8 Aug. 1938, 201 L.N.T.S. 163, Art. X; Greece, 15 Nov. 1938, 195 L.N.T.S. 145, Art. III.

[2] Above, pp. 31-4.

[3] The first general conference was held in Brussels in 1920; the second in Genoa in May 1922; the third in Geneva in May 1927; the fourth in Geneva in Oct. 1927; the fifth in London in 1935. For a brief but illuminating discussion of these conferences, see W. A. Brown, *The United States and the Restoration of World Trade* (1950) pp. 29-46.

[4] League of Nations, Monetary and Economic Conference, *Reports Approved by the Conference on July 27th, 1933 and Resolutions Adopted by the Executive Bureau and the Executive Committee*, II. Economic and Financial (1933. II. Spec. 4) p. 5, para. 12.

aware of the necessity of co-operating on the multilateral level
in order to achieve currency stability and to regulate the introduction and administration of exchange controls, were not yet
prepared to submit this aspect of their sovereignty to international legal regulation, but rather preferred to conduct their
inter-State monetary relations within the traditional framework
of the gold-standard mechanism. Nevertheless, certain recommendations and resolutions were adopted by these conferences,
and although these did not have the force of law, they represented a common consensus of opinion among the leading
nations of the world on monetary matters. As such they were
the precursors to the more dynamic post-1945 developments in
international monetary law and will for this reason be briefly
considered here.

The first Conference,[1] referred to as 'a gathering unique in
the history of the world',[2] called by the League of Nations
and attended by thirty-nine countries, met in Brussels in the
autumn of 1920 when the post-war economic difficulties and
in particular the problem of currency instability were still very
rampant. Although a strongly worded resolution condemned
the unrestricted expansion of currency, and stated that such
practice was in fact simply another method of debasing currency,[3] the Conference advocated a return to the gold standard
as the only feasible solution to the problem of currency instability, and rejected other more novel suggestions: 'We
believe that neither an international currency nor an international unit of account would serve any useful purpose or
remove any of the difficulties from which international exchange
suffers today.'[4] (It is interesting to note, in light of the International Monetary Fund's special drawing rights facility, that
the attitude of the majority of States towards the creation of an
international currency has, over the past half century, come
round full circle.) Similarly, while the Conference condemned
exchange restrictions as being 'artificial', 'futile', and 'mis-
chievous',[5] and recommended their progressive withdrawal,[6]
it did not find it necessary to pursue the matter further. Never-

---

[1] For a report of the conference, see League of Nations, 'International Financial
Conference. Report of the Conference', 1 *Official Journal* (1920) pp. 414–40.

[2] Ibid. p. 423.　　　　　[3] Ibid. p. 427.　　　　　[4] Ibid. p. 430.

[5] Ibid. p. 431.　　　　　　　　　　　　　　　　　[6] Ibid. p. 432.

theless, when viewed in retrospect, the approach adopted by the Conference in 1920 proved, in fact, to be a satisfactory one. The general outline of the pre-war international pattern of trade based on the gold standard—that is, a multilateral trading system operating through convertible currencies and achieving through indirect settlements a world-wide clearing of trade balances—reappeared unmistakably and functioned quite adequately in the three or four years following 1925 until it was irreparably damaged by the economic collapse in 1929. In the wake of the great depression, one would have expected the Monetary and Economic Conference held in London in 1933 and attended by sixty-four nations to have been much more dynamic in its approach to international monetary problems.[1] On the contrary, the following resolution adopted unanimously by Sub-Commission II, which was concerned with the issue of 'Permanent Measures for the Re-establishment of an International Monetary Standard', shows that the problem of currency instability, and the recommended methods of dealing with it, were still much the same as they had been thirteen years earlier during the Brussels Conference:

(a) That it is in the interests of all concerned that stability in the international monetary field be attained as quickly as practicable;

(b) that gold should be re-established as the international measure of exchange values, time and parity being for each country to determine.[2]

Similarly, although the Preparatory Committee of Experts made it clear in their report that exchange restrictions constituted a serious impediment to the exchange of goods and that their abolition was an essential precondition to world economic recovery, no positive action was taken in this respect by the Conference. Indeed, Sub-Commission I of the Monetary and

---

[1] For a list of resolutions adopted by this Conference, see League of Nations, Monetary and Economic Conference, *Reports Approved by the Conference on July 27th, 1933 and Resolutions Adopted by the Executive Bureau and the Executive Committee*, II. Economic and Financial (1933. II. Spec. 4). See also League of Nations, Monetary and Economic Conference, *Draft Annotated Agenda, submitted by the Preparatory Commission of Experts*, II. Economic and Financial (1933. II. Spec. 1), and 'Report of the World Economic Conference', *Supplement to The Economist*, 29 July 1933.

[2] League of Nations, Monetary and Economic Conference, *Reports Approved by the Conference*, ibid. p. 12, para. 4.

Financial Commission, which had been charged with the responsibility—*inter alia*—of reaching agreement on the application of exchange controls, simply reported that 'the discussion
of the other subjects on the agenda [of which exchange control
was one] did not proceed far enough to do more than outline
the main problems to be solved'.[1] The failure of the London
Conference[2] to reach common agreement at the global level
was responsible for the emergence of co-operation on a regional
level (a development which has not only continued but has in
fact accelerated in the post-Second World War period). In this
respect the Declaration on 3 July 1933 of the gold-bloc countries
was the first of several such attempts. The countries concerned
(France, Belgium, Italy, the Netherlands, Switzerland, and
Poland) declared that it was 'their intention to maintain the
free functioning of the gold standard in their respective countries at the existing gold parities and within the framework of
existing monetary laws'.[3] As early as 1934, however, Poland,
Italy, and Belgium were unable to abide by the policies of the
bloc and therefore withdrew. The demise of the gold bloc was
completed in 1936 when France, the Netherlands, and Switzerland were similarly forced to abandon the gold-bloc policies.
Finally the 'Tripartite Agreement'[4] concluded between France,
Great Britain, and the United States on 24 September 1936
and joined in November of that year by Belgium, the Netherlands, and Switzerland must also be considered. Identical
declarations were issued by the French Ministry of Finance and
by the United States[5] and British[6] Treasuries to the effect that:

. . . they welcome this opportunity to reaffirm their purpose to
continue the policy which they have pursued in the course of
recent years, one constant object of which is to maintain the
greatest possible equilibrium in the system of international ex-

---

[1] *Reports*, p. 11.

[2] *The Economist*, 8 July 1933, enumerates the reasons for failure.

[3] J. W. Wheeler-Bennett, *Documents on International Affairs 1933* (1934) p. 45.
See also 1 *Foreign Relations of the United States* (1934) pp. 594–614; Hudson, 6
International Legislation (1937) pp. 945–6; *The Economist*, 8 July 1933.

[4] For a survey of the diplomatic history before and after the joint declaration
of 24 Sept. 1936, see I *Foreign Relations of the United States* (1936) pp. 535–65.

[5] For the actual American Declaration, see ibid. pp. 560–1; 22 *Federal Reserve
Bulletin* (Oct. 1936) pp. 759–60.

[6] For the British Declaration, see J. W. Wheeler-Bennett, *Documents on International Affairs 1936* (1937) pp. 668–9.

changes and to avoid to the utmost extent any disturbances of that system . . .

and furthermore that:

. . . the success of the policy set forth above is linked with the development of international trade. In particular, they attach the greatest importance to action being taken without delay to relax progressively the present system of quotas and exchange controls with a view to their abolition.

However, it has subsequently been pointed out that:

Through the Tripartite Declaration, the signatory countries affirmed that problems connected with foreign exchange and world payments were matters of international concern . . . the adherents were few in number and agreement was reached only in principle. The Declaration involved no binding commitment, and there was no machinery for continuous consideration of the problems involved.[1]

The Declaration was discontinued following the establishment of the International Monetary Fund.

In conclusion, as far as the international legal regulation of international monetary relations was concerned in the period before 1945, only one thing is fairly certain: that States, as a matter of customary international law, were free to alter the rate of exchange of their currency as well as to introduce and administer exchange controls or otherwise manipulate their currency. The notion that such measures, if prejudicial to foreign nationals, constituted an illegal interference with the property rights of aliens if not compensated must at best be viewed with caution, and the efficacy of the notions *abus de droit* and unfair discrimination, in providing a measure of protection against the arbitrary exercise of the currency prerogative, would appear to be severely limited. Multilateral treaty arrangements were not forthcoming, and such bilateral treaties as dealt with these issues were, by and large, not of a regulatory but of a protectionist nature. Nevertheless, the necessity for greater co-operation had been realized and the stage was now set for the more dynamic developments which were to take place after 1945.

[1] C. L. Merwin, 'The Road to Bretton Woods', 1 F.D. (Sept. 1964) p. 61. Cf. Röpke, 'Economic Order and International Law', 86 R.C. (1954–II) p. 261.

Part Two

POST-FUND PERIOD
(A) GLOBAL MONETARY
ARRANGEMENTS

If I were asked to indicate in the briefest possible terms
the result of my reflections, I would say: whereas the
text-books on international trade show that international trade rests on the law of comparative costs, its
foundation is, in the last resort, the categorical impera-
tive 'pacta sunt servanda'.

w. RÖPKE, 'Economic Order and International Law',
86 R.C. (1954–II) p. 212.

INTRODUCTION

PROVISIONS prescribing a code of monetary conduct to which
all member States of the international community may accede
(the provisions are therefore, at least potentially, of universal
applicability) are set out in the following two instruments:
the Articles of Agreement of the International Monetary
Fund[1] and the text of the General Agreement on Tariffs and
Trade.[2] Of these two international conventions the Fund
Agreement is, for the student of international monetary affairs,
of greater importance, since it represents the most comprehensive introduction of the rule of law into what had formerly been a closely guarded area of State sovereignty. The
genesis of the Fund Agreement can be traced to the Second
World War and the period immediately thereafter, a period
which clearly represents a high-water mark in the history of
international economic co-operation.[3] It was one of two agreements drafted at the United Nations Monetary and Financial
Conference attended by forty-four nations at Bretton Woods,
New Hampshire, from 1 to 22 July 1944. This Conference had
been preceded by several years of careful preparation and study,
particularly on the part of the United Kingdom and the United
States of America, and indeed the resultant agreement constitutes a compromise between the so-called (British) Keynes
Plan and the (American) White Plan, although in the main
the Fund's legal structure is based on the American model.[4]
(It is interesting and only just to note at this point, however,

[1] For references see above, p. 2 n. 2.

[2] For the original text of the General Agreement on Tariffs and Trade
(G.A.T.T.), see 55 U.N.T.S. 187. For the current text, see B.I.S.D. vol. IV (Mar.
1969).

[3] R. N. Cooper, 'National Economic Policy in an Interdependent World
Economy', 76 Y.L.J. (1967–II) pp. 1276–8.

[4] See Scammell, op. cit. pp. 117–53, where he examines both the Keynes and
the White Plans in some detail as well as surveying the preparatory work which
took place before the Bretton Woods Conference. For the Conference records, see
Proceedings and Documents of the United Nations Monetary and Financial Conference, 2 vols.
(United States Government Printing Office, Washington, 1948). For a more con-
cise review of the events leading up to Bretton Woods, see C. L. Merwin, 'The Road
to Bretton Woods', 1 F.D. (1964) pp. 50–64, and B. K. Maddon, 'Echoes of Bretton
Woods', 6 F.D. (1969–2) pp. 30–8.

that the amendment to the Fund Agreement which sets forth
the provisions for the special drawing rights facility incorporates
the basic concept set out by Keynes in the original plan for the
establishment of an international clearing union.[1] Phoenix rising
out of the ashes?) The Fund Agreement entered into force on
27 December 1945 when twenty-two countries adhered. Since
this modest beginning, membership in the Fund has steadily
increased and currently stands at 113.[2] Although the current
membership encompasses countries in various stages of economic development and with varying forms of economic and
political structures, the Fund has, in spite of certain fundamental differences of opinion, succeeded in reconciling these
diverse interests, and has therefore come to play an increasingly
dominant role as keeper of the ring in the international monetary arena. The following pessimistic observation made by
a prominent monetary lawyer twenty-eight years ago when the
Fund was on the threshold of its career is surely no longer
tenable:

The writer whole-heartedly agrees with the opinion that the
necessary post-war reconstruction in monetary matters cannot be
achieved except by international cooperation. Still the question is
whether for this purpose the strait-jacket of a treaty, and of a long-
term treaty with a multitude of reliable and unreliable partners, is
the commendable solution for a beginning.[3]

The Fund Agreement and the monetary provisions contained
therein, however, cannot be considered in isolation, because
it is clear that without the concurrent regulation of commercial
controls, for example, tariffs, quantitative import restrictions,
etc., which are the concern of G.A.T.T., the Fund's monetary
code could easily be circumvented. It was accordingly recognized at the Bretton Woods Conference that if the defined
purposes of the Fund were to be achieved, they would have to
be integrated into a broad programme aimed at the regulation

---

[1] *Proposals for an International Clearing Union*, Cmd. 6437.

[2] For Fund Membership on 15 Nov. 1969, see XXII *International Financial
Statistics* (1969–12) pp. iv–v. Only four States have ceased their membership,
Poland in 1950, Czechoslovakia in 1954, Cuba in 1964, and Indonesia, which
withdrew on 17 Aug. 1965 but subsequently rejoined on 12 Feb. 1967. The most
important non-members are the U.S.S.R., all the Eastern European Communist
States (with the exception of Yugoslavia), the People's Republic of China, and
Switzerland.

[3] A. Nussbaum, 'International Monetary Agreements', 38 A.J.I.L. (1944) p. 257.

of both financial and commercial barriers. The delegates at the Bretton Woods Conference, in response to this recognition, adopted a resolution in which they recommended to the participating governments that

they seek, with a view to creating in the field of international economic relations conditions necessary for the attainment of the purposes of the Fund and of the broader primary objectives of economic policy, to reach agreement as soon as possible on ways and means whereby they may best: (1) reduce obstacles to international trade and in other ways promote mutually advantageous international commercial relations.[1]

This initiative was taken up at the first meeting, in February 1946, of the United Nations Economic and Social Council, where it was decided by the Council to convene an international conference on trade and employment.[2] A Preparatory Committee was established and charged with the task of preparing for the proposed Conference a draft convention for an international trade organization.[3] The Conference met in Havana from November 1947 to March 1948, and, on the basis of the Preparatory Committee's draft convention, drew up the Charter for the International Trade Organization (the Havana Charter).[4] Meanwhile, in Geneva, during the summer of 1947, the members of the Preparatory Committee decided to proceed with tariff negotiations among themselves without waiting for the Charter of the I.T.O. to be completed. To provide a legal framework for the tariff reductions which they had negotiated, pending the completion and entry into force of the I.T.O., the participants drew up the text of the General Agreement on Tariffs and Trade (G.A.T.T.). Owing to the failure of the Havana Charter to enter into force,[5] the G.A.T.T., in spite of its loose organizational framework and its intended transitory character,[6]

---

[1] *Proceedings and Documents of the United Nations Monetary and Financial Conference*, vol. I (1948) resolution VII, p. 941.

[2] *United Nations Journal of the Economic and Social Council*, First Year (Jan.–July 1946) pp. 133–4.

[3] Ibid., p. 134, para. 3.

[4] United Nations/Economic and Social Council/Conference on Trade and Employment (E/Conf. 2/78). For a review of the salient features of the I.T.O., see Claire Wilcox, *A Charter for World Trade* (1949).

[5] W. Diebold, 'The End of the I.T.O.', 16 *Princeton Essays in International Finance* (1952).

[6] For an excellent review of the unusual circumstances in which the G.A.T.T. was created and the subsequent legal problems that this unorthodox birth has

has come to play an important role in international commercial relations.[1]

The G.A.T.T.'s contribution to international monetary law lies primarily in its jurisdiction over the introduction and administration of quantitative import restrictions. The regulation of such controls is of direct relevance to the code of monetary conduct within the jurisdiction of the Fund for the following reasons: (i) similar economic results can be achieved through the introduction of quantitative import restrictions as through the imposition of exchange restrictions; and (ii) it is provided within the present framework of these two agreements that in correcting an adverse balance of payments situation, the principal[2] direct control (both of a financial and of a commercial nature) to which a State may resort is the quantitative import restriction. Apart from the basic area of interdependence, it will be seen that other G.A.T.T. provisions—for example, Schedules of Concessions,[3] Anti-dumping and Countervailing Duties,[4] Valuation for Customs Purposes,[5] etc.—are also inextricably linked to the Fund's monetary code.

In recognition of the interdependence of these two agencies, the G.A.T.T. agreement requires the Contracting Parties to seek co-operation with the Fund to ensure that both agencies may pursue a co-ordinated policy with regard to exchange questions within the jurisdiction of the Fund and commercial

given rise to, see J. Jackson, 'The Puzzle of G.A.T.T.', I J.W.T.L. (1967) pp. 137–44.

[1] The original signatories to the G.A.T.T. numbered twenty-three. On 1 January 1970 there were seventy-six full contracting parties; in addition, two States have acceded provisionally and twelve others are applying the Agreement on a *de facto* basis until such time as they have made a definite decision on G.A.T.T. membership. In all, therefore, ninety nations use the provisions of G.A.T.T. as the basis of their mutual trading relations. G.A.T.T. has thus acquired a universal character, for like the Fund, its membership includes countries in all stages of economic development and with different political systems. The accession of Poland in late 1967 and the applications in 1968 for accession by Romania and Colombia confirm this trend. For membership of G.A.T.T. in Apr. 1968, see *The Activities of G.A.T.T. 1967/68* (Geneva, Mar. 1969) p. 29 or *Keesings Contemporary Archives* (1965–6) p. 21366 and (1967–8) p. 22663.

[2] Although quantitative restrictions are the 'principal' method, it should be pointed out that exchange restrictions during the whole of the transitional period (Art. XIV of the Fund Agreement), and if the Fund so approves (Art. VIII of the Fund Agreement), may also be utilized to correct balance of payments disequilibrium.

[3] Art. II.   [4] Art. VI.   [5] Art. VII.

questions within the jurisdiction of the G.A.T.T. More particularly in respect of certain external financial matters—namely, problems concerning monetary reserves, balances of payments, or foreign exchange arrangements—the Contracting Parties are required to consult fully with the Fund and to accept all findings of statistical and other facts presented by the Fund relating thereto.[1] In addition, the Contracting Parties are obliged to accept the determination of the Fund: (i) whether action by a contracting party in exchange matters is in accordance with the Fund Articles or the terms of a special exchange agreement; and (ii) in relation to the criteria set forth in Article XII, paragraph 2 (*a*) or Article XVIII, paragraph (9).[1] In accordance with a further provision of the G.A.T.T.,[2] the Fund and the Contracting Parties have concluded informal agreements concerning consultation and co-operation.[3]

The two instruments acting in concert prescribe on a global multilateral treaty basis a comprehensive code of monetary conduct in respect of matters affecting (*a*) exchange stability and (*b*) direct controls, that is, quantitative import restrictions and exchange restrictions.[4] An examination of these and other provisions forms the basis of study of Chapters VI and VII respectively. The object of this examination will be twofold: (i) to describe the legal substance of these provisions; and (ii) to ascertain the impact that these rules of conventional monetary law have had on the customary law of money, as it was described in Part One of this study. Finally, in the light of the recent speculation over the future role of gold in the international monetary system, Chapter VIII will examine briefly the relationship between monetary gold and international law. Chapter IX will be concerned with an analysis of Fund provisions affecting international liquidity.

---

[1] Art. XV, para. (2).
[2] Art. XV, para. (3).
[3] See B.I.S.D. vol. I (May 1952) pp. 120–3; B.I.S.D., Third Supplement (June 1955) pp. 195–201.
[4] For a practical example of how the G.A.T.T. and Fund work together to liberalize international trade and payments, see Y. Ohara, 'Legal Aspects of Japan's Foreign Trade', 1 J.W.T.L. (1967) p. 7 ff.

VI

EXCHANGE STABILITY

1. *The Economic Background*

THE notion that exchange rates are matters of international concern and should therefore be the subject of international scrutiny and regulation is from the point of view of economic history, economic theory, and economic practice incontestable. Historically, the hard experience of the competitive devaluations of the 1930s with the resultant deterioration in the international economic climate provided clear evidence that the arbitrary and uncontrolled manipulation of exchange rates would contribute to economic disorder.[1] Theoretically, the very rationale behind an alteration in a nation's rate of exchange is to change its cost-price structure *vis-à-vis* other nations and thereby either increase or decrease its competitive position abroad. It is not surprising, therefore, that prominent contemporary economists, when considering the issue of exchange rate alteration, frequently voice the opinion that such measures 'have a great impact on the entire economic and social life of the nation concerned and of other countries as well',[2] and should therefore be 'under some control from an international agency, and their use should be restricted'.[3] Practically, it has been suggested that exchange rate instability constitutes one of the greatest obstacles to regional economic integration. So in the Latin American context it has been said that:

Another crucial aspect of the L.A.F.T.A. problem is to be found in the monetary field. In the short time that the contracting parties' reciprocal concessions have been in effect, in compliance with the liberalization mechanism provided for in the treaty, marked fluctuations in the value of the national currencies have had a disturbing influence on the trade prospects generated by the customs negotiations and even on the normal currents of intrazonal interchange.

[1] 'Introduction to the Fund', 1 F.D. (1964) p. 3.
[2] I. S. Friedman, 'The International Monetary System,' 10 *I.M.F. Staff Papers* (1963) p. 238.
[3] J. Tinbergen, *International Economic Integration* (2nd, rev. ed., 1965) p. 85.

Deriving from successive devaluations in the past, abrupt changes in the par value of the monetary units of certain of the countries in the zone have distorted commercial relations and are obstructing the normal expansion of the export industries.[1]

The contemporary economic controversy, therefore, is not concerned with the issue of whether exchange rates should be regulated (clearly the need for some type of regulation is accepted), but rather with the issue of what form the regulation should assume. Three principal schools of thought prevail:[2] (i) that rates of exchange should be allowed freely to fluctuate (float) and find their own level in response to the forces of supply and demand with official intervention taking place only in case of very wide fluctuations; (ii) that rates of exchange should be fixed with only occasional alterations being permitted; and (iii) a hybrid between (i) and (ii)—that is, that rates of exchange should be neither completely free to fluctuate nor rigidly fixed with only infrequent alterations. Rather it is advocated by protagonists of the third school that rates of exchange should continue to be internationally regulated, but in such a way as to permit more frequent and freer alteration. Various methods whereby this could be achieved have been suggested—for example, by permitting variations in exchange rates around the established par value beyond the present 1 per cent (perhaps by 3 per cent),[3] or by adopting a 'crawling' or 'sliding' peg system whereby a country would be allowed in any year to raise or reduce its exchange rate by a specified amount (say 2 or 3 per cent above or below parity).[4] The Fund has to

[1] M. S. Wionczek (ed.), *Latin American Economic Integration* (1966) p. 136. See similarly W. J. Sedwitz, 'Economic Aspects of Latin American Integration', 61 *Proceedings of the American Society of International Law* (1967) pp. 182–3. With respect to integration and exchange rate stability in the E.E.C., see Hans van der Groeben, *European Monetary Policy* (1968).

[2] Academic discussion of this issue is voluminous. The following articles are chosen at random: I. S. Katz, 'Two Approaches to the Exchange-Rate Problem: the United Kingdom and Canada', 26 *Princeton Essays in International Finance* (1956); A. Lanyi, 'The Case for Floating Exchange Rates Reconsidered', 72 *Princeton Essays in International Finance* (1969). See also Scammell, op. cit., pp. 88–106, Hirsch, op. cit. pp. 283–315.

[3] Decision No. 3463–(71/126) of 18 December 1971 permits members to increase the margin to $2\frac{1}{4}$ per cent.

[4] For a discussion of these various methods, their economic advantages and disadvantages, and their legal compatibility with the Articles of Agreement, see Hirsch, loc. cit. These alternative methods are also being studied by the Fund; see the *Financial Times*, 4 June 1969, p. 1, and *The Economist*, 7 June 1969, p. 72.

date opted for the second alternative. Studies are currently
being undertaken, however, both by the Fund and by academic
institutions as to the practicability of adopting the third alternative.[1]

2. *The Fund's Exchange Rate Regime*

(i) *Initial par value.* The first positive step towards the international regulation of exchange rates was taken at the Bretton
Woods Monetary and Financial Conference, when at a relatively early stage in the preliminary discussions agreement
was reached on the following point of principle, 'that an exchange rate in its very nature is a two-ended thing, and that
changes in exchange rates are therefore properly matters of
international concern'.[2] This principle was given positive legal
expression in Article I, paragraph (iii) of the Fund Agreement
which states the following to be one of that institution's guiding[3]
purposes: 'To promote exchange stability, to maintain orderly
exchange arrangements among members, and to avoid competitive exchange depreciation'. The major provisions setting
out the legal mechanism through which the Fund is to discharge this principal obligation are set out in Article IV,
Sections 1–7. Under Section 1, each member is required to
establish an initial par value for its currency in terms of gold
as a common denominator or in terms of the United States
dollar of the weight and fineness in effect on 1 July 1944. This
represents no real option, however, as the dollar is itself defined
in terms of gold, being equivalent to 0·888671 gram of fine
gold.

The actual procedure by which members establish initial
par values differs according to whether the member concerned
is an original Fund member or a Fund member admitted under
the terms of Article II, Section 2.

For original members, the procedure to be followed in
establishing an initial par value is set out in Article XX, Section
4 which prescribes that the initial par value of members, apart

---

[1] *The Times,* 19 and 25 Feb. 1970.

[2] *Proceedings and Documents of the United Nations Monetary and Financial Conference,*
vol. I (1948) p. 867.

[3] The last sentence of Art. 1, as amended, reads: 'The Fund shall be guided in
all its policies and decisions by the purposes set forth in this Article.'

from those whose territory had been occupied by the enemy, should be based on the rates of exchange prevailing on the sixtieth day before the entry into force of the Agreement. It is further provided, however, that should the par value so communicated be considered, either by the Fund or by the member, to be unsatisfactory, 'the Fund and the member shall, within a period determined by the Fund in the light of all relevant circumstances, agree upon a suitable par value for that currency'.[1]

For other members, the initial par value is determined in accordance with the criteria set out in their respective membership resolutions.[2] However, it is important to note that a modification which has been incorporated into all of the membership resolutions adopted since 1 June 1964 introduces a liberalizing element into Fund practice. This change authorizes the Executive Directors to permit a member to engage in exchange transactions with the Fund, under such conditions and in such amounts as may be prescribed by the Executive Directors, before the establishment by that member of an initial par value and the payment to the Fund of its subscription. The relevant decision reads as follows:

The following paragraph shall be adopted in future membership resolutions submitted to the Board of Governors:

6. *Exchange Transactions with the Fund*: [Member] may not engage in exchange transactions with the Fund until both (a) the par value of its currency has been agreed in accordance with paragraph 5 above and put into operation and (b) its subscription has been paid in full; provided, however, that at any time before the requirements under (a) and (b) have been met, the Executive Directors are authorized to permit exchange transactions with

---

[1] In accordance with these provisions the Fund, on 12 Sept. 1946, requested members to communicate their par values based upon exchange rates which were effective on 28 Oct. 1945, *I.M.F. First Annual Meeting of the Board of Governors. Report of the Executive Directors and Summary Proceedings* (1946) pp. 16–18. In consequence, thirty-two of the original members established initial par values on 18 Dec. 1946. The remaining seven original members all subsequently established par values.

[2] See, for example para. 4 of the Membership Resolution for Turkey, 2 Oct. 1946, *I.M.F. First Annual Meeting of the Board of Governors. Report of the Executive Directors and Summary Proceedings* (1946) p. 54 and paragraph 5 of the Membership Resolution for Sweden, 11 July 1951, *I.M.F. Summary Proceedings, Sixth Annual Meeting* (1951) p. 51.

[member] under such conditions and in such amounts as may be prescribed by the Executive Directors.[1]

This is a departure from the provisions contained in Article XX, Section 4 (c) of the Fund Agreement and paragraph 6 of previous membership resolutions which provided that members would be eligible to enter into exchange transactions with the Fund only after a par value had been established for that member's currency, and only after payment by that member of its subscription. The rationale behind this latest change is to 'encourage members to follow policies leading to the establishment of realistic exchange rates and to the adoption at the earliest feasible date of effective par values',[2] a task which for many of the new members which are by and large still in the initial stages of economic development poses many difficulties. This is not to suggest, however, that such members are free to engage in arbitrary currency manipulations. By a standard provision in its membership resolution, a new member is under an obligation not to change, without prior Fund agreement, the rate of exchange prevailing for its currency at the time it accepted Fund membership. So even in these cases, exchange rates are still subject to international scrutiny and regulation.[3]

(ii) *Par value as the basis of exchange rates.* The agreed par values constitute the principal element in the Fund's exchange rate system. The relevant Fund provisions (Article IV, Sections 3 and 4 (b)) oblige each member to ensure that all exchange transactions taking place within its territories between its currency and the currencies of other members are carried out at rates based upon the agreed par value and within limited margins thereof. The agreed par value is not tantamount to the foreign exchange rate, but rather furnishes the base upon which foreign exchange rates are calculated. The Fund agreement permits buying and selling of Fund members' currencies within a range of 1 per cent on either side of par[4] for

[1] Executive Board Decision no. 1686–(64/22) of 22 Apr. 1964, *I.M.F. Annual Report* (1964) p. 141.   [2] Ibid.

[3] For an example of the current form of the Membership Resolution, see Membership Resolution for Malawi of 10 Sept. 1964, *I.M.F. Summary Proceedings, Nineteenth Annual Meeting* (1964) pp. 263–6.

[4] The 1 per cent margin on either side of par has been modified by Executive Board Decision no. 3463–(71/126) of 18 December 1971.

all spot exchange transactions,[1] and in the case of other exchange transactions, such as forward exchange sales, the permitted margin may exceed the spot margin by 'no more than the Fund considers reasonable'. Although as regards 'other exchange transactions' the Fund has, to date, not defined the term 'reasonable' and has left it to each member to determine for itself what the forward rate should be, it could nevertheless, within the combined provisions of Article IV, Section 3 (ii) and Section 4 (a), affirm its jurisdiction over such rates, should they constitute a threat to international monetary stability. The obligation to maintain the rate within the 1 per cent margin applies only to exchange transactions taking place within the member's territories, and only when the other currency involved in the transaction is the currency of another Fund member.[2] Each member is allowed to determine for itself the measures it will adopt to maintain the proper rate of exchange for its currency, provided only that the adopted measure is consistent with the Agreement (for example the unilateral imposition of exchange restrictions would not be an acceptable method since exchange restrictions may be introduced only

---

[1] In practice, most members have defined their currencies in terms of the $U.S. If the rate of exchange of such a currency *vis-à-vis* the $U.S. fluctuates within a margin of one half of 1 per cent, giving rise therefore to a total spread of 1 per cent, the exchange rate between two such currencies would be within a margin of 1 per cent of the par rate or a total spread of 2 per cent. Consequently, margins of more than one half of 1 per cent *vis-à-vis* the $U.S. would give rise to margins of more than 1 per cent between two such currencies or to a total spread of more than the permitted 2 per cent. A decision taken by the Fund in July 1959, however, permits 'exchange rates which are within 2 per cent of parity for spot exchange transactions between a member's currency and the currencies of other members taking place within the member's territories, whenever such rates result from the maintenance of margins of no more than 1 per cent from parity for a convertible, including externally convertible, currency', *I.M.F. Annual Report* (1960) p. 31. For an excellent account of the foreign exchange market in practice and in particular the nature of official intervention in the market, see P. Einzig, *A Textbook on Foreign Exchange* (2nd ed., 1969).

[2] However, under the terms of Art. XI, entitled 'Relations with Non-Member Countries', members undertake not to engage in any transactions with non-members or with persons in a non-member's territories which would be contrary to the purposes of the Fund. Since it is one of the purposes of the Fund to promote exchange stability, to maintain orderly exchange arrangements among members, and to avoid competitive exchange depreciation, a Fund member who permitted exchange transactions with non-members or residents thereof, at rates greatly depreciated *vis-à-vis* those applicable to all other members, would frustrate this Fund purpose. In such cases, therefore, it would appear that the Fund could, under the auspices of Art. XI, oblige the member to prevent such transactions.

with prior Fund approval). The measure most commonly utilized is intervention by the member's monetary authority (central bank, stabilization fund) in the exchange markets.[1] Finally, although the combined effect of Sections 1 (*a*), 3, and 4 (*b*) of Article IV is to impose an obligation on all members to establish and maintain exchange rates which are both fixed (as opposed to fluctuating) and single or unitary (as opposed to multiple), it should be remembered that the terms 'fixed' and 'unitary' are, within the context of the Articles of Agreement, terms of art. Consequently, members, even when in strict compliance with Fund exchange rate requirements, still retain a wide measure of flexibility. For example, a member may utilize several buying rates; it may have one buying rate for the proceeds arising out of the export of certain manufactured commodities, another rate for the proceeds arising out of the export of primary products, and a third rate for the proceeds arising from tourist expenditures. But as long as all the various rates are within the prescribed margins, the member will be deemed for the purposes of the Fund Agreement to have a single rate structure. A single rate system will become a multiple rate system only when one or more of the officially permitted rates is outside the prescribed margin.[2] Similarly, an exchange rate which is allowed to fluctuate freely within the prescribed margin, but is not permitted to go beyond the legally prescribed limits, will constitute a fixed rate system. However, should the rate be permitted at any time to move beyond the prescribed margins in response to normal market forces, it would, for the purposes of the Fund Agreement, constitute a fluctuating rate.

(iii) *Changes in exchange rate.* 'The Fund Agreement makes it clear that the provisions for the regulation of exchange rates are not intended to impose upon the Fund the duty of perpetuating in the name of stability exchange rates which have

---

[1] *Statement by Ministers of the Group of Ten and Annex prepared by their Deputies* (H.M.S.O., London, 1964) p. 4: 'Official intervention in the foreign exchange markets has now become the general practice for keeping the exchange rate within the agreed parity limits.'

[2] Fund Decision no. 649–(57/33) of 26 June 1947 states that: 'An effective buying or selling rate which, as the result of official action, e.g. the imposition of an exchange tax, differs from parity by more than one per cent, constitutes a multiple currency practice', *I.M.F. Annual Report* (1948) p. 72.

lost touch with economic realities. Stability and rigidity are different concepts.'[1] An exchange rate loses touch with 'economic realities' when it no longer contributes to the maintenance of an equilibrium in the balance of payments, and in such cases the Fund permits the member to adopt another, more economically viable, rate of exchange.[2] Such changes are affected through the adoption of a new par value for the currency of the member suffering from the disequilibrium. The criteria which must be observed in carrying out such alterations are set forth in Article IV, Sections 5–7. Although hedged round with many other rules[3]—of both a procedural and a substantive nature— the key element in the formula rests with the concept 'fundamental disequilibrium'.[4] On the one hand, a member cannot propose 'a change in the par value of its currency except to correct a fundamental disequilibrium', and on the other hand, the Fund must consent to any proposed change 'if it is satisfied that the change is necessary to correct a fundamental disequilibrium'. Unlike the notions of 'fixed' and 'unitary', however, the concept 'fundamental disequilibrium' is not within the context of the Fund Agreement a term of art and has not been given a rigid legal definition.[5] On the whole, such an approach seems wise, since it is extremely difficult to define specifically beforehand the phenomenon of fundamental disequilibrium.[6] Furthermore, if a rigid legal definition had been given in the Agreement, the Fund would have been prevented

---

[1] *I.M.F. Annual Report* (1948) p. 21.

[2] *I.M.F. Annual Report* (1948) pp. 22–4.

[3] As pointed out by Fawcett, however, the rules are 'a little obscure . . . On the one hand a Member may propose a change *only* to correct a fundamental disequilibrium which suggests that the Fund must, even within the 10-per-cent range, be satisfied that this criterion is met; on the other hand, the language of the provision is peremptory, and the express requirement in the Article that the Fund must be so satisfied is confined to changes beyond the 10-per-cent range', 'The International Monetary Fund and International Law', 40 B.Y.I.L. (1964) pp. 38–9.

[4] 'A member desiring to change the par value of its currency shall give the Fund as much notice as the circumstances allow, and shall submit a full and reasoned statement why, in its opinion, such a change is necessary to correct a fundamental disequilibrium', *By-Laws, Rules and Regulations* (26th ed., 1966) p. 23, rule F. 3.

[5] For an interpretation rendered by the Executive Directors under Article XVIII concerning fundamental disequilibrium, see *I.M.F. First Annual Meeting of the Board of Governors, Report of the Executive Directors and Summary Proceedings* (1946) pp. 105–6.

[6] See, however, J. E. Meade, 'The International Monetary Mechanism', *Readings in Macroeconomics*, ed. M. G. Mueller (1969) pp. 386–7.

'from adopting an elastic policy in the treatment of subsequent cases'.[1] Assuming that a fundamental disequilibrium does exist and that a change in par value is imminent, a further difficulty which arises is ascertaining the extent of the alteration. Here again, it is obvious that the question 'cannot be determined with precision'.[2] The Fund Agreement, however, does prescribe certain guiding principles, albeit of a rather imperfect nature, which must be taken into account when alterations in par value are being contemplated. First, since it is a purpose of the Fund to promote a 'balanced' growth of international trade,[3] the proposed change must be large enough to correct the disequilibrium, thereby enabling the affected member to maintain its normal share in the total volume of international trade without experiencing payment difficulties. Secondly, since it is another avowed purpose of the Fund 'to avoid competitive exchange depreciation',[4] the proposed change must not be so great as to bestow upon the member an unfair advantage in international trade over that enjoyed by other Fund members. One of the reasons for the Fund's refusal to concur in the 1948 adjustment of the French exchange rate was that it considered the proposed alteration (or certain aspects thereof) as being tantamount, at least potentially, to a competitive depreciation.[5]

Finally, it is important to note that the Articles of Agreement provide that the member itself must take the initiative in proposing a change in its par value, so that the Fund's part is limited to affording international scrutiny to the proposal. However, the Fund's share in the process, though passive, is still important, for two reasons:

One, a country wishing to change its par value has to convince the other Fund members that it is justified in doing so, and that the new parity which it seeks to establish is a fair one. Two, the cumulative experience of the Fund in watching the changes in par values since 1949 has helped to bring into being a body of knowledge about the usefulness and effects of changes in par values which was not previously available, but which can now be drawn upon by any country. As a consequence of these two developments, the world

---

[1] S. Horie, *The International Monetary Fund, Retrospect and Prospect* (1964) p. 106.
[2] Executive Board Decision no. 278-3 of 1 Mar. 1948, *Selected Decisions*, pp. 17-18.
[3] Art. I, para. (ii).   [4] Art. I, para. (iii).
[5] *I.M.F. Annual Report* (1948) p. 36.

can be better assured than ever before that, if a country devalues, it does so for good reason and to no greater extent than its circumstances warrant.[1]

(iv) *Exceptions to the Fund's ideal rate structure.* In an ideal world, the Fund provisions just discussed would give rise to a system of exchange rates which would, in the short term, be both fixed and unitary, and which, in the long term, could, in collaboration with the Fund, be varied from time to time to adjust to fundamental changes in the international economy. In fact, however, exceptions to the Fund's ideal regime do exist, and members are legally entitled not only to engage in (*a*) multiple currency practices and (*b*) fluctuating rates (when part of a multiple rate system), but also (*c*) unilaterally— that is, without Fund concurrence—to alter their par values within the context of Article IV, Sections 5–7. It must be emphasized, however, that the above practices are only exceptions and that the Fund system is always tending towards the establishment of the ideal—a goal which in the real world, however, can probably never be achieved.[2]

(*a*) Multiple exchange rates. Article VIII, Section 3 states:

No member shall engage in, or permit any of its fiscal agencies referred to in Article V, Section 1, to engage in, any discriminatory currency arrangements or multiple currency practices except as authorized under this Agreement or approved by the Fund. If such arrangements and practices are engaged in at the date when this Agreement enters into force the member concerned shall consult with the Fund as to their progressive removal unless they are maintained or imposed under Article XIV, Section 2, in which case the provisions of Section 4 of that Article shall apply.

This provision outlaws the use by Fund members of multiple currency practices, except to the extent that they are permitted either by Fund approval or in the Articles of Agreement. To determine the extent to which Fund members will, under the terms of this provision, be permitted to circumvent the general

---

[1] 'Introduction to the Fund', 1 F.D. (1964) p. 10. For a breakdown of the devaluations which have been undertaken by Fund members since 1948, see M. G. de Vries, 'The Magnitudes of Exchange Devaluation', 5 F.D. (1968–2) pp. 8–12.

[2] See M. G. de Vries, 'The Decline of Multiple Exchange Rates, 1947–67', 4 F.D. (1967) pp. 297–303, and 'Fluctuating Exchange Rates: the Fund's Approach', 6 F.D. (1969–2) p. 45.

prohibition and to engage in multiple currency practices, a distinction must be drawn between Article VIII and Article XIV members.[1]

Before considering the effect of this distinction, however, it should be noted that the Fund has enunciated the following policy decisions which apply to all Fund members engaging in multiple currency practices regardless of their status: (1) members are required, as a minimum, to consult the Fund before introducing, adapting, or reclassifying multiple currency practices; (2) since multiple currency practices are, in most cases, both systems of exchange rates and restrictions on the payments and transfers for current international transactions, priority in elimination should be given to those features which effect exchange stability; (3) multiple currency practices should be removed when no longer justified for balance of payments reasons.[2] As mentioned, these policy decisions apply to all members engaging in multiple currency practices regardless of their Article VIII or Article XIV status. Moreover, they provide the general background against which the Fund applies the following more specific rules.

Article VIII members are entitled to introduce new multiple rates only with prior Fund approval.[3] Similarly, they may maintain, adapt, or reclassify any multiple currency practices which are in force by virtue of Article VIII only with prior Fund approval.[3] From a legal viewpoint it is clear that Fund members which have accepted Article VIII status are, in respect to multiple exchange rates, subject to a very strict regime.

Article XIV members are subject to what would appear, prima facie, to be a less rigorous regime. Under Article XIV,

---

[1] An Art. VIII member is one that has notified the Fund, as required under the terms of Art. XIV, Sect. 3, that it is prepared to accept the obligations of Art. VIII, Sects. 2, 3, and 4. It should be noted that, by virtue of Art. XIX (d), the currency of an Art. VIII member is, for the purposes of the Fund Agreement, deemed to be convertible. For a list of the members that had acquired Art. VIII status as of 30 Apr. 1969, see *I.M.F. Annual Report* (1969) p. 139. On the other hand, Art. XIV members are those countries that have notified the Fund, in accordance with Art. XIV, Sect. 3, that they intend to avail themselves of the transitional arrangements of Art. XIV, Sect. 2.

[2] Communication sent by Fund to Members on Multiple Currency Practices, 19 Dec. 1947, *I.M.F. Annual Report* (1948) pp. 65–72 at 66–7. See also *Selected Decisions* pp. 84–91 at 85–6.

[3] *Selected Decisions* pp. 88–9.

Section 2 they are entitled for the whole of the post-war transitional period to maintain and adapt to changing circumstances (and, in the case of members whose territories have been occupied by the enemy, introduce where necessary) restrictions on payments and transfers for current international transactions. Since multiple exchange rates are in most instances restrictions on payments and transfers as well as rates of exchange, the effect of Article XIV, Section 2 would be to bestow upon Article XIV members the privilege of maintaining, introducing (to the extent permitted), and adapting to changing circumstances multiple currency practices, without obtaining prior Fund approval. Article XIV members constituted, therefore, a potential source of exchange instability. To eliminate this potential weakness, the Fund in 'The December 1947 Letter on Multiple Currency Practice' adopted the following decision:

Multiple currency practices, besides being in most cases restrictive practices, also constitute systems of exchange rates. Since exchange stability depends on effective rates, the general purposes of the Fund and the members' undertakings of Article IV, Section 4 (a) 'to collaborate with the Fund to promote exchange stability, to maintain orderly exchange arrangements with other members, and to avoid competitive exchange alterations' are fundamental considerations in an interpretation of the rights and obligations of members under Article XIV, Section 2 or Article VIII, Section 3, to maintain, introduce, or adapt multiple currency practices . . .[1]

The effect of this decision was to subject Article XIV members to the same strict regime as Article VIII members. As a result of this decision, members availing themselves of the transitional arrangements of Article XIV, Section 2 are required, in respect of those restrictions which also constitute rates of exchange, to observe the exchange rate provisions of the Fund—that is, Article IV, Section 4 (a) and Article I, paragraph (iii). Under the terms of those provisions they are obliged to seek prior approval of the Fund for the introduction or adaptation of multiple rates of exchange.[2] Before granting the necessary approval the Fund would satisfy itself that the introduction or adaptation of multiple exchange rates was in conformity with the provisions of Article VIII as well as of Article IV, Section

---

[1] *Selected Decisions* p. 88.   [2] Ibid. p. 90.

4 (a) and Article I, paragraph (iii)—namely, that the introduction of multiple rates by a member which had been occupied by the enemy was in fact 'necessary', that any adaptation was in fact dictated by 'changing circumstances',[1] and that in either case (introduction or adaptation) the action was consistent with a member's duty to promote exchange stability, to maintain orderly exchange arrangements, and to avoid competitive exchange alterations.[2]

Since members, whether of Article VIII or Article XIV status, may not maintain,[3] introduce, or adapt multiple exchange rates without prior Fund approval, the Fund has been able to assume rigid control over all multiple currency practices. In the exercise of this control the Fund has been slow to grant approval for the introduction of new multiple rates, and in keeping with its basic policy decision has, as a general rule, sanctioned the imposition of new multiple rates only for balance of payments reasons.[4] Moreover, in a subsequent decision on multiple currency practices adopted in 1957,[5] the Fund suggested that it would approve only those adaptations which would 'simplify complex multiple rates systems'[5] and that it would be reluctant 'to approve changes in multiple rate systems which make them more complex'.[5]

Two conclusions may be drawn from the above discussion, one of a specific and the other of a more general nature. (1) Although multiple exchange rates may be legally approved by the Fund, the strict jurisdictional position adopted by the Fund clearly illustrates that its primary objective remains the establishment and maintenance of a unitary rate structure, and that multiple exchange rates will, at best, be tolerated only in

---

[1] *Selected Decisions* p. 90.

[2] Ibid. See also J. Gold, 'The Duty to Collaborate with the International Monetary Fund and the Development of Monetary Law', *Law, Justice and Equity, Essays in Tribute to G. W. Keeton*, ed. R. H. Holland and G. Schwarzenberger (1967) pp. 139–42.

[3] While Art. VIII members may not maintain multiple currency practices without Fund concurrence, Art. XIV countries may maintain, without Fund approval and for the duration of the transitional period, those multiple currency practices which were in effect upon their becoming Fund members. However, even this privilege is subject to a number of important qualifications, see *Selected Decisions* pp. 89–90, para. 3.

[4] J. E. S. Fawcett, 'The Place of Law in an International Organization,' 36 B.Y.I.L. (1960) p. 330.

[5] *I.M.F. Annual Report* (1957) pp. 161–2, or *Selected Decisions* pp. 91–2.

exceptional circumstances.[1] (2) More generally, the Fund attitude towards multiple currency practices

clarifies the extent to which the members of the Fund had departed from the view that the sovereign authority of a state entitled it to determine unilaterally the rates of exchange for its currency and had substituted for it the principle that rates of exchange were the subject of international concern and therefore international regulation.[2]

(b) *Fluctuating rates.*[3] The Fund's exchange rate system is based on the establishment and maintenance not only of unitary rates but of fixed rates as well. The lesson of experience has shown, however, that in certain economic conditions the adoption of a fluctuating rate system, that is, a rate which moves beyond the permitted margins in response to normal market forces, may prove to be preferable 'for a limited period of time'[4] to the maintenance of a fixed exchange rate. Consequently, although under the Articles of Agreement a Fund member is unable to abandon its official par value and adopt in its stead a fluctuating rate, it may nevertheless inform the Fund that it is unable to carry out its obligations under Article IV, Sections 3 and 4 (b). If the Fund finds that the arguments of the member are persuasive, it may say so, but unless the fluctuating rate is part of a multiple currency system, it cannot give its official approval to the action.[5]

[1] H. A. Aufricht, 'The Fund Agreement and the Legal Theory of Money', 10 *Österreichische Zeitschrift für öffentliches Recht* (1959–60) p. 40.

[2] J. Gold, 'The Duty to Collaborate with the International Monetary Fund and the Development of Monetary Law', *Law, Justice and Equity* (1967) p. 142.

[3] The Fund's position with regard to fluctuating exchange rates was set out in *I.M.F. Annual Report* (1951) pp. 36–41. For a succinct review of Fund policies with respect to fluctuating rates as they have evolved over the past twenty-five years, see M. G. de Vries, 'Fluctuating Exchange Rates: the Fund's Approach', 6 F.D. (1969–2) pp. 44–8.

[4] *I.M.F. Annual Report* (1951) p. 39.

[5] This stems from the fact that the Fund has jurisdiction to approve multiple exchange rates under Art. VIII, Sect. 3 and may thereunder legalize such regimes. Accordingly, when the Fund in 1947 examined the multiple currency practices of members prevailing at the time, it took cognizance of the fact that certain of the members' multiple rate systems included fluctuating exchange rates. It, therefore, informed its members that when a multiple rate system includes a free market with a fluctuating rate, the member should agree with the Fund on the scope of transactions permitted to take place in that market. Moreover, any changes in the scope of that free market should be agreed upon with the Fund. Hence the Fund can authorize a regime of fluctuating exchange rates when such a regime is part of a larger pattern of multiple exchange rates. *Ipso facto,* a fluctuating rate

The Fund has recognized the use of freely fluctuating exchange rates in two sets of circumstances. First, a fluctuating
exchange rate has been used in many of the stabilization programmes with which the Fund has in recent years been associated.[1] The rationale of this approach, particularly in respect of
those countries which previously had a complex multiple rate
structure in effect, has been that mutliple exchange rates could
be removed by stages. 'First, a broadening of a free market
might accompany removal of complex fixed rates; later, a single
free rate might be introduced. Free market forces could then
determine a new realistic exchange rate which could gradually
be stabilized and eventually become a par value.'[2] Secondly,
the Fund has tolerated, although to a much lesser extent than
in the case of stabilization programmes, the introduction of a
fluctuating rate by members who were experiencing domestic
inflation owing either to the large inflow of foreign capital
or to over-buoyant and rapidly expanding economies. For
example, when the Canadian Government, owing to a heavy
inflow of private foreign capital from the United States which
gave rise to serious inflationary pressures, suspended its fixed
rate of exchange and announced that the rate would be permitted to fluctuate in response to market forces, the Fund,
although unable to approve the Canadian measure, nevertheless 'recognized the exigencies of the situation that led Canada
to the proposed plan and took note of the intention of the
Canadian Government to remain in consultation with the
Fund and to re-establish an effective par value as soon as
circumstances warranted'.[3] After eleven years with a fluctuating
rate, Canada returned to a fixed par value in May 1962.[4]

In either of the above two cases—that is, where a fluctuating

per se, that is, which is not part of a multiple rate structure, cannot legally be
approved by the Fund. See *Selected Decisions*, p. 87, para. 3 (*a*).

[1] *I.M.F. Annual Report* (1962) pp. 62–3: 'Except when adopted temporarily,
as part of a comprehensive program of exchange reform, "a system of fluctuating
exchange rates is not a satisfactory alternative to the par value system".'

[2] M. G. de Vries, 'Fund Members' Adherence to the Par Value Regime:
Empirical Evidence', 13 *I.M.F. Staff Papers* (1966) p. 504.

[3] *I.M.F. Annual Report* (1951) pp. 44–5. For a short period in Sept. 1969, the
deutsche mark, again to check the large inflow of foreign capital, was allowed to
float. *Financial Times*, 30 Sept. 1969, pp. 1, 14.

[4] *The Economist*, 4 Oct. 1969, pp. 75–6. The Canadian dollar was again allowed to
float in June 1970.

rate is introduced as part of a stabilization programme or to deal with an inflationary situation—it should be understood that the Fund will tolerate the use of a fluctuating rate only for a limited period of time and only if such rates are not simultaneously utilized by a large number of member States.[1]

(c) Unauthorized change in par value. A member may change the par value of its currency without obtaining the prior concurrence of the Fund as required under Article IV, Sections 5 (c) and (f). Such unilateral alterations are, by virtue of Article IV, Section 6, deemed to be unauthorized changes. From the point of view of the delinquent member, such alterations cannot be made ineffective by the Fund Agreement. Nor, however, on its part, is the Fund without a sanction. Initially, unless the Fund otherwise determines, the delinquent member will be barred access to the Fund's resources. Furthermore, if, after the expiration of a reasonable period of time, the difference between the member and the Fund continues, the member may become subject to compulsory withdrawal. Article IV, Section 6, then, clearly represents a compromise. A member, on the one hand, ultimately retains the right to regulate its currency by altering the par value in spite of Fund objections. The Fund, on the other hand, although it cannot forestall the alteration, can nevertheless show its disapproval by withholding resources and demanding withdrawal.[2] The nature of this compromise has been so adequately summarized in Oppenheim that his remarks merit citation in full:

The general effect of the arrangements governing changes in par values may be described as being that neither the Fund nor the Member can, by taking or declining to take action, leave the other without a remedy, but that each, in determining its course of action,

[1] *I.M.F. Annual Report* (1951) pp. 39–40.

[2] France became ineligible to use the Fund's resources on 25 Jan. 1948, *I.M.F. Annual Report* (1948) p. 37: 'The French Government found that it could not accept the modifications suggested by the Fund and decided to go forward with its own proposals. Accordingly, the Fund considered that France had made an unauthorized change in its par value and had therefore become ineligible to use the Fund's resources.' In Sept. 1949, following the sterling devaluation, France consulted with the Fund on a proposal to unify her exchange system on the basis of the free market dollar rate. 'The French Government did not feel, however, that it was possible to declare a new par value for the franc', *I.M.F. Annual Report* (1950) p. 37. On 15 Oct. 1954, the Executive Directors restored France's eligibility to use the Fund's resources, *I.M.F. Annual Report* (1955) p. 88. France agreed a new par value with the Fund to take effect on 29 Dec. 1958.

must take into account the probable attitude and reaction of the other. If the Fund does not concur in a proposed change in the par value of a currency, the Member can in the last resort make the change unilaterally, but if the Member does so it becomes ineligible to use the resources of the Fund unless the Fund otherwise determines, and it is liable to be required, after the expiration of a reasonable period, to withdraw from the Fund. The system is one of checks and balances so designed that while the Fund is not given, and in the present stage of development of international organization and international economic and financial relationships cannot properly be given, final authority over national policies concerning currency depreciation, these policies no longer result from unilateral decisions which no international authority is formally entitled to appraise or, if necessary, to counteract.[1]

(v) *The system in practice.* In its early years the Fund fell far short of realizing the ideal exchange rate regime envisaged in its Articles of Agreement.[2] Not only were member States who engaged in multiple rate systems on joining the Fund unwilling to eliminate them, but in the 1947–55 period the use of multiple currency practices actually increased among the Fund's membership.[3] Indeed, by the end of 1955, thirty-six Fund members out of a total membership of fifty-eight had 'some kind of economic device which the Fund considered a multiple currency practice'.[4] In January 1948 France changed the par value of its currency despite objections by the Fund,[5] and in September 1949 the devaluation of sterling and the resultant realignment by other members of their par values took place with only nominal Fund approval.[6] The adoption in 1950 by Canada of a fluctuating exchange rate[7] was a further blow to Fund authority. All these events led one prominent Fund economist to describe the 1947–55 period in the Fund's history as 'a frustrating time for the Fund and for its members'.[8]

---

[1] Oppenheim, I *International Law* (8th ed., by H. Lauterpacht, 1955) pp. 1005–6.
[2] For a résumé of the first ten years of Fund activities, see *The First Ten Years of the International Monetary Fund* (Washington, 1956).
[3] M. G. de Vries, 'The Decline of Multiple Exchange Rates, 1947–67', 4 F.D. (1967) p. 299.   [4] Ibid. p. 300.
[5] *I.M.F. Annual Report* (1948) pp. 36–8, 76–8.
[6] F. A. Mann, 'Money in Public International Law', 96 R.C. (1959–I) pp. 43–4.
[7] *I.M.F. Annual Report* (1951) pp. 44–5.
[8] M. G. de Vries, loc. cit. See also R. A. Mundell, 'The International Monetary Fund', 3 J.W.T.L. (1969) pp. 476–9, where he suggests that the French devaluation in 1948, the devaluation of the pound sterling in 1949, and the Canadian

Since the mid fifties, however, the fortunes of the Fund have gradually improved, and indeed the contemporary situation reveals that a majority of member States are complying with the legal obligations incumbent upon them in respect of their exchange rate practices.[1] On 31 December 1967, Fund membership stood at 109, of which eighty-seven had agreed par values with the Fund and had therefore complied with the legal obligations of Article IV, Section 1. However, this compliance may be no more than what has aptly been described by S. D. Metzger 'as a sort of international singing for supper'.[2] Members may agree on initial par values in order to get access to Fund resources and then not conduct their exchange transactions at the agreed parity rates.[3] Since a par value in itself has no intrinsic value, and only has efficacy if exchange transactions are carried out at rates based on the par value, the success or failure of the Fund's exchange rate regime can be judged therefore only by determining the number of countries that are in fact actively utilizing the par value rate in accordance with Article IV, Sections 3 and 4 (*b*). Of the eighty-seven members with agreed par values, sixty-eight were in fact conducting their exchange transactions at parity rates.[4] Of

fluctuating rate were three of the four most damaging blows (the fourth being the effects of the Marshall Plan) to the Fund's prestige in its early years of operation.

[1] The following analysis is based on the statistical table outlining the 'Principal Features of Member Countries' Exchange Systems' set out in the *I.M.F. 19th Annual Report on Exchange Restrictions* (1968) pp. 490–3. It does not take into account events since 18 Dec. 1971 including I.M.F. Executive Board Decision No. 3463–(71/126). For a more detailed and comprehensive survey of members' compliance with the Fund's par value regime from the Fund's inception through to 15 Sept. 1966, see M. G. de Vries, 'Fund Members' Adherence to the Par Value Regime: Empirical Evidence', 13 *I.M.F. Staff Papers* (1966) pp. 504–32.

[2] S. D. Metzger, 'Exchange Controls and International Law', *University of Illinois Law Forum* (1959) p. 319.

[3] Under the terms of Art. XX, Sect. 4 (*c*) and the relevant paragraph of the membership resolutions (before the Fund's decision in 1964 which authorized the Executive Directors to permit a member to engage in exchange transactions with the Fund without that member's having established a par value), members were permitted to engage in exchange transactions only, *inter alia*, after having agreed on an initial par value for their currency. It is curious to note, however, that a similar provision was not adopted requiring members to comply with Art. IV, Sects. 3 and 4 (*b*). In such cases the Fund would, however, be able to invoke Art. XV, Sect. 2.

[4] Nine of the sixty-eight countries (Australia, Belgium–Luxemburg, Guyana, Iraq, Iceland, Jamaica, Trinidad and Tobago, Turkey, United Kingdom) had special rate(s) for some or all capital transactions and/or some or all invisibles,

the remaining nineteen countries, six conducted some of their exchange transactions at parity[1] while the remaining thirteen did not conduct any of their transactions at parity rates.[2] Of the remaining twenty-two members who had not yet established a par value, nineteen, although not complying with the provisions on a *de jure* basis, were complying on a *de facto* basis, that is, even though they had not yet agreed on an initial par value with the Fund, they nevertheless maintained fixed unitary exchange rates. Of the three remaining members who had not yet established a par value, one was conducting the majority of its transactions at a fixed unitary rate while the other two were engaging in fluctuating and multiple rate systems.[3]

3. *The Fund's Par Value Regime and the G.A.T.T.*

The par values established by the Fund members under the auspices of the Fund Agreement play a prominent role in those G.A.T.T. provisions concerned with: (i) Schedules of Concessions (Article II); (ii) Anti-dumping and Countervailing Duties (Article VI); (iii) Valuation for Customs Purposes (Article VII).[4]

Under Article II, Section 6 (*a*), the specific duties and charges (including margins of preference) included in the Schedules of Concessions relating to contracting parties which are members of the International Monetary Fund are to be expressed in the appropriate currency at the par value accepted by the Fund. It is apparent, therefore, that should a Fund member alter the par value of its currency, the effect of such an alteration would

while Nicaragua had import rates different from export rates, *I.M.F. 19th Annual Report, Exchange Restrictions* (1968) pp. 490–3. The remaining fifty-eight conducted all transactions at parity rates.

[1] The other rates applied in addition to rates based on par varied. Compare the exchange rate regimes maintained by Afghanistan and Costa Rica, ibid., pp. 15 and 113 respectively (both of which maintained free market rates in addition to official rates), to the voucher system maintained by Pakistan, ibid. p. 328.

[2] The rate structures adopted by these countries varied. Compare, for example, the complex multiple rate system maintained by Brazil, ibid. p. 50, to the unitary fluctuating rate maintained by Lebanon, ibid. p. 263.

[3] Vietnam had a fixed unitary rate for all transactions except for a special subsidy on the sale of exchange for certain study purposes abroad, ibid. p. 475. Korea had a fluctuating rate, ibid. p. 251, and Laos had a multiple rate system, ibid. p. 260.

[4] For a general discussion of these and other Fund provisions affecting the Fund, see E. Hexner, 'The General Agreement on Tariffs and Trade and the Monetary Fund', I *I.M.F. Staff Papers* (1950–1) pp. 432–64.

be to disturb the relative value of the concessions granted under the appropriate Schedules. To meet this contingency it was provided that should the par value be reduced by a margin in excess of twenty per cent,[1] the concessions—that is, the duties and charges granted in the Schedules—could be adjusted to take account of the reduction, provided: (i) that the Contracting Parties concur that such adjustments will not impair the value of the concessions provided for in the appropriate Schedule or elsewhere in the Agreement; and (ii) that the devaluation was consistent with the Fund's Articles of Agreement. The response of the Contracting Parties in practice has been favourable and several adjustments have been undertaken.[2] A recent case arose in 1961 when the Contracting Parties approved an adjustment in the Uruguayan Schedule of Concessions due to the devaluation of the Uruguayan peso from 1·90 pesos per $U.S. to 11·03 pesos per $U.S., a reduction of 82·8 per cent approved by the Fund and well beyond the necessary 20 per cent limit.[3] Moreover, under paragraph (3) of Article II, all contracting parties undertake not to alter their method of determining dutiable value or of converting currencies so as to impair the value of any concessions provided for in the appropriate Schedule.

In the operation of G.A.T.T. Article VI, entitled 'Anti-dumping and Countervailing Duties',[4] the Fund's exchange

---

[1] The provision does not apply to any currency appreciations. This contingency would probably never arise since currency appreciations are relatively infrequent, and when they do occur the change does not normally approach the twenty per cent requirement. The revaluation of the deutsche mark from 4·20 to 4·00, in Mar. 1961, amounted to only 5·00 per cent, and from 4·00 to 3·66, in Oct. 1969, to 9·29 per cent.

[2] See, inter alia, B.I.S.D. vol. II (May 1952) pp. 12–13 for the adjustment of specific duties and charges in Schedule II (Benelux) to take account of a reduction, of more than twenty per cent, of the par value of the Netherlands guilder. and B.I.S.D., Second Supplement (Jan. 1954) pp. 24–5 for similar adjustments following the devaluation of the Greek drachma.

[3] B.I.S.D., Tenth Supplement (Mar. 1962) pp. 34, 199–201. For a further adjustment, see B.I.S.D., Thirteenth Supplement (July 1965) p. 20.

[4] To give effect to the provisions of Art. VI, the G.A.T.T. has drafted a formal Agreement: Agreement on Implementation of Article VI. Anti-Dumping Code (Geneva, 1969), which entered into force on 1 July 1968. In general this Agreement interprets the provisions of Art. VI of the General Agreement and lays down rules for their application in order to provide greater uniformity and certainty in their implementation. For a general discussion of this Code, see E. L. Symons, Jr., 'The Kennedy Round G.A.T.T. Anti-dumping Code', 29 University of Pittsburgh Law Review (1967–8) pp. 482–516.

rate regime and in particular the multiple exchange rate exception play yet another important role. Under the terms of Article VI, contracting parties are authorized to offset or to prevent dumping by anti-dumping duties, and to offset any bounties or subsidies by levying countervailing duties. By an interpretative note to this Article, the Contracting Parties recognized that multiple exchange rates can in certain circumstances constitute a subsidy to exports or can constitute a form of dumping by means of a partial depreciation of a country's currency. Contracting parties are therefore authorized to retaliate against such measures by the introduction of countervailing and anti-dumping duties respectively. Conversely they are obliged to remove those retaliatory measures when the country against whom the measures are directed replaces its multiple rate system with a unitary rate structure.[1]

Finally it is provided in Article VII, paragraph 4 (*a*), (*b*), (*c*), and (*d*) that where conversion is necessary for customs valuation purposes—that is, where a contracting party needs to convert into its own currency the price of imported merchandise expressed in the currency of another country—then the rate of exchange at which the foreign currency is to be converted into the local currency must be undertaken, for each currency involved, on the basis of one of the following criteria: (*a*) the par value established pursuant to the Fund Articles or pursuant to the Special Exchange Agreement;[2] (*b*) on the rate of exchange recognized by the Fund; (*c*) where options (*a*) and (*b*) do not exist, then the conversion rate shall

---

[1] B.I.S.D. vol. III (Nov. 1958) pp. 67–8.

[2] Art. XV, paras. 6, 7 of the G.A.T.T. oblige any contracting party which is not a member of the Fund to enter into a special exchange agreement with the Contracting Parties. The agreement is a substitute for Fund regulations and subjects non-members to rules similar to those applying to Fund members in respect of exchange stability and exchange restrictions. The Fund and the G.A.T.T. co-operated in drafting the agreement, see B.I.S.D., vol. II (May 1952) pp. 115–38. In its early years the G.A.T.T. concluded several such agreements, see 64 U.N.T.S. 439 for the Special Exchange Agreement entered into on 28 Jan. 1950 between Ceylon and the Contracting Parties. More recently the policy of the G.A.T.T. has been to waive this obligation. under Art. XXV, para. 5 of the General Agreement. See B.I.S.D., Thirteenth Supplement (July 1965) pp. 23–4 for waiver of this obligation in respect of Cuba. See also B.I.S.D., Third Supplement (June 1955) pp. 42–4 and Sixth Supplement (Mar. 1958) p. 38 for waiver of this obligation in respect of New Zealand and Czechoslovakia. For a general discussion of special exchange agreements, see J. Gold, 'The Fund and Non-Member States. Some Legal Effects', 7 *I.M.F. Pamphlet Series* (1966) pp. 12–24.

reflect effectively the current value of such currency in commercial transactions; and (d) where multiple rates of exchange are applied consistently with the Fund Agreement, then the Fund in collaboration with the G.A.T.T. shall formulate rules to govern conversion of such a currency and contracting parties are required to convert according to such rules. Pending the adoption of such rules, however, the contracting parties are permitted to convert at a rate which reflects the effective commercial value of such a currency. Since the G.A.T.T. and the Fund have not yet agreed on rules to govern conversion of a currency with multiple rates, contracting parties are obliged to convert such a currency at a rate which reflects its effective commercial value. In fact, therefore, only the first three alternatives mentioned above are relevant, and contracting parties must base their conversions either: (a) on Fund-established par values; or (b) on Fund-recognized exchange rates; or (c) on rates which effectively reflect the current commercial value of the currency.

The first alternative presents no difficulties and is in fact the basis on which most conversions by contracting parties are undertaken.[1] The second alternative—that is, where conversions are to be based on the rate of exchange recognized by the Fund—would apply to (1) the conversions of new Fund members who have not yet agreed on initial par values and (2) the currencies of those members who, having initially agreed with the Fund on a par value, either allow the rate to fluctuate freely or utilize a multiple rate structure. In the former case

---

[1] In 1955 the G.A.T.T. undertook a 'Comparative Study of Methods of Valuation for Customs Purposes'. The results of this study were published in B.I.S.D., Third Supplement (June 1955) pp. 103–25. Question 11, ibid. p. 114, was one of several questions listed in a general questionnaire addressed to G.A.T.T. members and read in part as follows: 'What is the system adopted by your Administration for the conversion of foreign currencies for valuation purposes? Do you apply the official rate of exchange based on the par value recognized by the International Monetary Fund or market rates?' Country-by-country replies to this question are listed, ibid. pp. 118–25. When considered as a whole, the replies indicated that 'Nearly all countries apply the official rates or market rates (which include par values where such values have been recognized by the Fund)', ibid. p. 114. For the currency conversion provisions applicable in the United States of America, see Sect. 522 of the Tariff Act 1930, 31 U.S.C., 1964 ed., 372. For a discussion of this provision as it was in 1955, see G. Bronz, 'Conversion of Foreign Currency in Customs Administration', 34 *Texas Law Review* (1955–6) pp. 78–102. See also Mann, *Legal Aspect of Money*, p. 389.

there is no par value upon which one can undertake a conversion, while in the latter case the par rate is ineffective. Nevertheless, in both cases the Fund would have a 'recognized exchange rate' for the purpose of carrying out computations in that currency which affect the Fund, and contracting parties would be obliged to undertake conversions at such rates.[1] The third alternative—that is, where conversion is to be based on the effective commercial rate—would apply to the conversion of currencies of non-member countries who would have neither a par value established with the Fund nor an exchange rate recognized by the Fund. The conversion of the currencies of the State-trading countries of eastern Europe is the most obvious example to which this provision would be applicable.

[1] In respect of new members who have not agreed on a par value, see Executive Board Decision no. 1687-(64/22), *I.M.F. Annual Report* (1964) p. 141, para. (*a*). For further analysis of this procedure, see R. Kroc, 'The Financial Structure of the Fund. Part 1: Quotas and Charges', 2 F.D. (1965) p. 42. In respect of a member who has abandoned a par value rate in favour of a fluctuating rate and a multiple rate, see 'Decision on Transactions and Computations Involving Fluctuating Currencies', *I.M.F. Annual Report* (1955) pp. 125–7, and J. Gold, 'Maintenance of the Gold Value of the Fund's Assets', *I.M.F. Pamphlet Series* (1965) pp. 12–13.

VII

DIRECT CONTROLS

1. *Introduction*

THE use by States of direct controls—that is, controls over the movement both of the means of payment and of goods as a device for achieving external financial equilibrium—has assumed a position of such importance that one prominent authority has made the candid admission that 'we can no longer preserve the polite fiction that they are mere temporary aberrations thrown up by the war and its aftermath. For good or ill they have established a large foothold as means to control balances of payments . . .'[1] Indeed the recent imposition of import surcharges,[2] quantitative import restrictions,[3] and exchange controls[4] by several States, members of both the Fund and the G.A.T.T., clearly indicates that such measures will, in times of national economic stress, be readily resorted to. The necessity, therefore, of providing an international legal

---

[1] W. M. Scammell, op. cit. p. 106. For a general review of the main developments in the use of restrictive practices, i.e. trade and payments restrictions, multiple currency practices, import surcharges, advance deposits, export subsidies, and bilateral payments arrangements during 1968, see *I.M.F. Twentieth Annual Report on Exchange Restrictions* (1969) pp. 2–6.

[2] Canada imposed import surcharges in the period June 1962 to Apr. 1963, *I.M.F. Fourteenth Annual Report on Exchange Restrictions* (1963) p. 62. The United Kingdom similarly imposed import surcharges in the period Oct. 1964 to Nov. 1966, *I.M.F. Annual Report* (1968) p. 50.

[3] France introduced quantitative import restrictions on certain manufactured commodities following the general strike in May and June 1968, *I.M.F. Twentieth Annual Report on Exchange Restrictions* (1969) pp. 150–60.

[4] The United States of America introduced in Sept. 1964 the Interest Equalization Tax designed to stem the flow abroad of private capital, D. G. Carreau, 'The Interest Equalization Tax', 2 J.W.T.L. (1968) pp. 47–88. See also C. J. Hynning, 'Balance of Payments Controls by the United States', 2 *The International Lawyer* (1967–8) pp. 400–36; D. R. Young, 'Governmental Regulation of Foreign Investment', 47 *Texas Law Review* (1968–9) pp. 421–47. France in Nov. 1968 imposed stringent exchange control measures designed to tighten up foreign exchange transactions by importers and exporters and to restrict capital movements, *Official Gazette* (Paris, 25 Nov. 1968) and *I.M.F. Twentieth Annual Report on Exchange Restrictions* (1969) pp. 160–2.

order designed to regulate the introduction, administration, and ultimate removal of such practices is no less important today than it was in the immediate post-war period.[1] In this respect, the Fund, in conjunction with the G.A.T.T., has played and continues to play a prominent role.

Although the necessity of co-ordinated action between these two agencies has been described earlier, it should be re-emphasized that such concerted action is of particular importance in the area under consideration. This results from the recognition that restrictive trade and payment measures are both symptoms of, and cures for, the same ailment—namely, a balance of payments deficit—and are therefore frequently indistinguishable one from the other. A Special Working Party established by the Contracting Parties to consider the interdependence of the two agencies similarly concluded that 'In many instances it is difficult or impossible to define clearly whether a government measure is financial or trade in character and frequently it is both.'[2] The Working Party went on to say: 'It follows that certain measures come under the jurisdiction of both the IMF and the CONTRACTING PARTIES and that decisions in relation to such measures have to be taken against a background of the objectives and rules both of the Fund and the General Agreement.'[2] It is clear, therefore, that the desired objective of establishing a multilateral trading system free of direct controls and operating through a regime of convertible currencies can be achieved only through the simultaneous regulation of both trade and payment restrictions. In discharging its allotted function in the realization of this objective, the Fund Agreement prescribes a series of rules in respect of exchange restrictions while the G.A.T.T., for its part, provides a similar code in respect of quantitative restrictions. These various provisions will be examined in turn in the subsequent two sections of this chapter.

2. *The Fund and Exchange Restrictions*

(i) *The general prohibition of exchange restrictions.* The central expression of the Fund's position on exchange restrictions is

---

[1] In this regard see G. Crowther, *An Outline of Money* (rev. ed., 1948) p. 275, and Nussbaum, *Money in the Law* p. 513.

[2] B.I.S.D., Third Supplement (June 1955) para. 2, p. 196.

contained in Article VIII, Section 2 (*a*) which states that no member shall, subject to certain exceptions, impose restrictions on the making of payments and transfers for current international transactions.[1] In short, the effect of this provision is to deny to member States the use of foreign exchange restrictions in respect of current transactions. As has been mentioned earlier, however, the notion 'foreign exchange restriction' has, neither for the purposes of international economic relations nor for the purposes of international monetary law, been given a rigid definition. It can be, and frequently is, given a wider or narrower scope depending upon the objectives of the particular arrangement in question, and can be defined with any degree of precision only when considered in the context of the Agreement in which it is found.[2] For the purposes of the Fund regime, since the term is nowhere defined in the Articles of Agreement, its scope must be gleaned from the Articles in general as well as from subsequent Fund practice. The principal single clue provided by subsequent Fund practice is contained in a decision delivered by the Executive Directors in June 1960 which reads in part as follows:

Article VIII provides in Sections 2 and 3 that members shall not impose or engage in certain measures, namely restrictions on the making of payments and transfers for current international transactions, discriminatory currency arrangements, or multiple currency practices, without the approval of the Fund. The guiding principle in ascertaining whether a measure is a restriction on payments and transfers for current transactions under Article VIII, Section 2, is whether it involves a direct governmental limitation on the availability or use of exchange as such. Members in doubt as to

---

[1] At Bretton Woods there was general agreement on the following point of principle: '. . . that the peace and prosperity of all will be served by countries agreeing to avoid . . . exchange restrictions on their current international transactions . . .', *Proceedings and Documents of United Nations Monetary and Financial Conference*, vol. I (Washington, 1948) Document 472, p. 867. This principle was given positive legal effect in Art. 1 (iv): 'To assist in the establishment of a multilateral system of payments in respect of current transactions between members and in the elimination of foreign exchange restrictions which hamper the growth of world trade'.

[2] H. Aufricht, 'Exchange Restrictions under the Fund Agreement', 2 J.W.T.L. (1968) p. 298. See also J. E. S. Fawcett, 'The International Monetary Fund and International Law', 40 B.Y.I.L. (1964) pp. 42–5; J. Gold, 'The International Monetary Fund and Private Business Transactions', *I.M.F. Pamphlet Series* (Washington, 1965) pp. 7 ff.

whether any of their measures do or do not fall under Article VIII may wish to consult the Fund thereon.[1]

The key phrase in the above pronouncement is 'direct governmental limitation on the availability or use of exchange'. It clearly implies that any governmental measures which either prohibit (a prohibition amounts to nothing more than a total limitation) or limit (the limitation can be less than total) either the availability or the use (an exchange control regime which freely makes available foreign exchange, but only for certain transactions, is restrictive) of exchange required for the consummation of current international transactions will, for the purposes of the Fund Agreement, constitute a restriction. Another clue is provided in Article VI, Section 3, a provision about which more will be said later; however, for our immediate purpose attention will be focused on that part of the provision which states that no member may exercise controls over international capital movements in a manner 'which will restrict payments for current transactions or which will unduly delay transfers of funds in settlement of commitments'. This provision suggests that governmental measures which have the effect of prolonging or protracting financial settlements in respect of current international transactions may also be tantamount to restrictions.[2] The combined effect of the above two factors indicates that any 'governmental prohibition of, limitation on, or hindrance to the availability or use of exchange'[3] in respect of the making of financial settlements for current international transactions will, for the purposes of the Fund Agreement, constitute a restriction. It follows from this interpretation that the Fund Agreement draws a distinction between exchange controls and exchange restrictions and seeks to prohibit only the latter—that is, it prohibits only those aspects of domestic exchange control systems which constitute a real interference rather than a mere nuisance to the making

---

[1] *I.M.F. Annual Report* (1960) pp. 29–30; *Selected Decisions*, pp. 81–2.

[2] However, note the following remark by H. Aufricht, 'Exchange Restrictions', 2 J.W.T.L. (1968) p. 304; 'It appears that in Fund practice delay as such has not been treated as an exchange restriction requiring approval by the Fund or authorisation under the Fund Agreement.'

[3] J. Gold, 'The International Monetary Fund and Private Business Transactions', *I.M.F. Pamphlet Series* (1965) p. 7. See also H. Aufricht, 'Exchange Restrictions', 2 J.W.T.L. (1968) p. 304.

of financial settlements. Under the Fund regime, therefore, the requirements that a resident trader surrender all foreign exchange proceeds to the official monetary agency or that a resident comply with certain licensing requirements as a prerequisite to the allocation of foreign exchange will not in themselves constitute restrictions. Such requirements may create additional complications for the resident trader, but they do not negate his ability to consummate international transactions owing to the unavailability of exchange. But monetary authorities must proceed with caution. In particular they must not require compliance with intermediary measures which are unreasonable. This caveat was aptly put by J. Gold in the following comment:

> But one must be careful in looking at the facts. I said that the procedure must not be 'unreasonable'. Thus, although a licensing or similar procedure is not in itself a restriction, it would be regarded as one if it unduly delayed the making of payments or transfers. There would be no doubt that it was a restriction if it went beyond delay in its effect and involved the actual prevention of payments or transfers.[1]

This fundamental distinction in determining what is and what is not legally acceptable conduct by a member can be further clarified by practical example. Following the disturbances in France in the spring of 1968, the French Government, to protect its currency, introduced certain exchange control measures. Under these regulations, importers were permitted to obtain foreign currency only eight days before the bills fell due, and only after having produced documentary evidence that the imported goods had passed through French customs. Moreover, if delivery of the goods was subsequently cancelled, the foreign currency which had previously been allocated would have to be surrendered to the authorities immediately. Similarly strict rules were applied to French exporters, who were not permitted to extend the deadline for payment beyond ninety days after the delivery of goods, and were obliged to surrender such foreign currency proceeds to the

[1] J. Gold, 'The International Monetary Fund and Private Business Transactions', *I.M.F. Pamphlet Series* (1965) p. 8.

central monetary authority within a month of payment.[1] In both cases—that is, (i) where the importers could receive foreign exchange only under certain conditions, and (ii) where the exporters had to collect and surrender foreign currency proceeds within a defined time period—the requirements were clearly tantamount to a form of exchange control. But although these measures detracted from the trader's former unlimited freedom of action in this regard, they did not restrict his ability to consummate the transaction for lack of means of payment, and they were not therefore a restriction within the meaning of Article VIII, Section 2 (a) of the Fund Agreement.[2]

Article VIII, Section 2 (a) further requires that a member avoid the imposition of restrictions on the making of payments and transfers. Since the prohibition extends only to the 'making' of payments, a member is not prevented from regulating the receipt of payments and may require its exporters to accept payment only in certain specified currencies.[3] On the other hand, the prohibition extends to both the making of payments and the making of transfers. The former—that is, the prohibition on the making of payments—ensures that the resident payer will be able to settle a money obligation (regardless of the amount involved) arising out of current transaction either by using his own domestic currency or by using any other foreign currency freely acquired on the exchange markets. The latter—that is, the prohibition on the making of transfers—ensures that the non-resident payee will be able to enjoy freely the use of such proceeds either by converting them into his domestic currency or by using them to consummate another current international transaction.[4] Should the resident payee,

[1] *Official Gazette* (Paris, 25 Nov. 1968); *I.M.F. Twentieth Annual Report on Exchange Restrictions* (1969) pp. 160–2.

[2] See similarly the Promatex case, in M. Waelbroeck, 'Free Movement of Goods in the E.E.C. Decisions of the National Courts', 2 J.W.T.L. (1968) pp. 567–8.

[3] Such specification of currencies may constitute a discriminatory currency arrangement and be contrary to the provisions of Art. VIII, Sect. 3. See Fawcett, 'I.M.F. and International Law', 40 B.Y.I.L. (1964) p. 45. See also J. Gold, 'The I.M.F. and Private Business Transactions', *I.M.F. Pamphlet Series* (1965) p. 16. But note the position of H. Aufricht, 'Exchange Restrictions', 2 J.W.T.L. (1968) p. 302, who suggests that restrictions on the making of inward payments as well as of outward payments are covered by Art. VIII, Sect. 2 (a).

[4] This distinction is explained in practical terms by J. Fawcett, 'Trade and Finance in International Law', 123 R.C. (1968–I) p. 282.

however, not repatriate such proceeds within a reasonable period of time, they may come to be considered by the country of the resident payer as capital, and thereby become subject to capital controls. What constitutes a reasonable period of time has not yet been considered by the Fund, but factors such as normal business practices in respect of working balances and repatriation of profits would be of prime importance in any such determination.[1] Finally, the provision applies only to those transactions which are 'current' and 'international'. The distinction between current and capital is a central feature of the Fund regime and will therefore be considered in more detail later. It will suffice to say at this point that transactions of a capital nature do not fall within the purview of Article VIII. As a general rule an 'international' transaction for the purposes of the Fund Agreement is one between two members or between the residents of two members. Transactions between a member and a non-member or between the residents of a member and the residents of a non-member are not subject to the regime of Article VIII, Section 2 (*a*) unless the Fund determines otherwise in accordance with Article XI, Section 2.[2]

In addition to the general prohibition on the use by members of exchange restrictions contained in Article VIII, Section 2 (*a*), members undertake not to engage, subject to certain exceptions, in discriminatory currency arrangements or multiple currency practices.[3] Both these devices can constitute restrictions on payments and transfers, and the Fund has accordingly sought, as part of its attack on exchange restrictions in general, their elimination.

The combined effect of the above provisions, that is, Article VIII, Sections 2 (*a*) and 3 (if one ignores for the moment the permitted exceptions), would be to promote the establishment and maintenance of a multilateral system of payments—that is, a system devoid of all the diverse forms of currency control

[1] For a review of the regulation which a Fund member may undertake of any balances of its currency held by a non-resident, see J. G. Evans, 'Current and Capital Transactions: How the Fund Defines Them', 5 F.D. (1968–3) p. 32.

[2] The Fund has in fact concerned itself with bilateral payments agreements concluded between members and non-members, see S. A. Silard, 'The Impact of the International Monetary Fund on International Trade', 2 J.W.T.L. (1968) pp. 142–4.   [3] Art. VIII, Sect. 3.

enumerated above, in respect of current international transactions. Under such a regime, traders would be able to conclude international commercial transactions without being hampered by payments restrictions. However, it was recognized by the drafters of the Fund Agreement that in certain circumstances the introduction of restrictions on international payments would be necessary. Accordingly, provisions were included in the Fund Agreement to cover any such contingencies. Before considering these exceptions, however, it should be emphasized that they will be tolerated only as temporary measures. In the long term the Fund's objective remains constant—that is, the establishment of a multilateral system of payments and the elimination of all foreign exchange restrictions. This objective will always prevail in spite of any short-term deviations.

(ii) *Exceptions to the prohibition of exchange restrictions.* As mentioned, various provisions in the Articles of Agreement recognize the need for exchange restrictions and accordingly authorize their imposition. Article VII, Section 3 allows the introduction of restrictions when the Fund declares that a currency is scarce; Article XIV, Section 2 permits the use of restrictions during the whole of the post-war transitional period, and Article VIII, Sections 2 (*a*) and 3 allows such practices to be introduced whenever prior Fund approval has been granted.

Before discussing these exceptions, however, a consideration of the distinction which the Articles draw between 'current' and 'capital' transactions is necessary. While the above-mentioned provisions are only temporary exceptions to the general prohibition of restrictions, and are to be utilized only in well-defined conditions and withdrawn when such conditions no longer exist, the distinction between restrictions on current and capital transactions is a continuing and permanent feature of the Fund regime and therefore merits special consideration.

It has been shown that the prohibition of exchange restrictions contained in Article VIII, Section 2 (*a*) applies only to payments in respect of transactions which are current and international. It follows, therefore, that a payment in respect of a transaction which is not current (that is, of a capital nature) can be freely restricted by a member[1] without being

---

[1] In a more positive sense, it has been suggested by one prominent publicist that the right of States to regulate capital movements is so firmly established

contrary to its obligation under Article VIII, Section 2 (*a*). Indeed, under Article VI, Section 3 it is expressly provided that a member may exercise such controls as are necessary to regulate international capital movements so long as such controls do not restrict payments or unduly delay transfers in respect of current transactions.[1] Moreover, under Article VI, Section 1 (*a*) (amended) a member may even be requested by the Fund to restrict capital movements. Whether a transaction is of current nature and subject to the provisions of Article VIII, or whether it involves an international capital transfer and is subject to the requirements of Article VI, is clearly therefore of fundamental importance to the Fund.[2]

To facilitate the determination of what constitutes, for the purposes of the Fund Agreement, a current transaction in respect of which payments cannot be restricted, Article XIX (i) of the Fund Agreement sets out a number of broad and not altogether satisfactory criteria.[3] The basic test is contained in the first sentence of paragraph (i) which states that 'Payments for current transactions means payments which are not for the purpose of transferring capital . . .' Since, from an economic point of view, (and as a general rule only) 'a capital transfer is one that has as its counterpart a claim to a future return,

---

by the provisions of the Fund Agreement that it 'is about as close as one is likely to get to an international law rule on any subject'. S. D. Metzger, 'Exchange Controls and International Law', *University of Illinois Law Forum* (1959) p. 320.

[1] Although Art. VIII, Sect. 3 simply states that members shall not engage in discriminatory currency arrangements and multiple currency practices without specifying whether or not the prohibition applies to both current and capital transactions, subsequent Fund practice has clearly established that the prohibition applies—as in the case of restrictions under Art. VIII, Sect. 2 (*a*)—only to current transactions. Consequently, while a multiple exchange rate which restricts current transactions would be subject to eventual elimination under Art. VIII, Sect. 3, a multiple exchange rate which restricted only capital transfers could be maintained indefinitely. See *Selected Decisions*, pp. 86–7. Similarly, members may control capital transfers on a discriminatory basis, that is, permit capital transfers to or from some members but not others. It is only in respect of current transactions that discrimination must be avoided. See J. Gold, 'I.M.F. and Private Business Transactions', *I.M.F. Pamphlet Series* (1965) pp. 15–16.

[2] This distinction is of practical importance as is well illustrated by *Tabar Claim (No. 3)* (1953) I.L.R. pp. 242–3.

[3] The following analysis of Art. XIX (i) and of the distinction which the Fund makes between current and capital transactions for the application of the Agreement is based on a study made of this problem by James G. Evans, Jr., who is a member of the Fund's legal department. See J. G. Evans, 'Current and Capital Transactions: How the Fund Defines Them', 5 F.D. (1968–3) pp. 30–5.

while the counterpart to a payment for a current transaction
is the receipt of goods or services',[1] one is able to determine by
looking to the counterpart of a payment whether that payment
is for a current transaction or for the purpose of transferring
capital. In other words, if a payment made by a resident to a
non-resident results in goods or services being brought to, or
performed in, the territorial jurisdiction of the member in
which the payer is resident, the payment is a payment for a
current transaction. If, on the other hand, the payment does
not result in such an immediate return of goods or services,
it will be treated as a capital transfer. Subject to certain obvious
exceptions, such as tourist expenditures and transfer payments,[2]
this test would appear to provide an adequate basis for distinguishing payments for current transactions from those which
are for the purpose of transferring capital. It should be noted,
however, that should a controversy arise between members as to
whether a transaction is current or capital in spite of the general
economic test, the Fund would assume the role of final arbiter
in settling the dispute.[3] The Fund has to date not made any
such pronouncements. Article XIX (i) also enumerates a
series of payments which, for the purposes of the Fund Agreement, are to be considered as payments for current transactions. Certain of these payments—for example, those due as
interest on loans or as net income from other investments, or
those made in moderate amounts for amortization of loans
or for depreciation of direct investments—are, when considered
from the economic viewpoint, more akin to capital than to
current payments. Nevertheless, for the purposes of the Fund
Agreement they are to be treated as current payments and

---

[1] Evans, p. 30.

[2] Tourist expenditures do not fall within this general economic test. Expenditures
on food, lodgings, services, etc. are clearly current and not capital payments, but
under the economic test, since no goods or services are brought back into the
country of the resident payer, they would not be considered as current. Transfer
payments, such as donations, gifts, inheritances, and wages sent out by foreign em-
ployees to their families, 'refer to transactions which have no *quid pro quo*', P. Høst-
Madsen, 'Balance of Payments', 3 F.D. (1966) p. 34. Accordingly they are difficult
to classify by the use of the economic test. But subject to these difficulties the test,
as pointed out by Evans, has as a general rule been found adequate.

[3] The Fund's authority to do so springs from the last sentence of Art. XIX
(i): 'The Fund may, after consultation with the members concerned, determine
whether certain specific transactions are to be considered current transactions or
capital transactions.'

accordingly may not be restricted.[1] It has been suggested that
the rationale for treating these particular payments as current
payments is to encourage the growth of private foreign investment by assuring foreign investors that the net income from
their investments or the interest due on loans, etc., will be
repatriable.[2]

Before concluding this discussion, a further observation on
the nature of the obligation undertaken by member States in
respect of Article VI, Section 3 should be made. It has already
been mentioned that members, when introducing controls
in respect of capital movements, must so exercise such controls as not to restrict payments for current transactions. In
addition, members when acting under Article VI, Section 3 are
subject to a second condition. They must make certain that
when capital controls are introduced they are compatible
with the terms of Article IV, Section 4 (a)—that is, such controls must not jeopardize international monetary stability.
The recent imposition by the United States of America of the
Interest Equalization Tax (I.E.T.),[3] a form of capital control,[4]
is a case in point. In conformity with its obligation not to
contravene Article IV, Section 4 (a) by the introduction of the
I.E.T., Congress included the following paragraph in the
enabling legislation:

If the President of the United States shall at any time determine
that the application of the tax imposed by section 4911 will have such
consequences for a foreign country as to imperil or threaten to imperil the stability of the international monetary system, he may by
Executive order specify that such tax shall not apply to the acquisition by a United States person of stock or a debt obligation of the

[1] For a discussion of some of the problems raised by these provisions, see J. G.
Evans, op. cit. pp. 34–5.
[2] J. Gold, 'I.M.F. and Private Business Transactions', *I.M.F. Pamphlet Series*
(1965) p. 12. See also H. Aufricht, 'Exchange Restrictions', 2 J.W.T.L. (1968)
pp. 307–8.
[3] 26 U.S.C.A. Chap. 41. For a study of the factors leading up to the introduction
of the tax, its nature and effects, and subsequent legislative history, see D. G.
Carreau, 'The Interest Equalization Tax', 2 J.W.T.L. (1968) pp. 47–88. For a discussion of the international legality of the I.E.T., see ibid. pp. 81–4.
[4] In general the tax is designed to curb the outflow of United States capital
by raising the cost of borrowing on the capital markets of the United States. This is
achieved by the imposition of an *ad valorem* tax on the acquisition by a United
States person of foreign debt obligations and securities. The rate of tax varies
according to the nature of the transaction.

government of such foreign country or a political subdivision thereof . . .[1]

Turning now to a discussion of the three general exceptions enumerated above,[2] the first—that is, the scarce currency exception (Article VII, Section 3)—need not delay us long since it has never been put into active operation by the Fund. This non-activation policy of the Fund has been criticized as 'A most serious failure of the Fund',[3] since it removed the burden of dealing with an external payments disequilibrium from the collective shoulders of both surplus and deficit countries and placed it squarely in the lap of the latter. This is the case because a country running a surplus in its balance of payments will be able to add indefinitely to its holdings of international reserve assets without suffering any repercussions, while a country running a deficit can do so only as long as it has available international reserve assets with which to finance the deficit. When such facilities are exhausted or approaching depletion, it will be forced to take certain defensive measures. To shift this burden, Article VII, Section 3 (a) empowers the Fund to declare a member's currency scarce if it becomes evident to the Fund that the demand for that member's currency seriously threatens the Fund's ability to supply it. (This will normally be the case when a member is in a chronic surplus position, with the result that the demand for its currency far exceeds the available supply.) There are two consequences of a currency being declared scarce: (1) the Fund must ration the existing and accruing supply of the scarce currency among the various members requesting it with due regard to (a) the relative needs of members, (b) the general international economic situation, and (c) any other pertinent considerations; (2) more significantly, such a declaration acts as an authorization to any member, after due consultation with the Fund, to impose temporary limitations on the freedom of exchange operations in the scarce currency. In addition to being subject to the provisions of Article IV, Sections 3 and 4, however, these limita-

---

[1] 26 U.S.C.A. § 4917 (a).   [2] Above, p. 146.

[3] E. A. Birnbaum, 'Gold and the International Monetary System: an Orderly Reform', 66 *Princeton Essays in International Finance* (1968) p. 22. The author at pp. 22–6 reviews the intended objectives of these provisions and discusses as well the reasons for their non-implementation.

tions must not go beyond what is necessary to restore equilibrium between the demand for and the accruing and existing supply of the scarce currency. Furthermore, the restrictions are to be relaxed and ultimately abolished as soon as conditions permit.[1] In any event they are immediately to expire whenever the Fund formally declares the currency in question to be no longer scarce.[2]

The intended operation and effect of Article VII, Section 3 should now be apparent. A formal declaration by the Fund that a currency is scarce would authorize members of the Fund to discriminate against the exports of such a member. Accordingly, members in chronic surplus which did not pursue policies appropriate for restoring external-payments balance, or which did not at least extend adequate amounts of capital exports or external assistance, would face the threat of world-wide discrimination against their products.

The grand design of Bretton Woods would thus retain the possibility of trade discrimination in the postwar world. But this would not be the insidious bilateral discrimination associated with Hjalmar Schacht and the 1930's. Rather, like the possibility of a currency devaluation under the Articles, discrimination would require the sanction of an international consensus—a majority decision of the nations participating in the Fund.[3]

To date, however, these provisions have not been activated. From the economic viewpoint, the disadvantage of the resultant unilateral approach to the solution of a problem which essentially requires a multilateral approach is manifest.[4] From the legal viewpoint, the Fund has clearly failed to carry out one of the main duties entrusted to it at Bretton Woods. The gravity of this failure and the effect that it has had on the development of international monetary law are succinctly expressed by a Fund critic as follows: 'By preventing the Fund from acting under its scarce-currency provisions, one of the most important delegations of power originally entrusted to the IMF at Bretton

[1] Art. VII, Sect. 3 (b).
[2] Art. VII, Sect. 3 (c).
[3] E. A. Birnbaum, op. cit. p. 22. It was suggested that the scarce currency clause be activated to deal with the speculative rush into deutsche marks during 1968-9, *Financial Times*, 10 May 1969, p. 12.
[4] See R. A. Mundell, 'The International Monetary Fund', 3 J.W.T.L. (1969) pp. 466-8.

Woods was returned to the sovereign countries.'[1] When one
bears in mind the tenacity with which States cling to their
economic sovereignty, the seriousness of this loss becomes all
too obvious.

A more important exception is contained in Article XIV,
Section 2. It authorizes a member (if it so elects), for balance
of payments reasons, to maintain and to adapt to changing
circumstances those restrictions on payments and transfers for
current international transactions which were in effect when
the country became a member of the Fund. In the case of those
members who had been occupied by the enemy, the provision
permits the introduction of such restrictions 'where necessary'.
Originally this exception was intended to be of limited duration,
sufficient to enable members to resort to foreign exchange
restrictions while they reconstructed their war-exhausted
economies.[2] To date, however, only thirty-one members[3]
have abandoned their Article XIV status in favour of Article
VIII status, and, as one observer has pointed out, Article XIV
has in fact 'turned into a continuing escape clause'.[4] However,
the continued use of Article XIV has not had as disruptive an
impact upon the Fund's activities as is commonly believed.
This is due both to Fund policy in the interpretation and application of Article XIV and to certain built-in limitations.

In the first place, it is only when an adverse payments situation exists that a member may maintain and adapt existing
restrictions.[5] The member is obliged gradually to remove these
measures as its balance of payments position improves, and

[1] E. A. Birnbaum, op. cit. p. 25; cf. *Financial Times*, 28 Nov. 1968, p. 21.

[2] It would appear that the transitional period was originally intended not to last
much beyond five years. Under the terms of Art. XIV, Sect. 4, the Fund, three
years after the date on which it began to operate (1 Mar. 1947), was to report
on any restrictions still in force, and after five years, if a member still retained
controls, it was to consult with the Fund as to 'their further retention'. The Fund
if it deemed such action necessary, could require the member to abandon the
restrictions. To date the Fund has not utilized this coercive power. In Mar. 1947
only five members did not resort to the transitional arrangements of Art. XIV,
Sect. 2, and at the end of the five years (Mar. 1952), forty-four of the fifty-one
members were still availing themselves of Art. XIV. *I.M.F. Annual Report* (1952)
p. 60.

[3] For a list of Art. VIII members on 30 Apr. 1969, and the dates at which they
adopted Art. VIII status, see *I.M.F. Annual Report* (1969) p. 139.

[4] J. E. S. Fawcett, 'International Monetary Fund and International Law',
40 B.Y.I.L. (1964) p. 48.

[5] *I.M.F. Eighteenth Annual Report on Exchange Restrictions* (1967) p. 2.

indeed, when its payments position is favourable, the member must abandon any restrictions maintained under Article XIV and accept the obligations of Article VIII, Sections 2, 3, and 4. Furthermore, apart from those members whose territories had been occupied by the enemy, an Article XIV member like an Article VIII member may not, without prior Fund approval, introduce new restrictions or reimpose any that have been eliminated.[1] Moreover, in cases where an Article XIV member seeks to adapt existing restrictions to changing circumstances and it is not absolutely clear-cut that the contemplated measure is in fact an adaptation and may in fact be an introduction, the member is obliged to consult the Fund before proceeding. The issue—that is, whether the proposed measure is an adaptation or an introduction—will then be decided 'by the Fund on the facts of each case'.[1] By assuming the role of final arbiter in such cases, the Fund has further restricted the freedom of action which members possess under Article XIV. Finally, if one adds to this list of limitations the Fund's decision that all alterations—that is, adaptations and introductions (where permitted) in those restrictions which are also multiple exchange rates—require Fund approval,[2] it is apparent that Article XIV constitutes a narrower exception to Article VIII than is generally realized. Additionally, all Article XIV members are required to consult annually with the Fund about the further retention of any restrictions.[3] These annual consultations 'are among the main activities of the Fund',[4] and provide the forum in which the Fund and members alike can air their separate views on exchange matters, and more important, provide the Fund with the opportunity to place moral pressure on members to remove restrictions which are no longer justified for balance of payments reasons. It should also be noted at this point that Article VIII members who are maintaining restrictive measures by virtue of Sections 2 and 3

[1] *I.M.F. Eighteenth Annual Report on Exchange Restrictions* (1967) p. 2.
[2] See above, pp. 127-8.
[3] Art. XIV, Sect. 4.
[4] Jean van der Mensbrugghe, 'Consultations with the Fund', 2 F.D. (1965) p. 91. For a description of the actual procedure of consultations under Art. XIV, see ibid. pp. 92-4. See also a similar remark made by Per Jacobsson in a speech delivered at the 1962 Annual Meeting of the Board of Governors, *I.M.F. Summary Proceedings of the Seventeenth Annual Meeting* (1962) p. 24; *International Monetary Problems 1957-63, Selected Speeches of Per Jacobsson* (Washington, 1964) p. 289.

of Article VIII are also required to consult with the Fund concerning the further maintenance of such measures. Although Article VIII members who are not maintaining restrictive measures under the auspices of Article VIII are not required to consult with the Fund, consultations nevertheless do take place between the Fund and such members. These latter two policy decisions in respect of consultations with Article VIII members were adopted by the Executive Board on 1 June 1960:

3. If members at any time maintain measures which are subject to Sections 2 and 3 of Article VIII, they shall consult with the Fund with respect to the further maintenance of such measures. Consultations with the Fund under Article VIII are not otherwise required or mandatory. However, the Fund is able to provide technical facilities and advice, and to this end, or as a means of exchanging views on monetary and financial developments, there is great merit in periodic discussions between the Fund and its members even though no questions arise involving action under Article VIII. Such discussions would be planned between the Fund and the member, including agreement on place and timing, and would ordinarily take place at intervals of about one year.[1]

Finally, it should be emphasized that Article XIV represents only a temporary exception to the permanent obligation, incumbent upon all members, contained in Article VIII. Consequently, even Article XIV members are subject to the provisions of Article VIII, except to the extent that they are exempt from those provisions by virtue of Article XIV. For example, and as already mentioned, an Article XIV member (other than one who had been occupied by the enemy) who seeks to introduce a new restriction can do so only if the necessary approval has been granted by the Fund under Article VIII.[2]

The granting of Fund approval to the introduction by members of new foreign exchange restrictions brings us to a consideration of the last of the three enumerated exceptions. The Fund Agreement nowhere lays down explicit standards by

[1] Executive Board Decision no. 1034–(60/27), *Selected Decisions*, pp. 82–3; *I.M.F. Annual Report* (1960) p. 30.

[2] It has been suggested, however, that the Fund would be more prone to grant approval to an Art. XIV member than to an Art. VIII member. J. Gold, 'I.M.F. and Private Business Transactions', *I.M.F. Pamphlet Series* (1965) p. 18. But note Fund Decision no. 144–(52/51) in which a member for national or international security reasons may introduce exchange restrictions without prior Fund approval, *Selected Decisions*, pp. 75–6.

which it will decide whether or not to approve restrictions under Article VIII, Section 2 (*a*) or 3. The absence of specific criteria seems commendable in the light of economic realities, and accordingly the Fund's 'judgment must rest on an appraisal of the total circumstances of the nation concerned, the broad objectives of the Fund other than the elimination of restrictions which hamper the growth of world trade, and a delicate appraisal of whether the growth of world trade would be hampered more, in the circumstances, by the imposition of restrictions than by their non-imposition'.[1] Although pragmatism and flexibility are essential, the Fund does provide, as the following Fund directive illustrates, general terms of reference to which members should direct their attention when contemplating the imposition of restrictions:

. . . If members, for balance of payments reasons, propose to maintain or introduce measures which require approval under Article VIII, the Fund will grant approval only where it is satisfied that the measures are necessary and that their use will be temporary while the member is seeking to eliminate the need for them. As regards measures requiring approval under Article VIII and maintained or introduced for nonbalance of payments reasons, the Fund believes that the use of exchange systems for nonbalance of payments reasons should be avoided to the greatest possible extent, and is prepared to consider with members the ways and means of achieving the elimination of such measures as soon as possible . . . [2]

This pronouncement indicates that the Fund will be loath to grant approval to members to introduce restrictions under Article VIII. Only if the proposed measures are necessary, temporary, and justified on balance of payments grounds, will the Fund view any such proposals with sympathy.[3] The importance attached by the Fund to the balance of payments position of the member in deciding whether to grant approval under Article VIII is significant, particularly when one recalls that under the G.A.T.T. the primary justification for the introduction of quantitative import restrictions is an adverse balance of payments position of the contracting party. Direct

[1] S. D. Metzger, 'Exchange Controls and International Law', *University of Illinois Law Forum* (1959) p. 321.

[2] Executive Board Decision of 1 June 1960, *I.M.F. Annual Report* (1960) p. 30, para. 2; *Selected Decisions*, p. 82.

[3] See *I.M.F. Annual Report* (1955) p. 124, para. 4; *Selected Decisions*, pp. 76–7.

commercial and financial controls clearly have a distinct role to play in international monetary affairs. However, unlike the situation which prevailed in the pre-war period, their role is specifically defined and their use strictly regulated. The regulation of foreign currency restrictions has been dealt with; it now remains to consider the regulation of quantitative restrictions through the instrumentality of the G.A.T.T.

3. The G.A.T.T. and Quantitative Import Restrictions

(i) *Article XII (developed countries)*. Quantitative import restrictions, normally through the mechanism of a licensing system, fix the total quantity or value of certain or all commodities allowed to be imported into the restricting country.[1] The object of such regulation is to improve the balance of payments position of the restricting country by permitting only that amount of goods to be imported which can be paid for out of current export earnings. Since quantitative import restrictions, unlike tariff and other non-tariff barriers[2] to trade, do not merely burden competition in international trade but in fact tend to 'destroy competition altogether',[3] their use is prohibited in sweeping language in the G.A.T.T.:

No prohibitions or restrictions other than duties, taxes or other charges, whether made effective through quotas, import or export licences or other measures, shall be instituted or maintained by any contracting party on the importation of any product of the territory of any other contracting party or on the exportation or sale for export of any product destined for the territory of any other contracting party.[4]

Under the terms of this provision, contracting parties are

[1] Generally see *The Use of Quantitative Restrictions for Protective and Other Commercial Purposes* (G.A.T.T., Geneva, Nov. 1951).

[2] Among the other non-tariff barriers regulated by the G.A.T.T. are internal taxes (Art. III); anti-dumping and countervailing duties (Art. VI); freedom of transit (Art. V). Only quantitative import restrictions are of immediate relevance to this study, since not only are they historically the most significant non-tariff barrier to trade, but more important, their use (as permitted within the G.A.T.T.) is inextricably linked to the international payments performance of the contracting parties.

[3] G. Bronz, 'An International Trade Organization: The Second Attempt', 69 *Harvard Law Review* (1955–6) p. 451.

[4] Art. XI, para. 1. The G.A.T.T. Articles cited hereinafter will be those of the revised text as reproduced in B.I.S.D., vol. IV (Mar. 1969), unless otherwise indicated.

obliged to remove existing quantitative restrictions and undertake not to introduce new ones. This sweeping prohibition, however, is robbed of much of its force by various escape clauses, the most important of which is contained in Article XII. Under Article XII, contracting parties are permitted, in order to safeguard their external financial position and balance of payments, to restrict either the quantity or the value of merchandise permitted to be imported, provided that the restrictions do not exceed those necessary:

(i) to forestall the imminent threat of, or to stop, a serious decline in its monetary reserves, or

(ii) in the case of a contracting party with very low monetary reserves, to achieve a reasonable rate of increase in its reserves.[1]

Moreover, members are obliged to relax progressively and ultimately abolish any restrictions applied under this provision in response to improvements in their reserve position.[2] The conditions which have to be satisfied before any contracting party can either maintain, intensify, or institute quantitative import restrictions are, therefore, clearly defined in the G.A.T.T. The determination of whether such conditions exist rests with the Fund, and the Contracting Parties are obliged to accept the Fund's findings (Article XV, paragraph 2).[3] It should be emphasized, however, that the Fund's role under paragraph 2 of Article XV is purely consultative, since quantitative restrictions and measures with equivalent effect fall exclusively within the jurisdiction of the G.A.T.T. Accordingly, while the Contracting Parties are obliged to accept the findings of the Fund with respect to reserves, the answer to the question 'Are the commercial restrictions introduced to deal with the payments difficulty legal?' rests with the Contracting Parties.

In practice this provision was activated for the first time in the G.A.T.T.'s twenty-year history following the introduction in November 1968 by the United Kingdom of the import deposit scheme. Although in this instance the Fund supported the United Kingdom's action, finding that 'In

---

[1] Art. XII, para. 2 (*a*). It should be noted that contracting parties are also permitted to utilize quantitative import restrictions to safeguard their domestic agricultural industry, Art. XI, para. 2.

[2] Art. XII, para. 2 (*b*).

[3] See the last sentence of Art. XV, para. 2.

present circumstances, the import deposits scheme does not go beyond the extent necessary—in conjunction with other measures—to achieve a reasonable strengthening of the United Kingdom's reserve position',[1] the decision was not completely free from doubt. Although it was clear when the scheme was introduced that the British economic position was not strong, from the viewpoint of reserves—which is the only relevant criterion for determining the legality of the restrictive measures under paragraph 2 (a) of Article XII—Britain stood about tenth in the order of the Western world's reserve holders, and this position had not changed much since 1964. In fact, Britain's reserves stood at about £1,000m. at the end of 1968 after losses of some £125m. during the year. Nevertheless, the measures were accepted by the Fund as satisfying the criteria of Article XII, paragraph 2 (a), and on the basis of the Fund's findings the scheme was subsequently approved by the Contracting Parties of the G.A.T.T.

In the light of these specific provisions, the singular lack of success which the G.A.T.T. experienced in its early years in dismantling quantitative restrictions[2] is attributable in the main to the following two causes: (a) some contracting parties blatantly flouted their legal obligations and maintained restrictions even when not justified on payments grounds; and (b) other contracting parties were able, by a manipulation of the subsequent provisions of Article XII,[3] to generate balance of payments deficits and thereby, without breaching the letter of paragraph 2 (a), to maintain quantitative restrictions. (a) There is no doubt that in the early years the of G.A.T.T.'s existence, many contracting parties were maintaining, in direct contravention of their legal obligations, quantitative restrictions

[1] *Financial Times*, 1 Feb. 1969, p. 11. For further reports see *The Times*, 16 and 31 Jan. 1969, at pp. 17 and 30 respectively.

[2] The G.A.T.T. was more successful in its efforts to prevent the introduction of new restrictions. This was due to the terms of Art. XII, para. 4 (a) (of the original text) which obliged any contracting party contemplating such a move to consult with the Contracting Parties before instituting such restrictions (or, in circumstances in which prior consultation was impracticable, immediately after doing so). It should be noted that in the revised text of Art. XII, para. 4 (a) the above obligation is reversed, that is, contracting parties are obliged to consult only after introducing such restrictions, and prior consultation is required only in circumstances where it is practicable.

[3] Of the original text.

which were no longer justified on balance of payments grounds. Wyndham White, the Executive Secretary to the G.A.T.T., in reviewing the early efforts of the G.A.T.T. in this field, frankly admits that 'many countries chafed under the restrictions which the rules imposed on their traditional freedom of action in commercial policy and were distrustful of submitting to international discussion the delicate matters which had hitherto been jealously guarded national and bilateral preserves . . .'[1]

(b)[2] On the other hand, many contracting parties were, in fact, able to satisfy the payments criteria of Article XII, paragraph 2 and therefore validly retain restrictions. This was made possible through the combined effect of paragraph 3 (b) and sub-paragraph 3 (b) (i) of Article XII. Under the terms of paragraph 3 (b), contracting parties were permitted to engage in inflationary domestic policies. Such inflationary measures would in turn give rise to payments deficits and so justify the continued maintenance of quantitative restrictions under paragraph 2 (a). Moreover, it was expressly stated in sub-paragraph 3 (b) (i) that contracting parties would not be required to modify their domestic programmes even though such modifications could quite feasibly render unnecessary the continued maintenance of restrictions under paragraph 2 (a). In other words, domestic considerations were given preference over one of the basic objectives of the G.A.T.T., namely the elimination of quantitative restrictions.[3] The two provisions constituted a built-in device for generating payments deficits, and in effect turned Article XII into a continuing escape clause. International economic co-operation was sacrificed to narrow nationalistic objectives, and the intended elimination of quantitative restrictions remained, by and large, a dead letter until the mid fifties when the G.A.T.T. was revised.

Under the revised text of Article XII, contracting parties are still permitted to deviate from the obligation of Article XI, paragraph 1, if, as under the original text, they satisfy

---

[1] E. W. White, *The First Ten Years of the G.A.T.T.* (Geneva, 1958) p. 5.

[2] In the following discussion of reason (b) for the failure of the G.A.T.T. to eliminate quantitative restrictions in its early years, all Articles cited refer to the original text, B.I.S.D. vol. I (Geneva, May 1952), 55 U.N.T.S. 187.

[3] These particular provisions were severely criticized by the International Chamber of Commerce when they first appeared in the I.T.O. Charter; Curzon, *Multilateral Commercial Diplomacy* (London, 1965) p. 133.

the criteria set out in Article XII, paragraph 2 (*a*). However, to prevent the continued abuse of this exception, the subsequent paragraphs of Article XII have been considerably altered.

First, to ensure that contracting parties do not maintain restrictions which are no longer justified under Article XII, paragraph 2 (*a*), all contracting parties applying such restrictions are required, under the terms of Article XII, paragraph 4 (*b*), to enter into annual consultations with the Contracting Parties.[1] If as a result of these consultations the Contracting Parties find that the restrictions are being applied in a manner which is inconsistent with the provisions of Article XII, the delinquent member may become subject to certain sanctions. If the inconsistency is of a minor or technical nature, the Contracting Parties shall simply indicate the nature of the inconsistency and recommend a suitable modification.[2] If, on the other hand, the inconsistency is of a more serious nature, that is, the trade of another contracting party is actually damaged or threatened with damage thereby, the Contracting Parties shall make appropriate recommendations for correcting the inconsistency and the delinquent member is obliged to carry out the recommendations within a specified period of time. Failure to comply would give rise to retaliatory economic measures by any contracting party whose trade was adversely affected by the inconsistent restrictions.[3] In practice these consultations, which take place on a country-to-country basis, have been a regular feature of the activities of the G.A.T.T. since 1958, when a general review of all restrictions was undertaken,[4] and have been the main force behind the

[1] Provision was made for consultation under the original text (Art. XII, para. 4 (*b*)), but unlike the revised text (Art. XII, para. 4 (*b*)), the consultations did not take place on an annual basis. The Working Party established in 1955 to consider the revision of the G.A.T.T. was of the opinion that the best method of insuring against an abuse of Art. XII, para. 2 (*a*) was to establish a more rigid and demanding consultative procedure. B.I.S.D., Third Supplement (June 1955) p. 171, para. 4.

[2] Art. XII, para. 4 (*c*) (i). See also B.I.S.D., Third Supplement (1955) pp. 172–3, para. 9.

[3] Art. XII, para. 4 (*c*) (ii). See also B.I.S.D., Third Supplement (1955) p. 173, para. 10.

[4] A Committee on Balance of Payments Restrictions was established in 1958 and charged with the responsibility of conducting the consultations. The Committee is composed of governmental representatives and reflects various characteristics of the contracting parties such as their geographical location, external financial position, and stage of economic development, B.I.S.D., Seventh Supplement

successful dismantling of such restrictive practices in recent years.[1]

Secondly, to ensure that contracting parties would no longer be able freely to frustrate the gradual elimination of quantitative restrictions by indulging in inflationary domestic policies, the hitherto *carte blanche* right to engage in such programmes was curtailed. Under the revised Article XII, contracting parties, although still permitted to pursue inflationary domestic policies,[2] are also obliged, by virtue of paragraph 3 (*a*), 'in carrying out their domestic policies, to pay due regard to the need for maintaining or restoring equilibrium in their balance of payments on a sound and lasting basis and to the desirability of avoiding an uneconomic employment of productive resources'. However, it was the inclusion of the following new sentence in paragraph 3 (*a*) which tipped the scales against the predominance of domestic objectives and in favour of international co-operation. That sentence states: 'They [that is, the Contracting Parties] recognize that, in order to achieve these ends, it is desirable so far as possible to adopt measures which expand rather than contract international trade.' The operative words are 'which expand rather than contract international trade'. Contracting parties are no longer entitled indiscriminately to pursue domestic programmes regardless of their international repercussions, but must as far as possible order their affairs in such a way as to encourage the growth and development rather than the contraction of international trade.[3]

Following the G.A.T.T. amendment in 1955, the Contracting Parties achieved considerable success in the dismantling of quantitative restrictions, and indeed it has been suggested that the G.A.T.T.'s 'greatest achievement after tariff reductions, was the part it played (along with the IMF and

---

(Feb. 1959) pp. 94–5. As a general rule, the following four subjects are the main points of discussion: (1) Balance of payments position and prospects; (2) Alternative measures to restore equilibrium; (3) System and methods of restriction; (4) Effects of the restrictions. (Ibid. pp. 97–8.) For a complete list of references of the consultations which have taken place since 1957–66, see B.I.S.D., Fourteenth Supplement (July 1966) p. 211.

[1] *I.M.F. Annual Report* (1965) p. 12. [2] Art. XII, para. 3 (*d*).

[3] Referring to the addition of the new provision in para. 3 (*a*), Curzon, op. cit. p. 137, states: 'This was no mean achievement ... Now it was clear that sovereignty over domestic policies was recognized provided only it did not interfere with the trade of other Contracting Parties.'

OEEC) in getting quotas reduced or dismantled'.[1] Although some contracting parties still rely on quantitative restrictions, they pose no real threat to international commerce since their use is subject to international scrutiny through the consultative procedure which takes place on an annual or biennial basis, as the case may be.[2] In addition it will be seen that the use of such restrictions is also the subject of rigid international regulation and scrutiny at both the regional and the bilateral treaty levels.

(ii) *Article XVIII (developing countries)*. The revised G.A.T.T., in recognition of the special needs of those contracting parties with developing economies, that is, those contracting parties whose economies can support only low standards of living and are in the early stages of development,[3] introduced into Article XVIII, Section B provisions which enable such contracting parties 'to apply quantitative restrictions for balance of payments purposes in a manner which takes full account of the continued high level of demand for imports likely to be generated by their programmes of economic development'.[4] Although, in the main, the provisions of Article XVIII, Section B do not differ from those of Article XII, certain liberalizing elements have been introduced into Section B. For example, before an Article XVIII (B) contracting party can restrict imports, its reserves need not be 'very low' but only 'inadequate'.[5] Similarly, it can restrict imports if its reserves are threatening to decline; the threat need not be 'imminent'.[6] Moreover, in recognition of the long-term nature of developing countries' payments difficulties and in view of the practical difficulties which such countries may have in the preparation of the necessary documents, consultations are biennial rather than annual.[7] Furthermore, under Article XVIII, Section B, paragraph 12 (*e*)

---

[1] J. H. Jackson, 'The Puzzle of GATT', 1 J.W.T.L. (1967) p. 149.

[2] Consultations with contracting parties applying restrictions under Art. XII take place on an annual basis (Art. XII, para. 4 (*b*)), while consultations with contracting parties applying restrictions under Art. XVIII, Sect. B take place on a biennial basis (Art. XVIII, Sect. B, para. 12 (*b*)). For a list of contracting parties with whom consultations took place during 1964–5, see B.I.S.D., Fourteenth Supplement (1967) p. 161.

[3] Art. XVIII para. 1; these concepts are further defined in Annex 1 of the G.A.T.T.

[4] Art. XVIII, para. 2.

[5] Art. XVIII, Sect. B, para. 9.

[6] Ibid.; also B.I.S.D., Third Supplement (June 1955) p. 183, para. 44.

[7] Art. XVIII, Sect. B, para. 12 (*b*).

a contracting party is allowed to withdraw from the Agreement at shorter notice (sixty days) than is provided in Article XXXI (six months) for all other contracting parties if it finds that the operation of its programme and policy of economic development is adversely affected by any retaliatory measures authorized by the Contracting Parties in accordance with paragraph 12 (c) (ii) and 12 (d) of Article XVIII, Section B. Finally, in contrast to the provisions of Article XII, paragraph 3 (a), it should be noted that in Article XVIII, Section B, no suggestion is made that the contracting parties, in carrying out their domestic policies, should endeavour to achieve payments equilibrium on a sound and lasting basis through the adoption of measures 'which expand rather than contract international trade'. Domestic policies are clearly given preference over international co-operation.[1] It would appear that contracting parties with developing economies have, in the application of quantitative import restrictions, been given virtually a free hand.

(iii) *Discriminatory administration of quantitative restrictions.* Restrictions, whether applied under Article XII or under Article XVIII, Section B, must, subject to the provisions of Article XIV, be applied on a non-discriminatory basis.[2] Principal among the exceptions enumerated in Article XIV are those which permit contracting parties to deviate from the non-discrimination provision of Article XIII in a manner having equivalent effect to restrictions on payments and transfers for current international transactions which contracting parties may at that time be applying under Article VIII, Article XIV, and Article VII, Section 3 of the Articles of Agreement of the International Monetary Fund. In other words, if the Fund under Article VIII, Sections 2 (a) or 3 permits member A to introduce discriminatory currency practices or if the Fund under Article VII, Section 3 declares a currency scarce and thereby authorizes member A to impose temporary limitations on the freedom of exchange operations in that scarce currency, then, if member A is also a contracting party, it would *ipso facto*, by virtue of Article XIV, paragraphs 1 and

---

[1] See B.I.S.D., Third Report (June 1955) pp. 179–80, paras. 35 and 36.
[2] Art. XIII, para. 1.

5 of the G.A.T.T., be permitted to engage in similar discriminatory trade practices. Moreover, by an explanatory note to Article XIV, paragraph 1, it is further stated that the Fund need not actually declare a currency scarce under Article VII or actually approve the introduction of discriminatory currency practices under Article VIII before a contracting party would be permitted to adopt parallel trade practices, but only that the Fund would approve such discriminatory currency practices if requested.[1] Although it is not expressly stated in Article XIV, paragraph 1, discriminatory trade practices would presumably have to be eliminated when the Fund member was no longer permitted to maintain discriminatory currency arrangements under Article VIII, or when the Fund declared a currency to be no longer scarce under Article VII.[2]

4. *Non-tariff Distortions to Trade*

While the Fund and the G.A.T.T. have successfully subjected to international scrutiny and regulation two of the principal direct controls—namely exchange and quantitative import controls—utilized by countries to obstruct the free flow of international trade, a new and more serious threat to the flow of international commerce has emerged, the so-called 'Non-Tariff Distortions to Trade'.[3] The increased reliance made by governments on such devices to deal with payments difficulties was made abundantly clear during the November 1968 monetary crisis. Three of the countries most affected by the crisis—Britain, France, and Germany—all resorted to such back-door methods to regulate the flow of imports and exports. Britain introduced the import deposit scheme which in effect is tantamount to a tariff surcharge on certain imports.[4] France altered its tax structure in such a way as to provide an additional barrier to importers and an additional incentive to exporters.[5] Germany amended its turnover tax law so as to add 4 per cent

---

[1] B.I.S.D., Third Supplement (June 1955) p. 177, para. 28.

[2] Art. XIV enumerates other, more minor, permitted deviations from the general principle of non-discrimination, see paras. 2, 3, and 5 (*b*).

[3] See 'Non-Tariff Trade Barriers: New Liberalization or New Protectionism?', 63 *Proceedings of the American Society of International Law* (1969) pp. 203–21.

[4] *I.M.F. Twentieth Annual Report on Exchange Restrictions* (1969) p. 494.

[5] Ibid. pp. 156 ff.

to the cost of exports and to reduce the cost of imports by 4 per cent.[1]

The danger of these measures to the future development of international trade is apparent:

Clearly, international rules are being stretched to and beyond breaking point. Whatever answer the lawyer may in the end come up with, there can be no doubt that the measures taken in Germany, Britain and France offend against the spirit of various international Agreements, whether it be the GATT, the Treaty of Rome or the EFTA Convention. The precedent having been set, what is to stop others from following it?[2]

However, the important lesson to be learned by international organizations is that States, in times of financial crisis, have opted not for the imposition of quantitative restrictions (which is the only method permitted in the G.A.T.T. to deal with such difficulties) but for other, more surreptitious devices.[3]

Accordingly the international rules should be modified to reflect the established norm. If this were done, the G.A.T.T., for example, rather than dealing with such measures by granting waivers under Article XXV, paragraph 5, would bring these irregular devices within its purview and would be able to regulate, in a positive way, their introduction, administration, and ultimate removal. In short, it would be in a position to handle such matters in foresight rather than, as at present, in hindsight. In response to this challenge the G.A.T.T., through its Committee on Trade in Industrial Products, is currently exploring 'the possibilities for concrete action toward the reduction or elimination of these obstacles or, for example, the elaboration of codes of conduct where appropriate'.[4] Similarly the Working Party of the Committee on Trade and Development has considered amending the provisions of Article XVIII of the G.A.T.T. in order to enable the less developed countries to apply temporary import surcharges, rather than quantitative restrictions, to safeguard their balance of payments.[5] It is intended that these various studies shall result in the conclusion

[1] Ibid. pp. 175 ff.
[2] *Financial Times*, 27 Nov. 1968, p. 14.
[3] B. Tew, op. cit. p. 93.
[4] 5 *The Activities of GATT 1967/68* (Mar. 1969) p. 10.
[5] *EEC Bulletin* (Dec. 1965) p. 45. See also J. T. Lang, 'An Anglo-Irish Free Trade Area', 1 J.W.T.L. (1967) p. 220.

of new international agreements that shall have as their object the regulation of these increasingly important forms of State interference with the free flow of international trade and payments.

VIII

MONETARY GOLD AND INTERNATIONAL LAW

1. *Introduction*

RECENT suggestions that gold should be demonetized[1]—that is, that it should no longer be used as a means of settling international payments—have sparked off a raging controversy as to the future role of gold in the international monetary system. Those who support the continued use of gold see it as a substance 'which is eternally and universally accepted as the unalterable fiduciary value *par excellence*',[2] while those who seek its abolition view it as nothing more nor less than 'an archaic relic of a primitive monetary past'.[3] Whatever the eventual outcome of this continuing dialogue, there is no doubt that gold plays a prominent role in contemporary international monetary affairs. Indeed, it was recently stated by the Managing Director of the Fund, M. Schweitzer, that gold constitutes 'the basic element in the world monetary system'.[4]

Although the majority of the functions performed by gold in the international financial arena are based on long-standing tradition and practice, certain of its functions have been given a legal expression by the Fund's Articles of Agreement and these will be briefly examined here.

[1] See *The Economist*, 28 Sept. 1968, p. 64; *Sunday Times*, 29 Sept. 1968, p. 29; *Financial Times*, 20 June 1969, p. 38.

[2] Portion of the famous remark made by General de Gaulle at a press conference on 4 Feb. 1965. Reprinted in English in *Keesing's Contemporary Archives* (1965–6) p. 20667.

[3] *The Times*, 19 July 1968, p. 23.

[4] *The Times*, 3 Oct. 1968, p. 24. See similarly a United Nations report on the international monetary system, *International Monetary System—Issues Relating to Development Finance and Trade of Developing Countries* (TD/B/198) p. 23. For other studies on the place of gold in the international monetary system, see Stefan Mendelsohn, 'Gold Double or Quits', 8 *The Economist Brief Booklets* (London, 1968); W. J. Busschau, 'The Role of Gold in World Monetary Arrangements', 2 J.W.T.L. (1968) pp. 363–74; H. G. Johnson, 'The Future of Gold and the Dollar', 3 J.W.T.L. (1969) pp. 117–29; F. Hirsch, op. cit. pp. 194–215.

2. *The Fund and Monetary Gold*

(i) *Gold and par values.* Principal among the functions attributed to gold by the Fund regime are those in respect of par values. It will be remembered that all Fund members are required to express the par value of their basic monetary unit either directly in terms of gold or indirectly in terms of the United States dollar of a fixed gold content,[1] and that exchange rates are to be based on the agreed par values.[2] To ensure that members do not frustrate the operation of the Fund's exchange rate regime by buying or selling gold at prices other than those based on par, it is provided in Section 2 of Article IV that the Fund shall prescribe a margin above and below par value for transactions in gold by members.[3] Unfortunately, the effectiveness of this provision in preventing the erosion of the Fund's exchange rate regime has been somewhat impaired by the second half of Section 2.[4] Under Section 2 (last part) members are precluded from purchasing gold at a premium or selling gold at a discount, but by implication they are free to sell gold at a premium or buy gold at a discount. Such transactions will not be contrary to Section 2 so long as the other party to the transaction is a non-member or a private party. Moreover, the provision does not affect transactions between private parties, who are therefore free to buy and sell gold at any price.[5]

---

[1] Art. IV, Sect. 1 (*a*). [2] Art. IV, Sects. 3 and 4 (*b*).

[3] For the prescribed margin, see *By-Laws Rules and Regulations* (26th issue, 1966) p. 23, Rule F-4.

[4] The latter part of Art. IV, Sect. 2 provides: '. . . and no member shall buy gold at a price above par value plus the prescribed margin, or sell gold at a price below par value minus the prescribed margin'.

[5] The wide range of exceptions introduced by the second part of Sect. 2 have been and continue to be a source of international monetary instability. An early attempt by the Fund to regulate gold transactions not covered by Sect. 2 ended in failure. See J. Gold, 'The Duty to Collaborate with the International Monetary Fund and the Development of Monetary Law', *Law, Justice and Equity: Essays in Tribute to G. W. Keeton* (1967) pp. 146–50. See also W. M. Scammell, op. cit. pp. 215–19. More recently, the demise of the gold pool (whose very object was to keep all transactions in gold, both official and private, at the same price, i.e. $35 an ounce) and the emergence of the two-tier gold price system (i.e. the price of gold on the private market is determined by what the market will bear, while the official price remains at $38 an ounce), are again threatening to disrupt international monetary stability. In particular, if the differential between the official and private prices becomes too great, it is feared that certain central banks may be tempted to exchange their official dollar holdings for gold at the official rate and then resell the gold at the higher private rate. For a discussion of the history and functioning of the gold pool, see Stefan Mendelsohn, 'Gold Double or Quits', 8 *The Economist*

(ii) *Gold as a means of international payment.* Under Article IV, Section 4 (*b*), a Fund member is deemed to be fulfilling its obligation to maintain within its territories exchange rates between its currency and the currencies of other members within the prescribed limits (Article IV, Section 3 (i)), if in fact it freely buys and sells gold at a price which is within the limits prescribed under Section 2 of Article IV for its currency in the settlement of international transactions. A member availing itself of this provision need take no other measures, such as intervention in the foreign exchange markets, to maintain the exchange rate of its currency. Prior to August 1971, the United States of America was the only Fund member utilizing Section 4 (*b*).[1] (Additionally, however, the Federal Reserve Bank periodically intervened in the foreign exchange market to maintain the value of foreign currencies in terms of the dollar.) The United States was prepared to buy and sell gold in unlimited amounts and on demand at $35 an ounce (plus or minus one quarter of 1 per cent for handling charges) with monetary authorities of other member countries.[2]

To stop the drain on United States gold resources and to prevent any abuse of the two-tier gold system—that is, the exchange by foreign monetary authorities of dollars for gold at the official rate and the resale of the gold so obtained at the higher rate on the private market—it had been suggested that the United States should no longer satisfy its legal obligation to maintain all exchange transactions in its territories within the prescribed margins by the free purchase and sale of gold, but by intervention in the exchange market,[3] the method

---

Brief Booklets (1968) pp. 12–14. For a review of the events leading up to and following the establishment of the two-tier gold system, see *Keesing's Contemporary Archives* (1967–8) pp. 22597–601.

[1] The practice of the United States of selling gold bullion to, and purchasing gold bullion from, the monetary authorities of governments at the price of $35 (minus or plus a charge of one quarter of 1 per cent for handling) dated back to 1936. See H. Aufricht, 'The Fund Agreement: Living Law and Emerging Practice', 23 *Princeton Studies in International Finance* (1969) pp. 48–50. The United States discontinued this practice in August 1971.

[2] The gold stock held by the United States has been run down from $23 billion in 1950 to around $10·5 billion in mid 1968, while during the same period the total amount of dollars in foreign hands has increased from $9 billion to $33 billion, which is more than three times as much as the United States could redeem, if required, from its present gold stock.

[3] See John Parke Young, 'United States Gold Policy: the Case for Change',

adopted by all other Fund members. Such a change, from the legal viewpoint,[1] would be in conformity with the United States' obligations under the Fund Agreement, since under the Articles no member is legally obliged to buy or sell gold in transactions with other Fund members. Members may, at their own option as in the case of the United States, buy and sell gold in exchange for currencies among themselves at prices within the margins prescribed by the Fund, but the willingness to do so is not obligatory and rests either on the option set forth in Article IV, Section 4 (*b*) or, as is more commonly the case, on the longstanding custom that gold constitutes an acceptable means of international payment.[2] As mentioned, on 14 August 1971 the United States ceased to buy and sell gold for the purposes of Article IV, Section 4 (b). To this extent, therefore—that is, as between Fund members—gold has not been given the legal status of constituting an international means of payment.

The position of certain gold transactions between Fund members and the Fund itself is, however, quite different, since the Fund is legally obliged to buy gold from the members at par on demand of members, and conversely, members are legally obliged to buy gold from the Fund at par on the demand of the Fund. The latter obligation—that is, the sale of Fund gold in exchange for member currencies—stems from Article VII Section 2 which states in part:

> The Fund may, if it deems such action appropriate to replenish its holdings of any member's currency, take either or both of the following steps:
>
> (i) . . .
> (ii) Require the member to sell its currency to the Fund for gold.

The legal obligation incumbent upon members as a result

56 *Princeton Essays in International Finance* (1966); E. A. Birnbaum, 'Changing the United States Commitment to Gold', 63 *Princeton Essays in International Finance* (1967); E. A. Birnbaum, 'Gold and the International Monetary System: an Orderly Reform', 66 *Princeton Essays in International Finance* (1968).

[1] For an excellent analysis of some of the legal problems which such a change would give rise to, see 'Legal Problems of International Monetary Reform', 20 *S anford Law Review* (1968) pp. 983–91.

[2] See E. A. Birnbaum, 'Gold and the International Monetary System: an Orderly Reform', 66 *Princeton Essays in International Finance* (1968) p. 5. See also Shannon, *International Liquidity* (1966) p. 1: 'Gold is international money. Because it is acceptable over national boundaries a country may keep gold as a reserve to meet net international debts.'

of the Article is clear, and the Fund has resorted to this provision to raise currencies needed by it to finance drawings
by members.[1] The former obligation—that is, the purchase
of members' gold by the Fund in exchange for currencies
—stems from Article V, Sections 2, 6, and 7. While Sections 2
and 7 (a) and (b) have created no difficulties, the interpretation
of Section 6 has, in the wake of the establishment of the two-
tier gold system, given rise to much legal argument. Section 6
entitled 'Purchases of currencies from the Fund for gold' reads
as follows:

(a) Any member desiring to obtain, directly or indirectly, the
    currency of another member for gold shall, provided that it
    can do so with equal advantage, acquire it by the sale of gold
    to the Fund.

(b) Nothing in this Section shall be deemed to preclude any member
    from selling in any market gold newly produced from mines
    located within its territories.

It is argued on the one hand, primarily by South Africa (which
is the Western world's largest producer of gold,[2] and therefore
stands to gain the most by any increase in the price of gold)
and its supporters,[3] that this provision gives Fund members
the unconditional right to sell gold to the Fund for other
members' currencies. On the other hand it is argued, primarily
by the United States (which wishes to force South Africa
to sell the bulk of its gold production on the private
market, thereby depressing the buoyancy of that market and
bringing the price of free gold near or equal to that of the
official price), that some meaning must be attached to the

---

[1] R. Kroc, 'The Financial Structure of the Fund', 5 *I.M.F. Pamphlet Series* (1967)
p. 5. More particularly, in June 1968 the United Kingdom made a drawing of
$1,400,000,000 from the Fund. For the United Kingdom drawing, the Fund
used three sources: its own currency holdings ($559 million), currencies borrowed
from five members under the provisions of the General Arrangements to Borrow
(G.A.B.) ($476 million), and the equivalent of $365 million in currencies purchased from members against the sale of gold: see 5 F.D. (Sept. 1968) p. 52, and
The Times, 20 June 1968, p. 24. Total gold sales by the Fund since the beginning of
operations in 1947 to July 1968 have amounted to $2,438 million: see 5 F.D.,
loc. cit.

[2] South Africa currently produces about 70 per cent of the total world output
of gold, S. Mendelsohn, op. cit. p. 10.

[3] Of whom France has been one of the most avid, ibid. pp. 7–10; *The Times*,
1 Jan. 1970, p. 21; J. Rueff, 'Yet Another Expedient: Special Drawing Rights',
119 *The Banker* (1969) pp. 854–63.

phrase 'provided that it can do so with equal advantage', and that *a priori* the right of sale to the Fund is something less than an unconditional one.[1] In solution to this dispute, a compromise was reached between South Africa and the Fund[2] which, for all practical purposes, establishes a support level for the free market price of gold.

It is important to note, however, that the compromise is not intended to be permanent, nor is it to serve as an answer to, or in any other way affect the controversy over, the legal inter-pretation of Article V, Section 6. The Fund made this clear in its Communiqué: 'The Fund decision, which is taken without prejudice to the determination of the legal position under the fund's articles of agreement, is to be reviewed whenever re-quested because of a major change in circumstances and in any event after five years.'[3] Indeed, to have done otherwise would have been both practically and legally unwise. Practically, with the introduction of special drawing rights, the position of gold in the international monetary system is bound, over the next few years, to alter radically. Flexibility, therefore, with regard to its future place and use in that system is essential. Legally, the compromise does attach conditions as to when, how much, etc. gold a Fund member may sell to the Fund. And it is generally agreed that Article V, Section 6 gives all Fund members an unconditional right of sale.[4] For the moment, therefore, it is suggested that the legal question 'has been blandly ignored in the interests of realpolitik'.[5]

However, regardless of the eventual outcome of the legal

[1] For a résumé of the arguments put forward by the two opposing camps, see the three issues of *The Economist*, 6 July 1968, p. 62, 13 July 1968, p. 61, 20 July 1968, pp. 56–7.

[2] For the text of the Fund Communiqué setting out the compromise, see *The Times*, 1 Jan. 1970, p. 21.

[3] Ibid., para. 7 of the Communiqué.

[4] *The Economist*, 3 Jan. 1970, p. 50; *Financial Times*, 7 Aug. and 10 Dec. 1969. A similar conclusion was reached in a United Nations report on the international monetary system, *International Monetary System—Issues Relating to Development Finance and Trade of Developing Countries* (TD/B/198) p. 20. M. Schweitzer, Managing Director of the I.M.F., speaking in a strictly personal capacity on 27 Sept. 1968 at a press conference before the opening of the Fund's annual meeting, said that he believed that the Fund had a legal obligation to buy all gold offered by a member (see *Keesing's Contemporary Archives* (1969–70) p. 23387). Other member countries expressed a similar opinion (see ibid.).

[5] *The Economist*, 3 Jan. 1970, p. 50.

controversy over Article V, Section 6, it is nevertheless clear that the Fund, either conditionally or unconditionally, is under a legal obligation to buy gold in exchange for currencies from its members, and conversely its members are legally obliged to buy gold in exchange for currencies from the Fund. To this extent, therefore—that is, between Fund members and the Fund—the use of gold as a means of international payment no longer rests solely on tradition, as it did under the gold standard, but on specific legal obligations incumbent on all Fund members.

(iii) *Maintenance of gold value of Fund assets.*[1] In order 'that the Fund may have neither losses nor profits out of its holding foreign currencies',[2] it is provided in Article IV, Section 8 that the gold value of all Fund assets shall be maintained, notwithstanding changes in the par or foreign exchange value of the currency of any member. Consequently, whenever a member's currency has been devalued—that is, its par value in terms of gold has been reduced in accordance with Article IV, Section 5 or depreciated (the par value in terms of gold reduced without the adoption of a new par value under Article IV, Section 5)—the member is required to pay the Fund an amount of its own currency equal to the reduction in the gold value of its currency presently held by the Fund. Conversely, if a member's currency is revalued or appreciated, the Fund is required to pay the member an amount of its currency equal to the increase in the gold value of its currency held by the Fund. Similarly, all Fund transactions under Article V[3] and Fund borrowings under the General Arrangements for Borrowing[4] are subject to a gold (maintenance of value) clause.[5]

---

[1] For an informative review of this aspect of the Fund's activities, see J. Gold, 'Maintenance of the Gold Value of the Fund's Assets', *I.M.F. Pamphlet Series* (1965).

[2] *Proceedings and Documents of United Nations Monetary and Financial Conference,* vol. I (1948) p. 313.

[3] J. Gold, 'Maintenance of the Gold Value', pp. 3 ff.

[4] Ibid. pp. 27–9.

[5] Most other internatonal financial institutions, such as the International Bank for Reconstruction and Development, Inter-American Development Bank, and the Asian Development Bank have similar maintenance-of-value provisions.

IX

INTERNATIONAL LIQUIDITY AND INTERNATIONAL LAW

1. *Introduction*

THE entry into force on 28 July 1969[1] of the amendments to the Fund's Articles of Agreement marked the opening of an important new phase in the development of international monetary law. The amendments not only modified certain of the already existing Fund provisions, but more significantly brought into being a new facility, namely special drawing rights, which provides for the deliberate creation or diminution of international liquidity. This recent development has aptly been described as 'the most significant new departure in international monetary affairs since the signing of the original Articles of Agreement of the I.M.F. at Bretton Woods in 1944'.[2] It gives positive legal expression to a sentiment expressed as long ago as 1943 by Lord Keynes:

> We need a *quantum* of international currency, which is neither determined in an unpredictable and irrelevant manner as, for example, by the technical progress of the gold industry, nor subject to large variations depending on the gold reserve policies of individual countries; but is governed by the actual current requirements of world commerce, and is also capable of deliberate expansion and contraction . . .[3]

---

[1] This is the only *de jure* amendment of the Articles to date.

[2] *Special Drawing Rights in the International Monetary Fund*, Cmnd. 3662 (June 1968) p. iii, para. 3. But not all international economists are in agreement with this observation; see J. Rueff, 'Yet Another Expedient: Special Drawing Rights', 119 *The Banker* (1969) p. 859.

[3] *Proceedings and Documents of United Nations Monetary and Financial Conference*, vol. 2 (1948) p. 1551. See also J. E. Meade, 'The International Monetary Mechanism', *Readings in Macroeconomics* (ed. M. G. Mueller, 1969) p. 393: 'But finally I personally dislike anything which perpetuates the silly, irrational, primitive, magical idea that sound money consists in digging gold in one place and burying it in another. Let us go forward to a more rational control over our monetary arrangements, which is a matter for book-keepers and not for mining engineers.'

and as recently as 1962 by Lieftinck:

... it is difficult to believe that the solution of the problem of maintaining adequate world liquidity for the future can be left to one or two countries running sufficiently large balance-of-payments deficits. It seems obvious that this problem will have to be solved by some international monetary institution.[1]

However, as appears to have been the case in all major advances in international economic co-operation, it was not until the situation became acute that the suggestions of Keynes, Lieftinck, and others were acted upon. In the case of liquidity, the impetus to reach agreement stemmed from the phenomenon that in recent years the rate of increase of world liquidity has not kept pace with the rate of increase of international trade.[2] Although the ratio at which the volume of international liquidity should increase (or decrease) in relation to the increase (or decrease) in the volume of international trade cannot be determined with arithmetical precision, it is generally accepted that some such correlation does exist.[3] Consequently, while in the short term the existing supply of liquidity—that is, gold, foreign exchange, and reserve position in the Fund—[4] could feasibly expand at a rate sufficient to finance the growth of international trade, it was realized that in the long term reliance on the expansion of the conventional sources of liquidity would not suffice.[5] The special drawing rights facility

[1] P. Lieftinck, 'Recent Trends in International Monetary Policies', 39 *Princeton Essays in International Finance* (1962) p. 18.

[2] In the period 1951 to 1965, world reserves in countries other than the Soviet bloc and the Chinese People's Republic rose from $49·3 billion to $70·2 billion (comprising gold, foreign exchange, and members' reserve positions in the Fund). This represents an annual average rate of increase of only 2·6 per cent, while world trade has grown at an average of about 6 per cent per annum; as a result, reserves as a proportion of annual world imports have fallen from 67 to 43 per cent, *I.M.F. Annual Report* (1966) p. 12.

[3] For an enumeration, description, and explanation of the economic criteria on which it is suggested the volume of reserves (i.e. their adequacy or inadequacy) can be determined, see Gottfried Haberler, 'Money in the International Economy' 31 *Hobart Papers* (Institute of Economic Affairs, 1969) pp. 56 ff. See also F. Hirsch, op. cit. pp. 373 ff.

[4] Art. XXXII, Sect. (c) (amended): 'A participant's reserve position in the Fund means the sum of the gold tranche purchases it could make and the amount of any indebtedness of the Fund which is readily repayable to the participant under a loan agreement.'

[5] See J. J. Polak, 'The Outline of a New Facility in the Fund', 4 F.D. (1967) p. 276.

was established specifically for the purpose of bridging this potential liquidity gap. Through this facility the volume of international liquidity can be objectively determined on the basis of 'deliberate international decisions'.[1] It can be increased or decreased according to prevailing economic requirements and will no longer depend

on the deficits of the reserve currency countries, nor on the somewhat erratic fluctuations in the supply of gold: the creation of additional liquidity will hinge on a concerted assessment of the need for finance generated by the healthy expansion of international transactions. True, it will never be possible to determine with absolute accuracy the amount of liquidity needed; but there is no reason to believe that this method will be less efficient than the relatively hit-or-miss methods of creating liquidity that have been used so far.[2]

Although the significance of the new facility to the development of international monetary law is apparent (the greater part of this chapter will accordingly be devoted to an analysis of its many legal implications), it should also be remembered that the Fund, with its pool of gold and currencies, has constituted a valuable source of liquidity since its inception.[3] An impressive body of international law and practice has developed over the past twenty-five years in respect of the use, by Fund members, of these resources. And in spite of the fact that the Fund has been charged with the additional responsibility of acting as the overseer of the new special drawing rights facility, this aspect of the Fund's activities will not thereby be adversely affected. Indeed, the Fund amendments make it abundantly clear that not only are the existing Fund liquidity activities to be retained, but in certain aspects they are to be strengthened: for example, gold tranche purchases which before the amendment enjoyed *de facto* automaticity now enjoy *de jure* automaticity. Furthermore, it will be seen that several of the provisions of the new facility are based either on the

---

[1] *I.M.F. Annual Report* (1968) p. 16.

[2] *Bulletin of the European Communities* (Feb. 1968) p. 21.

[3] 'I have said on other occasions that liquidity is the business of the Fund—indeed, it was created to provide a pooling of gold and currencies which could be used to supplement the other reserves of its members.' Extract from a speech one by Pierre-Paul Schweitzer, Managing Director of the Fund, delivered before the Commercial Club of Chicago, 24 Mar. 1966: reprinted in 3 F.D. (1966) pp. 99–106 at p. 100.

Fund's existing policies governing the use of its resources (for example, the criterion for determining which participants are to be designated to provide currency convertible in fact under the new facility is similar to the criterion established in 1962 and used by the Fund for determining which currencies are to be drawn by a member in a transaction with the Fund), or on other similar Fund experiences. (For example, under the new facility the currency to be provided by a designated participant must be convertible in fact. This reflects the Fund's experience that while a member's currency may enjoy *de jure* convertibility for the purpose of the Fund Agreement—in other words it is the currency of a member who has accepted the obligations of Article VIII, Sections 2, 3, and 4—the currency may in fact be subject to restrictions introduced in agreement with the Fund under the authority of Article VIII, Section 2 (*a*). On the other hand, a member may not have accepted the obligations of Article VIII, Sections 2, 3, and 4, but its currency may not in fact be subject to restrictions. Such a currency, for the purposes of the Fund Agreement, though not *de jure* convertible is *de facto* convertible.)[1] Accordingly, owing to the continued and strengthened importance of the Fund's original liquidity functions as well as to the impact which the original liquidity provisions have had on shaping the form of certain provisions of the new facility, a brief review of this aspect of the Fund's activities will be instructive.

2. *Fund Resources as a Source of Liquidity*

(i) *The need for Fund resources.* As has been shown in the preceding two chapters, all Fund members are subject to a monetary code of conduct which—*inter alia*—obliges them to establish and maintain fixed and unitary rates of exchange and to refrain from the imposition of exchange restrictions. Fund members may not alter this established par value except when

---

[1] J. Gold, 'The Next Stage in the Development of International Monetary Law: the Deliberate Control of Liquidity', 62 A.J.I.L. (1968) p. 384. It must be remembered that the concept of currency convertibility as it is defined in the Fund Agreement applies only for the purposes of that Agreement. It is not an all-embracing definition of that concept and does not encompass the totality of possible forms which convertibility may, and does in fact, assume in the practical commercial world. In this respect see the observations made by Fawcett, 'Trade and Finance in International Law', 123 R.C. (1968–I) p. 285.

such alterations are necessary to correct a fundamental payments disequilibrium, nor may they deviate, except for the few
minor exceptions already discussed, from their obligation to
maintain fixed and unitary exchange rates. Similarly they
may not impose restrictions on payments except when such
measures are deemed by the Fund to be 'necessary' in the light
of adverse payments developments. The right of Fund members
to deal with a deteriorating payments situation either by
introducing direct controls or by devaluation is, therefore,
severely restricted by the Fund's monetary code of conduct.
Devaluation is a remedy which can be utilized only if the disequilibrium is of a fundamental nature, while restrictions on
payments, as the term 'necessary' implies, can be utilized only
when other corrective measures less disruptive to international
trade are not available. But a monetary code which prohibits
(at least for short-term or for temporary payments difficulties)
the use of two of the principal economic adjustment devices—
exchange rate alteration and direct controls—must ensure that
sufficient financial resources are available to finance any short-
term deficits while other corrective devices, more compatible
with the growth of international trade, are pursued.[1] As suggested in Article I, paragraph (v), the Fund's pool of gold and
currencies was established to provide this assurance: 'To give
confidence to members by making the Fund's resources temporarily available to them under adequate safeguards, thus
providing them with opportunity to correct maladjustments
in their balance of payments without resorting to measures
destructive of national or international prosperity'.[2] This
provision makes it clear that the Fund's pool of resources
constitutes a supplementary source of liquidity which is to be
made available to members for the purpose of financing payments deficits, thereby enabling them to pursue adjustment
policies which are compatible with, and not destructive of, the
growth of international trade. The Fund's pool of resources,
therefore, fulfils a twofold function: (a) it provides members
with additional resources with which to finance foreign account

[1] J. E. Meade, 'The International Monetary Mechanism', *Readings in Macroeconomics* (ed. M. G. Mueller 1969) p. 387.
[2] This is the amended version of Art. 1, para. (v) and differs from the original
provision only by the introduction of the word 'temporarily'.

deficits; and (*b*) it extends the period of time available to members in which they can constructively deal with payments difficulties, thereby avoiding recourse to other, more immediate measures such as direct commercial or financial controls.

(ii) *Sources of Fund resources*. The principal source of the Fund's pool of gold and currencies is members' subscriptions. The subscription of each member is equivalent to its quota, which is a fixed sum of money expressed in United States dollars and which reflects the relative economic strength of each member *vis-à-vis* other members:[1] for example, on 28 February 1971 the quota of the United States of America was $6,700 million,[2] while that of India was $940 million.[2] In paying their subscription to the Fund, original members were required to pay in gold, either 25 per cent of their quota or 10 per cent of their net official holdings of gold and United States dollars whichever was the less,[3] while the amount payable in gold by other than original members varies according to that prescribed in the relevant paragraph of the membership resolution.[4] In both instances the balance of the quota is payable in the member's own currency. However, in lieu of the member's own currency, the Fund may agree to hold non-negotiable, non-interest-bearing securities payable at their par on demand.[5]

Quotas are not immutable but may, with the concurrence of the member or members concerned, be either increased or decreased.[6] Appropriate adjustments are made in members' subscriptions following any quota alterations. The aggregate of Fund quotas on 28 February 1971 was $28,493 million, of which $28,288·7 million consisted of paid-up subscriptions in gold and currency and $204·3 million consisted of subscriptions

---

[1] The size of each member's quota is determined by the Fund on the basis of a not altogether satisfactory formula which takes into account various economic factors, e.g. national income, imports, exports, etc. For a discussion of this formula see R. Kroc, 'The Financial Structure of the Fund, Part 1: Quotas and Charges', 2 F.D. (1965) pp. 40–3. See also R. Kroc, 'The Financial Structure of the Fund', 5 *I.M.F. Pamphlet Series* (1967) pp. 1–3, and Oscar L. Altman, 'Quotas in the International Monetary Fund', 5 *I.M.F. Staff Papers* (1956–7) pp. 129–50.

[2] 24 *International Financial Statistics* (Apr. 1971) p. 8.

[3] Art. III, Sect. 3 (*b*).

[4] See H. Aufricht, 'The Fund Agreement: Living Law and Emerging Practice', 23 *Princeton Studies in International Finance* (1969) p. 29.

[5] Art. III, Sect. 5.

[6] Art. III, Sects. 2 and 4.

receivable.[1] Finally, it should be noted at this point that quotas play an important role in the new special drawing rights facility, since they are the basis upon which special drawing rights will be allocated to the participants in the scheme.

A secondary method by which the Fund is able to augment its pool of resources is by borrowing the currencies of the Fund members. Under Article VII, Section 2 (i), the Fund is empowered to replenish its holdings of a member's currency either by (a) borrowing the currency directly from the member, or (b) with the approval of the member, borrowing that member's currency from some other source either within or without the territories of the member. No member, however, is under any legal obligation either to lend its own currency directly to the Fund or to approve the borrowing of its currency by the Fund from some other source. The Fund utilized this provision for the first time in 1962, when it entered into the 'General Arrangements to Borrow'[2] (G.A.B.) with the ten industrial countries which compose the so-called 'Group of Ten'.[3] Under the G.A.B. the Fund is able to borrow up to $6 billion in currencies of the ten countries whenever supplementary resources are needed by it 'to forestall or cope with an impairment of the international monetary system'.[4] The arrangement, however, does have certain limitations which detract from its liquidity value. First, the finances are not available to all Fund members, but only to the other participants in the scheme.[5] Secondly, under the terms of the arrangement, the participants are not legally bound to lend their currencies to the Fund whenever the Fund deems that its resources should be supplemented; rather, any proposal to lend becomes

[1] 24 *International Financial Statistics* (Apr. 1971) p. 9.

[2] These arrangements consist of a decision of the Executive Directors, Decision no. 1289-(62/1) 5 Jan. 1962, *Selected Decisions*, pp. 56–66, and a letter exchanged among the ten participants, ibid. pp. 67–8. For the decision and the letter, see also *Arrangements for Borrowing by the International Monetary Fund*, Mar. 1962, Cmnd. 1656. For a discussion of this arrangement, see H. Aufricht, *The International Monetary Fund. Legal Bases, Structure Functions* (1964) pp. 67–72.

[3] Belgium, Canada, France, Germany, Italy, Japan, the Netherlands, Sweden, the United Kingdom, the United States. Switzerland, although not a Fund member or a member of the Group of Ten, has also entered into an arrangement to make money available. See *I.M.F. Annual Report* (1964) pp. 138–40; *I.M.F. Annual Report* (1968) p. 108; *Selected Decisions*, pp. 69–72.

[4] Preamble of the 1962 Decision.

[5] Ibid. para. 6.

'effective only if it is accepted by participants'.[1] In this respect, therefore, as pointed out by Fawcett, the arrangement constitutes 'at most a *pactum de contrahendo*'.[2] Nevertheless, since the arrangement came into effect on 24 October 1962, it has been frequently activated and has enabled the Fund to fulfil more adequately its liquidity function.[3]

Finally, it should be mentioned—although only in passing at this point—that under the new special drawing rights facility, the Fund can augment its supply of any participant's currency by requiring a participant to provide its currency in exchange for special drawing rights held in the General Account.

(iii) *Fund control over the use of its resources.* The access to the Fund's pool of resources is by necessity not automatic[4] but is subject to a number of conditions, some of which had been specifically provided for in the original Articles of Agreement (for example, quantitative limitations on the amount drawn), and some of which are the result of subsequent Fund practice (for example, drawings are available on a temporary basis only). To ensure the proper observance of these various conditions and thereby prevent any abuse in the use of its resources, the Fund in an early decision (10 March 1948)[5] decided that all drawings were subject to prior Fund scrutiny and required prior Fund approval. It based its adopted position on an interpretation of Article V, Section 3 (*a*) (i). Under this provision, a member is required to represent that any proposed drawing 'is presently needed for making in that currency payments which are consistent with the provisions of this Agreement'. The Fund, in its interpretation of this Article, decided that it had the power to challenge the correctness of any such representation. Furthermore, if it found that the representation was incorrect—that is (1) that the currency to be drawn was not 'presently needed', or (2) that the currency to be drawn was not needed to make payments 'in that currency', or (3) that the payments were not 'consistent with the provisions of this

[1] Ibid. para. 7 (*a*).
[2] Fawcett, 'The International Monetary Fund and International Law' B.Y.I.L. (1964) p. 75.
[3] *I.M.F. Annual Report* (1968) pp. 107–8.
[4] Scammell, op. cit. p. 157.
[5] Executive Board Decision no. 284–4, *I.M.F. Annual Report* (1948) pp. 97–8; *Selected Decisions*, p. 19.

Agreement'—it could shelve or reject the request or accept it subject to condition. These three points merit further clarification. First, care must be taken not to misconstrue the meaning of the phrase 'presently needed'. The Fund, in considering a member's request for a drawing, is not concerned with the immediacy of the drawing beyond ensuring that the economic policies to be pursued by the drawing member will be such as to correct the disequilibrium within a three- to five-year period, and that the drawing will be instrumental in achieving this objective. Second, since the adoption of the Executive Board decision of 20 July 1962 on 'Currencies to be Drawn and to be Used in Repurchase',[1] the phrase 'making in that currency payments' is no longer literally applied. In practice, especially with regard to large drawings, the drawings will be made in several currencies which will subsequently be converted by the drawing country—with or without the co-operation of the country whose currency is drawn[2]—either into the currency in which payments are to be made, into gold (a practice adopted by South Africa for all rand drawings), or into the currency in which the drawing country holds its reserves. Thirdly, the phrase 'consistent with the provisions of this Agreement' refers, for example, to the provisions of Article VI, Section 1, which prohibits the use of Fund resources to meet a large or sustained outflow of capital (however, under Article VI, Section 2 (amended), a member is entitled to make gold tranche purchases to meet capital transfers), or to those of Article XIV, Section 1, which states that the Fund 'is not intended to provide facilities for relief or reconstruction or to deal with international indebtedness arising out of the war'.

Finally, it should be noted that Article V, Section 3 (*a*) (i), and the adopted interpretation thereof, sets out only the conditions precedent to a drawing. To provide some measure of protection against the abusive use of resources, once drawn, the following provisions apply. Should the Fund subsequently be of the opinion that a member is, in fact, using Fund resources in a manner contrary to the purposes of the Fund, it may, by virtue of Article V, Section 5, set out its opinion of improper use in a report addressed to the delinquent member and,

[1] *Selected Decisions*, pp. 33–9.   [2] Ibid. pp. 38–9.

immediately upon delivery of the report, limit the use of its resources by the member. If the member does not suitably reply to the report within a prescribed period of time, the Fund may continue to limit the member's use of its resources, or may, after giving reasonable notice to the member, declare the member ineligible to use the resources of the Fund.

Although the adopted interpretation of Article V, Section 3 (*a*) (i) produced, from the Fund's viewpoint, the desired effect —that is, it ensured that the Fund would retain ultimate control over the use of its resources—its legal validity was doubtful.[1] Nevertheless, it had over the years become the established practice, and to remove any lingering doubts as to its legality the recent amendments to the Articles of Agreement bestowed *de jure* validity on what had become the *de facto* position. Accordingly Article V, Section 3 (*d*) of the amended Articles states: 'A representation by a member under (a) above shall be examined by the Fund to determine whether the proposed purchase would be consistent with the provisions of this Agreement and with the policies adopted under them, with the exception that proposed gold tranche purchases shall not be subject to challenge.' This provision makes it explicit that a member's representation under Article V, Section 3 (*a*) must be examined by the Fund to determine whether the requested drawing is consistent with the relevant Fund Articles and with the policies adopted by the Fund from time to time on the use of its resources. Under the amended Articles, therefore, it is clear that the Fund has not only a legal right but a legal obligation to ensure that a member's use of its resources is in conformity with the relevant Fund provisions. To this extent, therefore, all Fund drawings, with the sole exception of gold tranche purchases, are conditional.[2] Principal among these provisions

---

[1] See 'Legal Problems of International Monetary Reform', 20 *Stanford Law Review* (1968–II) p. 883 n. 48: 'It is difficult to find explicit support in the IMF Agreement for the Fund's practice of requiring this approval, except perhaps in the general grant of powers in article XII to the IMF governing bodies. Nevertheless, the practice is certainly well established.' For a more general criticism of the Fund's policies on the use of its resources, see E. A. Birnbaum, 'Gold and the International Monetary System: an Orderly Reform', 66 *Princeton Essays in International Finance* (1968) pp. 14–22. See also R. N. Gardner, *Sterling–Dollar Diplomacy* (1956) pp. 296–7.

[2] E. A. Birnbaum, 'Gold and the International Monetary System: an Orderly Reform', pp. 17–22.

are the following: temporary use of resources; tranche policies; currencies to be drawn; repurchase obligations; and use of resources for capital transactions. These will be briefly examined in turn.

(iv) *Temporary use of resources.* In the original Fund provisions there was no express suggestion that the Fund's pool of resources was to be made available to members on a short-term basis only.[1] Indeed the principal criterion for determining how long a drawing could remain outstanding was to have been the subsequent performance of the drawing member's reserve position.[2] No direct reference was made to the length of time that a drawing could remain outstanding. The first suggestion that time, in addition to the subsequent reserve performance of the member, was to be a determining factor was given on 26 September 1946 when the Executive Directors, in response to a question put by the Governor for the United States,[3] replied that 'authority to use the resources of the Fund is limited to use in accordance with its purposes to give temporary assistance in financing balance of payments deficits . . .[3] In a subsequent statement of policy on the use of Fund resources issued in February 1952,[4] the Fund, after reiterating its policy that 'the task of the Fund is to help members that need temporary help',[5] went on to state:

In view of the Executive Board's interpretation of September 26, 1946, concerning the use of the Fund's resources, and considering especially the necessity for ensuring the revolving character of the Fund's resources, exchange purchased from the Fund should not remain outstanding beyond the period reasonably related to the payments problem for which it was purchased from the Fund. The period should fall within an outside range of three to five years. Members will be expected not to request the purchase of exchange from the Fund in circumstances where the reduction of the Fund's

---

[1] 'The Fund Agreement does not specify the period within which a member that has purchased from the Fund the currency of another member has to reverse the transaction by "repurchase" of its currency from the Fund.' H. Aufricht, 'The Fund Agreement: Living Law and Emerging Practice', 23 *Princeton Studies in International Finance* (1969) p. 27.

[2] Art. V, Sect. 7 (*b*) and Schedule B of the original Fund Agreement text.

[3] For the content of the question see *First Annual Meeting of the Board of Governors, Report of the Executive Directors and Summary Proceedings* (1946) p. 106.

[4] *Selected Decisions*, pp. 21–4.

[5] Ibid. p. 21.

holdings of their currencies by an equivalent amount within that time cannot reasonably be envisaged.[1]

The Fund reiterated this policy frequently over the years,[2] and, as in the case of its interpretation of Article V, Section 3 (*a*), the adopted Fund practice resulted in what must be considered as a *de facto* amendment of the Fund's original provisions. Accordingly, in the recent amendment, by a modification of Article 1, paragraph (v), under which the Fund's resources are now only 'temporarily available' to members, and by the inclusion of a new Section 3 (*c*) to Article V, under which the Fund is required to 'adopt policies on the use of its resources that will assist members to solve their balance of payments problems in a manner consistent with the purposes of the Fund and that will establish adequate safeguards for the temporary use of its resources', the *de facto* amendment was given a *de jure* status.

It is important to note, however, that in law as well as in practice the three- to five-year period can be effectively extended by a process that in Fund parlance is referred to as 'rolling over the debt'. By this procedure, when repayment becomes due at the end of a five-year period on an outstanding credit, a new credit arrangement can be negotiated between the Fund and the member. To meet repayments on the original drawing, the member then draws on the newly negotiated line of credit which will itself become payable in a three- to five-year period. This method was resorted to by the United Kingdom in 1969 to meet repayments arising out of U.K. Fund drawing in 1965.[3] More particularly it was specifically stated in paragraph 3 of the letter of intent accompanying the 1969 stand-by credit negotiated between the U.K. and the Fund that:

The purpose of this stand-by is to support the Government's economic objectives and policies. It will facilitate the repayments of external debt now falling due, including the scheduled repurchase of sterling from the Fund in respect of the 1965 drawing by the

---

[1] *Selected Decisions*, p. 22. See also *I.M.F. Annual Report* (1952) pp. 38–43 for a résumé of the circumstances surrounding the adoption of this decision and its rationale.

[2] For such pronouncements see, *inter alia*, the following Annual Reports of the I.M.F.: 1955, 1957, 1958, 1962, at pp. 84–6, 118–19, 23–4, 31–3 respectively.

[3] *The Times*, 17 July 1969, p. 25.

U.K., and will assist in maintaining stability in the international monetary system.[1]

Repayment on an original drawing can thus effectively be extended for a further specified period. However, the extension is by no means automatic. Rather, the same conditions as for an original purchase have to be met. Accordingly, a credit can be terminated at the end of any particular five-year period should circumstances so dictate.

(v) *Tranche policies (quantitative and qualitative restrictions on the use of resources)*. A Fund member, after having established an initial par value and paid its subscription in full to the Fund, is entitled to enter into transactions with the Fund—that is, it may purchase from the Fund the currency of another member in exchange for an equivalent amount of its own currency. In making such drawings, however, two basic factors are always applicable: one of a quantitative nature (that is, a member is restricted in the amount of currency it may purchase in relation to certain periods of time), and the other of a qualitative nature (that is, not all drawings are of the same value or quality to members because the difficulty of drawing from the Fund increases as the drawings outstanding increase).

Under the first factor, member's drawings, as a general rule, are limited to 25 per cent of the purchasing member's quota in any twelve-month period.[2] For example, member A, which has been allotted a quota of $100m. and which has paid its subscription 25 per cent in gold and 75 per cent in its own currency, is entitled in any twelve-month period to purchase from the Fund, in exchange for an equivalent amount of its own currency, the equivalent of $25m. (25 per cent of its quota) of another member's currency. However, two important exceptions to the 25 per cent rule exist. First, the Fund under Article V, Section 4 can waive the 25 per cent limit (provided that it does so on terms that safeguard its interests) and allow a member to draw more than the permitted 25 per cent in a twelve-month period. Waivers of this nature have, since 1953,

---

[1] For the entire text of the letter of intent (dated 22 May 1969) see the *Financial Times*, 24 June 1969, p. 10.

[2] Amended Art. V, Sect. 3 (*a*) (iii).

become commonplace.[1] Secondly, drawings may exceed the
25 per cent limit provided that they are within the gold tranche.
A member's gold tranche corresponds to the total amount of
gold paid by it in subscription to the Fund, plus any net use
by the Fund of that member's currency.[2] In our example,
member A paid 25 per cent of its quota in gold; this 25
per cent is equivalent to its gold tranche. Should member
B, however, purchase an amount of A's currency held by the
Fund equivalent to $15 m., the Fund will have made a
15 per cent net use of A's currency, thereby increasing A's
gold tranche by 15 per cent (this 15 per cent is, in Fund parlance, known as the super gold tranche)[3] to a total of 40 per
cent of A's quota. Member A would therefore be entitled to
purchase from the Fund an amount of foreign currency equivalent to 40 per cent of its quota in any twelve-month period.
Apart from the 25 per cent rule, which places, subject to the
two exceptions already discussed, one quantitative limitation
on the amount any member may draw in a twelve-month
period, the Fund imposes a second quantitative limitation on
the total drawings which a member may have outstanding at
any given time. This second ceiling is restricted to 200 per
cent of quota,[4] and although waivers may be granted under
Article V, Section 4, allowing a member to exceed this limit,
the Fund has to date granted waivers of this variety only on a
few occasions.[5]

Under the second factor—that is, qualitative restrictions— .
the Fund's tranche policies are of prime importance. As

---

[1] *I.M.F. Annual Report* (1968) p. 102.

[2] Gold tranche has been given a legal definition in the amended Articles.
See Art. XIX, para. J.

[3] The *I.M.F. Annual Report* (1968) p. 16 defines the term 'super gold tranche'
as the amount by which 75 per cent of a member's quota exceeds the Fund's
holdings of its currency.

[4] Art. V, Sect. 3 (*a*) (iii).

[5] In 1967/8 a waiver of this type was granted to Ceylon, whose drawing equi-
valent to $19·3 million under the compensatory financing decision brought the
Fund's holdings of that member's currency to approximately 205 per cent of its
quota, *I.M.F. Annual Report* (1968) p. 102. It should be understood, however, that
'In order to implement the Fund's policies in connection with compensatory
financing of export shortfalls, the Fund will be prepared to waive the limit on
Fund holdings of 200 per cent of quota, where appropriate . . .', Decision on
Compensatory Financing, *I.M.F. Annual Report* (1967) p. 160; *Selected Decisions*,
p. 42.

mentioned, a member may in any twelve-month period purchase from the Fund an amount of currency equivalent to
25 per cent of quota. Returning to our example, therefore,
member A would in its initial purchase be entitled to bring the
Fund's holdings of its currency from 75 per cent to 100 per
cent of its quota, provided that the Fund had not made a net
use of A's currency, in which case A would be entitled to
purchase in its initial drawing an additional amount of currency equivalent to the net use. In subsequent purchases, the
Fund's holdings of A's currency would be increased from 100
to 125 per cent, then from 125 to 150 per cent, and so on until
the maximum holding of 200 per cent of quota had been
reached. In general, each percentage increase is classified in
Fund terminology as a tranche. More particularly, the first
increase—that is, the one that would raise the Fund's holdings
of the drawing member's currency to 100 per cent of quota—
is called a gold tranche purchase, while all subsequent increases which cause the Fund's holdings to increase by 25 per
cent of quota are called credit tranches. A number of important
policies, some of which have been given positive legal expression
in the recent amendments concerning the accessibility of
drawings within these various tranches, have been evolved by
the Fund.

(a) Gold tranche. Before the recent amendments to the Fund's
Articles of Agreement, it had been the policy of the Fund to
give members the overwhelming benefit of the doubt[1] in relation
to requests for transactions within the gold tranche. In other
words, requests for drawing which did not increase the Fund's
holdings of the currency of the drawing member beyond
an amount equal to the member's quota were granted on a
virtually automatic basis. In fact requests for gold tranche
purchases enjoyed *de facto* automaticity. One of the effects of the
amendments was to make the use of the Fund's resources in the
gold tranche legally automatic. Under the amended provisions
of Article V, Section 3, any member making a request for a
drawing in the gold tranche is still subject to the provisions
of Article V, Section 3 (a) (i)—that is, still required to make

---

[1] *Selected Decisions*, p. 23: 'Each member can count on receiving the overwhelming benefit of any doubt respecting drawings which would raise the Fund's
holdings of its currency to not more than its quota.'

a representation of need in accordance with the terms of that provision. However, by virtue of a new provision, namely Article V, Section 3 (d),[1] the Fund will not have the power to challenge such a representation. Although the legal automaticity of gold tranche purchases makes it possible for a member to abuse the principle of need set forth in Article V, Section 3 (a) (i), the Fund proposes to meet this contingency if and when it arises by an appropriate adjustment of its policies 'with respect to the currencies to be used in purchases in order to bring about a correction of the effects of any misuse by a member . . .[2] In terms of a practical example, therefore, should member A make a gold tranche purchase without satisfying the representation of need test of Article V, Section 3 (a) (i) and thus bring the Fund's holding of its currency up to 100 per cent of quota, the Fund could correct this abusive use of its resources by directing other members to purchase A's currency until the Fund's holding of A's currency is reduced to 75 per cent of A's quota. In any event, it will be remembered that the Fund has general authority under Article V, Section 5 to declare any member ineligible to use the Fund's resources if the member uses the resources in a manner contrary to the purposes of the Fund.

Finally, it should be noted that the understanding that the gold tranche could be drawn against virtually on demand induced a number of members to include such drawing rights in their official reserves along with gold and foreign currencies,[3] thus making their 'reserve positions in the Fund' a valuable part of their monetary reserves. Indeed it has been suggested by one prominent Fund official that these reserve assets were in many respects 'the forerunners of the special drawing rights'[4] provided for under the new Fund liquidity provisions. The comparison, as will be seen, is in many respects a valid one, since the new special drawing rights and members' reserve positions in the Fund represent similar forms of liquidity, in

---

[1] For text of Art. V, Sect. 3 (d), see above, p. 183.

[2] *Proposed Amendment of Articles of Agreement, a Report by the Executive Directors to the Board of Governors* (I.M.F. Apr. 1968) p. 23, para. 32. This document will hereinafter be referred to as *The Report*.

[3] H. Aufricht, *Comparative Survey of Central Bank Law* (1965) pp. 77–82; J. Gold, 'The Next Stage in the Development of International Monetary Law', 62 A.J.I.L. (1968) pp. 371–3.

[4] J. J. Polak, 'The Outline of a New Facility in the Fund', 4 F.D. (1967) p. 276.

that both are unconditional in character—that is, 'the kind of liquidity that countries can use without being subject to any commitments or discussion as to policy'[1]—and both are the product of international agreement.

(b) Credit[2] tranches. Unlike drawings in the gold tranche, drawings in the credit tranches are not automatic either on a *de facto* or on a *de jure* basis. On the contrary, Article V, Section 3 (d), by obliging the Fund to examine whether a proposed purchase by a member is consistent with the provisions of the Agreement and with the policies adopted under them, by implication, prohibits the Fund from extending the unconditional use of its resources beyond the gold tranche. Accordingly, the Fund's established policies with respect to drawings within the various credit tranches will continue to be applied. This means that requests within the first credit tranche—that is, transactions which bring the Fund's holdings of a member's currency above 100 per cent but not above 125 per cent of its quota—will be treated on a liberal basis, provided that the member itself is making reasonable efforts to solve its problems, while requests for drawings beyond the first credit tranche will require substantial justification.[3] Since the Fund is legally prohibited from granting *de facto* automaticity—that is, the overwhelming benefit of any doubt or treatment having the same effect—to requests for drawings in the credit tranches, it is envisaged that all future requirements of unconditional liquidity will be met by the activation of the special drawing rights facility.

[1] Polak, op. cit. p. 277.

[2] *I.M.F. Annual Report* (1958) p. 26: '. . . the Fund's resources are not credit facilities in the legal sense . . .' As the Fund points out, it does not extend credit to its members. Members purchase with their own currency an equivalent amount of the currency of another member held by the Fund. This process is reversed when the purchasing member repurchases its own currency with either gold or the convertible currency of another member acceptable to the Fund.

[3] The Fund has frequently reiterated its credit tranche policies, see *I.M.F. Annual Report* (1963) pp. 16–17 and *I.M.F. Annual Report* (1962) pp. 31–3. This policy was succinctly stated by P.-P. Schweitzer, Managing Director of the Fund, as follows: 'The Fund expects any member requesting assistance against its credit tranches to be taking active steps to restore its external payments to a healthy balance, and the larger the amount required, in relation to the member's quota, the more stringent the criteria which must be satisfied: P.-P. Schweitzer, 'International Liquidity and the Fund', 3 F.D. (1966) p. 102.

The nature of the conditions which are attached to drawings in the credit tranche category are difficult to ascertain, as it has not been the policy of the Fund to make public the conditions under which such facilities are made available. However, several letters of intent, which are concluded in conjunction with stand-by credit arrangements and which set out the undertakings of the drawing member, have been made public and therefore give some insight into the nature of the imposed conditions.For example, in connection with the 1968 $45m. stand-by agreement with Chile, the following details of the Chilean letter of intent to the Fund have been made known:

  (i) It is hoped to achieve equilibrium in the balance of payments in 1968. There will be no intensification of import restrictions.
 (ii) It is intended to unify the present dual exchange market (banks' and brokers') during 1968.
(iii) Outstanding Banco Central loans to the Government are not to exceed 3,230m. escudos by the end of this year.
 (iv) The Government will take measures to increase revenue and achieve greater economies in current expenditure, so as to obtain a budget surplus on current account to be channelled into investment projects.[1]

Similarly, in connection with the 1969 $1,000m. stand-by agreement with the United Kingdom, the following aspects of the British letter of intent to the Fund are germane:

  (i) In the financial year ending in March 1970, the objective is to obtain a surplus of at least £300m. on the current and long-term capital account of the balance of payments.
 (ii) Public expenditure will again be held within the totals announced in January 1968, which allowed for an increase of 1 per cent in real terms over the planned level for 1968-9.
(iii) In 1969-70 the Central Government's accounts (again excluding import deposits) are intended to be in surplus by at least £850m.
 (iv) The Government's objectives and policies imply a domestic credit expansion for the private and public sectors in the year ending 31 March 1970, of not more than £400 millions.
  (v) It is the Government's policy to maintain the present degree of trade liberalization, and to abolish as soon as the balance of payments allows the restrictions which it currently maintains

---

[1] 2 *Bolsa Review* (June 1968) p. 349.

on travel expenditure and small cash gifts, and also the import deposit scheme.[1]

In general, these two letters, and in particular the latter, demonstrate that the conditions attached to drawings in the credit tranches may affect not only external but also internal economic measures. This gradual encroachment by an international organization of internal economic policies is significant in that it illustrates the ever-increasing extent to which States are relinquishing the regulation of 'matters which are essentially within the domestic jurisdiction of any State'[2] to international law. Indeed it has been suggested that this process is bound to continue, and will in time give rise to 'a growing body of practices which may well be recognized some day as rules of customary international economic law'.[3]

(vi) *Currencies to be drawn.* As mentioned, a Fund member, in exchange for an equivalent amount of its own currency, purchases from the Fund's pool of currencies the currency of another member. Before 1958, the currency so purchased was almost exclusively the United States dollar.[4] Since then, however, owing to the return to *de facto* convertibility in 1958 and *de jure* convertibility in 1961 of the currencies of the major trading nations, there has been a movement away from the United States dollar and into these other currencies. As a result, the number of currencies used in drawings has gradually increased from eight at the end of 1960 to sixteen at the end of 1965 and twenty-two at the end of April 1968.[5]

To assist members in their selection of currencies, the Fund adopted on 20 July 1962 a major policy decision[6] according to which a member contemplating a purchase is required to consult the Managing Director on the selection of currency or currencies to be drawn. The Managing Director, in determining which currencies are to be drawn, takes into account the balance of payments and reserve positions of the members

---

[1] For text of this agreement in full, see the *Financial Times*, 24 June 1969, p. 10.
[2] Art. 2, para. 7 of the United Nations Charter.
[3] S. Silard, 'The Impact of the International Monetary Fund on International Trade', 2 J.W.T.L. (1968) pp. 130–1.
[4] *Selected Decisions*, p. 34.
[5] *I.M.F. Annual Report* (1968) p. 20.
[6] *I.M.F. Annual Report* (1962) pp. 36–41; *Selected Decisions*, pp. 33–9.

whose currencies are considered for use,[1] as well as the Fund's holdings of these currencies. In all cases, however, the Managing Director is required to consult with the Executive Director representing the member whose currency is being considered as a prospective drawing candidate.

In practice, requests for drawings of small amounts are normally executed in one currency, while requests for larger amounts are normally distributed over several currencies. For example, the $1,400 million drawing made by the United Kingdom in June 1968[2] was distributed over several currencies including Belgian francs, German marks, Italian lire, and Netherlands guilders, while the drawing made by the United Kingdom in June 1969 was made in Argentine pesos, Australian dollars, Canadian dollars, German marks, Italian lire, Japanese yen, Mexican pesos, Netherlands guilders, and U.S. dollars.[3] Frequently, a member which has drawn one or more currencies will convert either the whole or part of the amount drawn in a particular currency into the currency of a third member.

(vii) *Repurchase obligations.* The Fund's original repurchase provisions have been aptly described by Nussbaum as 'the most involved part of the whole Agreement—in fact, perhaps the most intricate norm ever found in an international treaty'.[4] Unfortunately it would appear that these provisions have been made even more complex by the recent amendments to the Articles of Agreement, and accordingly no attempt will be made in this study at a detailed examination of the provisions. Rather, attention will be focused on their more salient features only.[5]

---

[1] In keeping with this policy of selling the currencies of members with strong balance of payments and reserve positions, the Fund has in recent years drawn heavily upon its stock of European currencies because of the large surpluses in balance of payments which these countries have been achieving. As a result, on 30 Apr. 1968 the Fund's holdings of the currencies of six European members, namely Austria, Belgium, France, Germany, Italy, and the Netherlands, were about 19 per cent of their combined quotas, *I.M.F. Annual Report* (1968) p. 20.

[2] *I.M.F. Annual Report* (1968) p. 19.

[3] *Financial Times*, 24 June 1969, p. 1.

[4] Nussbaum, *Money in the Law* (1950) p. 538.

[5] For a more detailed review of the Fund's repurchase obligations as they existed before the amendments, see H. Aufricht, *The International Monetary Fund* (1964) pp. 61–4. For a review of the effects of the amendments on these provisions, see *The Report*, pp. 25–8.

First, the provisions of Article V, Section 7 (*b*) and (*c*) (amended), in conjunction with Schedule B (amended), establish the formula for determining the amount of its own currency held by the Fund in excess of 75 per cent of its quota which a member is legally obliged to repurchase at the end of each Fund financial year—that is, 30 April. Although the specific terms of these provisions are somewhat complex, the general criteria by which the extent of a member's repurchase obligation in any particular year is determined are two: (i) by the movements (either increases or decreases) in that member's monetary reserves; and (ii) by the movements (either increases or decreases) in the Fund's holdings of that member's currency.[1] A member will remain under an obligation to repurchase until the Fund's holdings of its currency are reduced to 75 per cent of its quota. Repurchases which would reduce the Fund's holdings below that point are not required.[2] Similarly, a member is not required to repurchase if its monetary reserves are below 150 per cent of its quota[3] or to repurchase in any one financial year an amount greater than 25 per cent of its quota.[4] Moreover, since the repurchase provisions do not in all cases ensure the restoration within a short period of the Fund's holdings of a member's currency to 75 per cent of quota, the Fund, to protect the revolving nature of its resources, has adopted a policy which requires members, regardless of the repurchase provisions (Article V, Section 7 and Schedule B), to restore their holdings to that position within a period of from three to five years.

Apart from meeting its repurchase obligation by actually repurchasing its own currency as just described, a member's repurchase obligation can also be satisfied by the sale of that member's currency held by the Fund to another member. For example, suppose that member A has brought the Fund's holdings of its currency to 100 per cent of quota. Member A would therefore be under a legal obligation to reduce that holding to 75 per cent of its quota, and in normal circumstances would do so by repurchasing an amount of its own currency

---

[1] Art. V, Sect. 7 (*b*) (i) (amended).
[2] Art. V, Sect. 7 (*c*) (ii) (amended) and Schedule B, para. 1 (*c*) (amended).
[3] Art. V, Sect. 7 (*c*) (i) (amended) and Schedule B, para. 1 (*c*) (amended).
[4] Art. V, Sect. 7 (*c*) (iv) (amended) and Schedule B, para. 1 (*e*) (amended).

held by the Fund equivalent to 25 per cent of quota. However, if member B drew an amount of A's currency equivalent to 20 per cent of A's quota, then the Fund's holdings of A's currency would be reduced to 80 per cent of quota and A's repurchase obligation would be reduced from 25 to 5 per cent of its quota. In practice, this method of discharging a member's repurchase obligationwas until very recently almost non-existent. However, in recent years, owing to the increase in the number of members with convertible currencies and also to the Fund's policy of diversifying the range of currencies drawn, the number of instances in which repurchase obligations were so satisfied has gradually increased.[1]

Finally, a member in executing the repurchase is obliged to repurchase its currency in exchange for gold[2] or convertible currencies of other members.[3] Although currencies used in repurchase need not be the same as those initially drawn, only those currencies which are formally convertible—that is, the currencies of those members which have accepted the obligations of Article VIII, Sections 2, 3, and 4—are acceptable in settlement of repurchase obligations.[4] Consequently, before 1961 repurchases were executed almost exclusively in United States dollars. However, beginning with the return to *de jure* convertibility of the major European currencies in 1961, the number of Article VIII members has steadily increased,[5] with the result that the range of currencies used in repurchase has also increased.[6]

(viii) *Use of Fund resources for capital transactions.* As a general rule, the Fund's resources may not be utilized by members to finance transactions of a capital nature.[7] However, several exceptions to this general rule exist. First, Section 1 of Article VI states that 'A member may not use the Fund's resources to meet a large or sustained outflow of capital . . .' By implication,

---

[1] See *I.M.F. Annual Report* (1968) p. 20.

[2] Art. V, Sect. 7 (*a*).

[3] Schedule B, paras. 1 and 2 (amended).

[4] In addition the Fund's holdings of such currencies must be below 75 per cent of quota: Art. V, Sect. 7 (*c*) (iii); Schedule B, para. 1 (*d*) (amended); *Selected Decisions*, pp. 34–8.

[5] The number of members with Art. VIII status on 30 Apr. 1969 was thirty-four, *I.M.F. Annual Report* (1969) p. 139.

[6] *I.M.F. Annual Report* (1968) pp. 20, 102–3.

[7] Art. VI.

therefore, it follows that a member may use the Fund's pool of resources to finance capital outflows which are not 'large or sustained'. Although to date the Fund has not decided what constitutes a 'large or sustained' outflow, it has been suggested by one Fund official that factors such as the 'size and duration'[1] of the outflow, the 'size of the country's economy',[1] and the 'size of the Member's quota'[1] in relation to the outflow might need to be considered in any case where a member attempted to justify its use of Fund resources to finance a capital outflow on the grounds that the outflow was not 'large or sustained'. Secondly, a member may use the resources of the Fund to finance 'capital transactions of reasonable amount required for the expansion of exports or in the ordinary course of trade, banking or other business . . .'.[2] Finally, Section 2 of Article VI (amended) provides that 'A member shall be entitled to make gold tranche purchases to meet capital transfers.' The effect of this provision is to extend the legal automaticity of gold tranche purchases not only to drawings intended to finance current transactions, but also to drawings intended to finance capital transactions, even when such payments arise out of capital outflows which could be regarded as 'large or sustained'. In other words, for drawings within the gold tranche, no distinction will be made between current and capital transactions.

(ix) *Stand-by credit arrangements and compensatory financing facility*. Before concluding this discussion on the nature and use of Fund resources, two further innovations in Fund practice, not foreseen in the original scheme of the Agreement, but which have assumed great importance in current Fund conduct, require brief mention—namely stand-by arrangements and compensatory financing of export fluctuations.

(*a*) Stand-by credit arrangements.[3] In essence, a stand-by credit arrangement is an agreement entered into between

---

[1] J. G. Evans, Jr., 'Current and Capital Transactions: How the Fund Defines Them', 5 F.D. (1968–3) p. 33.

[2] Art. VI, Sect. 1 (*b*) (i).

[3] For the relevant Fund decisions on Stand-by Credit Arrangements, see *Selected Decisions*, pp. 21–32. For a discussion of this aspect of Fund practice, see J. Gold, 'The Law and Practice of the International Monetary Fund with Respect to "Stand-by Arrangements"', 12 I.C.L.Q. (1963) pp. 1–30; C. H. Alexandrowicz, op. cit., pp. 182–3; G. Nicoletopoulos, 'Stand-By Arrangements', 1 F.D. (1964) pp. 192–7; S. Mookerjee, 'Policies on the Use of Fund Resources', 13 *I.M.F. Staff Papers* (1966) pp. 421–42.

a Fund member on the one hand and the Fund on the other, whereby the latter, in exchange for assurances from the former (such assurances are normally set out in an unpublished letter of intent),[1] provides the former with an undertaking that it shall be able to draw immediately, without further negotiation, and during a defined period of time (normally twelve months), an agreed amount of currency from the Fund's pool of resources. The arrangement is analogous to a commercial overdraft limit in municipal law. It arose in response to the general feeling that some technique should be devised whereby members who did not require immediate Fund assistance could nevertheless be assured of prompt financial assistance from the Fund should the need arise in the near future. Economic planning, which depended in part on adequacy of reserves, could then be more safely undertaken. This method was first used in June 1952, when the Fund entered into a stand-by credit arrangement with Belgium,[2] and has since that time so grown in popularity that it is now the principal method whereby the Fund's resources are made available to members.[3]

(b) Compensatory financing of export fluctuations.[4] Primary producing countries—that is, countries which depend mainly on the export of one or two staple products for their foreign exchange earnings—can, owing either to a falling off of commodity prices on the world market or to serious crop failures, suddenly be faced with a shortage of foreign exchange. To assist countries experiencing such payments difficulties, and to obviate recourse by them to trade and exchange restrictions, the Fund decided in 1963 to make its resources available to members experiencing such difficulties provided that:

(a) the shortfall is of a short-term character and is largely attributable to circumstances beyond the control of the member; and
(b) the member will cooperate with the Fund in an effort to find,

---

[1] For the United Kingdom letter of intent of 22 May 1969, see the *Financial Times*, 24 June 1969, p. 10.

[2] *I.M.F. Annual Report* (1953) p. 50.

[3] *I.M.F. Annual Report* (1968) pp. 19, 100.

[4] For relevant Fund Decisions, see *Selected Decisions*, pp. 40–3; *I.M.F. Annual Report* (1967) pp. 131–2, 159–61; 5 I.L.M. (1966) pp. 81–91, 1047–89. For a general discussion of these decisions, see S. Silard, 'The Impact of the International Monetary Fund on International Trade', 2 J.W.T.L. (1968) pp. 156–9; S. Mookerjee, loc. cit.; J. K. Horsefield, 'The Fund's Compensatory Financing', 6 F.D. (1969–4) pp. 34–7.

where required, appropriate solutions for its balance of payments difficulties.[1]

Originally, the amount of drawings outstanding under this arrangement could not exceed 25 per cent of the drawing member's quota. Following the 1966 amendment to the original decision, the amount was increased to a maximum of 50 per cent of quota.[2] Additionally, the 1966 amendment provides that any drawings under the compensatory facility will not be taken into account should the member subsequently apply to the Fund for a 'normal' drawing under Article V.[3] In other words, in keeping with U.N.C.T.A.D. proposals,[4] compensatory credits are placed entirely outside the structure of the gold and successive credit tranches, so that the drawing of compensatory credits does not directly or indirectly prejudice a member's ability to make an ordinary drawing.

3. *Special Drawing Rights*[5]

(i) *Role of special drawing rights in world liquidity.* As mentioned, the *raison d'être* of the special drawing rights facility is to provide a mechanism whereby the quantum of international liquidity can be objectively regulated—that is, either increased or decreased in the light of the prevailing economic climate. It is accordingly expressly stated in Section 1 of Article XXI (significantly, the first of the twelve Articles which deal with the new facility) that the Fund, to meet the need, as and when it arises, for a supplement to existing reserve assets, is authorized to allocate special drawing rights to members that are parti-

---

[1] *Selected Decisions*, p. 42.   [2] 5 I.L.M. (1966) p. 1087.
[3] Ibid. p. 1088.   [4] Ibid. p. 1063.
[5] For further economic and legal discussions of this new facility, see F. Machlup, *Remaking the International Monetary System. The Rio Agreement and Beyond* (1968); H. Aufricht, 'The Fund Agreement: Living Law and Emerging Practice', 23 *Princeton Studies in International Finance* (1969) pp. 60–6; M. A. Heilperin, 'International Monetary Order: the Missing Link', 119 *The Banker* (1969) pp. 865–9; J. Rueff, 'Yet Another Expedient: Special Drawing Rights', ibid. pp. 854–63; M. Barrett and M. Greene, 'Special Drawing Rights: a Major Step in the Evolution of the World's Monetary System', *The International Monetary System. Problems and Proposals* (ed. L. Officer and T. Willett, 1969) pp. 143–50; J. Gold, 'The Next Stage in the Development of International Monetary Law', 62 A.J.I.L. (1968) pp. 365–402; F. L. Deming, 'Special Drawing Rights: the Urgent Need for a New Global Monetary Reserve', 3 *The Journal of Law and Economic Development* (1968) pp. 1–7.

cipants in the Special Drawing Account. Once allocated, however, drawing rights do not thereby necessarily become a permanent element in the world's stock of reserve assets, but may subsequently be cancelled,[1] if a decision to that effect is adopted by the requisite majority. In this way, therefore—that is, by allocating special drawing rights when additional liquidity is required and by cancelling special drawing rights when there is too much liquidity—the Fund, at least potentially, will be able to influence the world's liquidity position.

It must be remembered, however, that at least initially, special drawing rights are intended only to supplement and not to supplant existing reserve assets—that is, gold, foreign exchange, and members' reserve positions in the Fund. For example, it was provided in the first allocation that the value of special drawing rights to be created in the next three years (1970, 1971, 1972) should be restricted to an amount equivalent to $9,500 million, of which $3,500 million[2] was allocated on 1 January 1970 and $3,000 million was to be allocated in each of the years 1971 and 1972.[3] By 1972, therefore, special drawing rights would value only $9,500 million, while traditional reserve assets (assuming stability in their value over the next three years) would value approximately $75,000m. This means that the equivalent of only 13 per cent of existing monetary reserves will be added to the world's stock of international liquidity. In the short term, therefore, the percentage of drawing rights in total world reserves would be small, and accordingly the degree of liquidity regulation which could be undertaken through the allocation or cancellation of special drawing rights would be commensurately small. In the medium term, however, should special drawing rights continue to be allocated, their importance as a regulatory device would also proportionately increase. In the longer term, on the other hand, it has been suggested from time to time that

[1] Although Art. XXI refers only to the allocation of special drawing rights, Art. XXIV, entitled 'Allocation and Cancellation of Special Drawing Rights,' sets out the procedure for both the creation and the cancellation of drawing rights.

[2] The total allocation was in fact only $3,414m. The Fund intended to allocate $3,500m. of S.D.R.s, but the amount was reduced by the decision of Formosa not to take up its portion.

[3] *The Economist*, 10 Jan. 1970, p. 62.

there exists a real possibility that special drawing rights could at some stage in the future constitute the principal element in the world's stock of monetary reserves. The first thing is to get confidence. Once that is established there is no reason why special drawing rights should develop not just as a complement to gold but as an alternative.[1] The importance of the special drawing rights facility to the future development of world liquidity is, therefore, twofold: (i) it could, in the medium term, become an effective regulator of the quantum of world liquidity; and (ii) it could, in the longer term, replace gold as the principal element in the world's stock of monetary reserves. Both these possibilities represent a movement away from the fortuitous past developments in international liquidity to a more orderly, planned future development, through the instrumentality of international law.

(ii) *What are special drawing rights?* Various commentaries on the new facility have referred to special drawing rights as either 'the beginnings of real supranational currency',[2] or 'a new international currency',[3] or 'a kind of legal tender',[4] or 'international fiat money'.[5] Although all these descriptions contain some measure of legal validity, upon closer examination the analogies to certain features of muncipal monetary systems upon which their validity depends do not in all cases stand up. Accordingly, although it may seem logically inconsistent in doing so, this section of the study will examine the principal legal and economic features of the new facility. It will then be followed in subsequent sections (iii)–(x) by a more detailed examination of the separate provisions of the scheme. Such an approach is necessary in order to dispel at the outset any preconceived and in some cases misleading notions, such as those referred to above, as to the general nature of the new facility.

From the legal aspect the following three issues will be examined: (*a*) are drawing rights money or credit? Assuming

[1] See H. G. Johnson, 'The Future of Gold and the Dollar', 3 J.W.T.L. (1969) p. 120.

[2] M. Heilperin, 'International Monetary Order: the Missing Link', 119 *The Banker* (1969) p. 865.

[3] 'Legal Problems of International Monetary Reform', 20 *Stanford Law Review* (1968–II) pp. 896–7.

[4] 'Paper Gold', 8 *Index, Svenska Handelsbanken Economic Review* (1969).

[5] W. J. Busschau, 'The Rule of Gold in World Monetary Arrangements', 2 J.W.T.L. (1968) p. 371.

that they are in fact money, (*b*) are they a form of international legal tender? and (*c*) do they constitute international fiat money?

It may be that the opinions I am about to put forward in reply to these questions will differ from those of the individual readers. This is to be expected. Special drawing rights are both a novel and a unique legal creation, and controversies as to their basic legal nature are therefore bound to occur. These will be settled only in the course of time and in the light of practical experience, because commercial matters such as these 'sont nécessairement conditionnés et influencés par la réalité sociale, politique et juridique qui les environne et où ils s'insèrent',[1] and not solely by legislative enactments.

First, are special drawing rights money or credit? The answer to this question is widely disputed both by international monetary economists[2] and by international monetary lawyers.[3] No conclusive authoritative answer can be reached. Rather, it is generally acknowledged that the Articles of Agreement were so drafted as to allow either interpretation,[4] thereby accommodating those members which favoured the expansion of credit facilities as well as those members which favoured expansion of owned reserve assets as the appropriate method of dealing with the liquidity problem. Nor is the issue clarified by reference to the legal nature of money in its municipal context. Controversy as to what is money exists here as well.[5] The question then is a moot one and will, as suggested above, be answerable with any degree of certainty only in the light of State practice. For the moment, one can only agree with Machlup's observation: 'Just as it has been possible to conclude that SDR's are and are not credit, depending on what meaning is given to the word, one may state that SDR's are money and are not money.'[6]

Secondly, assuming for the sake of the following discussion

---

[1] M. Giuliano, 'Quelques aspects juridiques de la coopération intergouvernementale en matière d'échanges et de paiements internationaux', 124 R.C. (1968–II) p. 557.

[2] F. Machlup, *Remaking the International Monetary System* (1968) pp. 77–95.

[3] J. Gold, 'The Next Stage in the Development of International Monetary Law', 62 A.J.I.L. (1968) pp. 379–80.

[4] F. Machlup, op. cit. pp. 8–12.

[5] Compare the State theory of money adhered to by Mann, *The Legal Aspect of Money* (1953) pp. 12–19, with the societary theory of money adhered to by Nussbaum, *Money in the Law* (1950) pp. 5–10. [6] F. Machlup, op. cit. p. 92.

that special drawing rights are money, not credit, do they constitute an international form of legal tender? In the municipal context the legal tender attribute of currency has been described as 'money which a creditor is not privileged to refuse if it is tendered by a debtor in payment of his debt'.[1] By analogy, therefore, whether special drawing rights constitute an international form of legal tender depends on whether other States participating in the scheme are under a legal obligation to accept special drawing rights when these are tendered to them in discharge of international monetary obligations. In this respect the Fund Articles provide in essence that a member having both special drawing rights and international monetary obligations cannot directly use the former to settle the latter. It must first obtain from another participating member (or several other members) currencies convertible in fact for its special drawing rights, and with the currencies so obtained settle its obligation. Thus convertible currencies (or gold) remain the means of settling international accounts, while special drawing rights are simply an additional means of borrowing the traditional means of international payments. As pointed out by J. Gold, therefore: 'The asset should not be classified as a form of legal tender, however, even among monetary authorities. The asset will not be usable directly for the compulsory discharge of obligations.'[2] Although from the strictly 'black letter' approach Gold's contention is not disputable, if one adopts a more dynamic approach and looks to the 'spirit' rather than to the 'letter' of the facility, it is arguable that at least to the extent that special drawing rights must in the intermediate stages be accepted in discharge of international obligations, they do constitute an international form of legal tender.

The final question to be considered is: 'do special drawing rights constitute international fiat money?' Again in answering this question one must first look to municipal law. Mann suggests:

The combination of legal tender and inconvertibility constitutes

---

[1] Nussbaum, *Money in the Law* (1950) pp. 45–6. See also Mann, *The Legal Aspect of Money* (1953) pp. 34 ff.

[2] J. Gold, 'The Next Stage in the Development of International Monetary Law', 62 A.J.I.L. (1968) p. 381.

what is called forced issue or compulsory tender or fiat money
(*cours forcé*, *Zwangskurs*). Thus *The Encyclopaedia Britannica* defines
fiat money as irredeemable money issued and made legal by government order but not secured by gold or silver or other adequate
reserve. Or, perhaps more correctly, it may be said that the issue
is a forced one if paper money is the only circulating medium and
if nothing but paper money can be tendered to or demanded by the
creditor.[1]

Today, fiat money circulates in most municipal monetary
systems, that is to say, the issuing authority is under no obligation to exchange the notes issued by it into gold, silver, or any
other commodity. Likewise, special drawing rights will be
issued by the Fund to the participants in the scheme. There
will be no pool of gold and foreign exchange to act as backing
for the new facility and the Fund will be under no obligation
to exchange the special drawing rights issued by it for other
reserve assets.[2] Rather: 'Backing will consist entirely of two
kinds of promises: those by creditor nations to provide hard
currency in exchange for SDRs, and those by debtor nations
to reconstitute their positions. Thus, the SDRs will be start-
lingly close to money by fiat.'[3] Thus the new facility dispensed
with the notion of backing in the traditional sense—that is,
the notion that the issuer of the debts, the central legal debtor
(in this case the Fund which issues the special drawing rights),
is supposed to hold assets (gold, foreign currencies) as security
against the issued liabilities (special drawing rights)—and
introduced in its place the notion that backing would consist
merely of the mutual legal obligation of the participants to
accept drawing rights in exchange for their currencies. The
essence of this concept is succinctly stated by Machlup:

All that matters for the acceptability of anything as a medium
of exchange is the expectation that others will accept it. If over a
hundred central banks or national monetary authorities including
those of the major trading nations of the world agree to accept

---

[1] Mann, *The Legal Aspect of Money* (1953) p. 38.

[2] In case of termination by a participating member or liquidation of the entire
facility, the Articles provide for redemption of special drawing rights in certain
instances. See Arts. XXX, XXXI, and Schedule I.

[3] 'Legal Problems of International Monetary Reform', 20 *Stanford Law Review*
(1968–II) p. 939. See similarly J. J. Polak, 'The Outline of a New Facility in the
Fund', 4 F.D. (1967) p. 277.

SDR's from one another in exchange for convertible currencies, this is all that is needed to establish the moneyness of the SDR's in inter-central-bank transactions. Money needs takers, not backers; the takers accept it, not because of any backing, but only because they count on others accepting it from them.[1]

On the basis of analogy to fiat money in municipal law, special drawing rights clearly do constitute a form of international fiat money. However, here again much will depend on State practice and in particular the confidence which participants place in the new facility. If in practice that confidence grows, and special drawing rights are readily accepted, then the new facility will flourish. Should that confidence wane and special drawing rights be rejected, then the new facility will perish.

In conclusion, definitive pronouncements on whether special drawing rights are a supranational currency, or international legal tender, or international fiat money cannot be made. Certainly, when compared with the legal nature of money in its municipal context, they appear to possess many similar attributes. However, such analogies are not in themselves conclusive. Much will depend on subsequent State practice. Indeed, all that can be stated with certainty at this point is that special drawing rights are *sui generis* in the law.

From the economic viewpoint, special drawing rights are unique in that they are in fact tantamount to free goods. Countries participating in the scheme will be credited with special drawing rights without surrendering to the Fund any of their existing international reserves and without the payment of their own currencies into a 'pool'. Thus there will be an immediate increase in world reserves and not merely a change in the distribution of an existing total of reserves. For example, following the first allocation of special drawing rights on 1 January 1970, the United Kingdom was credited with special drawing rights valued at $409·92 million[2] (each special drawing right is equivalent to 0·888671 gram of fine gold which was the gold value of $U.S.1, prior to 8 May 1972)[3] so that merely by a book-keeping entry the United Kingdom's

---

[1] Machlup, op. cit., pp. 65–6.
[2] *The Times*, 3 Jan. 1970, p. 11.
[3] Art. XXI, Sect. 2 of the Fund's Articles of Agreement.

total reserve assets were increased by that amount.[1] Hitherto a country acquired reserves only in exchange for real resources, that is to say, a country normally added to its reserves (gold, dollars, sterling) only when it sold more goods and services (real resources) on the international market than it bought. Discounting capital movements, a surplus on the current account was reflected by an increase in reserve assets. In contrast, one of the striking economic features of the new special drawing rights facility is that reserves can be created costlessly, without such a surrender of real resources. Unlike the situation which existed before their introduction, where one country's surplus was another country's deficit, the new facility allows all countries to increase their reserve asset positions without any commensurate decreases. They are, in effect, free claims to other countries' real resources.

(iii) *Who is eligible to join the scheme?* The Articles provide for two distinct categories of membership in the scheme. These are classified in the Articles as (*a*) participating members and (*b*) other holders.[2] The basic distinction between the two is that allocation of special drawing rights will be made only to the former. The latter will never be allocated special drawing rights. However, they, in conjunction with the former, will be able to accept, hold, and use special drawing rights.

(*a*) Participating members. Participation in the scheme, although only open to Fund members, is not compulsory— that is, Fund members are not legally obliged to participate in the new facility and may limit their transactions with the Fund to a use of the Fund's pool of resources. In other words, all participants must be Fund members, but not all Fund members need participate. In fact, only ten Fund members decided not to participate in the first allocation of the new facility. They were Ethiopia, Iraq, Kuwait, Lebanon, Libya, Nepal, Portugal, Saudi Arabia, Singapore, and Thailand.[3] To become

---

[1] Other participants received the following allocations (these are expressed in millions of $U.S.); United States, 867; Germany, 202; France, 166; Canada, 124; Japan, 122; Italy, 105; other industrial countries, 281; other developed countries, 285; India, 126; other less developed countries, 726, *The Economist*, 10 Jan. 1970, p. 62. For the second allocation of drawing rights see 23 *International Financial News Survey* (13 Jan. 1971) p. 1.

[2] Art. XXIII.

[3] *The Times*, 3 Jan. 1970, p. 11.

a participant the member must deposit with the Fund an instrument setting forth that it undertakes all the obligations of a participant in the Special Drawing Account in accordance with its municipal laws and that it has taken all the steps necessary to enable it to carry out those obligations.[1] The principal legal obligations that are incumbent upon a participant are: (i) to accept any special drawing rights allocated to it under a decision to allocate;[2] and (ii) to provide on demand, when designated by the Fund, currency convertible in fact to another participant in exchange for that participant's special drawing rights.[3] The relevant legislation which enables the United Kingdom to comply with these principal obligations provides in part as follows:

(2) The purposes for which the Exchange Equalisation Account is to be used shall include the purpose of carrying out any of the functions of the Government under the amendments; and accordingly— (a) any special drawing rights received or disposed of by the Government in pursuance of the amendments shall, in the case of receipts, be treated as assets of the Account and, in the case of disposals, be transferred from the Account; (b) the Treasury may cause any funds in the Account to be invested in the acquisition of special drawing rights in pursuance of the amendments . . .[4]

Under the terms of this legislation the United Kingdom will, on the one hand, accept into the Exchange Equalisation Account any special drawing rights allocated to it and consider them to be reserve assets (Section 2 (a)), and, on the other hand, it will, when designated, provide funds from the Account in exchange for special drawing rights (Section 2 (b)).

(b) Other holders. Although only Fund members may become 'participants' in the Special Drawing Account, that is to say, only they may be allocated special drawing rights under any decision to allocate, it is provided in Section 2 of Article XXIII that the Fund itself may accept and hold special drawing rights in, and use them through, what will now be called the General Account.[5] In addition, Section 3 of Article XXIII

---

[1] Art. XXIII, Sect. 1.   [2] Art. XXIV, Sect. II (e).
[3] Art. XXV, Sect. 4.
[4] International Monetary Fund Act 1968 (16 & 17 Eliz. II, c. 58).
[5] The General Account must be kept separate from the Special Drawing Account. Transactions and operations involving special drawing rights will be conducted through the Special Drawing Account, while all other transactions

provides that the Fund, by an eighty-five per cent majority of the total voting power, may allow special drawing rights to be accepted, held, and used, in certain prescribed transactions and operations,[1] by non-members (for example, Switzerland would appear to be a likely candidate), by non-participating members (for example, any of the ten Fund members enumerated above who are not participants would be potential candidates), or by institutions performing the function of a central bank for more than one member (for example, the Bank for International Settlements, or certain regional organizations in which members pool some of their resources, would fall within this category).

(iv) *Decision-making process to allocate/cancel.* The procedure laid down in the Articles for activating the scheme—that is, either to allocate or to cancel special drawing rights—is intentionally elaborate, and is so designed to ensure that any activation has the broad support of the majority of participants.[2] From the procedural viewpoint, the plan provides that a decision to activate must proceed through the following sequence: first, informal consultations by the Managing Director with national representatives, then concurrence by the Executive Directors, and finally approval by the Board of Governors. More particularly the decision-making process can, in all instances, only be begun by a proposal of the Managing Director.[3] Before making a proposal, however, the Managing Director must satisfy himself that it is consistent with the principle set out in Article XXIV, Section 1 (*a*), which governs all decisions to allocate or cancel special drawing rights. That principle requires that the Fund must seek to meet the long-term global need, as and when it arises, to supplement existing reserve assets

between members and the Fund, e.g. subscriptions, adjustments of quota, direct purchases, will be conducted through the General Account. In general see Art. XXII.

[1] All these operations and transactions will require Fund approval, Art. XXIII, Sect. 3 (ii) and (iii).

[2] *I.M.F. Annual Report* (1968) p. 15. See similarly J. J. Polak, 'The Outline of a New Facility in the Fund', 4 F.D. (1967) p. 280.

[3] The Managing Director was required to make a proposal for the first allocation of special drawing rights as soon after the establishment of the Special Drawing Account as he was satisfied that the conditions precedent to activation were complied with. In fact, this process was begun in the autumn of 1969 and allocation took place on 1 Jan. 1970. He is now required to make proposals at certain times and in certain circumstances, as prescribed in Art. XXIV, Sect. 4 (*c*).

in a manner that will promote the attainment of the Fund's purposes as set forth in Article 1 and will avoid economic stagnation and deflation as well as excess demand and inflation in the world. Moreover, the first decision to allocate special drawing rights had to take into account, as special considerations, a collective judgment that there was a global need to supplement reserves, and the attainment of a better balance of payments equilibrium, as well as the likelihood of a better working of the adjustment process in the future.[1] Having satisfied himself that the proposal would be consistent with the above principle, or both principles in the case of the initial allocation, the Managing Director is then obliged to conduct such consultations as will enable him to ascertain that there is broad support among the participants for the proposal.[2] This provision probably serves to avoid the embarrassment of a veto—that is, to ensure that there is not a greater than fifteen per cent opposition. Although it is not stated with whom he must so consult, it is probably correct to assume that such consultations would be conducted with the relevant national authorities, for example, the Finance Ministers and/or the Central Bank Governors of the participating members. However, if one examines the manner in which the first decision to allocate was reached, it would appear that in actual practice 'broad support' really only means 'support of the Group of Ten'. Following their Paris agreement on 24 July 1969 that the initial allocation of special drawing rights would be restricted to $9,500m. over the period 1970–2, it was clear that apart from observing the legal formalities, the decision had then been made.[3] Once 'broad support' is assured, the legal formalities require that the proposal be concurred in by the Executive Directors.[4] Finally, the proposal must be approved by the Board of Governors by an eighty-five per cent majority of the total voting power of the participants.[5] The requirement

[1] Art. XXIV, Sect. 1 (b).
[2] Art. XXIV, Sect. 4 (b).
[3] See the following reports which considered the importance of this agreement: *The Times*, 29 July 1969, p. 22; *Financial Times*, 25 July 1969, pp. 1, 20.
[4] Art. XXIV, Sect. 4 (a).
[5] Art. XXIV, Sect. 4 (d). However, Art. XXVII, paragraph (a) (ii) and (iii) provides that if a decision is to be taken on an item that pertains exclusively to the Special Drawing Account—for example, on a proposal by the Managing Director to allocate or cancel special drawing rights—only Governors for members that are

of the eighty-five per cent majority means that in practice the Common Market countries (if they vote as a unit), like the United States, having more than fifteen per cent of the total voting power, could veto any activation of the scheme.

(v) *Basis of allocation/cancellation.* It is intended as a general rule that decisions to allocate or to cancel special drawing rights will be made for basic periods which will normally be five years[1] in duration, and which will run consecutively. For example, the first basic period includes the years 1970–5, while the second would cover the years 1975–80, the third 1980–5, and so on. Moreover, while the decision covering the first period, 1970–5, provides for an allocation of at least $9,500m. worth of special drawing rights,[2] the second period, 1975–80, might be an 'empty' period—that is, a period in which there were neither allocations nor cancellations. A basic period can be an empty period either because the Managing Director was unable to formulate a proposal as required under Article XXIV, Section 4 (*b*) or because after a proposal had been formulated it failed to command the required eighty-five per cent majority from the Board of Governors. Finally, the Fund may decide that, for example, during the third basic period, 1980–5, the volume of liquidity should be reduced, and accordingly provide for the cancellation of special drawing rights during that period.

Although it is intended that decisions should be effected for basic periods of five years, the rule is not an inflexible one. Section 2 (*c*) (i) of Article XXIV provides that the Fund may decide that the duration of a basic period should be other than five years, while Section 3 permits the Fund, even after the commencement of a basic period for which a decision has been taken, to change the length of the basic period or start a new basic period if at any time it finds it advantageous to do so because of 'unexpected major developments'. Even though no

participants may vote, and each Director will be able to cast only the votes of the Fund members appointing or electing him that are participants.

[1] Art. XXIV, Sect. 2 (*a*). The choice of the five-year basic periods is significant. See Polak, 'The Outline of a New Facility', 4 F.D. (1967) p. 278.

[2] These are to be distributed during the first three years of the 1970–5 period. The participants will decide at a later date (presumably during 1972) on the last two years' allocations in the light of the evolution of the international payments balance. Thus the principle of the basic five-year allocation period has been observed.

indication is given in the Articles as to what constitutes an 'unexpected major development', a severe reduction or expansion in the volume of international trade would presumably so qualify. In both cases, however—that is, an alteration of the basic five-year period under Article XXIV, Section 2 (*c*) (i), or an alteration under Section 3—the proposed change could only be undertaken if sanctioned by eighty-five per cent of the total voting power.[1]

Allocations will normally be made to participants at yearly intervals[2] and will normally be expressed as percentages of quotas[3] on the date of the relevant decision to allocate.[4] For example, the first allocation took place on a non-discriminatory basis, with each of the participants receiving special drawing rights computed on the basis of 16·8 per cent of its quota with the Fund on 31 December 1969. The amounts allocated varied from $504,000-worth each of drawing rights for Botswana and Lesotho to $886·8m.-worth for the United States.

As in the case of basic periods, however, the rule that the rates at which allocations are to be made must be expressed as percentages of quotas on the date of the decision to allocate, or that allocations are to take place at yearly intervals, is not an inflexible one. The Fund may decide that allocations are to be made at intervals other than a year,[5] or are to be based on quotas other than those which exist at the time of the relevant decision to allocate.[6] Moreover, under Article XXIV, Section 3, the Fund, even after the beginning of a basic period, may, in the light of unexpected major developments, change the

---

[1] Art. XXIV, Sect. 4 (*d*).   [2] Art. XXIV, Sect. 2 (*a*).

[3] The allocation of S.D.R.s on this basis has been severely criticized; see 'Legal Problems of International Monetary Reform', 20 *Stanford Law Review* (1968–II) p. 955. This criticism has much validity when one considers that on this basis of allocation, of the $3,414m. allocated on 1 Jan. 1970 almost half ($1,645m.) went to the four leading Western industrial countries, the United States, Britain, Germany, and France, while only $852m. went to other less developed countries. Other formulas were put forward, e.g. that the S.D.R.s should be brought into circulation in the first instance through development aid, but failed for lack of support from the industrial countries. This latter suggestion, however, is still much favoured; see E. R. Fried, 'International Liquidity and Foreign Aid', 48 *Foreign Affairs* (1969) pp. 139–49; P. Streeten, 'Linking Currency and Development', 46 *International Affairs* (1970) pp. 23–9; *International Monetary Reform and Co-operation for Development. Report of the Expert Group on International Monetary Issues* (TD/B/285/Rev. 1).

[4] Art. XXIV, Sect. 2 (*b*).   [5] Art. XXIV, Sect. 2 (*c*) (ii).

[6] Art. XXIV, Sect. 2 (*c*) (iii).

rates or intervals of allocation which are to apply for the rest
of a basic period.[1]

Similar provisions apply in the case of cancellations, except
that they are to be expressed as percentages of net cumulative
allocations of special drawing rights on the date of each decision
to cancel.[2] For the purposes of this facility, net cumulative
allocation of special drawing rights has been defined as 'the total
amount of special drawing rights allocated to a participant less
its share of special drawing rights that have been cancelled
under Article XXIV, Section 2 (a)'.[3]

Any member who is a participant at the time a decision to
allocate is made will be obliged to accept its proportion of the
the allocation unless: (i) its Governor did not vote in favour of
the decision (that is, voted against or abstained) under which the
allocation is to be made; and (ii) before the first allocation
under that decision the participant gives the Fund notice in
writing that it does not wish to receive the allocation. However,
even where notice has been given, the Fund, on the request of
the participant, may terminate the effectiveness of the notice
and permit the participant to receive any subsequent allocations still due under the decision. In this case, however, the
participant will receive only those allocations made after the
termination of the notice; any allocations that were made while
the notice was in effect will not be recoverable.[4] Finally, it is
provided in Article XXIV, Section 2 (d) that unless the Fund
decides otherwise,[5] a member who becomes a participant after
a basic period has started shall not be eligible to receive any
allocations made during the remainder of that period.

(vi) *Use of special drawing rights.* General observations. Unlike
other components in a participant's monetary reserves—that is,
gold and foreign exchange, which as to usability are not subject

---

[1] All such alterations, except for the decisions under Sect. 3 of Art. XXIV with
respect to a decrease in the rates of allocation, require an 85 per cent majority,
Art. XXIV, Sect. 4 (d).

[2] Art. XXIV, Sect. 2 (a), (b), (c), and Sect. 3.

[3] Art. XXXII, para. (a). With respect to cancellations, note also the provisions
of Art. XXIV, Sect. 2 (f).   [4] Art. XXIV, Sect. 2 (e).

[5] It has been suggested, see *The Report* (1968) p. 9, that in practice the policy
of the Fund will be to permit a new participant to receive any allocations made
during the remainder of an existing basic period. For example, Iraq and Thailand, which were not participants on 1 Jan. 1970 when the first allocation was made,
subsequently became participants, and received allocations in 1971.

to any international legal regulation—special drawing rights will be usable only in those operations and transactions,[1] and only under those terms and conditions, that are authorized by, or under, the Articles of Agreement. The terms and conditions of usage, however, vary according to the nature of the operation and/or transaction. Four distinct categories of operations and/or transactions are envisaged. For the purposes of this study these will be classified and examined under the following four headings: (a) transactions between participants subject to designation; (b) transactions between participants not subject to designation; (c) operations and transactions between participants and the Fund; (d) operations and transactions between participants and other holders.

(vii) Transactions between participants subject to designation. Article XXV, Section 2 (a) provides that 'A participant shall be entitled to use its special drawing rights to obtain an equivalent amount of currency from a participant designated under Section 5 of this Article'. Under the terms of this provision, a participant (member A) having satisfied certain requirements—for example, the requirement of need—is entitled to obtain from another participant (member B), designated by the Fund, an equivalent amount of currency convertible in fact in exchange for special drawing rights. In other words, member A, having satisfied certain criteria, has a legal right to obtain an equivalent amount of currency convertible in fact in exchange for its special drawing rights, while member B, having been designated by the Fund, is under a legal obligation to provide currency. It is upon this legal right–legal obligation relationship that the success or failure of the scheme will depend. The new facility has no intrinsic value; it will not be backed by reserves received from participants and held by the Fund, but rather it will derive its value 'from the obligation of participants to accept it, in much the same way as the value of domestic fiduciary money derives from its status as legal tender'.[2] To use a practical example, suppose that the United Kingdom, which has been allocated approximately $410m. worth of special drawing rights, were in balance of payments deficit and required dollars to engage in market

[1] See *The Report* (1968) p. 10, para. 10.
[2] Polak, 'The Outline of a New Facility in the Fund', 4 F.D. (1967) p. 277.

operations to maintain the value of the pound sterling.[1] Suppose further that France were in payments surplus and enjoyed a strong gross reserve position as well. The United Kingdom would approach the Fund,[2] which in turn could designate France. Once designated, France would be under a legal obligation to deliver currency convertible in fact (dollars) to the United Kingdom in exchange for an equivalent amount of special drawing rights.

However, the conditions under which the United Kingdom or any other participant will be permitted to use its drawing rights to acquire currency, the conditions under which France or any other participant will be legally obliged to provide currency in exchange for the drawing rights, the type of currency which must be so provided, and finally the extent to which the United Kingdom or any other participant which has used its drawing rights will be obliged to reconstitute its holdings of drawing rights are all strictly defined in the Articles of Agreement. These matters will now be considered in turn under the headings: (a) requirement of need, (b) designation, (c) currency convertible in fact, and (d) reconstitution.

(a) Requirement of need. Although Section 2 (a) of Article XXV unconditionally endows participants with the legal right to use their drawing rights in transactions with other participants to acquire currency, the right is not an indiscriminate one. In particular, it is intended that only if participants are able to satisfy the requirement of need criterion should they enter into such transactions. That criterion is set out in Section 3 (a) of Article XXV and states:

In transactions under Section 2 of this Article, except as otherwise provided in (c) below, a participant will be expected to use its special drawing rights only to meet balance of payments needs or in the light of developments in its official holdings of gold, foreign exchange, and special drawing rights, and its reserve position in the Fund, and not for the sole purpose of changing the composition of

[1] It has been suggested that in practice S.D.R.s will probably be largely used to buy dollars, since dollars are used in market intervention, Machlup, *Remaking the International Monetary System* (1968) pp. 15–16.

[2] To prevent any secret use of S.D.R.s, which could be contrary to the treaty provisions, it is provided in Sect. 3 of Art. XXII that all changes in holdings of special drawing rights, to be legally effective, must be recorded by the Fund in the Special Drawing Account.

the foregoing as between special drawing rights and the total of gold, foreign exchange, and reserve position in the Fund.

This criterion is, in fact, made up of several individual parts and can therefore be best understood if each part is examined separately. First, drawing rights can be used only to meet 'balance of payments needs'; all other uses, for example, to acquire currency to finance development projects, are specifically excluded. However, the reference to 'balance of payments needs' in general implies that for the purposes of the facility, no distinction is to be made between payments difficulties attributable to the current, and those attributable to the capital account. Unlike the Fund's pool of currencies, therefore, which as a general rule is available only to finance current account deficits, special drawing rights will be available to deal with difficulties arising in either the current or the capital account. Secondly, the reference to 'developments' in a participant's holdings of gold, foreign exchange, special drawing rights, and reserve position in the Fund indicates that any such 'developments', 'even if attributable to conversions of balances of the member's currency and not to a balance of payments deficit',[1] would justify the use of drawing rights under this provision. For example, a reserve currency participant such as the United States of America, in complying with its obligations under Article IV, Section 4 (*b*),[2] could lose gold from its reserves to other participants even though its payments balance was not in deficit. Under the combined terms of Article XXV, Section 3 (*a*) and Article XXV, Section 2 (*b*) (i), it could, therefore, in agreement with these other participants, use its drawing rights to repurchase any dollars held by them. Such a use of drawing rights by the United States would be in response to 'developments' (the loss of gold) in its reserve assets, and would therefore be in accordance with the terms of the provision. Finally, the last part of Section 3 (*a*) prohibits the use of special drawing rights for the sole purpose of changing the composition between the participant's holdings of special drawing rights and its holdings of other reserve assets. In other words, the use of drawing rights merely to reduce holdings of such

[1] *The Report* (1968) p. 14.
[2] The United States ceased to buy and sell gold for the purposes of Article IV, Section 4 (*b*) in August 1971.

rights and to increase holdings of foreign exchange owing to the 'distrust of the former or preference for the latter'[1] would not be in conformity with the requirement of need criterion.

Although every participant is expected (subject to the exceptions to bè discussed) to use its drawing rights only when such a use is in compliance with the requirement of need criterion just described, it is expressly provided in Section 3 (b) of Article XXV that any improper use—that is, a use not in compliance with that criterion—will not be subject to challenge by the Fund. The Fund may make representations to a participant making an improper use, and in the case of persistent abuse the Fund may even suspend the right of the delinquent participant to use any drawing rights acquired after the notice of suspension,[2] but under no circumstances can the Fund prevent a participant from utilizing any drawing rights already held by challenging the appropriateness of the use under Article XXV, Section 3 (a). The special drawing rights facility, therefore, clearly constitutes an unconditional as distinct from conditional form of liquidity.[3] As mentioned, unconditional liquidity is liquidity to which countries have access without being subject to any prior commitments or discussions as to economic policy, while conditional liquidity is liquidity which is made available to countries only on the prior condition that they agree to undertake certain prescribed economic measures. In this respect, therefore, the new facility is akin to drawings in the gold tranche, which, unlike drawings in the credit tranches, are automatically accessible to all Fund members.

(b) Designation. As mentioned, the principal legal obligation incumbent upon participants is the duty to provide currency convertible in fact in exchange for special drawing rights when designated to do so by the Fund.[4] The importance of this obligation to the effective functioning of the facility cannot be

---

[1] J. Gold, 'The Next Stage in the Development of International Monetary Law', 62 A.J.I.L. (1968) p. 384.

[2] Art. XXIX, Sect. 2 (b). In addition to what may be described as negative sanctions, i.e. representation and suspension, the Fund may take another, more positive measure to redress any improper use of drawing rights by designating delinquent participants to provide currency in exchange for drawing rights (Art. XXV, Sect. 5 (a) (ii)).

[3] M. A. Heilperin, 'International Monetary Order: the Missing Link', 119 *The Banker* (1969) p. 866.   [4] Art. XXV, Sect. 4.

overstated. Special drawing rights, *per se*, have no intrinsic value. They exist, in fact, only as book-keeping entries. They are valuable only in so far as they can be used to procure foreign currencies. Failure to comply with this central obligation—that is, unwillingness by participants to provide currency when designated to do so by the Fund—would necessarily mean failure for the facility. That the drafters of the scheme viewed this particular obligation seriously is reflected by the fact that for its violation is reserved the most serious sanction in the facility, that is, suspension of the use of all special drawing rights held by the violator. Failure to comply with any other obligations gives rise to a less serious sanction, that is, suspension of the use of those drawing rights acquired after the commission by the participant of the violation, or—in Fund parlance—suspension of after-acquired rights.[1]

In selecting participants for designation, the Fund is obliged to act in accordance with the following general principles which may be supplemented by such other principles as the Fund may from time to time adopt: (i) a participant will be subject to designation if its balance of payments and gross reserve position is sufficiently strong, though it might still be selected if it has a strong reserve position combined with a moderate balance of payments deficit;[2] (ii) a participant will be subject to designation if it needs drawing rights to promote reconstitution, to reduce a negative balance in its holdings of drawing rights, or to offset a failure to fulfil the expectation under the requirement of need criterion.[3] In designating participants under (i) and (ii) above, it is intended that the Fund will normally give priority in designation to those participants needing to acquire drawing rights to meet the objectives of designation under (ii).[4] If, for example, member A has made an improper use of its drawing rights—that is, has not complied with the requirement of need criterion—then A would, under the terms of this provision, be designated by the Fund, in preference to other participants with stronger reserve and balance of payments positions, to provide currency in exchange for special drawing rights until such time as the improper use had been offset. However, in designating participants who

[1] Art. XXIX, Sect. 2 (*a*), (*b*).   [2] Art. XXV, Sect. 5 (*a*) (i).
[3] Art. XXV, Sect. 5 (*a*) (ii).   [4] Art. XXV, Sect. 5 (*a*) (iii).

fall into the second category in preference to those who fall into the first category, the Fund will have to proceed with caution. Participants who have found it necessary to use their special drawing rights to such an extent that they fall within one of the three categories enumerated in Article XXV, Section 5 (*a*) (ii) will more probably than not be suffering from an unsatisfactory payments and reserve position. Accordingly, to apply the priority rule strictly in all cases would clearly be inappropriate. Perhaps it was in recognition of this fact that the strictness of the rule was somewhat mitigated by the introduction of the phrase 'normally shall give priority' into Section 5 (*a*) (iii), which accords the Fund some measure of flexibility in dealing with such contingencies.

In cases where the Fund designates participants under the first criterion—that is, those with a strong balance of payments and reserve position—it is obliged to select participants in such a way as to promote over a period of time a balanced distribution of holdings of special drawing rights among them.[1] More particularly, the designations are to be such as to promote over a period of time equality in the ratios of their holdings of special drawing rights in excess of their net cumulative allocations to their official holdings of gold and foreign exchange.[2] This is to ensure that no one participant of several with strong reserve and payments positions is singled out too frequently for designation, thereby accumulating more than its proportionate share of drawing rights. Rather, the intention is to achieve an equal distribution of holdings among the participants. In any event, no participant is legally obliged to increase its holdings of special drawing rights beyond an amount equivalent to three times its net cumulative allocation. For example, the United Kingdom, whose first allocation amounted to $410m.-worth of special drawing rights, is not obliged to accept more than $820m. drawing rights, so that its total holdings need never exceed $1,230m.-worth of drawing rights. A participant may, however, either voluntarily or in agreement with the Fund, provide currency in excess of the obligatory amount.

(*c*) Currency convertible in fact. A participant which has

[1] Art. XXV, Sect. 5 (*a*) (i).
[2] Art. XXV, Sect. 5 (*b*), (*c*), and Schedule F. For an explanation of these somewhat complex provisions, see *The Report* (1968) pp. 11–13.

been designated by the Fund is under a legal obligation to provide on demand 'currency convertible in fact' which for the purposes of the Fund Agreement has been given the following legal definition:

Currency convertible in fact means:

(1) a participant's currency for which a procedure exists for the conversion of balances of the currency obtained in transactions involving special drawing rights into each other currency for which such procedure exists, at rates of exchange prescribed under Article XXV, Section 8, and which is the currency of a participant that

  (i) has accepted the obligations of Article VIII, Sections 2, 3, and 4, or
  (ii) for the settlement of international transactions in fact freely buys and sells gold within the limits prescribed by the Fund under Section 2 of Article IV; or

(2) currency convertible into a currency described in paragraph (1) above at rates of exchange prescribed under Article XXV, Section 8.[1]

Under paragraph (1) of the above provision, a designated participant is entitled to provide, in exchange for special drawing rights, the currency of any participant including its own, but only if that currency possesses the following attributes. First, the currency provided must enjoy *de jure* convertibility—that is, it must be the currency of a participant which either freely buys and sells gold under Article IV, Section 4 (*b*), or has accepted the obligations of Article VIII, Sections 2, 3, and 4.[2] Secondly, the currency must belong to a select group of currencies which, in respect of balances arising in connection with the use of special drawing rights, are interconvertible. The currencies of participants which are to be included in this special group of currencies and the procedure whereby their interconvertibility will be carried out will presumably be determined by the Fund in collaboration with the participants.[3] Thirdly, the currency must be convertible into any one of the other currencies in the special group at appropriate rates of exchange. An appropriate rate of exchange is one that is established in accordance with

---

[1] Art. XXXII, para. (*b*).
[2] See above, p. 177.
[3] Under Art. XXVIII, all participants are obliged to collaborate with the Fund.

Section 8 of Article XXV, and ensures that whatever the currency into which the currency initially provided is subsequently converted, the participant will receive the same value.[1]

Under paragraph (2) a designated participant may provide any other currency—for example, the currency of a non-participating member or even a non-member—so long as the currency provided is freely convertible (unlike the currency provided under paragraph (1), which must be *de jure* convertible, the currency provided in paragraph (2) need be only *de facto* convertible), at rates of exchange prescribed by the Fund, into any one of the currencies mentioned in paragraph (1), that is, into a currency which belongs to the select group of interconvertible currencies. Through one or more conversions, a currency provided under paragraph (2) can, therefore, be converted into any one of that group of currencies.

Although the procedure just described is rather complex, its objective, as pointed out by the following observation made by the Fund itself, is quite straightforward:

The provisions of Article XXXII (*b*) are designed to ensure that any participant using special drawing rights to obtain 'currency convertible in fact' from a designated participant can obtain, directly or indirectly, any one of a number of convertible currencies that he may choose, in amounts determined by the exchange rates prescribed under Article XXV, Section 8, in accordance with the principle of equal value.[2]

In short, whether a participant receives currency under paragraph (1) of Article XXXII (*b*) (currency which is *de jure* convertible) or under paragraph (2) of Article XXXII (*b*) (currency which is *de facto* convertible), it will have the option according to its particular requirements of either holding the currency actually provided or converting it, at rates which will ensure equal value, into one of several other currencies.

---

[1] 'Under Art. XXV, Sect. 8, the exchange rates for operations and transactions are to be such as will ensure that a participant using its special drawing rights will receive the same value, on the basis of the exchange rates prevailing at the time the transaction takes place, whatever the currencies that might be provided and whichever the participant that provides the currency. The Fund will have to adopt regulations to give effect to this principle, and will consult a participant on the procedure for determining rates of exchange for its currency.' *The Report* (1968) p. 16.

[2] *The Report* (1968) p. 18.

As already suggested, however, if in practice the Netherlands, for example, transfers special drawing rights to Denmark, this will most likely be in exchange for United States dollars, since dollars are normally used by monetary authorities in market intervention. However, Denmark need not supply dollars, but may in fact supply Danish kroner, Italian lire (both of which are *de jure* convertible for Fund purposes), Swiss francs (which are only *de facto* convertible by Fund definition), or any other currency, so long as the currency tendered satisfies the qualifications enumerated above.

(*d*) Reconstitution. The answer to the question 'should a participant which has used its special drawing rights to acquire currency be obliged, at some future date, to reconstitute its holdings of drawing rights?' determines to a large extent the asset value[1] of the new facility. In other words, does the scheme in fact amount only to an extension of credit facilities (that is, a system under which a participant will be able only to borrow foreign exchange which must be repaid), or does the scheme in fact create owned reserve assets (that is, a system under which a participant will have direct and immediate access to foreign exchange without incurring a repayment obligation)? If, on the one hand, a participant which has used its special drawing rights is obliged to reconstitute its holdings to or near to their initial level at an early date, the facility would amount to nothing more than a short-term borrowing arrangement. If, on the other hand, drawing rights can be utilized without being subject to reconstitution provisions, at least for an extended period of time, their asset-like value is obviously greatly enhanced. Returning again to our example, if the United Kingdom transfers, say, $100m.-worth of special drawing rights to France in exchange for United States dollars, and simultaneously incurs an obligation to repurchase those drawing rights at some future date, the scheme will be no more than a sophisticated form of credit facility. If, on the other hand, no obligation to repurchase is incurred, then the scheme will generate a novel form of reserve asset.[2]

[1] J. Gold, 'The Next Stage in the Development of International Monetary Law', 62 A.J.I.L. (1968) pp. 379–82, 386–8; F. Machlup, *Remaking the International Monetary System* (1968) pp. 8–12, 38–9.

[2] See 'Legal Problems of International Monetary Reform', 20 *Stanford Law Review* (1968–II) pp. 896–7.

In the preparatory debates on the new facility, two schools of thought predominated as to the form which this aspect of the facility should assume: (*a*) one that supported the view that analogous to existing Fund repurchase provisions, special drawing rights should be reconstituted when the particular payments difficulty for which they had been used had been corrected; and (*b*) one that supported the view that the asset-like quality of drawing rights should have predominance, with the effect that reconstitution obligations should be kept to a minimum.[1] The adopted provisions, although they attempt to accommodate both views, tend on balance to favour the latter school of thought. Participants which use their drawing rights are under a legal obligation to reconstitute their holdings, but only to a limited extent. The specific rules as set out in Article XXV, Section 6 and Schedule G provide that a participant's net use of its special drawing rights must be such that the average of its holdings over a five-year period will not be less than 30 per cent of the average of its net cumulative allocations over the same five-year period. Participants may for some part of any five-year period use more than 70 per cent of their net cumulative allocation, but they must subsequently reconstitute their holdings to a point above 30 per cent and keep them at that level for a sufficient length of time to re-establish the required 30 per cent average. The rules governing reconstitution are to be reviewed at the end of each basic period, and with an eighty-five per cent majority of the total voting power, the established rules may be abrogated or modified and new rules may be adopted.[2] Indeed, it is envisaged that as confidence in the scheme develops, the reconstitution provisions can be gradually relaxed and finally abolished.[3]

However, for the present the reconstitution obligation remains a central feature of the facility, and accordingly a number of devices have been introduced into the Articles which are designed to promote reconstitution both on an obligatory and on a voluntary basis. First, as has been seen, the Fund, in designating participants to provide currency convertible in fact in exchange for drawing rights, is required as a general

[1] Cf. the *I.M.F. Annual Report* (1966) p. 17.
[2] Art. XXV, Sect. 6 (*b*).
[3] *The Economist*, 22 Sept. 1967, pp. 799–800.

rule to give priority in designation to those participants that need special drawing rights to comply with the reconstitution requirements of Schedule G. Secondly, it will be seen that under Article XXV, Section 2 (*b*) (ii), any participant may, in agreement with another participant, enter into a transaction which would promote reconstitution without satisfying the requirement of need criterion. Thirdly, participants are required to pay due regard to the desirability of pursuing over a period of time a balanced relationship between their holdings of special drawing rights and their other reserve assets.[1] A proper observance of this obligation in the management of its reserves would make it highly unlikely that a participant would find it necessary at any one point in a five-year basic period to adjust drastically its holdings of special drawing rights as a result of the obligation to reconstitute. Finally, drawing rights have been endowed with many attractive features: for example, their value is guaranteed in terms of gold, each right being equivalent to 0·888671 gram of fine gold;[2] and unlike the conventional reserve assets (that is, gold and foreign exchange), special drawing rights will earn interest.[3] These features should encourage participants not only to retain any drawing rights allocated to them and to use them sparingly, but also to acquire additional ones when possible. However, should a participant, in spite of all the measures just mentioned, need to acquire special drawing rights to comply with its reconstitution obligation, it is entitled and indeed required to obtain them, at its option for gold or currency acceptable to the Fund in a transaction with the Fund conducted through the General Account.[4] If the participant is unable to acquire sufficient drawing rights from the Fund, the participant is then obliged and entitled to

[1] Schedule G, para. 1 (*b*).

[2] Art. XXI, Sect. 2.

[3] Art. XXVI, Sects. 1, 2, 3, and 5. It should also be noted that under the terms of a new provision (Art. V, Sect. 9), the Fund is required to pay a return to members on the excess of 75 per cent of a member's quota over the average of the Fund's holdings of the member's currency, or, in other words, on the Fund's net use of a member's normal currency subscription. The rate of remuneration will be $1\frac{1}{2}$ per cent per annum. However, the Executive Directors would be able to specify other rates within the limits of 1 and 2 per cent per annum by a majority of the votes cast. The remuneration is payable in gold, or in the member's own currency, or partly in gold and partly in such currency.

[4] Schedule G, para. 1 (*a*) (iv).

obtain them with currency convertible in fact from a participant specified by the Fund.[1]

(viii) *Transactions between participants not subject to designation.* In addition to accepting transfers of special drawing rights in exchange for currencies convertible in fact when designated by the Fund to do so (that is, when legally obliged to do so), a participant may, in agreement with another participant, voluntarily accept transfers of special drawing rights. The principal distinction between this category of transaction and the one already discussed in the preceding section is the absence of legal obligation to surrender currencies for drawing rights. The varieties of transactions in which two participants may agree to this form of transfer of special drawing rights are set out in Article XXV, Section 2 (*b*):

A participant, in agreement with another participant, may use its special drawing rights:

(i) to obtain an equivalent amount of its own currency held by the other participant; or

(ii) to obtain an equivalent amount of currency from the other participant in any transactions, prescribed by the Fund, that would promote reconstitution by the other participant under Section 6 (*a*) of this Article; prevent or reduce a negative balance of the other participant; offset the effect of a failure by the other participant to fulfil the expectation in Section 3 (*a*) of this Article; or bring the holdings of special drawing rights by both participants closer to their net cumulative allocations. The Fund by an eighty-five per cent majority of the total voting power may prescribe additional transactions or categories of transactions under this provision. Any transactions or categories of transactions prescribed by the Fund under this subsection (*b*) (ii) shall be consistent with the other provisions of this Agreement and with the proper use of special drawing rights in accordance with this Agreement.

In addition to the principal distinction already mentioned—that is, absence of designation—between these two types of transaction, the one under discussion differs from the former in two vital respects: (1) any transactions in this category, except for the one in which drawing rights are exchanged for the other participant's own currency, need not satisfy the

[1] Ibid.

requirement of need criterion; and (ii) the currency given in exchange for drawing rights need not be currency convertible in fact. However, all transfers of special drawing rights made under the auspices of Article XXV, Section 2 (b) are subject to identical reconstitution provisions as apply to transfers made under the auspices of Article XXV, Section 2 (a).

(ix) *Operations and transactions between participants and the Fund.* The Fund is under a legal obligation to accept drawing rights from participants (i) in repurchases accruing in special drawing rights under Article V, Section 7 (b), and (ii) in reimbursements pursuant to Section 4 of Article XXVI.[1] In the first case, the Fund, having decided to include special drawing rights in members' monetary reserves for the purposes of Article V, Section 7 (b) and Schedule B, paragraph (1),[2] must *ipso facto* accept any drawing rights used by members in complying with their repurchase obligations under those provisions. More particularly, in Article V, Section 7 (b) it is stated that 'a member shall repurchase from the Fund with each type of monetary reserve . . . part of the Fund's holdings of its currency'. Since special drawing rights are for the purposes of the re-purchase provisions deemed to be monetary reserves,[2] any member with a repurchase obligation which holds drawing rights in its reserves must satisfy that repurchase obligation in part by using some of its drawing rights, and the Fund is accordingly under an obligation to accept any drawing rights so presented.[3] In the second case, the Fund accepts drawing rights from the participants as a result of assessments made under Section 4 of Article XXVI. Initially all expenses in conducting the business of the Special Drawing Account are to be met by the Fund from the General Account, and the Fund is to be periodically reimbursed on the basis of a reasonable estimate of such expenses.[4] For the purposes of such reimbursement, the Fund is permitted to levy assessments on all participants in

---

[1] Art. XXV, Sect. 7 (b).

[2] Art. XXV, Sect. 7 (a) reads in part: 'Special drawing rights shall be included in a member's monetary reserves under Article XIX for the purposes of Article III, Section 4 (a), Article V, Section 7 (b) and (c), Article V, Section 8 (f), and Schedule B, paragraph 1 . . .'

[3] The Fund has in fact accepted drawing rights from certain member States in repayments, see *The Times*, 3 Mar. 1970, p. 24.

[4] Art. XXII, Sect. 2.

proportion to their net cumulative allocations, and participants are required to pay, in special drawing rights, their portions of the assessment directly into the General Account.[1]

In addition to the two cases just discussed, the Fund may decide to accept drawing rights (1) in payment of charges, and (2) in repurchases other than those under Article V, Section 7 (b).[2] Unlike the situation in the former two cases, however, the Fund, in the latter two cases, is under no legal obligation to accept special drawing rights, but may elect to do so voluntarily.

Finally, subsections (d) and (e) of Article XXV, Section 7 describe the circumstances in which the Fund is authorized to enter into transactions with participants—that is, to obtain currencies from participants in exchange for drawing rights held in the General Account. Under subsection (d) the Fund, if it deems it appropriate to replenish its holdings of the participant's currency in the General Account and has consulted the participant on alternative means of replenishment under Article VII, Section 2, may require a participant to provide its currency to the Fund for special drawing rights. Under subsection (e) the Fund is authorized to provide a participant with special drawing rights from the General Account for gold or currency acceptable to the Fund in order to help a participant meet its reconstitution obligation, to prevent or reduce a negative balance, or to reverse the effects of a transaction engaged in inconsistently with the requirement of need criterion.

(x) *Operations and transactions between participants and other holders.* It has been seen that the Fund, by an eighty-five per cent majority of the total voting power, may prescribe as holders of drawing rights non-members, members that are non-participants, and certain classes of institution.[3] Furthermore, subject to the requirement that all uses of drawing rights must be consistent with the Articles of Agreement, the Fund has complete discretion in prescribing the terms and conditions on which such other holders and participants may be permitted to use drawing rights in operations and transactions with one another[3]. Since no mention is made in the Articles of the types of operations and transactions that will be permitted, the full

[1] Art. XXVI, Sects. 4 and 5.
[2] Art. XXV, Sect. 7 (c).   [3] Art. XXIII, Sect. 3.

effect of this provision on the future development of the facility can only be a matter of speculation. However, it is probably correct to suggest at this point that as a minimum those classes of operations and transactions which participants may enter into with either other participants or the Fund will be permitted.

Part Three

POST-FUND PERIOD
(B) REGIONAL AND BILATERAL
MONETARY ARRANGEMENTS

INTRODUCTION

WHILE Part Two of this study was concerned with an analysis of the legal regulation of international monetary affairs at the global treaty level—that is, through the instrumentality of the Fund Agreement and the G.A.T.T.—Part Three will be concerned with a similar analysis at the regional (Chapter X) and the bilateral (Chapter XI) levels.

During the course of this analysis it will become apparent that many of the monetary provisions contained in the various regional and bilateral arrangements being considered are similar to the provisions provided for in the Fund Agreement and the G.A.T.T. For example, provisions prohibiting the imposition of exchange restrictions in respect of current international transactions—provided for in the Fund Agreement—are also to be found in many of the regional trading arrangements and in most of the bilateral treaties of Friendship, Commerce and Navigation. Similarly, exchange rates which under the Fund Agreement are subject to a certain measure of legal control are also the object of regulation in certain of the regional and bilateral treaties considered in this part of the study.

However, there the similarity ends, and it must be made clear at the outset that the monetary provisions which are to be considered in this part of the study do not merely imitate at the regional and bilateral levels what the Fund and the G.A.T.T. have already provided at the global level. Rather it will be seen that in addition to complementing their global counterparts, the monetary provisions of the regional and bilateral arrangements very often surpass them. This point was made clear by one such regional organization, the Organization for European Economic Cooperation (O.E.E.C.) in a report published in 1961 dealing with that institution's activities in the field of commercial and exchange restrictions:

. . . balance of payments difficulties and national protectionism in some countries began to lead to increasingly severe forms of

restriction, which became almost universal in Europe when war
broke out in 1939.

Significant steps in the reversal of this trend after the war were the
establishment, under the auspices of the United Nations, of the
International Monetary Fund and the drawing up of the General
Agreement on Tariffs and Trade as a step towards the projected
world-wide trade organisation of the United Nations. The aims of
the O.E.E.C. in Europe have been in line with those of the I.M.F.
and the G.A.T.T.; its work has been complementary to theirs and
in some ways has gone beyond it.[1]

More particularly, while the Fund's monetary code of conduct
prohibits the imposition of exchange restrictions in respect of
current transactions only, certain regional organizations such
as the Organization for Economic Cooperation and Development (O.E.C.D.) and the European Economic Community
(E.E.C.) proscribe such restrictions not only in respect of current, but also in respect of capital, transactions. Similarly,
exchange rates are subject to more rigorous legal regulation
in the West African Monetary Union, for example, than they
are under the relevant Fund provisions. Moreover, several of
the regional trading blocks—for example, the Central American
Common Market and the European Common Market—have as
their ultimate objective the formation of a complete economic
and monetary union, and accordingly, monetary matters
which go to the very heart of a nation's internal economic life,
such as budget policies and central bank policies, are gradually
becoming the object of supranational control.[2] Indeed, the
member States of the West African Monetary Union have already established among themselves a common central bank,
which, as will be seen, is the creature of an international legal
instrument, and therefore possesses many unique and interesting legal characteristics.

The above examples serve to illustrate the fact that States
which have entered into these various regional and bilateral

---

[1] *Liberalisation of Current Invisibles and Capital Movements* (O.E.E.C., Paris, 1961,
Document no. C/60/98) p. 9.

[2] The point that membership in a monetary union necessarily results in the
transference of monetary sovereignty from the member States to the union as a
whole is made by René de Lacharrière, 'L'évolution de la Communauté franco-
africaine', *Annuaire français de droit international* (1960) p. 32. See similarly Guy de
Carmoy, 'Monetary Problems of the EEC', 120 *The Banker* (1970) pp. 21–5.

treaty arrangements have thereby accepted restriction of their monetary sovereignty well beyond that resulting from their membership in the Fund and in the G.A.T.T. Accordingly, the objects of this part of the study will be twofold, one of a particular and the other of a general nature: first, to define the contemporary position of international monetary law as it exists at the regional and bilateral levels, and second, thereby to draw attention to the fact, often overlooked in view of the Fund's prominent position in these matters, that the international legal regulation of money at the regional and bilateral levels has, in many respects, gone well beyond that yet achieved on the global plane.

X

REGIONAL MONETARY
ARRANGEMENTS

1. *Terms of Reference*

THIS chapter examines the monetary provisions contained in various regional monetary arrangements, and in it the notion 'regional monetary arrangements' is defined to mean those arrangements: (i) which prescribe on an international legal basis certain rules of monetary conduct for their respective members (as distinct from those arrangements which prescribe such rules of behaviour on a more informal basis—for example, the sterling area—though even here, as will be shown below, rules of behaviour emanating from international law have assumed some measure of importance); and (ii) which allow for restricted membership only (as distinct from global arrangements, such as the Fund and the G.A.T.T. in which membership is open to all the States of the world). Accordingly, only those economic associations which satisfy the two criteria set out in the above definition—that is, (*a*) they prescribe monetary rules of conduct on a legal basis, and (*b*) they allow for restricted membership only—will be considered in this chapter.

On the one hand, therefore, multilateral treaty arrangements such as free trade associations and customs unions created under the auspices of Article 24 of the G.A.T.T. clearly qualify for inclusion under the terms of this definition. In fact, these two varieties of economic association constitute the principal forms of regional monetary arrangement to be considered in this chapter. On the other hand, such nebulous groups as, for example, the 'Gnomes of Zürich', the 'Club of Basle', and the 'Paris Club', which have no formal institutional framework and which have respectively been defined as 'a league of private Central and West European bankers; a group at the fringes of the Bank for International Settlements; and a group

of German, Dutch, Italian, Swiss, and British private corpora-
tions . . .',[1] clearly fall outside the scope of this definition. They
will not, therefore, be the objects of examination. However, an
exception will be made with respect to the so-called 'Group
of Ten'. Like the other above-mentioned groups, the 'Group
of Ten' lacks a formal constitutional framework. However, it
exerts such an important influence on the development of
international monetary law that some mention of its structure
and activities must be made. Finally, the sterling area and the
franc area, both of which have restricted membership and which
prescribe certain rules of monetary behaviour for their respective members, will also be considered. These two arrangements
are, from the institutional viewpoint, neither completely nebulous nor completely formalized, but rather represent a hybrid
between these two extremes. Accordingly, in analysing them,
emphasis will be placed on those particular norms of behaviour
established by them that have been endowed with an international legal status.

The total number of regional monetary arrangements of
the first variety (that is, those which possess a formal institutional framework) currently in force stands at no fewer than
twenty, with additional arrangements being continually
created. Due to the great proliferation of these arrangements,
as well as to the tenuous nature and volatility of certain of them,
it is both impractical and unnecessary to examine separately
and in detail the monetary provisions of each agreement.
Accordingly, for this reason as well as for reasons of presenta-
tion, these various treaties (with the sole exception of the
O.E.C.D., which will be examined separately because the
diversity of its membership prevents it from being classified on a
geographical basis with the other arrangements) will be divided
up and grouped for examination on the following geographical
basis: Western Europe, Africa, and Latin America.[2] Where it is

---

[1] James K. Weeks, 'The Cross of Gold: United States Trade and Travel
Restrictions and Monetary Crisis', 19 *Syracuse Law Review* (1967–8) p. 871. See also
Hirsch, op. cit. pp. 244–5, who sets out in tabular form the various monetary
associations.

[2] Little economic and monetary co-operation exists among the countries of the
Middle and Far East. For comments plus relevant texts on the Arab Common
Market, Regional Cooperation for Development among Pakistan, Iran, and
Turkey, and the Federation of Malaya and Singapore Common Market, see
Miguel S. Wionczek (ed.), *Economic Cooperation in Latin America, Africa and Asia. A*

advantageous to do so, either because of the similarity of the monetary provisions in the various arrangements as in Western Europe, or because the stability of certain of the arrangements is open to question as in Africa, attention is focused on select arrangements within that particular geographic region. For example, in Western Europe, where no fewer than six such economic associations are currently in force, only the monetary provisions of the Treaty of Rome will be considered in detail, with the equivalent provisions of E.F.T.A., Benelux, etc., being referred to on a comparative basis only. Similarly, of the several associations in Africa, only two, the Monetary Union of West Africa and the East African Common Market, will be the subject of examination.

Finally, for reasons already mentioned, the 'Group of Ten' and the sterling and franc areas will be dealt with separately.

To summarize, therefore, the following review will consider: (1) the 'Group of Ten'; (2) the sterling and franc areas; (3) the O.E.C.D., and finally the monetary arrangements of: (4) Western Europe; (5) Africa; and (6) Latin America.

2. 'Group of Ten'

The 'Group of Ten' is composed of the ten leading industrial nations of the Western world, namely Belgium, Canada, France, West Germany, Italy, Japan, the Netherlands, Sweden, the United Kingdom, and the United States. It came into existence in 1961 when these ten countries in conjunction with the Fund concluded the General Arrangements to Borrow (G.A.B.).[1] As mentioned, the Group of Ten does not possess a formal institu-

---

Handbook of Documents (1969) pp. 284–303, 313–17, and 543–54 respectively. For a discussion of the economic features of the Arab Common Market, see Muhammad Diab, 'The Arab Common Market', 4 *Journal of Common Market Studies* (1964–5) pp. 238–50. However, a free trade agreement (with monetary provisions similar to those found in E.F.T.A.) entered into force between New Zealand and Australia on 1 Jan. 1966. For the text of this agreement see 5 I.L.M. (1966) pp. 305 –15. See S. I. Picker, Jr., 'Pacific Partnership: the New Zealand–Australia Free Trade Agreement', 7 *Melbourne University Law Review* (1969) pp. 67–96.

[1] Although not a permanent member, Switzerland also participates in the Group's activities and has agreed to lend money within the over-all framework of the General Arrangements to Borrow. See *I.M.F. Annual Report* (1964) pp. 138–40 and *I.M.F. Annual Report* (1968) p. 108. See also *Selected Decisions*, pp. 69–72. In July 1972, a "Committee of Twenty" was established within the framework of the Fund for the purpose of dealing with the matter of international monetary reform and related issues.

tional framework, but rather operates, by and large, on an informal pragmatic basis, meeting as and when the international monetary situation requires.

The Group is of interest to the student of international monetary law only to the extent that it represents the interests of the wealthiest nations of the Western world and is thereby able to influence the development of international monetary law in much the same way as, for instance, 'Parliamentary Lobbyists' are able to influence the form and substance of municipal legislation. The most recent example of this type of activity, apart from their participation in the General Arrangements to Borrow, is the prominent role which the ten countries played in the formation of the special drawing rights facility. In fact, a historical review of the events preceding the adoption of the Fund's draft amendments on special drawing rights in April 1968 clearly reveals that it was the Group of Ten which by and large determined the actual form and substance of the new facility.[1] Moreover, subsequent practice would suggest that the members of the Group of Ten also enjoy a privileged position in the actual operation of the scheme.[2]

In addition, the Group of Ten is able to exert considerable influence on the nature and substance of Fund policies and decisions because of the built-in privileged position which its members enjoy in that institution's principal executive body, that is, the Executive Directors. Of the five permanent Fund Directors, four (United States, United Kingdom, Germany, and France) are also members of the Group of Ten. Indeed, during the general review of quotas in 1965, Canada agreed to forgo the full quota increase that was its due because this would have cost India fifth place in the league table, and with it the right to have a permanent Executive Director with the Fund. However, when the 1970 quota changes came into effect

---

[1] For a detailed résumé of the events leading up to the adoption of the new facility, see *Keesing's Contemporary Archives* (1967–8) pp. 22691–7.

[2] In this respect it will be remembered that the provisions of the Agreement are so formulated (Art. XXIV) as to ensure that all participants in the scheme have a voice in deciding whether or not there is a need to increase reserves by the allocation of S.D.R.s. In fact, however, in the decision-making process which gave rise to the initial allocation, only the opinions of the member States of the Group of Ten appear to have been considered. See the *Financial Times*, 4 June, 6 June, 28 June, 30 June, 25 July 1969 at pp. 38, 32, 24, 1, and 1 respectively. See also *The Economist*, 19 July 1969, p. 65.

in 1970, fifth place in the league table went to Japan with a quota of $1,200 million compared with India's quota of $940 million.[1] This has further strengthened the predominance of the Group of Ten within the Fund, 'a tendency which the Fund officials understandably dislike'.[2] Moreover, when one considers that the membership of the Group of Ten nearly coincides with that of the Working Party No. 3 (a subcommittee set up by the Economic Policy Committee of the O.E.C.D. to review on a regular basis the monetary and fiscal policies of O.E.C.D. members in the light of current economic developments with special reference to balance of payments disequilibria), and that the central banks of much the same group of countries are represented at the monthly meetings of the Bank for International Settlements in Basle, the real influence of the countries composing the Group of Ten in shaping international monetary relations should not be underestimated.

However, it is not the object of this study to examine the underlying political and economic forces which influence the course of development of international monetary relations. That is, more properly, the concern of the economist and political scientist. From the lawyer's viewpoint, it will suffice to take note that such forces, of which the Group of Ten clearly is one, do exist, that they enjoy a privileged position in the international monetary arena, and that they are thereby able to influence both the substance and the application of international monetary law.[3]

3. The Sterling and Franc Areas

(i) *The sterling area.* Although the origins of what in common parlance is referred to as the 'sterling area' date back to the nineteenth century when the commercial and financial supremacy of Great Britain made sterling the key world

---

[1] 24 *International Financial Statistics* (Feb. 1971) pp. 8–9.

[2] *The Times,* 23 July 1969, p. 23. It has also been suggested by both prominent international monetary lawyers and international monetary economists that a shift of monetary power has occurred from the Fund to the 'Group of Ten'. See Fawcett, 'Trade and Finance in International Law', 123 R.C. (1968–I) p. 295.

[3] For a discussion of 'The Concept of International Monetary Power', see E. A. Birnbaum, 'Gold and the International Monetary System: an Orderly Reform', 66 *Princeton Essays in International Finance* (1968) pp. 5–6.

currency, it was not until 1931 that the sterling area became a clearly recognizable entity,[1] and it was not until 1947, under the aegis of the Exchange Control Act,[2] that the area acquired some degree of legal formality. In that Act the members of the sterling area are referred to as the 'scheduled territories' and are singled out for special treatment in respect of United Kingdom exchange control regulations. This special treatment stems from Sections 5 and 6 of the Act which provide—in essence—that all payments to persons resident *outside* the scheduled territories require Treasury permission.[3] The fact that the scheduled territories 'are excluded from the need for permission is the legal basis of their existence'.[4] Accordingly, when considered from the viewpoint of United Kingdom exchange control legislation, 'The area comprises the group of territories within which residents may pay or receive from other residents without conflicting with the provisions of the Exchange Control Act 1947 . . .'[5] In this respect, therefore, the term 'sterling area' is synonymous with the term 'scheduled territories', although the former term does not appear anywhere in the Act. Prior to June 1972, included in the scheduled territories—and therefore in the sterling area—were all the nations of the British Commonwealth (with the exception of Canada and Rhodesia) plus a small number of other non-Commonwealth countries.[6]

---

[1] For a description of the various phases in the historical evolution of the sterling area, see F. Hirsch, op. cit. pp. 347–60. See also J. E. S. Fawcett, *The British Commonwealth in International Law* (1963) pp. 235–9 for a brief discussion of the legal aspects of the sterling area.

[2] *Exchange Control: The Act and the Instruments as in operation on 1st November, 1968* (H.M.S.O., 1968).

[3] For a brief explanation of the legal effect of these provisions, see Mann, *The Legal Aspect of Money*, pp. 348–53. The economic rationale of those provisions is explained by Hirsch, op. cit. p. 351: 'The logic of allowing payments out of Britain freely to these countries was that they would themselves continue to hold the sterling; either building it up in their reserves or using it for payments to Britain . . . or between themselves.'

[4] F. R. Ryder, 'The Sterling Area', 1 J.W.T.L. (1967) p. 179.

[5] Ibid. p. 180.

[6] In addition to the United Kingdom which includes the Channel Islands and the Isle of Man, the members, in 1970 were: Australia, Barbados, Botswana, Ceylon, Cyprus, The Gambia, Ghana, Guyana, Iceland, India, Irish Republic, Jamaica, Hashemite Kingdom of Jordan, Kenya, State of Kuwait, Lesotho, Malawi, Malaysia, Malta, Mauritius, New Zealand, Nigeria, Pakistan, Western Samoa, Sierra Leone, Singapore, South Africa, South West Africa, People's Republic of Southern Yemen, Swaziland, Tanzania, Trinidad and Tobago, Uganda, and

As a financial institution, the sterling area, like the Commonwealth itself, 'is a free and loose association of countries working together for a common purpose. It has no formal constitution and no formal set of regulations'.[1] The monetary code of conduct to which the member States subscribe and which gives the area its cohesion, namely that

(a) the members use sterling as the normal means of external settlement;
(b) they hold the major part of their reserves in sterling;
(c) they look to the United Kingdom as a major source of external capital;
(d) they co-operate to maintain the strength of sterling . . .[2]

rests largely on tradition and usage, and not on legal obligation. However, even in this traditionally informal institution a certain measure of international legal formality has recently been introduced. Following the devaluation of sterling in November 1967, the sterling area countries, which, in keeping with the unwritten code of conduct, held a portion of their reserves in sterling, suddenly found their sterling holdings reduced by 14·3 per cent in terms of dollar purchasing power. To protect themselves against any such future losses (and as part of a more broadly-based effort to give the sterling reserve system greater stability),[3] each of the thirty-eight sterling area countries[4] entered into a formal agreement[4] (Exchanges of

Zambia, together with all British Dominions, Protectorates, Protected States, and Trust Territories not previously mentioned, except Canada and Rhodesia. The Maldive Islands are administratively treated as being within the sterling area. See *Exchange Control. The Act and the Instruments as in operation on 1st November 1968* (H.M.S.O., 1968). In June 1972 the sterling area was effectively reduced to four members only, the United Kingdom, the Channel Islands, the Isle of Man, and the Republic of Ireland.

[1] R. B. Looper, 'The Significance of Regional Market Arrangements', *University of Illinois Law Forum* (1959) p. 373.   [2] F. R. Ryder, op. cit. p. 184.
[3] See *The Basle Facility and the Sterling Area* (Oct. 1968) Cmnd. 3787, reproduced in the *Financial Times*, 15 Oct. 1968, p. 23. The object of this Facility was succinctly summarized in a United Nations Report entitled *International Monetary System— Issues Relating to Development Finance and Trade of Developing Countries, October 23, 1968* (TD/B/198) p. 11, para. 20. See also B. J. Cohen, 'The Reform of Sterling', 77 *Princeton Essays in International Finance* (1969).
[4] The main elements in these Agreements are uniform for all sterling area countries, although there are certain differences of form. However, in the cases of Australia and New Zealand, where the Voluntary Programme of restraint on investment from the United Kingdom applied, an additional provision was included that if during the life of the Agreements the United Kingdom imposed

Notes and Letters) with the United Kingdom in which the latter undertook to guarantee the value, in terms of the United States dollar, of a defined part of each country's official sterling reserves. Accordingly, in the event of any further devaluation of sterling against the United States dollar during the life of the Agreements, the United Kingdom would be legally obliged to make a payment in sterling to each country to restore the dollar value of the guaranteed portion of each country's sterling balances.[1] As a *quid pro quo* for the United Kingdom guarantee, each of the thirty-eight countries undertook to maintain not less than an agreed proportion of its total reserves in sterling. The agreed proportion is referred to as the Minimum Sterling Proportion and is fixed by consultation between the governments.[2]

The Agreements which came into force on 25 September 1968 were effective for an initial period of three years, and could be extended for a further two years by mutual consent. During the life of these Agreements and to the extent provided therein, the sterling reserve system no longer rested solely 'on informal undertakings, on political, historical, commercial and other facts',[3] but assumed a formal legal character. The introduction of this element of legal formality in turn injected a measure of certainty and confidence into the system which, as the following observation points out, was advantageous both to the United Kingdom and to the other sterling area countries:

By ensuring the smooth functioning of the sterling system the new arrangements are thus a contribution to world monetary stability. They will benefit sterling area countries who, although they have accepted certain limitations on their freedom as regards the disposition of their reserves, now have a guarantee and will benefit from the strengthening of confidence in sterling which the arrangements

further restrictions on the flow of capital from the United Kingdom to these countries, there would be immediate consultation between the parties. For the actual Agreements, see *Exchange of Despatches and Letters concerning the Guarantee by the United Kingdom and the Maintenance of the Minimum Sterling Proportion by Certain Overseas Sterling Area Governments* (Nov. 1968) Cmnd. 3834, Cmnd. 3835.

[1] For a practical explanation of this undertaking, see *The Economist*, 28 Sept. 1968, p. 64.

[2] In this respect, for example, Australia has undertaken to maintain a Minimum Sterling Proportion of 40 per cent of total reserves, Cmnd. 3834, p. 8.

[3] F. A. Mann, 'Money in Public International Law', 96 R.C. (1959–I) p. 35.

as a whole should bring. The United Kingdom too will gain. The arrangements do not make any direct contribution to the problem of the balance of payments, nor do they in any way lessen the need for the United Kingdom to earn substantial surpluses. But they do mean that the United Kingdom reserves will not be vulnerable to demands resulting from large-scale movements out of sterling by countries which hold their reserves in our currency.[1]

(ii) *The franc area.* The franc area, or as it is more commonly referred to in French literature, 'la zone franc', originated as a by-product of the French colonial empire. It was merely the financial and economic expression for the territories under French tutelage. Indeed, until the gaining of independence by the majority of the States concerned in the late 1950s and early 1960s, the franc area consisted of Metropolitan France (that is, continental France plus Corsica, the Overseas Departments, and the Overseas Territories) and only four other sovereign States.[2]

The zone during this period was characterized by a number of economic and monetary features common to the entire area, namely: (i) a unified monetary structure;[3] (ii) uniform exchange controls;[4] (iii) a common pool of reserves;[4] (iv) preferential treatment in matters of trade and commerce;[5] and (v) free and unlimited convertibility of franc area currencies.[6] However, as might be expected in the light of the predominantly colonial structure of the area, these features were regulated not on the basis of sovereign equality but, as the following comment verifies, on the basis of French superiority: 'En somme tout le système ancien de la zone franc impliquait une rigoureuse centralisation du pouvoir en faveur du Gouvernement français, qui posait les règles de l'émission, contrôlait les budgets, les changes, le commerce extérieur, aussi bien que les investissements et la planification.'[7]

Since 1958,[8] however, the date of accession to independence

---

[1] Cmnd. 3787, p. 7.

[2] For an account of the legal features of the franc area as it existed before 1958, see René de Saint-Legier, 'La zone franc. Mécanismes. Problèmes internationaux', *Annuaire français de droit international* (1956) pp. 260–78.

[3] Ibid. pp. 263–4.   [4] Ibid. pp. 264–5.

[5] Ibid. pp. 265–6.   [6] Ibid. pp. 266–7.

[7] René de Lacharrière, 'L'évolution de la Communauté franco-africaine', *Annuaire français de droit international* (1960) p. 33.

[8] For a general account of the legal developments which have occurred within

of the majority of the French colonial dependencies, the franc area has undergone a substantial legal alteration. While the area has by and large retained the five principal features enumerated above—at least, as will be seen, in respect of fourteen States—the underlying principle upon which these features are formulated has changed. They are no longer based on the principle of French superiority, but rather on the principle of sovereign equality between the newly emergent States and France.

The area today consists of three distinct groups of countries and territories. The three groups are distinguishable from one another according to the nature of their monetary links with France:[1] (a) those States which, upon gaining independence, decided to maintain close monetary links with France on an international legal basis; (b) those States which, upon gaining independence, decided to maintain monetary links with France of a looser and more informal nature; (c) those territories which have not yet attained independence, and whose monetary arrangements with France are therefore a matter of domestic jurisdiction.

The first group, which is by far the largest and of most importance and interest to the student of international monetary law, comprises fourteen countries, namely those which belong to the West African Monetary Union (Dahomey, Ivory Coast, Mauritania, Niger, Senegal, Togo, Upper Volta, and Mali[2]), those which belong to the Monetary Union of Equatorial Africa and Cameroon (Cameroon, Central African Republic, Chad, Congo, and Gabon), and the Malagasy Republic. On

the zone since 1958, see P. Velles, 'Development of the Franc Area and of Franco-African Monetary Co-operation', 2 J.W.T.L. (1968) pp. 89–96. For a recent account of the economic features of the zone, see 'The CFA Franc System', 10 I.M.F. Staff Papers (1963), pp. 345–96; J. V. Mládek, 'Evolution of African Currencies. Part I: The Franc Area', 1 F.D. (1964) pp. 81–8; 'Financial Arrangements of Countries Using the CFA Franc', 16 I.M.F. Staff Papers (1969) pp. 289–387. For more particular details of both an economic and a legal nature, see the annual report of the franc zone, La Zone franc, Rapport publié par le Secrétariat général du Comité monétaire de la Zone franc (Paris, 1956 to date).

[1] This is a distinction which is made by the Monetary Committee of the franc zone, see La Zone franc en 1967, pp. 7–9.

[2] By January 1970, Mali had not yet become a full member of the West African Monetary Union, but had entered into bilateral arrangements with France as a transitional step towards becoming a full member, see La Zone franc en 1967, p. 8.

gaining their independence, each of these fourteen countries entered into agreement with France for co-operation in economic, monetary, and financial matters (Accord de coopération en matière économique, monétaire et financière).[1] These Agreements placed on an international legal basis those five features of the franc area mentioned above that had previously owed their existence either to French municipal law or to long-standing usage and practice. Since all of these Agreements are in the main similar, only the provisions of one such treaty—that is, Accord de coopération en matière économique, monétaire et financière entre la République française et la République du Cameroun—will be referred to here for the purpose of illustration.

The first provisions of importance of this 'Accord' which merit special mention are Articles 1 and 2. These provisions make it clear that both parties, being sovereign States as well as members of the franc area, will continue to co-operate in monetary matters:

Article 1: The Cameroons Republic declares that it intends to promote its development in close association with the French Republic and the other countries of the Franc area, while availing itself of opportunities of trade with the other countries of the world.

Article 2: The contractual association of the Cameroons and the

---

[1] For the text of Accord de coopération en matière monétaire, économique et financière [hereinafter referred to simply as Accord] signé le 27 juin 1960 entre la République française et la République malgache, see *Journal officiel de la République française* [hereinafter referred to simply as J.O.] 20 juillet 1960, pp. 6612–15. For the text of this treaty in English, see 87 *Journal du droit international* (1960) pp. 1113–19. Accord conclus le 15 août 1960 entre la République française, la République centrafricaine, la République du Congo et la République du Tchad, see J.O. 24 nov. 1960, pp. 10461–3. Accord conclus le 17 août 1960 entre la République française et la République gabonaise, see J.O. 24 nov. 1960, pp. 10484–6. Accord conclus le 13 nov. 1960 entre la République française et la République du Cameroun, see J.O. 9 août 1961, pp. 7429–32. For the text of this treaty in English, see 88 *Journal du droit international* (1961) pp. 1205–15. Accord conclus le 24 avril 1961 entre la République française et la République de Côte-d'Ivoire, see J.O. 6 fév. 1962, pp. 1212–63. For the text of this treaty in English, see 89 *Journal du droit international* (1962) pp. 795–803. Accord conclus le 24 avril 1961 entre la République française et la République du Dahomey, see J.O. 6 fév. 1962, pp. 1277–9. Accord conclus le 24 avril 1961 entre la République française et la République du Niger, see J.O. 6 fév. 1962, pp. 1292–4. Accord conclus le 24 avril 1961 entre la République française et la République de Haute-Volta, see J.O. 6 fév. 1962, pp. 1307–9. Accord conclus le 19 juin 1961 entre la République française et la République islamique de Mauritanie, see J.O. 6 fév. 1962, pp. 1328–30.

French Republic within the franc area is based on two fundamental principles:

Each of the two States retains the totality of its economic and financial powers, which are a prerogative of sovereign States.

The member States agree to the coordination of their external and financial policies within the framework of joint institutions, so as to lend mutual assistance to one another and promote the economic development of each one of them as rapidly as possible.

Articles 12 to 17 deal with trade, and clearly illustrate that although the Cameroons Republic as an independent State has the sovereign right to determine the nature of its external commercial policy, its trading arrangements are to be established and maintained in such a way as to ensure preferential treatment for France and the franc area as a whole. In respect of commercial sovereignty, Article 12 states:

The external commercial and financial policies of the Cameroons Republic shall be a matter for its exclusive sovereignty. It shall, *inter alia*, as of right negotiate and sign with all countries, whether members of the Franc area or not, as well as with all international organisations, commercial treaties or agreements, customs agreements and financial agreements. The Cameroons Republic shall also sovereignly determine its tariffs and quotas policies.

However, this right of sovereign determination is extensively restricted by Articles 13–17. For example, under the relevant portion of Article 13 both States 'agree that their trade relations shall be governed by a reciprocally preferential régime' and that 'The object of such preferential régime will be to ensure privileged trade outlets to each of the Parties'. In the wider context of preferential treatment for the entire franc area, Articles 14, 15, and 17 provide respectively:

Article 14: The Cameroons Republic and the French Republic agree to coordinate their policies in regard to trade with third parties. It is agreed between the Parties that they shall hold consultations with each other within the Franco-Cameroons Commission on the subject of their imports plan. It is also agreed that consultations will be held within the same commission, or any other institution consisting of several members of the Franc area, or all of them, every time one of the Parties intends to prepare the negotiation of agreements, conventions, commercial and financial treaties, or payments agreements, whose content is of substantial interest to the partners.

Article 15: The two Governments shall keep each other informed of all steps which they envisage taking susceptible of bringing about a change in the customs régime, so as to enable the general customs régime of the Cameroons to be harmonised with those of other countries of the Franc area.

Article 17: The Cameroons shall benefit from the advantages flowing from the organisation of markets and financial association concerning basic products within the Franc area. It shall be a member of all bodies concerned with tropical products.

The Cameroons Government will be consulted prior to any modifications in the organisation of markets as well as prior to the setting up of new institutions. The Cameroons Government for its part undertakes to comply with the general rules and directives laid down in this field for the whole of the Franc area, subject to any adjustments deemed necessary and jointly agreed upon within the Franco-Cameroons Commission.

Articles 18–21 deal with international payments and the pooling and use of the reserves of the franc area. Article 18 requires that all foreign exchange transactions be conducted on the Paris exchange market: 'All takings from and payment to countries outside the Franc area by the Cameroons shall be executed by way of surrender or purchase of foreign currencies on the central exchange market of the Franc area.' For this purpose a special dollar account entitled 'Cameroons—drawing rights' is established with the French Stabilization Exchange Fund. Certain agreed international receipts and payments by the Cameroons Republic must be conducted through that account. Moreover, should the Cameroons Republic find that it requires more currency than is available in its account, Article 20 provides that the 'Cameroons—drawing rights' account may if necessary 'be credited by a supplementary allocation of drawing rights on the general reserves of the Franc area'.

Articles 22 and 23 ensure that the Cameroons exchange control regulations will conform with those prevailing in the franc area:

Article 22: Subject to any adjustments deemed necessary in the light of local requirements, determined within the Franco-Cameroons Commission, the Cameroons Republic undertakes to apply within its territory the exchange control regulations of the Franc area. The French and Cameroon authorities will cooperate to repress any infringements to these regulations.

Article 23: Coordination of exchange control and commercial and economic policy shall be ensured in the Cameroons by cooperation between the Cameroons Republic and the central authorities of the Franc area, in the conditions stipulated in the above paragraph . . .

Part IV of the Accord—entitled 'currency'—deals with the monetary unit of account and convertibility. Article 26 provides in part that 'the legal currency for the whole of the territory of the Cameroons shall be the C.F.A. Franc issued by the central bank of the States of Equatorial Africa and the Cameroons'. Since the C.F.A. franc is defined in terms of the French franc,[1] Article 31 states: 'Any modification in the parity between the monetary unit of the Cameroons and the French Franc shall be effected only by agreement between both parties'. As a *quid pro quo*, the second paragraph of the same Article provides: 'The Government of the French Republic will, as far as possible, consult the Government of the Cameroons Republic prior to any devaluation or revaluation of the French Franc.'[2] Finally, Article 27 states: 'There shall be full convertibility between the currency issued by the central bank of the States of Equatorial Africa and the Cameroons, and the French Franc. There is no restriction on transfers of funds between France and the Cameroons, and *vice versa*.'

The above provisions have been cited in detail in order to make it abundantly clear that in so far as the fourteen States which have concluded such Agreements with France are concerned, the principal features of the franc area, namely (i) preferential treatment in trade, (ii) pooling of reserves, (iii) common exchange controls, (iv) unified monetary structure, and (v) convertibility, have been placed on an international legal basis. For this group of States, therefore, the franc area

---

[1] The official currency unit, the C.F.A. franc, has a fixed relationship to the French franc of 50 C.F.A. francs per French franc. Transactions in French francs are made at fixed buying and selling rates, and exchange rates for other currencies move with the French franc rates for those currencies.

The C.F.A. franc was established as the monetary unit of the French non-metropolitan areas in Africa in Dec. 1945. The initials formerly stood for Colonies françaises d'Afrique, and now stand for Communauté financière africaine.

[2] For the procedure followed by France *vis-à-vis* the franc area countries with respect to the devaluation of the French franc on 8–10 Aug. 1969, see *The Times*, 9 Aug. 1969, p. 1.

has a definite legal content and shape. In addition to these bilateral treaties, however, certain of these States have concluded among themselves further monetary arrangements, such as the Monetary Union of West Africa. This development will be examined in more detail in Section 6 of the study under regional monetary arrangements in Africa.

The second group of States within the franc zone is made up of Algeria, Morocco, and Tunisia. These three States have for several years not allowed the free transfer of funds to the other countries of the zone and vice versa. Moreover, they have adopted independent policies on reserves, and their monetary units of account are not defined in terms of French francs but rather in terms of gold. However, they do maintain preferential commercial links with France, and are also extended special financial assistance by France. For example, by agreement with France, Morocco and Tunisia can have recourse in times of need—albeit to a limited extent—to the Stabilization Exchange Fund.[1]

Finally, the third group within the franc area comprises those territories which have not yet attained independence, namely the Overseas Departments and the Overseas Territories. Since these territories are deemed to be part of Metropolitan France, their monetary and economic associations with France fall outside the realm of international law and need not be considered here.

4. The O.E.C.D.

(i) *Terms of reference.* Of the several regional arrangements considered in this chapter, perhaps the most important and yet the most neglected—from the viewpoint of international monetary law—is the Organization for Economic Cooperation and Development (O.E.C.D.). The O.E.C.D. officially came into existence in September 1961 as successor to the Organization for European Economic Cooperation (O.E.E.C.), which had itself been created in 1945 to administer the Marshall Aid

---

[1] See *La Zone franc en 1967*, p. 8. These three countries plus Libya constitute the so-called Maghrib States. Some measure of economic co-operation has been undertaken by these four countries: see M. S. Wionczek (ed.), *Economic Cooperation in Latin America, Africa and Asia. A Handbook of Documents* (1969) pp. 304–12.

Plan and to aid in the general European economic recovery from the Second World War.[1] Unlike its predecessor, membership in the O.E.C.D., which currently numbers twenty-two, is not restricted to Western European countries, but includes as full members Canada, the United States of America, and Japan.[2] In addition, Australia and New Zealand participate in some of its activities.[3]

Frequently referred to as the 'rich men's club'[4] because its membership consists primarily of the leading industrialized nations of the world, its importance as an international monetary institution is probably second only to that of the International Monetary Fund.[5] Indeed, certain of the legal arrangements created and operated under the auspices of the O.E.C.D. exceed those of the Fund itself. This is particularly so in the case of exchange restrictions. Here the O.E.C.D.'s 'Code of Liberalisation of Capital Movements' (hereinafter referred to as the Capital Code), which has as its objective the progressive liberalization of restrictions on capital movements,[6] and the O.E.C.D.'s 'Code of Liberalisation of Current Invisible Operations' (hereinafter referred to as the Current Invisible Code), which specifically spells out item by item the current invisible operations which are to be freed of all

[1] For the text of both conventions, see Peaslee, *International Governmental Organizations, Volume II* (1961) pp. 1624–38. For the rules of procedure of the O.E.C.D., see XIV E.Y. (1966) pp. 131 ff. For a brief résumé of the historical events that led up to the signing of the Convention on 15 Apr. 1948, and a brief institutional analysis, see Donald Mallett, 'The History and Structure of O.E.E.C.', I E.Y. (1955) pp. 62–70. For a chronological review of the events leading to the change-over of the O.E.E.C. into the O.E.C.D., see VIII E.Y. (1960) pp. 275–363. For an institutional analysis of the O.E.C.D. with references, see A. H. Robertson, *European Institutions* (1966) pp. 65–85.

[2] Except for the subsequent addition of Finland (Finland became a full member of the O.E.C.D. only in Jan. 1969, see 39 *O.E.C.D. Observer* (1969)), the current European membership of the O.E.C.D. is the same as was the original European membership of the O.E.E.C., namely: Austria, Belgium, Denmark, France, Germany, Greece, Iceland, Ireland, Italy, Luxemburg, Netherlands, Norway, Portugal, Spain, Sweden, Switzerland, Turkey, and the United Kingdom.

[3] See Thorkil Kristensen, 'Five Years of O.E.C.D.', XIII E.Y. (1965) p. 103.

[4] G. Schwarzenberger, *Foreign Investments and International Law* (1969) p. 35; John Calmann (ed.), *Western Europe A Handbook* (1967) p. 624.

[5] Kristensen, op. cit. p. 103.

[6] Referring to the Capital Code, a report published by the O.E.E.C. states: 'The O.E.E.C. is the first international organisation to have adopted a legal instrument of this kind for international capital movements.' *Liberalisation of Current Invisibles and Capital Movements* (O.E.E.C., Paris, 1961, C/60/98) p. 20.

restrictions, both surpass the Fund's Article VIII provisions. Moreover, when one considers that the liberalization measures contained in both the above-mentioned codes are to be extended where possible not only to all O.E.C.D. member States and their overseas territories but to all other members of the International Monetary Fund as well,[1] it is apparent that the O.E.C.D.'s impact upon the contemporary development of international monetary law is very pronounced indeed.

In addition to the above-mentioned Codes, the O.E.C.D. also fulfils certain liquidity and exchange rate functions through its operation of the European Monetary Agreement (E.M.A.). However, the provisions of this latter agreement have a more restricted applicability owing to the E.M.A.'s exclusively European membership.

Before examining the two Codes and the E.M.A. in detail, however, a brief review of certain of the monetary activities of the O.E.C.D.'s predecessor, the O.E.E.C., will be undertaken. This preliminary review will examine the O.E.E.C.'s achievements in liberalizing and ultimately abolishing—through the instrumentality of international law—commercial and exchange restrictions[2] which had 'kept international trade, and particularly intra-European trade, in a kind of strait-jacket during the period immediately following the war'.[3]

(ii) *The O.E.E.C. (commercial and exchange restrictions)*. Article 4 of the Convention for European Economic Cooperation dealt with the issue of financial and commercial restrictions to trade and provided in part thus:

The contracting parties will develop in mutual cooperation the maximum possible interchange of goods and services. To this end they will continue the efforts already initiated to achieve as soon as possible multilateral systems of payments among themselves and will cooperate in relaxing restrictions on trade and payments between one another, with the object of abolishing as soon as possible those restrictions which at present hamper such trade and payments.[4]

[1] See *Code of Liberalisation of Capital Movements* (Jan. 1969), Art. 1, paras. (c) and (d), and *Code of Liberalisation of Current Invisible Operations* (Nov. 1967), Art. 1, paras. (c) and (d).

[2] In addition to dealing with exchange restrictions, the 1948 Convention also dealt with exchange rates, see Article 7.

[3] *Liberalisation of Current Invisibles and Capital Movements* (O.E.E.C., Paris, 1961, C/60/98) p. 12.

[4] Art. 6 of the Convention further provided: 'The contracting parties will co-

Although the aim of this provision was clear—namely the replacement of the existing bilateral trade and payments regime by a multilateral system—its phraseology was so vague as to leave the desired objective virtually unattainable. To give positive and precise effect to this and the other 'General Obligations'[1] of the Convention, the Council—the supreme organ of the O.E.E.C.[2]—was, under Articles 13 and 14, given the power to adopt legally binding decisions[3] for the purpose of realizing the Convention's general aims. The main corpus of O.E.E.C. law (and indeed of the current O.E.C.D. law) is to be found, therefore, not in the provisions set out in the Convention itself, but rather in the subsequently adopted Council decisions. It is to these decisions, therefore, which it should be emphasized 'create obligations in international law for the *Member States*',[4] that one must look in order to ascertain the exact nature and scope of the international legal obligations which the member States assumed under the O.E.E.C. and are currently assuming as members of the O.E.C.D.

Accordingly, in implementing the provisions of Article 4, the Council, under the auspices of Article 14, adopted a series of decisions which were periodically amended and codified into an international legal instrument entitled 'The Code of Liberalisation'.[5] It was through the operation of this Code as well as

operate with other like-minded countries in reducing tariff and other barriers to the expansion of trade, with a view to achieving a sound and balanced multilateral trading system such as will accord with the principles of the Havana Charter.'

[1] The 'General Obligations' are set out in Arts. 2–9.
[2] Art. 15 (A): 'A Council composed of all the members shall be the body from which all decisions derive.'
[3] For a discussion of the decision-making power of the Organization, see Alexander Elkin, 'The Organization for European Economic Cooperation. Its Structure and Powers', IV E.Y. (1958) pp. 114–36.
[4] Ibid. p. 125.
[5] The first Code was adopted by a Council decision [C(50)258] of 18 Aug. 1950 and was entitled 'The Code of Liberalisation of Trade'. This first Code, however, was concerned only with visible trade. On 20 July 1951, the Council adopted 'The Code of Liberalisation' [C(50)325] which dealt with both visible and invisible transactions. The 1951 Code remained—in essence—the same for the following ten years, although a large number of amendments were adopted. With the transformation of the O.E.E.C. into the O.E.C.D. in 1961, that part of 'The Code of Liberalisation' which dealt with visible trade was discontinued, and only that part which dealt with invisible trade was continued. This part of the Code is now called the 'Code of Liberalisation of Current Invisible Operations' and will be considered in more detail later in this chapter. In this immediate section all references will be to the July 1960 version of the Code.

through the operation of the European Payments Union (E.P.U.)[1]—'two of the most effective international institutions ever created'[2]—that the aims of Article 4 were realized.

The task of the E.P.U. in this concerted effort was to provide a mechanism whereby intra-European payments could be settled on a regional European basis rather than, as had previously been the case, on a bilateral basis. Briefly, the E.P.U. settlement mechanism operated as follows.[3] At the end of each accounting period—that is, once a month—each member of the Union calculated on a bilateral basis the balance of payments position between itself and each other Union member. These several bilateral balances, which were all calculated on the basis of a uniform unit of account,[4] were then offset, leaving the member with a single residual balance. This residual balance was then settled, according to prescribed rules, between the member and the Union.[5]

In fact, therefore, the E.P.U. amounted to nothing more than a multilateral clearing arrangement or, as stated by one authority, a 'plurilateral transfer machinery'.[6] The Union, *per se*, did not and indeed was not intended to deal directly with the root cause of bilateralism—that is, the underlying trade and exchange restrictions themselves. Rather, the attack against these restrictive measures was to be the direct concern of the other member of the partnership—that is, the O.E.E.C.'s

[1] Following two previous and less effective attempts at establishing a payments union in Europe in 1948 and 1949 respectively, the agreement establishing the E.P.U. was signed by all members on 19 Sept. 1950. This agreement—with several subsequent amendments—remained in force until 27 Dec. 1958, when the majority of the member countries re-established partial convertibility, and the European Monetary Agreement (E.M.A.) entered into force. In this section all references will be to the 30 Nov. 1958 version of the E.P.U.

[2] R. Marjolin, 'L' O. E. C. E. et le développement de la coopération économique européenne', I E.Y. (1955) p. 60.

[3] For a more detailed analysis of the European Payments Union see Yves Biclet, 'L'Union européenne des paiements', II E.Y. (1956) pp. 151–82; Hug, 'The Law of International Payments', 79 R.C. (1951–II) pp. 678–709.

[4] Art. 26, paras. (*a*) and (*b*).

[5] Art. 3: 'For the realisation of the purposes of the Union, operations (hereinafter referred to as the "operations") shall be carried out periodically whereby the bilateral surpluses and deficits of each Contracting Party shall be offset and the residual net surplus or deficit towards all other Contracting Parties taken together shall be settled with the Union in accordance with the provisions of the present Agreement.'

[6] Hug, op. cit. p. 578.

Code of Liberalisation. However, this is not to suggest that the E.P.U. did not play an important and indeed indispensable role in the liberalization of intra-European trade. On the contrary, by providing an automatic mechanism for the multilateral settlement of balances, the Union elevated the matter of payments equilibrium from the bilateral to the regional European level. It was, therefore, under the E.P.U. mechanism no longer necessary for each member of the Union to balance its accounts bilaterally with each other Union member, and consequently the trade and exchange controls which had previously been necessary to maintain these bilateral balances could be gradually dismantled. In this respect the relevant part of Article 2 of the E.P.U. Convention provided as follows:[1]

The purposes of the Union shall be to facilitate, by means of a multilateral system of payments, the settlement of all transactions between the monetary areas of the Contracting Parties . . . *and thus* to assist the Contracting Parties to implement the decisions of the Organisation on commercial policy and the liberalisation of trade and of invisible transactions . . . [my italics]

As has been mentioned, the abolition of these restrictions was carried out by the Council of the O.E.E.C. through a series of decisions which were codified and embodied in the 'Code of Liberalisation'. The Code's approach in dealing with the underlying restrictions was a comprehensive one. It attacked the restrictions at three levels. First, from the viewpoint of commercial restrictions to trade, the Code obliged the member States to remove all quantitative restrictions to the extent provided, and in respect of the commodities enumerated, in the Code.[2] Secondly, from the viewpoint of exchange restrictions, all member States were obliged to co-ordinate their liberalization of financial restrictions with their liberalization of commercial restrictions. In other words, it was agreed that where a particular commodity had been freed from commercial control (that is, it was no longer subject to quantitative restrictions), payment for that commodity would automatically have to be allowed (that is, exchange restrictions could not apply in respect of payments for that commodity). In this

---

[1] See also Hug, op. cit. p. 680.
[2] Arts. 1 and 2 of the Code.

respect Section I, paragraph 1 of Annex A of the Code provided:

Measures of liberalisation of trade shall consist in the abolition of quantitative restrictions on the importation of commodities which are the object of these measures, whether this abolition results from the admission of such commodities without licensing or from the automatic and immediate issue of licences for their importation. *Measures of liberalisation of trade must provide for the automatic allocation of the foreign exchange required for such imports* [my italics].

Thirdly, from the viewpoint of invisibles, all members were obliged automatically to permit all invisible transactions and payments for such invisible transactions when they related to trade in a liberalized commodity. In this respect Article 14 of the Code provided:[1] 'Member countries shall abolish all restrictions on current invisible transactions connected with the movement of commodities which are the object of measures of liberalisation of trade taken in accordance with Article I.' The combined effect of the above provisions was such that commodities liberated in accordance with Article 1 of the Code were freed not only from commercial restrictions—that is, quantitative restrictions—but also from exchange restrictions and from any restrictions on invisibles connected with the liberated goods. In this way, the O.E.E.C. was able, owing to the flexibility of its constitutional structure (that is, in the generality of its aims and in its wide powers to take legally binding decisions) and its jurisdiction over both financial and commercial matters (it will be remembered that at the global level there is a division of power between the Fund and the G.A.T.T. in respect of financial and commercial matters), to strike in one blow at the very heart of its members' restrictive regimes. Indeed, the effect of the O.E.E.C.'s programme was so immediate that in its First Annual Report, only one year after the initiation of the E.P.U. and the Code, the Board of Management of the E.P.U. was able to report:

The discrimination, at least on currency grounds, against countries such as Belgium, Switzerland and Germany, which was a disturbing factor in the relationships between the members in the past few

---

[1] In respect of invisibles see also Arts. 13, 15, and 16 of the Code.

years, has been brought to an end. The results of the abolition of this discrimination in visible trade are already striking.[1]

In its second report the Board was able to state still more emphatically:

> After four years, the Organization can claim that these objectives have, to a large degree, been attained, and that the European Payments Union has contributed considerably to their attainment. The trade of the Member countries between themselves and with the overseas territories and the countries of the sterling area, is, in general, conducted on a non-discriminatory basis, and there has been a progressive relaxation of the restrictions imposed on such trade.[2]

Indeed, by 1960, the greater portion of intra-European trade had been so liberalized. That international law played a leading role in this achievement was made clear in the O.E.E.C.'s report on the Liberalisation of Current Invisibles and Capital Movements:

> Since 1951 the Code of Liberalisation has been the instrument of the Organisation's policy for liberalising trade and current invisibles. The Code represents the agreed consolidation, in a legal instrument, of progress achieved over the years. While it exists, there can be no retreat from liberalisation except in a recognised emergency and under precise rules. By accepting its provisions, the Members have been able to guarantee their residents effective freedom for practically all current financial transfers abroad, and for most current transactions.[3]

(iii) *The O.E.C.D. (Capital and Current Invisible Codes)*. With the transformation of the O.E.E.C. into the O.E.C.D., that part of the O.E.E.C.'s Code of Liberalisation which dealt with restrictions to visible trade was discontinued. It was felt that the international legal regulation of commercial and financial restrictions to visible trade should henceforth be the concern of the G.A.T.T. and the Fund respectively.

Nevertheless, in spite of its discontinuance of this aspect of its activities, it still remains one of the aims of the O.E.C.D.

---

[1] *European Payments Union First Annual Report of the Managing Board* (1951) p. 33.
[2] *European Payments Union Second Annual Report of the Managing Board* (1952) pp. 49–50.
[3] *Liberalisation of Current Invisibles and Capital Movements* (O.E.E.C., Paris, 1961, C/60/98) p. 18.

to promote policies designed 'to contribute to the expansion of world trade on a multilateral non-discriminatory
basis . . .'[1] In pursuit of this aim the member States have
agreed that they will, both individually and jointly 'pursue
their efforts to reduce or abolish obstacles to the exchange of
goods and services and current payments and maintain and
extend the liberalisation of capital movements . . .'[2] As already
mentioned, the Council, in pursuance of this provision, has
adopted under the auspices of Article 5 (a)[3] two Codes, one
dealing with capital movements[4] and the other dealing with
current invisible transactions.[5] Both these Codes, which are
currently in force, apply to all O.E.C.D. member States[6] and
contain a number of monetary provisions that have no counterpart in any other international agreement. This is particularly
so in the case of the Capital Code.

Before examining the provisions of the two Codes in detail,
however, three observations of a preliminary nature need to be
made.

First, the O.E.C.D.'s approach to liberalization—like the
approach adopted by the O.E.E.C.—is a comprehensive one.
Liberalization within the meaning of the O.E.C.D.'s two Codes
applies to both transfers and transactions. By this means, the
O.E.C.D. ensures not only that exchange control permission
for payments will be given in respect of the items annexed to
the two Codes, but also that such permission will not be frustrated by other, non-monetary restrictions, imposed on the
underlying transaction.

---

[1] Art. 1, para. (c) of the Convention of the O.E.C.D.

[2] Art. 2 (d) of the Convention.

[3] Art. 5 reads in part: 'In order to achieve its aims, the Organisation may:
(a) take decisions which, except as otherwise provided, shall be binding on all
the Members.'

[4] Although the Organization agreed for the first time in Dec. 1957 on some firm
obligations to liberalize investment capital, it was not until Dec. 1959 that all the
obligations and recommendations already agreed upon were embodied in a
Code of Liberalisation of Capital Movements. That Code has subsequently been
amended several times. In this section, all references will be to the Capital Code
as it existed in Jan. 1969.

[5] For the purposes of this section, all references will be to the Nov. 1967 version
of the Current Invisible Code.

[6] Canada does not adhere to the Capital Code. It should be noted, however,
that Canada has no exchange restrictions in respect of capital movements, *I.M.F.
Nineteenth Annual Report on Exchange Restrictions* (1968) p. 68.

Secondly, it should be noted that the O.E.C.D. has made no attempt in either Code to give any theoretical definition of what constitutes a current invisible or a capital transaction.[1] Rather, the transactions are classified according to their objects and are set out in comprehensive lists annexed to both Codes. For example, in Annex A of the Capital Code, which Annex is further subdivided into List A and List B, are enumerated item by item (with explanatory remarks where necessary) all the transactions and transfers which are to be liberalized. From the viewpoint of legal regulation, the advantage to be gained by such an approach is apparent. By setting out in detail, item by item, which capital movements are to be freed of restrictions, many ambiguities and uncertainties are removed. Each contracting party knows to a fairly well-defined degree its rights and obligations *vis-à-vis* each other contracting party. Difficulties such as those which arise under Article VIII and Article XIX (i) of the Fund Agreement in ascertaining whether a particular transaction is current or capital are thereby avoided. From the viewpoint of the lawyer—who, it must be admitted, is accustomed to dealing with specifics—the 'List' approach adopted by the O.E.C.D. is clearly preferable to the 'blanket' approach adopted by the Fund.

Thirdly, since the provisions in both Codes are, in the main, identical (subject, of course, to the proviso that the transactions which are the objects of liberalization differ), this analysis will refer only to the provisions of the Capital Code. Any observations made on the Capital Code will apply equally to the Current Invisible Code. Reference will be made to the Current Invisible Code only if and when a provision in that Code differs substantially from the corresponding provisions in the Capital Code.

As a general undertaking, all O.E.C.D. member States which adhere to the Capital Code are obliged by the terms of Article 1 (*a*) of that Code gradually to remove obstacles impeding capital movements to the extent necessary to ensure efficient economic co-operation. This general undertaking to liberalize is given a more specific formulation in Article 2 (*a*) which provides that

[1] But note the definitions which are set out by the O.E.E.C. in its report, *Liberalisation of Current Invisibles and Capital Movements* (O.E.E.C., Paris, 1961), C/60/98) Annex III, p. 45.

members must 'grant any authorization required for the conclusion or execution of transactions and for transfers specified
in an item set out in List A or List B of Annex A to this Code'.
As mentioned, the Lists annexed to the Code set out in detail
the capital movements which members must progressively
liberate. The distinction between List A and List B is related
to the matter of reservations and will be discussed in more
detail subsequently. It will suffice to note at this point that a
member can lodge a reservation in respect of any item in List
B at any time, while reservations to items in List A can be
lodged only at specified times.[1] Since a reservation has the effect
of exempting the item to which it applies from liberalization,
the practical effect of the distinction is that the obligation to
liberalize items in List A is much more rigorous than is the
obligation to liberalize items in List B. Originally the Current
Invisible Code similarly adopted the dual-List approach. Since
June 1965, however, no distinction has been made and all
items have been treated uniformly.[2] On the basis of the
precedent established by the Current Invisible Code, it can
probably be assumed that the Capital Code will also at some
future date abandon List B, thereby subjecting all capital movements to the strict regime of List A transactions.

In addition to obliging member States progressively to
abolish existing restrictions on those capital movements enumerated in Annex A, members must also endeavour to avoid
(1) introducing any new restrictions on the movement of
capital, and (2) making existing restrictions more restrictive.[3]
This so-called 'standstill' provision is intended to discourage
members from frustrating the process of liberalization by the
introduction of new restrictions or the intensification of existing
ones. However, it should be noted that members are required

[1] More specifically, Art. 2 (b) of the Capital Code provides:
'A Member may lodge reservations relating to the obligations resulting from
paragraph (a) when:
  (i) An item is added to List A of Annex A to this Code;
  (ii) Obligations relating to an item in that List are extended;
  (iii) Obligations relating to any such item begin to apply to that Member; or
  (iv) At any time, in respect of an item in List B.

Reservations shall be set out in Annex B to the Code'.
[2] Art. 2 (b) of the Current Invisible Code is similar in wording to Art. 2 (b) of
the Capital Code, except that sub-para. (iv) does not appear in the latter.
[3] Art. 1 (e).

only to 'endeavour' to comply with the standstill, which suggests that the obligation is more akin to a moral than to a legal requirement. Again, a similar standstill clause was included in the early versions of the Current Invisible Code; however, as the list of items to be liberalized gradually became more comprehensive, the standstill clause became redundant and was abolished.

Although the above-mentioned provisions impose a strict duty on the various member countries to abolish restrictions, this duty is greatly restricted by several exceptions and escape clauses. These various escape clauses will now be considered under the headings of (a) reservations, (b) derogations, and (c) public order and security clauses.

(a) Reservations. As has already been mentioned, a country, by entering a reservation in respect of any item(s) in Annex A, is exempted from its obligation to abolish restrictions in respect of the item(s) to which the reservation applies. All reservations are set out on a country-by-country basis in Annex B of the Code. The Organization is obliged to examine each reservation at intervals of not more than eighteen months[1] with a view 'to making suitable proposals designed to assist Members to withdraw their reservations'.[1] In practice, the number of reservations which are currently being applied varies considerably from member country to member country.[2] Japan, for example, continues to apply extensive reservations, in spite of the fact that since the adoption of its policy on the Liberalization of Foreign Investments in June 1967,[3] the intensity of its reservations has been greatly reduced. At the other extreme, however, Germany makes no reservations, and the United States[4] makes reservations only to a very limited extent.

[1] Art. 12 of the Capital Code.

[2] For the reservations which were being applied as at Jan. 1969, see Capital Code of Jan. 1969, pp. 61–151.

[3] For the English text of the Japanese Cabinet Decision of 6 June 1967 concerning the Liberalization of Inward Investments, see 6 I.L.M. (1967) pp. 1164–73. For a discussion of the compatibility of Japan's municipal laws on capital movements with its international obligations under the Capital Code, see 'Foreign Investment in Japan, a Change of Policy', 33 *O.E.C.D. Observer* (1968) pp. 43 ff. See also Y. Kanasawa, 'Accession of Japan to the Organization for Economic Cooperation and Development (O.E.C.D.) and the Liberalisation of Capital Movements', 11 *The Japanese Annual of International Law* (1967) pp. 24–36.

[4] For a discussion of the compatibility of the United States controls over capital outflows and its obligations under the Capital Code, see D. G. Carreau, 'The U.S.

Reservations to the Current Invisible Code are very few and are made mainly in respect of transport, insurance, and films.

(b) Derogations. The Capital Code allows members to derogate from their obligations in two ways. The first permitted derogation is intended for countries suffering from economic difficulties of a relatively long duration. Thus, if a member's general economic and financial situation justifies such a course, it need not take the whole of the measures prescribed in Article 2 (a),[1] and indeed the member may withdraw any measures of liberalization already taken or maintained if such measures result in serious economic and financial disturbances.[2] Iceland,[3] Turkey,[3] Greece,[4] and Portugal (on behalf of its overseas provinces)[5] are currently invoking the terms of this provision, and are therefore temporarily exempt from the obligations of the Code. Greece,[6] Turkey,[7] and Portugal (on behalf of its overseas provinces)[8] are also invoking a similar provision in respect of their obligations under the Current Invisible Code.

The second permitted derogation is intended for members encountering a temporary strain on their foreign currency reserves. Thus, if a country finds its balance of payments developing adversely at a rate and in circumstances which it considers serious in view of the state of its foreign currency reserves, it may temporarily suspend liberalization.[9] Members which derogate from their obligations under this latter provision, however, must endeavour to restore the original position within a period of twelve months and must comply fully with their obligations under Article 2 (a) within eighteen months.[10]

In both cases, however—that is, whether a member's derogation is due to economic difficulties of a long-term or short-term

Balance of Payments Programs. New Developments in the American Regulations of Capital Movements', 2 J.W.T.L. (1968) pp. 647–50.

[1] Art. 7, para. (a) of the Capital Code.
[2] Art. 7, para. (b) of the Capital Code.
[3] Council decision C(62)21 (Final) of 3 May 1962.
[4] Council decision C(64)95 (Final) of 28 July 1964.
[5] Council decision C/M(68)3, Item 32 of 20 Feb. 1968.
[6] Council decision C(64)95 (Final) of 28 July 1964.
[7] Council decision C(62)21 (Final) of 3 May 1962.
[8] Council decision C/M(68)3, Item 32 of 20 Feb. 1968.
[9] Art. 7, para. (c) of the Capital Code.
[10] Art. 7, para. (d) of the Capital Code.

nature—it must derogate in such a way as to avoid unnecessary damage to the financial or economic interests of another member, and, in particular, it must avoid discriminating between member States.[1] Moreover, all derogations must be notified—with reasons for their introduction—to the Organization[2] who will keep them under review until they are withdrawn.[3]

(c) *Public order and security.* This last exception is in fact tantamount to a general escape clause, since it permits a member, irrespective of the other provisions of the Code, to take any action which it deems necessary for—*inter alia*—the maintenance of public order, the protection of its essential security interests, etc.[4] The introduction of exchange controls to stem large outflows of capital in times of serious economic difficulties such as were experienced in France during 1968[5] would undoubtedly fall within the ambit of this provision.

Finally, in concluding this examination of the provisions of the Capital Code, attention should be drawn to what might well be regarded as the Code's central feature—that is, the incorporation into the Code of the principle of non-discrimination. This fundamental principle is to be applied by members in their application of the Code in two varieties of situation. Firstly, by virtue of Article 9, members may not 'discriminate as between other Members in authorising the conclusion and execution of transactions and transfers which are listed in Annex A and which are subject to any degree of liberalisation'. Thus members are bound to extend equally to all their O.E.C.D. partners the measures of liberalization they have decided to adopt. That is to say, one member State is not permitted to bargain bilaterally with another member State to secure reciprocal concessions. Rather, measures of liberalization must be extended equally to all O.E.C.D. member States.[6] Secondly,

---

[1] Art. 7, para. (*e*) of the Capital Code.
[2] Art. 13, para. (*a*) of the Capital Code.
[3] See generally Arts. 13, 14, and 15 of the Capital Code.
[4] Art. 3 of the Code.
[5] For a discussion of these developments in detail—in particular, exchange control in respect of capital movements—and their compatibility or otherwise with France's international obligations as a member of O.E.C.D. and E.E.C., see Pierre Jasinski, 'The Control of Capital Movements in France', 3 J.W.T.L. (1969) pp. 209–18.
[6] However, members forming part of a special customs or monetary system may apply to one another, in addition to measures of liberalization taken in

if any member finds it necessary to mitigate the full effect of
the Code either by lodging reservations under Article 2 (*b*) or
by invoking the derogation provisions of Article 7, the other
members are nevertheless legally obliged to continue to give
the member in difficulties the full benefit of their own liberalization measures.[1] Thus a member which is in economic difficulties and cannot itself liberalize must not be discriminated
against and will continue to receive the economic advantages
of liberalization granted by other members.

(iv) *O.E.C.D.* (*European Monetary Agreement*).[2] As stated in
the Preamble to the European Monetary Agreement[3] (E.M.A.),
one of the principal reasons for the conclusion of the Agreement was 'to establish an institutional framework for the con-
tinuance of monetary co-operation in Europe . . .' Monetary
co-operation in Europe had previously been conducted through
the European Payments Union, and with the demise of that
institution in 1958, the E.M.A., the text of which had already
been drafted in 1955 in anticipation of the E.P.U.'s demise,
came into force. In the succeeding ten years the E.M.A.
contributed to European monetary co-operation,[4] and indeed
in deciding in 1968 to renew the Agreement for a further three
years—that is, until the end of 1971[5]—the Board of Management stressed the continuing need for such co-operation in
contemporary Europe:

Moreover, the Board felt that in conditions such as characterised
1968—namely, a very large imbalance in international payments,
instability in the exchange markets, fears about the general level

accordance with the provisions of Art. 2 (*a*), other measures of liberalization without extending them to other members. See Art. 10 of the Capital Code.

[1] Art. 8 of the Capital Code.

[2] For the original text of the Agreement in French and English, see III E.Y.
(1957) pp. 213–55. For text of original Directives for the application of the European Monetary Agreement, see Council decision C(55)222 of 29 July 1955. For a
discussion of the institutional as well as functional features of the E.M.A., see
Alexander Elkin, 'The European Monetary Agreement: its Structure and Working', VII E.Y. (1960) pp. 148–74. In the following study references will be to the
1 Mar. 1966 version of the E.M.A. and the 1 Mar. 1966 version of the Directives.

[3] Unlike the membership of the O.E.C.D. itself, which includes other than
European States, e.g. Japan, U.S.A., and Canada, the membership of the E.M.A.
is purely European.

[4] For a résumé of the activities of the E.M.A. in the period 1958–68, see *European
Monetary Agreement, First Annual Report of the Board of Management* (1959) through
to the *Tenth Annual Report* (1968).

[5] See *E.M.A. Tenth Annual Report* (1968) p. 57.

of currency parities and a tendency to reintroduce controls and restrictions on international transactions—it is of the utmost importance to maintain and reinforce co-operation between monetary authorities. The European Monetary Agreement is a modest but useful part of the framework for such co-operation.[1]

The E.M.A., which is administered by a committee of eight independent experts called the Comité Directeur (Board of Management),[2] has two principal functions: (1) to provide the member States with credit facilities, thus enabling them to withstand temporary over-all balance of payments difficulties without resorting to restrictive and discriminatory trade and payments policies—for this purpose a special European Fund has been created; (2) to provide the member States with a Multilateral System of Settlements to facilitate the settlement of select monthly balances between the central banks of the member States. Broadly speaking, the E.M.A. in discharging these two functions provides for its members on the European level what the I.M.F. provides for its members on a global scale. In the former instance, the European Fund, like the International Monetary Fund, has a pool of resources which is conditionally available to members in temporary payments difficulties. In respect of the latter function—that is, the Multilateral System of Settlements—the E.M.A. complements the Fund in two respects. Firstly, it obliges all members to fix buying and selling rates for their respective currencies and so limits fluctuations in the exchange rates of those currencies, and secondly, as is also provided in Article VIII, Section 4 of the Fund agreement (a provision which to date has not been activated),[3] the E.M.A. ensures that certain currency balances held by the central banks of the member States will be—in certain circumstances—convertible into United States dollars at predetermined rates of exchange. Both of these functions affect the state of European monetary law and each will, therefore, be briefly examined in turn.

(a) The European Fund. The Fund's capital consists of 607·5 million units of account (each unit of account is equivalent

---

[1] Ibid.

[2] The functions of the Board of Management of the E.M.A., its structure, and the scope of its work are described in *E.M.A. First Annual Report* (1959) pp. 41–3.

[3] See J. Gold, 'The International Monetary Fund and International Law. An Introduction', *I.M.F. Pamphlet Series* (1965) p. 17.

to 0·88867088 gram of fine gold[1] of which 335·925m. units
are contributed by the member States, 123·538m. units are
pledged by the United States Government, and the remainder,
148·037m. units, represent assets transferred to the Fund from
the E.P.U.[2] In addition to the subscribed capital which constitutes the European Fund's principal source of liquid assets,
the European Fund, like the International Monetary Fund,
is empowered to augment its resources by means of special
credits obtained, on conditions determined by the O.E.C.D.,
either directly from one or more of the member States,[3] or
from international financial institutions such as the Bank
for International Settlements whose registered offices are
within the territory of a participating country.[4]

As already pointed out, the purpose of this pool of resources
is, like that of the I.M.F.'s pool of resources, to provide an
additional source of liquid assets from which a member
State can draw to correct a temporary payments imbalance,
thus obviating the need to resort to other, more restrictive
trade and payment policies.[5] In practice, the E.M.A. works in
close co-operation with the I.M.F., and frequently their respective financial facilities are made available on a parallel basis,
as in the case of the $52 million credit made available to
Turkey in 1967 (of which $25 million came from the
European Fund and $27 million from the I.M.F.).[6] As is
the case with I.M.F. drawings, drawings on the European Fund
must be repaid within a period not exceeding from three to
five years.[7]

However, facilities available from the European Fund differ
from I.M.F. facilities in two fundamental respects: (1) Unlike

---

[1] Art. 24 of the E.M.A.

[2] Art. 3 of the E.M.A. and *E.M.A. Eleventh Annual Report* (1969) p. 52.

[3] Art. 7 bis of the E.M.A. states: 'The Fund may obtain special credits from
Contracting Parties on conditions which shall be determined by the Organisation.'

[4] The Board put forward early in 1967 its proposals for these new arrangements
under which the European Fund might obtain short-term financing from an
international financial institution. These arrangements, which are described in
detail in *E.M.A. Ninth Annual Report* (1967) p. 62, were adopted in June 1967.

[5] Art. 2 of the E.M.A. provides in part that: 'The purposes of the Fund shall
be: (i) to provide the Contracting Parties with credit in order to aid them to
withstand temporary overall balance of payments difficulties and to continue to
pursue liberal and non-discriminatory trade and payments policies.'

[6] *E.M.A. Ninth Annual Report* (1967) p. 64. See also *E.M.A. Eleventh Annual Report*
(1969) p. 31.   [7] Art. 7, para. (*c*) of the E.M.A.

drawings on the I.M.F., in which the drawing member must in fact purchase the required currency or currencies with an equivalent amount of its own currency, drawings can be made on the European Fund without any such equivalent payment. European Fund drawings, unlike I.M.F. drawings, therefore, represent lines of credit in the strict legal sense of that term. (2) Again, unlike I.M.F. drawings, only some of which are conditional—that is, those drawings in the so-called 'credit tranches'—all drawings on the European Fund are conditional. Paragraph (c) of Article (5) of the 'Directives for the Application of the European Monetary Agreement' specifically empowers the O.E.C.D. to grant credits subject to the condition that the member State concerned comply with such recommendations as 'the Organization may think fit to address to it when granting the credit'. Article 7 (a) of the E.M.A. itself provides more generally that in granting a credit the Organization may decide—*inter alia*—'on any financial or other terms attached to the credit'.[1]

Finally, all drawings and repayments of credits as well as interest and other service charges are payable in gold.[2]

Since it began operations in December 1958, drawings have been made on the European Fund by Greece, Iceland, Spain, and Turkey.[3] These countries, whose reserves and I.M.F. quotas are small in relation to their payments swings and which are unable to participate easily in other forms of credit arrangements, such as bilateral swap arrangements, find that the short-term credit facilities made available to them through the European Fund are an invaluable source of supplementary financial assistance.[4]

(b) Multilateral System of Settlements. Article 9 (a) of the European Monetary Agreement states:

Each Contracting Party shall, for the purpose of limiting the fluctuations of its currency, fix buying and selling rates for gold, the United States dollar or some other currency and shall notify each

[1] The provisions regulating the granting of credits are Arts. 7 and 7 bis of the E.M.A. and Part II of the Directives. [2] Art. 7 (b) of the E.M.A.

[3] For a breakdown, year by year, country by country, of the amounts drawn from the commencement of operations by the European Fund in Dec. 1958 to 31 Dec. 1968, see *E.M.A. Tenth Annual Report* (1968) p. 75.

[4] Ibid. p. 56.

of the other Contracting Parties and the Organisation of the rates so fixed, which shall be used as a basis for the calculations and settlements provided for in the present Part of the Agreement.

Under the terms of this provision, each member State is required to establish a buying and selling rate (that is, an exchange rate) for its currency in terms of either gold, or the United States dollar, or some other third currency. In practice, all member States have expressed their buying and selling rates in terms of the United States dollar.[1] Although the above provision does not prescribe any specific limits for either buying or selling rates, most member States have in fact declared rates which fluctuate within 0·75 per cent on either side of the declared parity.[1] The value of this provision in promoting exchange rate stability within Europe, however, should not be overstated, since the member States remain free to modify the established rate unilaterally at their discretion.[2] Moreover, when one considers that all E.M.A. members[3] are also members of the I.M.F. and are by virtue of their membership in that organization obliged to keep their rates of exchange within one per cent either side of the established parity, the value of Article 9 (a) in promoting exchange stability is more apparent than real.[4] However, this provision does fulfil another, more important function. The rates established under the auspices of Article 9 (a) are the basis upon which calculations and settlements, if any, under the Multilateral System of Settlements are made. In this respect, therefore, Article 9 (a) in concert with Article 13 constitutes an exchange rate guarantee. Member States are assured, by virtue of these two Articles, of the opportunity to settle certain balances held by their central banks in other members' currencies[5] at predetermined rates of

[1] See *E.M.A. Eleventh Annual Report* (1970) p. 57.
[2] Since early 1971, the 0.75 per cent margin has not been fully observed, see *Euromoney* (April 1972) p. 30.   [3] With the sole exception of Switzerland.
[4] From the viewpoint of the development of international monetary law, however, the exchange rate–exchange stability aspect of this provision should not be completely ignored, since it serves as yet another example of the post-war realization among States that exchange rates are by their very nature objects of international concern and should therefore be subject to some measure of supranational regulation. Indeed, Arts. 1 and 2 (c) of the O.E.C.D. Convention both make reference to 'financial stability'. The I.M.F. margin of one per cent was increased to two and one quarter per cent in December 1971.
[5] Up to Feb. 1963, there were no limits on the amounts of the balances which could benefit from the exchange guarantee. Since that date, limits have been

exchange. The currency balances which are subject to this special form of settlement fall into three separate groups. It is not intended to examine either the nature of these various balances or the procedure by which these balances may be settled through the E.M.A. machinery.[1] It will suffice to note that in practice settlement through the E.M.A. machinery is rarely resorted to, since the E.M.A. settlement provisions are so formulated as to make the settlement of such balances more advantageous through normal market operations. The real value of the scheme lies in its reserve capacity:

> . . . Governments and central banks know that they can count at all times on the E.M.A. system. When things go badly they can rely on a settlement of their currency claims, including all accumulated working balances, at a fixed rate and on the 50m. U.S. dollars guarantee in case of default. For, while each participant may notify *new* rates at any time, existing balances are settled at rates notified *before* the modification. This maintains an exchange rate guarantee . . .[2]

The Multilateral System of Settlements was activated in 1967 following the devaluation of the pound sterling and other European currencies, and again in 1968 and 1969 following the devaluation of the Icelandic króna and the French franc respectively. In November 1967, thirty-seven balances in sterling, Spanish pesetas, Danish kroner, and Icelandic krónur were settled, totalling some $19·8 million.[3] The system was activated again in November 1968 and August 1969 to settle balances in Icelandic krónur and French francs following those currencies' devaluations. The cumulative total of settlements under the multilateral system was, in December 1969, $82·6 million.[3]

5. *Western Europe*

(i) Introduction. In Western Europe the movement towards economic integration has, in recent years,[4] been particularly

agreed by the central banks concerned in relationships with the Bank of England, the amounts guaranteed remaining unlimited in all the other relationships between E.M.A. central banks. See *E.M.A. Eleventh Annual Report* (1969) pp. 46, 55.

[1] For a description of the balances which can be settled under the E.M.A. Settlements Scheme, see Alexander Elkin, 'The European Monetary Agreement', VII E.Y. (1960) pp. 162–8.   [2] Ibid. p. 167.

[3] *E.M.A. Eleventh Annual Report* (1969) p. 45.

[4] For a brief history of attempts at European economic integration, see Étienne-Sadi Kirschen, *Financial Integration in Western Europe* (1969) pp. 1–19. For a general

pronounced, with the result that not less than five separate economic groupings are currently in existence, namely the Belgium–Luxembourg Economic Union (B.L.E.U.), the Benelux Economic Union, the European Economic Community (E.E.C.), the European Free Trade Association (E.F.T.A.), and the Anglo-Irish Free Trade Area.

Chronologically, the oldest of these arrangements is the B.L.E.U. Originally established in 1921 as a customs union between Belgium and the Grand Duchy of Luxembourg,[1] it was transformed into a full-fledged economic[2] and monetary[3] union in 1963, thus currently becoming—from the monetary viewpoint—the most integrated of the several European groupings. The next formal effort at economic integration did not appear until during the Second World War, when the Belgian, Luxembourg, and Netherlands Governments-in-exile concluded a monetary agreement in 1943,[4] and the Netherlands, Belgium, and Luxembourg customs convention of 1944.[5] Co-operation between the Benelux countries continued and expanded during the post-war period[6] and finally culminated in 1958 in the conclusion of the 'Treaty Instituting the Benelux

bibliography of literature on European integration, see *Special Annotated Bibliography. Regional Integration*', vol. I (O.E.C.D., INF/BIB(69)11).

[1] Convention between Belgium and the Grand-Duchy of Luxembourg for the Establishment of an Economic Union between the Two Countries, 25 July 1921, 9 L.N.T.S. 223.

[2] Consolidated Convention between Belgium and the Grand Duchy of Luxembourg instituting the Belgo-Luxembourg Economic Union, 29 Jan. 1963, 547 U.N.T.S. 148.

[3] Special Protocol between Belgium and the Grand Duchy of Luxembourg relating to the System of Monetary Association, 29 Jan. 1963, 547 U.N.T.S. 141. Protocol of Application of the Special Protocol relating to the System of Monetary Association, 21 May 1965, 547 U.N.T.S. 144.

[4] Belgo-Luxembourg-Netherlands Monetary Convention, 21 Oct. 1943, 2 U.N.T.S. 294.

[5] Customs Convention between the Netherlands and the Economic Union of Belgium and Luxembourg, 5 Sept. 1944, II E.Y. (1956) pp. 283–7.

[6] It is interesting to note that these three States concluded on 8 July 1954 one of the first conventions on the removal of exchange restrictions on capital movements, Agreement . . . concerning the Removal of Restrictions on Capital Transfers between the Netherlands and the Belgo-Luxembourg Economic Union, 8 July 1954, 287 U.N.T.S. 36. For a more detailed résumé of economic co-operation between these States before 1960, see C. D. A. Van Lynden, 'Benelux', VII E.Y. (1961) pp. 132–51. See also E. J. E. M. H. Jaspar, 'Réalisations dans le domaine de la coopération Benelux', II E.Y. (1956) pp. 34–59, and M. A. G. van Meerhaeghe, *International Economic Institutions* (1966) pp. 228–33.

Economic Union'.[1] The treaty establishing the E.E.C.[2] or the common market between Belgium, the Federal Republic of Germany, France, Italy, Luxembourg, and the Netherlands followed shortly. Signed in Rome on 25 March 1957, it entered into force on 1 January 1958. Following the establishment of the E.E.C., negotiations took place within the O.E.E.C. for the establishment of some sort of association between the E.E.C. and the remaining members of the O.E.E.C. However, it became apparent during the course of these negotiations that they had no prospect of success, and as a result officials from seven countries, Austria, Denmark, Norway, Portugal, Sweden, Switzerland, and the United Kingdom, met in Stockholm to consider the establishment between these countries of a free trade area. These consultations culminated in the establishment of the European Free Trade Association (E.F.T.A.) which entered into force on 3 May 1960.[3] A Convention establishing a free trade area similar in most respects to the E.F.T.A. was concluded between the Republic of Ireland and the United Kingdom in 1965.[4]

Although all of these arrangements affect in varying degrees the monetary sovereignty of their respective member States by prescribing for them legal rules of monetary conduct, attention will be focused primarily on the E.E.C. monetary provisions. Reference will be made to the relevant provisions in the other treaties by way of comparison only. Such an approach is the most appropriate, because the E.E.C. has been and undoubtedly will continue to be the most important instrument for achieving European economic integration. Its activities not

[1] For text of this treaty plus protocols, see 381 U.N.T.S. 260; V E.Y. (1966) pp. 228–33.
[2] For text of this treaty together with Annexes and Protocols, see 298 U.N.T.S. 11. For the most recent review of the legal developments, i.e. case law, Council and Commission Regulations, Directives and Decisions in the Common Market, see Alan Campbell, *Common Market Law*, 2 vols. (1969).
[3] Convention establishing the European Free Trade Association, 4 Jan. 1960, 370 U.N.T.S. 3. For an exhaustive study of the legal aspects of this Association, see John S. Lambrinidis, *The Structure, Function, and Law of a Free Trade Area* (1965). For shorter articles, see H. G. Darwin, 'The European Free Trade Association', 36 B.Y.I.L. (1960) pp. 354–9, and F. E. Figgures, 'Legal Aspects of the European Free Trade Association', 14 I.C.L.Q. (1965) pp. 1079–88.
[4] For text of this Agreement, see Cmnd. 2858, Dec. 1965; for a discussion of the legal features of this Agreement, see John Temple Lang, 'An Anglo-Irish Free Trade Area', 1 J.W.T.L. (1967) pp. 216–23.

only overshadow those of its two 'sub-groups'—that is, B.L.E.U. and Benelux—and those of the other 'outer groups', but it also appears that in the future it may well absorb into its compass several of the member States now belonging to the 'outer groups'.[1]

Moreover, with the sole exception of the B.L.E.U., the E.E.C.'s monetary provisions are the most comprehensive of all the contemporary European arrangements. Its stated long-term objective[2] is the establishment of an economic and monetary union, which presupposes—*inter alia*—the total absence of restrictions, whether of a commercial or of a financial nature and whether in respect of current (visible or invisible) or capital transactions, a unified policy with respect to exchange rates, a common policy for dealing with balance of payments difficulties, and a harmonization of other national economic policies, for example, fiscal and monetary. Accordingly, in order to ascertain the contemporary stage of development of Community monetary law, the following review will examine those provisions of the Rome Treaty (together with the subsequent jurisprudence adopted thereunder) concerned with (i) exchange restrictions, (ii) exchange rates, (iii) balance of payments, and (iv) economic harmonization.

For the sake of perspective, however, the following words of caution are necessary. The contemporary extent of supra-national monetary regulation within the community represents only the thin edge of the wedge. The ultimate objective, namely monetary union, still remains distant and will, as the following observation suggests, be achieved only gradually:

The process of European integration should be carried to completion since failure to do so would result in irretrievable losses to prosperity. Completion of the process of integration includes the creation of conditions similar to those of a domestic market. This applies also to monetary policy. In the monetary field, conditions similar to those of a domestic market mean not only substantial measures of co-ordination on the part of the Member State but also

[1] At the time of writing, the United Kingdom, Ireland, and Denmark are in the process of becoming members of the E.E.C.

[2] See 'Commission Memorandum to the Council on the Co-ordination of Economic Policies and Monetary Co-operation within the Community', *Supplement to Bulletin of the European Communities* (Mar. 1969).

real sacrifices of sovereignty . . . However, since to waive additional national sovereign rights requires great self-restraint and in most cases even a victory over one's own political ego, the approach to be adopted in practice will have to be one of advancing step by step.[1]

The current community law, as it is discussed below, represents therefore only the early stage in a long evolutionary process and must be considered as such. Nevertheless, it is not only the basis upon which a more coherent Community monetary law will be built, but indeed the basis upon which a truly 'European' monetary law may well in future develop. It therefore merits careful examination.

(ii) *Exchange restrictions:* (*a*) *general observations.* The objective of creating within the European Community economic conditions similar to those prevailing within a domestic market necessitates the complete removal of all restrictions—whether administrative, financial, or commercial—on the movement of goods, services, capital, and labour within the Community. Accordingly, in Part II of the Rome Treaty (Articles 9–84), appropriately entitled 'Bases of the Community', are set out comprehensive provisions which oblige member States to establish such a restriction-free regime within a twelve-year transitional period. More particularly, Articles 9–17 and Articles 30–7 require the gradual abolition as between member States of customs duties, quantitative restrictions, as well as all other charges with equivalent effect on the importation and exportation of goods within the Community. Similar arrangements apply with respect to trade in agricultural products (Articles 38–47). Articles 48–51 and Articles 59–66 similarly require the elimination of restrictions on the movement of persons and the supply of services respectively. The abolition of restrictions on the movement of capital within the Community is dealt with in Articles 62–73.[2] (These latter provisions will be considered in more detail below.)

---

[1] Hans von der Groeben, *European Monetary Policy towards the Gradual Establishment of a European Monetary System*, Commission of the European Communities (1968), pp. 17–18.

[2] For a complete and detailed résumé of the provisions of Part II of the Rome Treaty plus the measures adopted thereunder during the first ten years of the Community's existence, see *Les Novelles, Droit des Communautés européennes* (Brussels, 1969) pp. 657–792 (hereinafter referred to as *Les Novelles*). For a much more limited review of a similar nature, see A. H. Robertson, *European Institutions* (1966) pp. 160–7.

In addition, the above provisions are complemented by Article 106. This Article ensures that the establishment of the restriction-free regime envisaged in Part II of the treaty will not be frustrated by financial restrictions.[1] Under Article 106 member States are obliged—as a minimum—to liberate payments and transfers to the extent that the underlying transactions themselves are freed of other restrictions in accordance with the provisions of Part II of the Rome Treaty. The relevant part of Article 106 reads as follows:

Each Member State undertakes to authorise, in the currency of the Member State in which the creditor or beneficiary resides, any payments connected with the exchange of goods, services or capital, and also any transfers of capital and wages, to the extent that the movement of goods, services, capital and persons is freed as between Member States in application of this Treaty.

Thus, where transactions—be they of a current or capital nature—are liberated in accordance with Part II of the Treaty, payment for such transactions must automatically be allowed. Moreover, where the free movement of goods, services, and capital is impeded only by exchange restrictions, that is to say, where there are no administrative, commercial, or other restrictions other than financial restrictions preventing the conclusion of a transaction, then such financial restrictions must also gradually be abolished.[2] In this respect, paragraph 2 of Article 106 provides:

To the extent that exchanges of goods and services and movements of capital are limited only by restrictions on payments connected therewith, the provisions of the Chapters relating to the abolition of quantitative restrictions, to the freeing of services and to the free movement of capital shall, for the purposes of the progressive abolition of such restrictions, apply by analogy.

What is particularly noteworthy about the above-mentioned provisions, however, is their comprehensiveness. By providing for the abolition of exchange restrictions both on current transactions—that is, goods and services—and on capital

---

[1] *Les Novelles*, p. 769.

[2] In compliance with Art. 106, para. 2, the Council adopted on 31 May 1963 a directive requiring the removal of all prohibitions on, or other obstacles to, payments for services where payment restrictions were the only limiting factor on their supply, J.O.C.E. (1963) p. 1609.

transactions, the Rome Treaty is, of the several international conventions already considered in this study, the most comprehensive in this regard. By comparison, it will be remembered that the I.M.F. limits its attention to current transactions, while the O.E.C.D. is concerned only with invisibles and capital transactions. Similarly comprehensive provisions are to be found in the Benelux economic union[1] and the B.L.E.U.,[2] while the E.F.T.A. and the Anglo-Irish free trade area limit their attention to current transactions only.[3]

However, it is also interesting to note that Article 106 of the Rome Treaty, irrespective of its comprehensive nature, does not in fact result in any significant alteration of the Six's international legal obligations with respect to exchange restrictions. All six member States of the Community are also party to the O.E.C.D.'s two Codes—that is, Current Invisible Code and Capital Code—and all six States have acquired Article VIII status under the Fund Agreement.[4] As a consequence of their participation in these arrangements, the Six are already obliged not to introduce exchange restrictions—subject to certain permitted exceptions—on all current as well as on certain capital transactions. Thus Article 106, apart from consolidating all these obligations into one legal instrument, does not otherwise

[1] See Arts. 1, 2, 3, 4, and 5 of the treaty instituting the Benelux Economic Union, 381 U.N.T.S. 260. For a discussion of these provisions, see M. A. G. van Meerhaeghe, *International Economic Institutions* (1966) p. 234.

[2] Art. 4 of the Special Protocol between Belgium and the Grand Duchy of Luxembourg relating to the System of Monetary Association, 547 U.N.T.S. 141 provides:

'The Luxembourg Government shall introduce and apply the same legislation as Belgium with respect to exchange control.

Such control shall be entrusted to a single body whose decisions shall be binding throughout the territory of the Economic Union. The Grand Duchy of Luxembourg shall be represented in that body.'

In fact the two countries share a fully unified capital market. See *O.E.C.D. Code of Liberalisation of Capital Movements* (Jan. 1969) pp. 65–7.

[3] See Arts. 3 (1), 11 (a), 29, and 37 of the E.F.T.A., 370 U.N.T.S. 3, and Arts. 24 and 21 of the Anglo-Irish Free Trade Agreement, Cmnd. 2858. See also F. E. Figgures, 'Legal Aspects of the EFTA', 14 I.C.L.Q. (1965) p. 1079, and *The Stockholm Convention Examined* (2nd ed., Geneva, 1963) pp. 65–7. It should also be remembered, however, that all the countries represented in these two treaties are party to the O.E.C.D.'s Capital Code.

[4] On 15 Feb. 1961, all six members of the E.E.C. accepted the obligations of Art. VIII, Sects. 2, 3, 4. Austria, Denmark, Norway, Sweden, United Kingdom, and Ireland (all of which are members of E.F.T.A.) have also acquired Art. VIII status.

significantly alter the Six's international legal obligations in this regard.

In addition to the provisions contained in Article 106, however, the Rome Treaty devotes an entire chapter (Articles 67–73) to the liberalization and harmonization of capital movements within the Community. In certain respects the provisions in this chapter and the measures adopted thereunder exceed those of the O.E.C.D.'s Capital Code, and they therefore merit further consideration.

(iii) *Exchange restrictions: (b) capital transactions.*[1]

The free movement of capital is distinct from transfers connected with goods, services, or the movement of manpower, and includes the unrestricted right of nationals of Member States to acquire, transfer, and utilize within the boundaries of the Community, capital originating within the Community.

By making more money available to finance investments and by allowing existing resources to be better deployed over a broader area, the freeing of capital movements leads to an improved use of the savings potential and a more rapid creation of the means of production. Normally speaking, capital movements should help to avoid disequilibrium between the balances of payments of different Member States and to harmonize the cost factor represented by rates of interest and other financial burdens.[2]

Although the economic advantages to be gained from the free flow of capital within the Community were made clear by the Spaak Report—as evidenced by the above-quoted excerpt from that Report[2]—the legal provisions adopted by the founding fathers of the Community and included in the Rome Treaty through which this objective is to be realized are particularly vague. The reasons put forward explaining the timidity of approach are primarily economic—for example, the fear that

---

[1] For a general discussion of the legal and economic aspects of capital movements within the Community, see Claudio Segré, 'Capital Movements in the European Economic Community', 15 *Banca Nazionale del Lavoro Quarterly Review* (1962) pp. 78–102; Étienne-Sadi Kirschen, *Financial Integration in Western Europe* (1969) pp. 41–86; *Les Novelles*, pp. 755–68; J. B. De La Giroday, 'The Effects of the European Economic Community on the Banking Business within it', 18 *Business Lawyer* (1962–3) pp. 1025–9; John Temple Lang, 'The Right of Establishment of Companies and Free Movement of Capital in the European Economic Community', *University of Illinois Law Forum* (1965) pp. 710–14; von Bodo Börner, 'Rechtsfragen des Zahlungs- und Kapitalverkehrs in der EWG', *Europarecht* (1966) pp. 97–128.

[2] Étienne-Sadi Kirschen, op. cit. pp. 41–2, where an unofficial tranlation of the quoted portion of the Spaak Report appears.

without control, capital would be directed away from the less developed regions most in need of it and towards those regions within the Community possessing a skilled labour force and highly developed infrastructure; and the fear that without control, the free movement of capital could cause havoc in a member State's balance of payments, etc.[1] However, an additional explanation of a legal nature, with which international lawyers are only too familiar, namely that the member States were not prepared to abandon beyond the necessary minimum their economic sovereignty in this respect, is also accorded considerable weight.[1] Nevertheless, in spite of its inherent inadequacies, the value of Chapter 4 (Articles 67–73) must not be underestimated, since it is the basis upon which a Community capital market is currently being, and will in future continue to be, developed.

The main provisions on capital flows are contained in Article 67 which reads as follows:

1. Member States shall, in the course of the transitional period and to the extent necessary for the proper functioning of the Common Market, progressively abolish as between themselves restrictions on the movement of capital belonging to persons resident in Member States and also any discriminatory treatment based on the nationality or place of residence of the parties or on the place in which such capital is invested.

2. Current payments connected with movements of capital between Member States shall be freed from all restrictions not later than at the end of the first stage.

In compliance with the specific obligation set out in paragraph 2 above, all restrictions on current payments connected with capital movements—for example, the transfer of profits arising from capital investments—have been liberated. However, since all six member States are already obliged to liberate such movements under Article VIII, Section 2 of the Fund Agreement, Article 67, paragraph 2 is of little practical importance. Of more importance is paragraph 1, which requires not only the progressive abolition of existing restrictions—both financial and others—on the movement of capital belonging to

---

[1] For a further discussion of the economic advantages and disadvantages of the free movement of capital within the Community, see Claudio Segré, op. cit. pp. 79–84.

Community residents, but also prohibits member States from discriminating as between nationals and non-nationals, residents and non-residents in respect of intra-Community capital movements. This latter prohibition against discriminatory treatment is of particular significance. Such discriminatory treatment is a fundamental feature of most exchange control regimes. By requiring its abolition, a principal source of inequality within the Community is removed. A member State cannot accord privileged treatment to a non-resident, such as exempting him from the effect of exchange controls over capital, without extending similar treatment to its own residents and vice versa.

Unfortunately these obligations are somewhat mitigated by virtue of the fact that they need be complied with only 'to the extent necessary for the proper functioning of the Common Market'. The determination of what constitutes 'proper functioning' is left to the two principal organs of the Community, namely the Council and the Commission, who, during the course of the first two stages of the twelve-year transitional period, by means of a unanimous vote and subsequently by means of a qualified majority vote, are to issue the directives necessary for the progressive implementation of the provisions of Article 67.[1]

In compliance with this latter obligation, the Council, acting on the proposals of the Commission, has adopted two directives (11 May 1960[2] and 18 December 1962[3]). The combined effect of these two directives (the latter is in fact just a refinement of the former) has been to create three categories of capital transactions within the Community, with each category being subject to a differing degree of liberalization.

For those capital movements in the first category, such as direct investments and their liquidation, investments in real estate, personal capital movements, short- and medium-term credits connected with commercial transactions, and operations in limited securities,[4] liberalization is complete and uncon-

[1] Art. 69.
[2] J.O.C.E. (1960) p. 921. For an unofficial translation of this text into English, see C. Segré, op. cit. pp. 90–8.
[3] J.O.C.E. (1963) p. 62.
[4] For a more detailed explanation of these transactions, see Les Novelles, pp. 760–1.

ditional,[1] that is to say, a member State is no longer able to maintain any exchange restrictions on this category of capital movement except under the safeguard clauses of Articles 73, 108, and 109 (of which more will be said below). The liberal regime accorded to these transactions is explained by the fact that these capital transactions are the corollaries to the basic principles of the Treaty. The free movement of persons necessitates the free movement of personal capital, the free movement of goods necessitates the free conclusion of commercial credits, and the right of establishment necessitates the free movement of direct investment capital. Finally, in certain member States (B.L.E.U.),[2] capital transfers are effected wholly or in part on special exchange markets where the exchange rates are allowed to fluctuate more widely than those relating to current transactions. To ensure that the fluctuations of rates on these special markets do not go beyond the limit where capital can still move freely, member States must not allow these rates to diverge appreciably and for a substantial period from those applying to payments relating to current transactions.[3]

For capital movements in the second category—such as the issue and placing of securities on the capital market, the acquisition of securities not quoted on the stock exchanges, etc.[4]—a conditional system of liberalization applies. Member States are obliged to grant any exchange required for the conclusion of such transactions; however, should the free movement of such capital threaten to impede a member State in attaining the aims of its economic policy, then that State may maintain or reintroduce any exchange restrictions on such movements of capital existing at the date of entry into force of the Directive.[5] Three member States—France, Italy, and the Netherlands—are currently maintaining restrictions on such capital movements. For the other member States, which had already liberalized these operations by 11 May 1960 (the date on which the Directive entered into force), liberalization has

---

[1] Art. 1, para. 1 and Art. 2, para. 2 of the First Directive.

[2] Code of Liberalisation of Capital Movements (Jan. 1969) p. 65.

[3] Art. 1, para. 2 of the First Directive. But note also Art. 2, para. 2 which, in respect of the transactions listed in Annex B, restricts the efficacy of this obligation.

[4] For a more detailed explanation of these provisions, see *Les Novelles*, pp. 761–2.

[5] Art. 3 of the First Directive.

become irrevocable, subject again to the safeguard provisions of Articles 73, 108 and 109.

The third category is concerned with capital movements of a short-term nature.[1] Due to the high mobility of this kind of capital—so-called 'hot money'—member States may control this type of capital transfer at their sole discretion.[2]

The provisions of Article 67, paragraph 1 and the measures adopted thereunder are complemented by Articles 68, paragraph 1, and 71. Under Article 68 (1), member States are obliged to grant 'in the most liberal manner possible such exchange authorisations as are still necessary' in respect of capital transactions. This obligation applies to those capital transactions not falling within the compass of Article 67, paragraph 1, and in respect of which, but for this provision, exchange restrictions would continue because their abolition was not judged necessary 'for the proper functioning of the Common Market'.[3] Under Article 71 member States must endeavour: (1) to avoid introducing within the Community new exchange restrictions which affect the movement of capital and current payments connected with such movement; (2) to avoid making existing rules more restrictive; and (3) to go beyond the required degree of liberalization of capital required by Articles 67–70 if their general economic and balance of payments situation allows. However, Article 71 does not establish any legal obligations; at best it constitutes only a declaration of intent, since the member States must only 'endeavour' to comply with its provisions.[4]

The liberalization of capital movements within the Community may disturb the normal functioning of a member State's capital market; for example, there might be an abnormal increase or decrease in the demands on the capital market or in rates of interest charged[5] thereon. A member State affected by

---

[1] *Les Novelles*, p. 762.

[2] A third Directive which at the time of writing had not yet been adopted but was being considered provides for the relaxation of exchange controls, mentioned above, applied by France, Italy, and the Netherlands. The object of this Directive is to establish a better balance among the commitments of the various member States. In addition, the Directive seeks to abolish obstacles other than exchange restrictions, e.g. of an administrative and fiscal nature, which interfere with the free movement of capital. *E.E.C. Bulletin* (Apr. 1967) p. 32; *E.E.C. Bulletin* (May 1968) p. 80; *Bulletin of European Communities* (May 1969) pp. 21–3.

[3] *Les Novelles*, p. 762, para. 1892.   [4] Ibid. para. 1893.

[5] *Les Novelles*, p. 763, para. 1894.

such difficulties may, under Article 73, take protective measures. As a general rule, only the Commission (subject to subsequent Council revocation or alteration) may authorize a member State to take protective measures, and only the Commission (again subject to Council action) may determine the conditions and particulars thereof. Only when such difficulties require secret and urgent attention may the affected State act unilaterally. However, even in such cases the Commission and the other member States must be informed of any measures so adopted not later than at the date of their entry into force.[1] Moreover, the Commission is entitled, after consulting the Monetary Committee, to modify or abolish the unilaterally adopted measures.[2]

In addition, any member State suffering from balance of payments difficulties may, in accordance with the provisions of Articles 108 and 109, deviate from its obligations in certain circumstances.[3]

The provisions discussed above are concerned only with the liberalization of intra-Community capital movements. However, if, as intended, a 'Community' capital market is to be established, the Six must also adopt a common policy with respect to the movement of capital between the Community as a whole and the rest of the world. Indeed, without such a co-ordinated policy, the liberalization of capital movements within the Community could be abused. (More particularly, assume that the point has been reached where there are no restrictions on capital movements within the Community. Assume further that the six member States maintain exchange

[1] Ibid.

[2] The resulting system of liberalization differs appreciably from that set out in the 'Code of Liberalisation' of capital movements adopted by the O.E.C.D. Council. The E.E.C. provisions are distinctly stricter from the legal angle. A member State is not free, under the E.E.C. provisions, to withdraw the measures of unconditional liberalization established by the Council except in accordance with the safeguard clauses contained in Arts. 73 and 109 of the Treaty. These clauses can be evoked only on specific conditions and following Community procedures. In the O.E.C.D. system, on the other hand, a member State may unilaterally withdraw measures adopted 'if they result in serious economic or financial disturbance' and may temporarily suspend their application 'if the balance of payments position . . . develops adversely at a rate and in circumstances which it considers serious . . .' See *The Development of a European Capital Market, Report of a Group of Experts Appointed by the E.E.C. Commission* (Brussels, 1966) p. 85.

[3] See below, pp. 282–8.

controls, of varying severity, over the movement of capital to non-Community member States. In such circumstances, a resident of a member State which has particularly severe controls over the movement of capital to third countries could easily avoid these controls by exporting capital to a member with less severe exchange controls *vis-à-vis* third countries.) Clearly, to prevent difficulties of this sort from arising, it is necessary to harmonize the Six's regulations pertaining to the movement of capital to third countries. Articles 70 and 72 provide the basis for such a co-ordinated Community policy. Article 70, paragraph (1) provides for the progressive co-ordination of the exchange policies of the member States in respect of the movement of capital between those States and third countries.[1] Article 72 provides that 'Member States shall keep the Commission informed of any movements of capital to and from third countries as are known to them'. In pursuance of these provisions, the Commission in 1965 submitted to the Council a proposal for a directive[2] providing for statistics on movements of capital to and from non-member countries to be supplied to the Commission, and a recommendation[3] for a Council decision laying down a procedure for consultation within the Community on national policies relating to capital movements to and from non-member countries.

(iv) *Exchange rates.* Although substantial progress has been achieved in the liberalization of payments and transfers within the Community, without an accompanying regulation of exchange rates at which such transactions take place, the full potential of such integration cannot be exploited:

Goods, services, capital and persons will be able to move freely within the Community only if efforts are made to dispel all shadow of doubt as to the irrevocability of the permission to effect the resultant payments and the accompanying transfers across the internal frontier.

This is, however, not enough. There will be certainty as to the present and future effects of the law only if businessmen are sure of being at any time able to effect the required payments and transfers

---

[1] In the event that such co-ordination is not realized or is incomplete, the provisions of Art. 70 para. 2, become applicable.

[2] J.O.C.E. (1967) p. 1015; *E.E.C. Commission Tenth General Report* (1967) p. 168.

[3] Ibid.

and if they know in advance at what rate of exchange the transfer from one currency into the other will be made . . .[1]

What is required, it is suggested,[2] is an exchange rate system in which: (i) there exists for each member's currency a single, fixed rate of exchange where, unlike Fund definitions, single means single and fixed means fixed—that is, all exchange transactions between Community members should take place at the parity rate;[3] and (ii) all parities are frozen with member States being able to change their parities only together and *vis-à-vis* non-member countries. Another suggested alternative is that the Community should establish a single common currency which would be legal tender and circulate freely throughout the Community.[4]

However, to date,[5] attempts to achieve for the Community either of the above-mentioned currency regimes on the basis of legal obligation have been unsuccessful. This is attributable, at least in part, to the inadequate attention given this matter in the Rome Treaty. In fact, reference to exchange rates is made only once in the Treaty. Article 107, paragraph (1) merely requires each member State to treat its policy with regard to exchange rates as a matter of common interest, an obligation which clearly detracts very little from a member's monetary sovereignty. Moreover, in paragraph 2 of Article 107, 'special provision is made for cases of devaluation in a manner "incompatible with the Community's objectives", making it clear that there is no prohibition of unilateral pegging of exchange rates'.[6] It is not surprising, therefore, that 'la réglementation du traité en cette matière a été considérée comme le point faible de tout le système'.[7] The unilateral devaluation of the French franc in August 1969, the revaluation of the German mark in October 1969, and the May 1971 European monetary crisis established beyond all doubt the inadequacy of this aspect of the Community's monetary arrangements.

[1] Hans von der Groeben, op. cit. p. 6.
[2] Ibid. pp. 6–8.
[3] At the moment this applies only to the Belgian and Luxembourg franc.
[4] *Financial Times*, 13 Mar. 1970, p. 40.
[5] The latest measure concerning exchange rates were adopted by the Council of Ministers on 21 March 1972; scc No. 9 European Community Background Information (March 29, 1972).
[6] O'Connell, op. cit. p. 1105.
[7] *Les Novelles*, p. 913.

However, for a variety of reasons, both legal and economic, it was thought (before the above-mentioned parity changes) that the regulation of exchange rates among the Six, although not as rigorous as the Commission had envisaged,[1] was not as imprecise as Article 107 would suggest. First, on 8 May 1964 the representatives of the member States meeting in the Council adopted a declaration requiring the holding of consultations between the member States before any change in their exchange rates. The declaration reads in part as follows:[2]

LES REPRÉSENTANTS DES GOUVERNEMENTS DES ÉTATS MEMBRES DE LA COMMUNAUTÉ ÉCONOMIQUE EUROPÉENNE, RÉUNIS AU SEIN DU CONSEIL,
DÉCLARENT
— que les gouvernements des États membres se consulteront préalablement à toute modification de la parité de change de la monnaie d'un ou de plusieurs États membres, selon des modalités appropriées qui seront précisées après avis du Comité monétaire:
— que la Commission sera associée à ces consultations.

Secondly, owing to the high level of economic integration already achieved—for example, in the field of capital markets, taxation, and agriculture—it was the opinion of the Commission that 'resort to the major monetary policy instrument of a change in currency exchange rates in order to adjust fundamental imbalances stemming from unduly wide divergences between national policies is now not at all what it was in the past'.[3] The most important of these factors was thought to have been the Common Market's agricultural policy. Under this policy, common prices expressed in units of account equal to the gold parity of the pre-8 May, 1972 United States dollar (0·888671 gram of fine gold) were established for Community agricultural products.[4] Should there be changes in the relative value of the various currencies, an immediate and automatic readjustment would occur in the prices of agricultural products, with the result that economic repercussions would be felt within the Community commensurate with

---

[1] Supplement to Bulletin of European Communities (Mar. 1969) pp. 3–4.
[2] J.O.C.E. (1964) p. 1226; E.E.C. Bulletin (Dec. 1962) pp. 57, 63; Supplement to E E.C. Bulletin (July 1963) p. 39.
[3] E.E.C. Commission Tenth General Report (1967) p. 165.
[4] See E.E.C. Bulletin (Feb. 1965) p. 13.

the devaluation or revaluation.[1] Indeed, it has frequently been suggested that, following the European currency crises in the autumn of 1968 and the spring of 1969 which were precipitated by the undervaluation of the German mark and the overvaluation of the French franc, the one major reason why the German Government did not revalue and the French Government did not devalue was the Common Market's agricultural pricing system.[2]

For these reasons it was suggested that member States were, as a minimum, legally obliged to consult with one another before undertaking any exchange rate alterations. 'Unilateral decisions in this area are a thing of the past.'[3] Furthermore, in its eighth annual report, the Commission implied that all that remained to be done to elevate the legal obligation from one of prior consultation to one of prior agreement was to bestow *de jure* status on what had become the *de facto* situation: 'The task of the Community institutions is now to render internal devaluation or revaluation impossible or unnecessary, instead of merely difficult and unlikely.'[4] As mentioned, the unilateral alterations of the French franc and German mark in 1969 demonstrated quite categorically that a Community exchange rate policy existed neither on a *de facto* nor on a *de jure* basis. With respect to three member States, however—namely the Netherlands, Belgium, and Luxembourg—such a *de jure*

---

[1] On 30 May 1968, the Council approved an obligatory set of rapid procedures to be followed for agreement on modifications in agricultural prices in the event of an alteration in existing exchange parities, J.O.C.E. (1968) no. L 123/4.

[2] *The Economist*, 30 Nov. 1968, pp. 62–3; *The Times*, 22 Nov. 1968, p. 26. In place of a revaluation by altering the exchange rate of the mark, a disguised revaluation ('Ersatzaufwertung') of about 4 per cent was carried out by reducing the import turnover tax from 11 per cent to 7 per cent and, where only 5½ per cent was normally levied, to 3½ per cent. Similarly, German exporters of goods which if sold within Germany were subject to value-added tax at 11 per cent, but on which this tax was rebated on export, received only 7 per cent back, which meant that such exports were effectively taxed at 4 per cent; goods which carried half the normal rate of TUA were taxed on export at 2 per cent. See *Economist Intelligence Unit, Quarterly Economic Reviews Germany No. 4* (1968) p. 4. France undertook a similarly disguised devaluation. See *Economist Intelligence Unit, Quarterly Economic Review France No. 4* (1968) p. 5. The E.E.C. Commission itself opposed any revaluation of the mark and any devaluation of the French franc. See *European Communities Bulletin* (Jan. 1969) pp. 16, 35.

[3] Étienne-Sadi Kirschen, op. cit. p. 115.

[4] *E.E.C. Commission Eighth General Report* (1965) p. 149.

situation has already been established by virtue of Article 12 of the Benelux Treaty.[1] Paragraph 1 of that Article provides that 'As regards the rate of exchange between the Netherlands guilder and the Belgian and the Luxembourg franc, the High Contracting Parties shall determine their policies by mutual agreement. Likewise, by mutual agreement they shall fix their exchange rates in relation to the currencies of third countries'. More significantly, paragraph 2 provides that 'In particular they shall not effect any alteration of rates of exchange except by mutual agreement'. Moreover, as a result of the monetary association concluded in 1963 between Belgium and Luxembourg, both these countries not only are legally prohibited from unilaterally altering their respective rate of exchange, but both have in fact also adopted identical parities (the par values are 0·0177734 gram of fine gold per Belgian franc and per Luxembourg franc, or B.F. 50·00 = $1 and Lux. F. 50·00 = $1). All transfers between the two currencies take place at the established parity rate.[2]

(v) *Balance of payments*.[3] The basic principle underlying the Community balance of payments provisions (Articles 108 and 109) is that the right and obligation to deal with any payments disequilibrium rests with the Community as a whole rather than with the individual affected member(s). It is only in very exceptional circumstances that a member State may act autonomously, and even in such cases the permitted exceptions are so formulated as to ensure that the Community interests will not thereby be unduly jeopardized.

In contrast, the basic principle within E.F.T.A.[4] is that the

[1] 381 U.N.T.S. 260.

[2] Art. 2 of the Special Protocol between Belgium and the Grand Duchy of Luxembourg relating to the System of Monetary Association, 547 U.N.T.S. 141. Moreover, notes of the Banque nationale de Belgique and notes of the Belgian State are legal tender for payments up to any amount in the Grand Duchy of Luxembourg. Coins of every kind minted by the Belgian State are similarly legal tender in Luxembourg, but only for payments up to agreed amounts, Art. 1, ibid.

[3] For a general discussion of the balance of payments provisions in the Rome Treaty, see *Les Novelles*, pp. 911–13; H. A. H. Audretsch, 'The E.E.C. and E.F.T.A. Two Solutions regarding Balance of Payments Difficulties', 4 *Common Market Law Review* (1966–7) pp. 419–39.

[4] Art. 19 of the E.F.T.A. Treaty and Art. XVIII of the Anglo-Irish Free Trade Agreement are concerned with balance of payments difficulties. The provisions in both Articles are virtually identical (in fact the entire Anglo-Irish Agreement is based on the E.F.T.A. model).

right of action rests with the individual member State which may, unilaterally and without prior notification[1] to the Council take the necessary safeguard measures. The only restrictions on this freedom of action are: (1) that such measures must be consistent with that member's other international obligations; (2) that the member must abolish such restrictions as soon as its balance of payments situation permits; and (3) if after eighteen months the difficulties persist and the safeguard measures applied 'seriously disturb the operation of the Association', the Council by a majority decision (legally binding) may 'devise special procedures to attenuate or compensate for the effect of such measures'.[2]

A second basic feature of the Community balance of payments mechanism, not to be found in the E.F.T.A. or indeed in the relevant provisions of the G.A.T.T., is its flexibility, in that it permits a variety of solutions for coping with a payments disequilibrium. While both the E.F.T.A. and the G.A.T.T. only permit the imposition of quantitative restrictions on imports to correct a deteriorating payments situation, the Rome Treaty, apart from requiring the Commission to proceed through a number of successive and predetermined phases of action (each phase is to be successively implemented in response to the seriousness of the situation), allows the Commission in the final phase to authorize the State in difficulties to take such measures of safeguard as it (the Commission) deems necessary.

The continued abuse of the G.A.T.T. and E.F.T.A. provisions suggests that the flexibility of the Community mechanism is more in harmony with current administrative and economic realities than the more rigid approach of the G.A.T.T. and E.F.T.A. For example, the United Kingdom in October 1964[3] and again in November 1968[4] introduced an import surcharge

---

[1] Notification, however, after the imposition of restrictions is required, Art. 19, para. 2.

[2] For a more detailed discussion of these provisions, see John S. Lambrinidis, *The Structure, Function, and Law of a Free Trade Area* (1965) pp. 170–6; *The Stockholm Convention Examined* (1963) pp. 50–2; John Temple Lang, 'An Anglo-Irish Free Trade Area', 1 J.W.T.L. (1967) p. 220.

[3] For the nature of the surcharge and the E.F.T.A. reaction to it, see 4 I.L.M. (1965) pp. 1–14, 1056–7; *Fifth Annual Report 1964/1965 of the EFTA* (1965) pp. 6–8, 39 ff; XIII E.Y. (1967) pp. 685–7.

[4] For the nature of the scheme, see *Ninth Annual Report of the EFTA* (1969) p. 34. For a discussion of the legality of the scheme in light of the United Kingdom's

and an import deposit scheme respectively as corrective measures, maintaining in defence of the former that 'the legal alternative, quota restrictions on imports, was not practicable because the apparatus of quota control had been dismantled and could not be brought into existence quickly enough to have any impact on the immediate crisis',[1] and in defence of the latter, 'that the Convention itself, by Article 19, gives the right to Member States to take far more drastic measures in order to protect their balance of payments than we have done by the terms of the Bill. Under Article 19 the stringent step of introducing quotas and licensing systems is permitted . . .'[2] Both the above explanations suggest the need and desirability of greater flexibility in the corrective measures legally available to countries in temporary payment difficulties.

Under phase one of the Community mechanism, which can be activated (i) only as soon as payments difficulties are imminent or when such difficulties have already arisen, and (ii) only if such difficulties are likely to prejudice either the functioning of the Common Market or the progressive establishment of the common commercial policy, the Commission is required to examine without delay the economic situation within the country experiencing the difficulties as well as the corrective measures which the Country has taken itself in accordance with Article 104.[3] As a consequence and on the basis of this examination, the Commission is to recommend to that member the adoption of certain corrective measures. Measures recommended under this initial phase, however, are intended to establish only general guidelines of conduct, rather then rigid obligations. First, Commission recommendations have no legally binding force,[4] and second, although there is no indication in the Treaty stating what the nature and scope of these measures should be, the Commission's recommendations to the French Government on 5 July 1968 following that Govern-

obligations under both the E.F.T.A. and the Anglo-Irish Agreement, see *House of Commons Parliamentary Debates*, vol. 774 (1968–9) cols. 1269 ff.

[1] *Fifth Annual Report 1964/1965 of the EFTA* (1965) p. 7.

[2] *House of Commons Parliamentary Debates*, vol. 774 (1968–9) col. 1277.

[3] Art. 104 reads as follows: 'Each Member State shall pursue the economic policy necessary to ensure the equilibrium of its overall balance of payments and to maintain confidence in its currency, while ensuring a high level of employment and the stability of the level of prices.'

[4] Art. 189.

ment's activation of Article 109 suggest that in practice such measures will be of a general economic nature.[1]

Community action under the second phase, however, is more substantial. In this phase the Commission, having sought and received the advice of the Monetary Committee—which advice it is legally bound to take into account[2]—recommends to the Council the granting of mutual assistance. Mutual assistance, as the term itself suggests, consists of corrective measures which are to be undertaken on behalf of the member State in difficulty by all the other Community members. Although some forms of mutual aid which may be granted are enumerated in Article 108, paragraph 2, that list is not exhaustive. For example, in response to the French crisis of June 1968, the Council's directive on mutual assistance to France provided for measures which went beyond those enumerated in Article 108. Member States, other than France, were obliged (it should be noted that Council decisions or directives on mutual aid, unlike Commission recommendations, are legally binding) to adopt any measures necessary (1) to achieve and maintain a high growth rate, (2) to pursue a policy of interest-rate stabilization, and (3) to allow, as far as possible, French borrowers to float loans on their capital markets.[3]

To date, however, the most important mutual aid provision —the one which deals with the granting of credits by other member States to a State in difficulties—has been a dead letter.[4]

The first occasion which the Council considered appropriate for exercising this clause arose when Italy ran into a payments crisis in 1964. Then the United States quickly came to Italy's aid while Brussels was still trying to decide on the procedures and conditions, and the conclusion was widely drawn that the E.E.C.'s arrangements for monetary cooperation were not the most appropriate, among those available, even for its own members.[5]

---

[1] *Bulletin of European Communities* (Aug. 1968) pp. 18, 21.

[2] Art. 4 of the Statute regulating the Monetary Committee provides: 'L'avis du Comité monétaire est obligatoirement recueilli soit par le Conseil, soit par la Commission dans les cas prévus à l'article 69, à l'article 71, dernier alinéa, à l'article 73, paragraphe 1, alinéa 1 et paragraphe 2, à l'article 107, paragraphe 2, à l'article 108, paragraphe 1, alinéa 2, et à l'article 109, paragraphe 3.' For entire text of the Statute, see J.O.C.E. (1958) p. 390.

[3] *Bulletin of European Communities* (Aug. 1968) pp. 18–23.

[4] See *Supplement to Bulletin of European Communities* (Mar. 1969) p. 8.

[5] *Economist Intelligence Unit. 18 European Trends* (Feb. 1969) p. 21.

Even with respect to France, the mutual aid measures adopted, quite apart from not providing any collective Community financial assistance, were minimal compared to the measures unilaterally adopted by France under Article 109.

To correct this serious inadequacy, a new mechanism has recently been established by the Commission.[1] The object of this new arrangement will be to reduce the need for member States to take unilateral action under Article 109 by putting teeth into the vague mutual assistance provisions of Article 108. The proposals include a suggestion for the creation of a new two-tier, six-nation monetary arrangement under which both short- and medium-term aid could be given to countries in financial difficulty. In order to provide short-term support, each country would put part of its reserves at the disposal of the other member States. These would be used to help any member State in difficulties under a sort of drawing rights system. When a drawing was to take place, the Six would together study methods of re-establishing equilibrium in the drawing country. If no agreement could be reached on such action, the drawing would be limited to the short term—that is, to a period of three months. If on the other hand agreement could be reached, the loan would be renewed or replaced by medium-term support— say three to five years. Medium-term aid would be decided by the Council, acting on a recommendation of the Commission. The nature of and conditions attached to medium-term support would be decided on an *ad hoc* basis according to the circumstances and in co-ordination with other international financial institutions.[2]

Should recommendations under phase one and mutual assistance under phase two prove to be insufficient, the Commission under phase three is given a virtual *carte blanche* authority to deal with the disequilibrium. This wide authority stems from the generality of the language employed in paragraph 3 of Article 108:

---

[1] For a discussion of the mechanism, see *The Economist*, 22 Feb. and 19 July 1969, at pp. 77 and 65 respectively, and also the *Financial Times*, 13 Dec. 1968 and 18 July 1969 at pp. 7 and 7 respectively. The mechanism was formally approved in Jan. 1970, see the *Financial Times*, 27 Jan. 1970, p. 15; *The Economist*, 31 Jan. 1970, p. 65.

[2] For more details of the scheme, see *Supplement to Bulletin of European Communities* (Mar. 1969) pp. 11–13; *Financial Times*, 23 Jan. 1970, p. 7.

If the mutual assistance recommended by the Commission is not granted by the Council or if the mutual assistance granted and the measures taken are insufficient, the Commission shall authorise the State in difficulties to take measures of safeguard of which the Commission shall determine the conditions and particulars.

Such authorisation may be revoked and such conditions and particulars may be amended by the Council acting by means of a qualified majority vote.

It was by the operation of Article 108, and in particular paragraph 3 of that Article, that the European Commission, by a process which at best can only be described as legalistic juggling, brought the unilaterally introduced French measures of July and November 1968 within the framework of the Rome Treaty.[1]

Finally, as has already been mentioned, a member State confronted with a sudden balance of payments crisis may, under Article 109, take unilateral countervailing measures. Under the rather strict terms of this provision, however, a State may act autonomously only subject to a number of conditions: (1) the crisis must be sudden and unexpected; (2) a decision by the Council to deal with the crisis within the meaning of Article 108, paragraph 2 (that is, the granting of some form of mutual assistance) is not taken immediately; (3) the measures adopted must cause the least possible disturbance to the functioning of the Common Market and in particular must not exceed those strictly necessary to remedy the difficulties; (4) the Commission and the other member States must be informed of the measures not later than at the time of their entry into force; and (5) the measures must be of a provisional nature.

However, in compliance with the basic principle underlying the Community's balance of payments provisions—that is, that payments disequilibria are primarily a Community problem requiring a concerted Community solution—the Commission, even after the unilateral measures have been introduced, may recommend mutual assistance to the Council under Article 108 (2). Moreover, to prevent any abuse of this emergency procedure, the autonomous action taken by a member State can be halted, since the Council may decide on the advice

[1] See *Bulletin of European Communities* (Aug. 1968) pp. 9–15; J.O.C.E. (1968) no. L 178/15; J.O.C.E. (1968) no. L 295/10.

of the Commission, and after consulting the Monetary Committee, that the member State concerned must either amend, suspend, or abolish the unilaterally adopted measures.

(vi) *Economic harmonization.*[1] (*a*) Internal economic relations. The establishment of a common market in which goods, services, and capital are free to move without restrictions and in which exchange rate alterations are to be kept to a minimum necessitates a simultaneous harmonization of national economic policies. Indeed, without the harmonization and supranational regulation of both short- and medium-term economic policies, the establishment of an economic and monetary union, which remains the ultimate objective of the E.E.C., will be impossible.

In recognition of this fact, Article 2 of the Rome Treaty provides in part that it shall be the aim of the Community to promote a harmonious development of economic activities throughout the Community 'by establishing a Common Market and progressively approximating the economic policies of Member States . . .'[2] More particularly, Article 103, entitled 'Policy Relating to Economic Trends', provides:

1. Member States shall consider their policy relating to economic trends as a matter of common interest. They shall consult with each other and with the Commission on measures to be taken in response to current circumstances.

2. Without prejudice to any other procedures provided for in this Treaty, the Council may, by means of a unanimous vote on a proposal of the Commission, decide on measures appropriate to the situation.

3. The Council, acting by means of a qualified majority vote on a proposal of the Commission, shall, where necessary, issue any requisite directives concerning the particulars of application of the measures decided upon under the terms of paragraph 2.

4. The procedures provided for in this Article shall apply also in the event of difficulties arising in connection with the supply of certain products.

Although paragraphs 2 and 3 specifically empower the Council to adopt legally binding measures[3] with respect to economic affairs, to date, the harmonization of economic matters has not

---

[1] *Les Novelles*, pp. 901–11; *Supplement to Bulletin of European Communities* (Mar. 1969) pp. 6–13; *Bulletin of European Communities* (Apr. 1969) pp. 41–3; European Community Background Information (March 29, 1972).

[2] See also Art. 3 (*g*).   [3] See also Art. 145.

progressed much beyond the consultative stage. In addition to the Monetary Committee, which is the principal forum of discussion of Community monetary affairs,[1] two new bodies also with a consultative function, the Committee of Governors of Central Banks of the European Economic Community[2] and the Budgetary Policy Committee,[3] have been established.[4] The purpose of the former Committee is to allow the six central bank governors to hold consultations on the main lines of central bank policy, to exchange information on the more important measures under this policy, and as far as possible to examine such measures before they are introduced by the competent national authorities. The task of the latter Committee, which is composed of officials drawn from the ministers of finance of the Six, is to examine, when national budgets are at an early stage of preparation, the broad lines of the member States' budgetary policies, particularly from the point of view of their repercussions on the economic development of the Community as a whole. These procedures were further augmented by a Council decision of 17 July 1969.[5] In this decision the members have agreed to prior consultations with other member States before their governments introduce any short-term economic policy measures that could affect the economies of other Community countries. Conversely, they have agreed that any one country can call for Community consultations if it thinks that the economic situation of another member State is exerting an unfavourable influence on its own. *Inter alia*, these consultations cover the budgetary, fiscal, and balance of payments policies of any member State. The Commission has

---

[1] Art. 105, para. 2. For a brief discussion of the nature and activities of the Monetary Committee, see H. K. Junckerstorff (ed.), *International Manual on the European Economic Community* (1963) pp. 124–5.

[2] See Council decision 64/300/CEE of 8 May 1964, J.O.C.E. (1964) p. 1206. For the text in English of the Commission recommendation to the Council and the Council's draft decision concerning collaboration between the central banks, see *Supplement to EEC Bulletin* (July 1963) pp. 35–7.

[3] See Council decision 64/299 C.E.E. of 8 May 1964, J.O.C.E. (1964) p. 1205. For the text in English of the Commission recommendation to the Council and the Council's draft decision concerning co-operation in matters of budgetary policy, see *Supplement to EEC Bulletin* (July 1963) pp. 39–40.

[4] In addition to these Committees, the Medium-term Economic Policy Committee and the Short-term Economic Policy Committee have been established; see *Supplement to Bulletin of the European Communities* (Mar. 1969) pp. 9–11.

[5] J.O.C.E. (1969) no. L 183/41.

also put forward far-reaching new proposals for the co-
ordination of the Six's medium-term economic policies, for
example, the growth rate of G.N.P., unemployment, the external balance of goods and services, and the over-all rate of
price increases.[1]

(b) External monetary relations. In order to promote the
harmonization of the policies of the six member States with
regard to their international monetary affairs, the Council
adopted on 8 May 1964 a decision which provides in part:

Des consultations ont lieu au sein du comité monétaire au sujet de
toute décision et de toute prise de position importantes des États
membres dans le domaine des relations monétaires internationales
et concernant en particulier:
— le fonctionnement général du système monétaire international;
— le recours par un État membre à des ressources mobilisables dans
le cadre d'accords internationaux;
— la participation d'un ou de plusieurs États membres aux actions
importantes de soutien monétaire au bénéfice de pays tiers.[2]

Through the operation of this decision the Community has
achieved some uniformity of action with regard to international
monetary problems and their solution. In practice, the approach of the Six has been to discuss any relevant topics among
themselves within the Monetary Committee, thus adopting a
common position before the topics come up for discussion in
other bodies or institutions. The concerted approach adopted
by the Six in respect to certain Fund matters is a case in point.
For example, the Monetary Committee held discussions before
the increase of Fund quotas and the extension of the General
Arrangements to Borrow in 1965.[3] More recently, during the
negotiations preceding the adoption of the special drawing
rights facility, the Six acting as a unit gained, in return for their
support of the scheme, the important concession that following
the entry into force of the Fund amendments all major Fund
decisions would require an eighty-five rather than an eighty
per cent majority for approval. Since the Six have between

[1] *Financial Times*, 18 Dec. 1969, p. 7.
[2] Council decision 64/301/CEE of 8 May 1964, J.O.C.E. (1964) p. 1207.
For the text in English of the Commission recommendation to the Council and
the Council's draft decision concerning co-operation in international monetary
relations, see *Supplement to EEC Bulletin* (July 1963) pp. 37–9.
[3] *EEC Bulletin* (July 1966) p. 55.

them over fifteen per cent of the total voting power, by acting in concert they will have a power of veto in regard to all major Fund decisions.[1]

6. Africa

(i) *Introduction.* Of the several regional economic and monetary associations currently existing in Africa,[2] only two will be considered in this study, namely the West African Monetary Union and the East African Common Market. These two arrangements are singled out for special examination, first, because they are among the oldest and therefore among the most stable regional institutions in contemporary Africa. Although both were formally established only during the past decade, their origins date back to the period of French and British colonial rule in Africa. The Treaty for East African Cooperation, for instance, which established a common market between Kenya, Tanzania, and Uganda in June 1967, represents in many respects only the formal institutionalization on an international legal basis of what had already been the established practice in the area[3] (for example, a common

---

[1] Similarly, in the case of deciding the size of the initial allocation of S.D.R.s, the six Common Market countries negotiated as a unit, having agreed a common position among themselves, *The Times*, 24 July 1969, p. 22, and the *Financial Times*, 25 July 1969, p. 1. For other practical examples of co-operation, see *Bulletin of European Communities* (Jan. 1969) pp. 15–17.

[2] Other arrangements include: (1) Union douanière des États de l'Afrique occidentale (UDEAO), signed in Abidjan, Ivory Coast, June 1966, by Dahomey, Ivory Coast, Mali, Mauritania, Niger, Senegal, and Upper Volta. For text of this agreement in English, see Miguel S. Wionczek (ed.), *Economic Cooperation in Latin America, Africa, and Asia. A Handbook of Documents* (1969) pp. 279–83. (2) Union douanière et économique de l'Afrique centrale (UDEAC), signed in Geneva, Dec. 1964, by Cameroon, Central African Republic, Congo (Brazzaville), Gabon, and Chad. For text of this treaty in English, see 4 I.L.M. (1965) pp. 699–718. (3) Union économique de l'Afrique centrale (UEAC), signed in Fort-Lamy, Chad, Apr. 1968, by Congo (Kinshasa), Central African Republic and Chad. For text in English, see 7 I.L.M. (1968) pp. 725–34. For other interim economic arrangements, see the Economic Community of Eastern Africa, 5 I.L.M. (1966) pp. 633–5; Agreement on Interim Organization for West African Economic Cooperation, 4 I.L.M. (1965) pp. 916–20; Articles of Association for the Establishment of an Economic Community of West Africa, 6 I.L.M. (1967) pp. 776–81. For a brief discussion of these and other arrangements, see Krishna Ahooja-Patel, 'Economic Co-operation in Africa. The Institutional Framework', 3 J.W.T.L. (1969) pp. 251–71.

[3] See Wionczek, op. cit. pp. 159–67.

currency area, administered by the East African Currency Board, was established among the three colonies in 1919/20).[1] Similarly, the West African Monetary Union (Dahomey, Ivory Coast, Mauritania, Niger, Senegal, Togo, Upper Volta, and Mali), which was formally established only on 12 May 1962 following the attainment by these States of full independence, is merely the successor to a previous long period of monetary and economic co-operation in the area under French tutelage. Secondly, the two arrangements merit special consideration because, of all the arrangements (global, regional, bilateral) considered in this study, they have attained the highest measures of supranational monetary co-operation. Indeed, while monetary union still remains a distant objective of the European Economic Community, it is already an existing reality in Equatorial[2] and French West Africa. In the East African Common Market, the provisions governing community monetary relations are so comprehensive that one authority has made the observation that 'The agreement on monetary matters makes the three currencies very close to a single currency'.[3]

As a result of this relatively advanced level of monetary integration, both arrangements contain a wide range of monetary provisions, some of which are unique. This is particularly so in the case of the West African Monetary Union. Accordingly, the following survey will consider first, and in some detail, the legal framework of the West African Monetary Union, and second, in less detail, the monetary provisions of the East African Common Market.

(ii) *West African Monetary Union.*[4] The principal legal instrument upon which the West African Monetary Union is based is the 'Traité instituant une Union monétaire ouest-africaine' (hereinafter referred to as traité) which entered into

---

[1] For a detailed discussion of the Board, see J. W. Krutz, 'The East African Currency Board', 13 *I.M.F. Staff Papers* (1966) pp. 229–55.

[2] Although they have not concluded a multilateral treaty to that effect, a monetary union also exists between Cameroon, Central African Republic, Congo (Brazzaville), Chad, and Gabon, see P. Robson, *Economic Integration in Africa* (1968) p. 202.

[3] A. Hazlewood, 'The Treaty for East African Co-operation', *Standard Bank Review* (Sept. 1967) p. 9.

[4] For a general discussion of the West African Monetary Union, see *La Zone franc en 1961*, pp. 145–8, and J. V. Mládek, 'Evolution of African Currencies, Part I: The Franc Area', 1 F.D. (1964) pp. 81–8.

force on 12 May 1962.[1] The traité is complemented by two further agreements, also adopted on 12 May 1962, namely the Accord de coopération entre la République française et les Républiques membres de l'Union monétaire ouest-africaine[2] (hereinafter referred to as the accord) and Statuts de la Banque centrale des États de l'Afrique de l'Ouest[3] (hereinafter referred to as statuts). These three instruments acting in concert establish between the member States a monetary regime which possesses a number of unique legal characteristics. Principal among these is the predominance of the supranational over the national regulation of monetary matters within the area. Unlike the other regional and indeed global arrangements already considered, where as a general rule international monetary rules are only grafted as exceptions on to the main corpus of municipal rules, in the West African Monetary Union the opposite situation prevails. The main corpus of law is international, and it is only in exceptional circumstances that the national interest, manifested through municipal regulations, may prevail.

More particularly, the definition of the monetary unit of account, such as dollar, pound, mark, franc, etc., which in most other currency systems is the function of the municipal legal system, is in the West African Monetary Union the function of international law. In this respect, Article 5 of the traité provides:

L'unité monétaire légale des États signataires est le franc de la Communauté financière africaine.

La définition et la parité du franc de la Communauté financière africaine sont celles en vigueur à la signature du présent traité pour l'actuel franc CFA. Elles ne pourront être modifiées que par accord entre tous les États de l'Union monétaire ouest-africaine et en conformité avec leurs engagements internationaux.

and Article 6 of the accord further provides:

La définition et la parité du franc de la Communauté financière africaine sont celles en vigueur à la signature du présent accord pour l'actuel franc CFA.

---

[1] For text of traité in French see *La Zone franc en 1961*, pp. 445–7.

[2] For text of accord in French, see ibid. pp. 448–50. For English text see 90 *Journal du droit international* (1963) pp. 871–3.

[3] For text of these statuts in French see *La Zone franc en 1961*, pp. 451–62.

Elles ne pourront être modifiées que par accord entre les États membres de l'Union monétaire et la République française.

The combined effect of these two provisions is to make 'le franc de la Communauté financière africaine' (commonly referred to as the C.F.A. franc) the sole legal monetary unit of account within the Union. Indeed, Article 1 of the traité categorically states that 'L'Union monétaire ouest-africaine . . . se caractérise par l'existence d'une même unité monétaire . . .'

Since the C.F.A. franc serves as a common currency for all the member States of the Monetary Union, its parity and alteration thereof is, by necessity, the object of a comparatively rigorous international legal regulation. Consequently, unlike the equivalent Fund provisions which merely require mutual consultation before any alteration of the par value, the parity of the C.F.A. franc cannot be altered except by the agreement of all the member States plus France. Finally, it is important to note that although all member States of the West African Monetary Union are also members of the Fund, they have not established with the Fund a par value for their currencies as required by Article IV, Section 1 (a) of the Fund's Articles of Agreement. Rather, in compliance with Article 5 and Article 6 of the traité and accord respectively, they have maintained from the inception of the Union a fixed relationship of fifty C.F.A. francs per French franc. Following the devaluation of the French franc in August 1969, the finance ministers of the franc area countries unanimously agreed to devalue the C.F.A. franc proportionately. Transactions between the C.F.A. franc and the French franc are carried out at fixed buying and selling rates, while exchange rates for other currencies move with the French franc rates for those currencies.

Secondly, complete freedom of transferability is a legal requirement within the Union. Article 4, paragraph 3 of the traité obliges all member States, under penalty of automatic expulsion from the Union, to permit 'La libre circulation des signes monétaires et la liberté des transferts à l'interieur de l'Union . . .' Of the two permitted exceptions to the rule of unrestricted transferability—that is, (a) the continued applicability of restrictions which were in force at the date of entry into force of the Union, and (b) the subsequent introduction of new restrictions—the latter constitutes a potentially greater threat to the maintenance of the free payments regime. However, to prevent abuse of this latter exception, such additional restrictions may be introduced only in specific circumstances (no indication is given of what will constitute 'conditions particulières'), and only if the Council of the Monetary Union agrees that their introduction will not cause serious damage to the other member States. The unrestricted right of internal convertibility is extended to external convertibility through the operation of Article 4 of the accord which provides as follows:

La République française assure la libre convertibilité en franc francais du franc de la Communauté financière africaine (franc CFA), émis par la Banque centrale des États de l'Afrique de l'Ouest. Un compte d'opérations est ouvert à cet effet au nom de la Banque centrale dans les écritures du Trésor français. Les modalités d'ouverture et de fonctionnement de ce compte feront l'objet d'une convention appropriée entre le Ministre des Finances de la République française et la Banque centrale.

Les États prendront toutes dispositions utiles pour que soient centralisés au compte d'opérations les avoirs extérieurs de l'Union monétaire.

This provision ensures the unlimited convertibility of the C.F.A. franc into French francs and thus into all other currencies or into gold in so far as is required by the member States of the Union and is permitted by the relevant franc area exchange controls. Accordingly, should the members of the Union as a whole run a deficit in their balance of payments, the French Treasury is obliged to advance them the funds necessary to finance the deficit. The *quid pro quo* for the unlimited convertibility of C.F.A. francs into French francs is an undertaking by all Union members to deposit with the French Treasury the whole of their external assets—that is, gold and foreign exchange.[1]

Thirdly, in order to ensure the proper functioning of the Monetary Union, the member States are obliged to adopt a uniform policy with respect to counterfeiting, bills of exchange and other commercial matters, banking, and credit.[2]

[1] The obligation to centralize all external assets of the Monetary Union in the operating account is established by the last sentence of Art. 4 of the accord and by Art. 4, para. 2 of the traité.
[2] Art. 10 of the traité.

Finally, the traité provides for the establishment of a central bank, the Banque centrale des États de l'Afrique de l'Ouest (hereinafter referred to as Banque centrale), which is to serve as the central bank for all member States of the Union. The statutory provisions of the Banque centrale are set out in an annex to the traité. Its functions, powers, etc., are therefore determined by an international rather than by a municipal legal instrument as is the case with other central bank statutory provisions.[1] The Banque centrale itself is endowed with international legal personality,[2] and in order that it may properly fulfil its functions, it is to be accorded in the territories of the member States all privileges and immunities normally accorded to international financial institutions.[3] More particularly, the Banque centrale is endowed with full legal personality for the purpose of suing, contracting, and buying and selling property (both moveable and immoveable). In addition it enjoys certain privileges and immunities accorded only to international organizations, such as inviolability of its archives, the exemption of its assets from all forms of requisition, confiscation, expropriation, and so on.[4]

Among the Banque centrale's principal functions, all of which are defined in the statuts and which can be modified only by the unanimous decision of its Administrative Council,[5] is the issuing of all legal tender, both notes and coins, within the Union.[6] The right of issue and matters pertaining thereto, such as face value of the notes and coins, impression, etc., are the exclusive prerogative of the Banque centrale.[7] In addition, the Banque centrale fulfils other traditional central bank functions:

---

[1] For a useful collection of statutes and related materials pertaining to central bank monetary and banking laws of twenty-one countries, see *Central Banking Legislation*, 2 vols. (I.M.F., 1961).

[2] Art. 1 of the statuts provides: 'La Banque centrale des États de l'Afrique de l'Ouest, ci-après désignée « la Banque », est un établissement public international régi par les accords conclus entre les États participant à la formation de son capital, ci-après dénommés « États membres », et par les présents statuts.'

[3] Art. 9 of the traité provides in part: 'En vue de permettre à la Banque centrale de remplir les fonctions qui lui sont confiées, les immunités et privilèges habituellement reconnus aux institutions financières internationales lui seront concédés sur le territoire de chacun des États membres de l'Union monétaire dans les conditions précisées par ses statuts.' See also Art. 3 of the accord.

[4] Art. 4 of the statuts.   [5] Art. 8 of the traité.
[6] Art. 6 of the traité.
[7] Arts. 6, 7, and 8 of the statuts.

it is empowered, for instance, to deal in gold and foreign exchange,[1] to buy and sell short-term treasury bills, etc.[2]

(iii) *East African Common Market*.[3] Although the monetary provisions of the Treaty for East African Co-operation are not as extensive as those of the West African Monetary Union just discussed, they nevertheless establish a relatively rigorous monetary regime within the area.

First, the retention and introduction of exchange restrictions on both current and capital account are, as a general rule, prohibited. Article 2 of the Treaty, which sets out the general aims of the Community, provides that the Community shall use its best endeavours to ensure, *inter alia*, 'the retention of freedom of current account payments between the Partner States, and freedom of capital account payments necessary to further the aims of the Community'. This objective is spelt out in more detail in Article 25. Paragraph 1 of that Article, which is concerned with payments for current account transactions, differs from equivalent provisions to be found in other treaties and merits special attention. It provides:

Each Partner State undertakes to permit, in the currency of the Partner State in which the creditor or beneficiary resides, all *bona fide* payments on current account falling within the definition of current account payments set out in Annex VII to this Treaty, and undertakes to ensure that all necessary permissions and authorities are given without undue delay.

This provision is of unique interest in that it enumerates, item by item, in Annex VII all those current account transactions for which the requisite payment must be permitted. To avoid rigidity and to allow alterations in the annexed items in response to actual experience, the list, which in fact includes most goods and services, may from time to time be amended or added to. Paragraph 2 of Article 25 similarly obliges each Partner State to permit all payments and transfers on capital account, except to the extent that a Partner State considers that 'control of

---

[1] Art. 9 of the statuts.   [2] Arts. 10 ff. of the statuts.
[3] For text of the Treaty see 6 I.L.M. (1967) pp. 932–1057; 7 *Journal of Common Market Studies* (1968) pp. 129–91. For a general discussion see N. Orloff, 'Economic Integration in East Africa: the Treaty for East African Co-operation', 7 *The Columbia Journal of Transnational Law* (1968) pp. 302–32; J. Kodwo Bentil, 'The Legal Framework and the Economic Aspects of the East African Common Market', 4 *The Journal of Law and Economic Development* (1969) pp. 27–47.

certain categories of such payments and transfers is necessary for furthering its economic development and an increase in trade consistent with the aims of the Community'. This rather broad exception to the free movement of capital was deemed necessary so that a partner State suffering from a serious outflow of capital would be legally entitled to take defensive measures.[1] However, such restrictions, if introduced, must not prejudice the ability of the Community or its organs from carrying out their functions under the treaty.

Secondly, although the Treaty makes no mention of exchange rates and their regulation, all three partner States of the Community are also members of the Fund and have accordingly established with the Fund identical rates of exchange for their respective currencies. (The established par value for all three currencies is 0·124414 gram of fine gold per currency unit or 7·14286 current units = $1.)[2] Subject to exchange control laws and regulations, which must not be in conflict with the provisions of the Treaty, all exchange transactions in the three currencies must take place at the official par value and without any exchange commission.[3]

Thirdly, the Treaty provides for two forms of collective defence measures should any member State suffer from a temporary balance of payments disequilibrium. As an initial corrective measure, the country in difficulty may introduce quantitative import restrictions. Such restrictions, however, may be introduced only under strictly defined conditions, and in particular only after prior consultation has taken place within the Common Market. Moreover, while such restrictions remain in force, the Common Market Council is obliged to keep them under review.[4] In addition to allowing the introduction of direct controls, provision is also made for a system of reciprocal credits. Thus, if a partner State is in balance of payments difficulties, and provided that it has already exercised its drawing rights under the first credit tranche beyond the gold tranche with the International Monetary Fund, such State may request assistance, up to a predetermined amount, in the way

---

[1] A. Hazlewood, 'The Treaty for East African Co-operation', *Standard Bank Review* (Sept. 1967) p. 9.

[2] *I.M.F. Nineteenth Annual Report on Exchange Restrictions* (1968) pp. 247, 405, 435.

[3] Art. 24.

[4] Art. 12, para. 4.

of credits from another partner State. A partner State from which the credit is requested is obliged to grant the credit only up to a certain amount (subject to an agreement to the contrary), and only if it has had, over a defined period, a payments surplus with the requesting partner State. All credits granted are to be denominated in the currency of the partner State granting the credit, and are not to remain outstanding beyond a period of three years. To encourage early repayment, the interest charges increase from 4 per cent in the first year to 5 and 6 per cent in the second and third years respectively.[1]

Finally, the partner States have agreed to harmonize their monetary policies to the extent required for the proper functioning of the Common Market. For this purpose, the Governors of the three central banks are to meet at least four times every year.[2]

7. Central and South America

(i) *Introduction.* In this section, the monetary provisions of three[3] regional economic arrangements will be examined— namely the Central American Common Market (C.A.C.M.), the Latin American Free Trade Association (L.A.F.T.A.), and the Caribbean Free Trade Association (C.A.R.I.F.T.A.). Other legal instruments associated with the above arrangements, such as the Agreement Establishing the Central American Clearing House, the Agreement on the Establishment of a Central American Monetary Union, etc., will also be briefly considered.

(ii) *Central American Common Market.*[4] Although economic co-operation has a long history in Central America, the major impetus for regional economic integration in the area began

---

[1] Art. 28.

[2] Art. 2, para. (*f*) and Art. 27, para. (2).

[3] A fourth arrangement, the so-called Andean Group, consisting of Bolivia, Colombia, Chile, Ecuador, Peru, and Venezuela, was formed in Feb. 1968. See *BOLSA Review* (Nov. 1968) pp. 626–7; ibid. (July 1969) pp. 426–9; I.L.M. (1969) pp. 940–58.

[4] For a general discussion of the evolution of the C.A.C.M. as well as of its principal legal features, see Simmonds, 'The Central American Common Market', 16 I.C.L.Q. (1967) pp. 911–45. More generally, see *BOLSA Quarterly Review* (Apr. 1961) pp. 186–99; ibid. (Jan. 1964) pp. 36–46; *BOLSA Review* (June 1968) pp. 312–32; J. W. Crow, 'Economic Integration in Central America', 3 F.D. (Mar. 1966) pp. 58–66; Miguel S. Wionczek (ed.), *Latin American Economic Integration* (1966) pp. 263–80.

with the conclusion on 13 December 1960 of the General Treaty of Central American Economic Integration.[1] Although the primary objective of the General Treaty was the creation of a regional common market between the five member States —Costa Rica, El Salvador, Guatemala, Honduras, and Nicaragua—the Treaty did not devote much attention to regional monetary relations.[2] Rather, the main provisions affecting Central American States' exchange rates and exchange restrictions spring from their membership in the Fund. For example, unlike many other Latin American countries, all five member States of the Central American Common Market have for several years past agreed par values with the Fund and have conducted exchange transactions within the permitted margins.[3] Similarly, as regards exchange restrictions, all five countries have accepted the obligations of Article VIII of the Fund Agreement[3] under which they are prohibited, subject to certain permitted exceptions, from introducing exchange restrictions on current transactions.

The General Treaty's sole reference to monetary affairs is contained in Article 10. Nevertheless, this provision, as evidenced by subsequent practice, has had a considerable impact on monetary relations within the Central American Common Market and will therefore be cited here in full:

The central banks of the signatory States shall closely cooperate in order to prevent currency speculations which might affect the exchange rates and so as to maintain the convertibility of the currencies of the respective countries on a basis which, under normal conditions, guarantees freedom, uniformity, and stability of exchange.

In the event of one of the signatory States establishing quantitative restrictions on international monetary transfers, it shall adopt the necessary measures to ensure that such restrictions will not affect the other States in a discriminatory manner.

---

[1] For the text of this Treaty plus several other treaties, declarations, etc., affecting Central American economic relations, see *Instruments Relating to the Economic Integration of Latin America* (Inter-American Institute of International Legal Studies, 1968) pp. 3–204.

[2] See J. Gonzales Del Valle, 'Monetary Integration in Central America: Achievements and Expectations', 5 *Journal of Common Market Studies* (1966–7) pp. 13–25.

[3] *I.M.F. Nineteenth Annual Report on Exchange Restrictions* (1968) pp. 113, 136, 175, 185, 313.

In the event of serious balance-of-payments difficulties which affect or might affect the monetary payment relations between the signatory States, the Executive Council either *ex officio*, or at the request of one of the Parties, shall immediately study the problem in collaboration with the central banks, for the purpose of recommending to the signatory governments a satisfactory solution compatible with the maintenance of the multilateral free trade system.

In compliance with the first paragraph of Article 10, the central bank presidents of the five member States concluded on 25 February 1964 an 'Agreement on the Establishment of a Central American Monetary Union'.[1] This agreement, which, it should be noted, is intended to serve only as a transitional arrangement and is to be superseded, when conditions permit, by a permanent agreement,[2] is designed to promote the co-ordination and harmonization of the monetary, exchange, and credit policies of the Central American countries and thereby progressively to create the basis for a Central American Monetary Union. More particularly, the five central banks have set themselves—*inter alia*—the following goals: (1) to promote a uniformity in the exchange systems, as well as stability and convertibility, of the Central American currencies; (2) to broaden the Central American system of multilateral clearing and encourage the use of national currencies in transactions between Central American countries; (3) to promote financial assistance, with the aim of correcting temporary maladjustments in the balance of payments; (4) to obtain a high degree of uniformity in legislation with respect to monetary, exchange, and credit policies; and (5) to establish a permanent system of information and consultation, with the aim of harmonizing

[1] For text of this Agreement, in English, see *Instruments Relating to the Economic Integration of Latin America*, pp. 161–7.

[2] See last sentence of Art. II of the Monetary Agreement. An important step forward in the establishment of a permanent arrangement was taken in Sept. 1969, when a formal agreement for the creation of the Central American Fund for Monetary Stabilization was signed in Washington by the presidents of the central banks of Guatemala, El Salvador, Honduras, Nicaragua, and Costa Rica. The Stabilization Fund is designed to provide short-term financial assistance to member countries of the Central American Common Market facing temporary balance of payments difficulties. Its policies will be orientated to encourage monetary discipline and to preserve free trade within the context of the Central American integration process. The fund will have resources totalling $20 million, to be subscribed equally by the five member countries. 21 *International Financial News Survey* (24 Oct. 1969) p. 344.

the course of action and the instruments relating to monetary, exchange, and credit policy.[1] In addition, the five central banks concluded on 28 July 1961 an 'Agreement Establishing the Central American Clearing House'.[2] The principal function of the clearing-house is to encourage the use of the five national currencies of the region for the negotiation of regional trade and financial transactions. In practice, the clearing-house has been an outstanding success, with over ninety per cent of total regional commercial transactions being settled through it in 1968.

In compliance with the second paragraph of Article 10, Central American States that have found it necessary to introduce exchange restrictions have, as a general rule, exempted all other C.A.C.M. countries from such restrictions. For example, Guatemala imposes a surcharge of 100 per cent of the customs duty on products originating in or imported from countries with which it has had an unfavourable trade balance. On 31 December 1967, this surcharge applied to certain imports from twenty-eight countries. However, all imports which were included in the agreed uniform tariff list of the countries participating in the General Treaty of Central American Economic Integration were exempt from the surcharge.[3] In El Salvador, for specified goods (including luxury goods, alcoholic beverages, cigarettes, perfumes and cosmetics, jewellery, certain types of automobiles, etc.) the Exchange Control Department does not permit importers to place orders abroad unless evidence is submitted that an advance deposit in colones equivalent to 100 per cent of the value of the goods to be imported has been lodged with the Central Reserve Bank, or at the option of the importer, that an irrevocable letter of credit will be established on which a 100 per cent margin deposit is made. However, imports of the same goods from other countries of the C.A.C.M. are exempt from these requirements.[4]

---

[1] Art. 1 of the Monetary Agreement.

[2] For text of this agreement in English, see *Instruments Relating to the Economic Integration of Latin America*, pp. 153–61. An 'Agreement on Clearance and Reciprocal Credits between the Central Banks Members of the Central American Clearing House and the Bank of Mexico' was subsequently signed at Mexico City on 27 Aug. 1963, see ibid. pp. 167–74.

[3] *I.M.F. Nineteenth Annual Report on Exchange Restrictions* (1968) p. 176.

[4] Ibid. p. 137.

Similarly, Costa Rica, which operates a multiple rate structure
—that is, an official rate of 6·62 Costa Rican colones per $1
and a free market rate of 7·77–7·80 Costa Rican colones
per $1—allows importers of goods from the other C.A.C.M.
countries to make payments at the official rate.[1] Foreign exchange for certain goods imported from other than C.A.C.M.
countries must be purchased at the free market rate. The free
market rate being higher than the official rate, is tantamount
to a form of exchange restriction.

Finally, in compliance with paragraph 3 of Article 10, which
requires the members of the C.A.C.M. to adopt a common
approach to Community balance of payments difficulties, the
Central American Economic Council agreed to introduce a new
Protocol to the General Treaty to ease the problem of the
region's balance of payments, which, because of an increase
in import prices and a decrease in export prices, showed a
deficit of $240 million in 1967. The Council recommended in
this Protocol the imposition of an additional duty of thirty per
cent on the import of certain goods from outside Central
America.[2]

(iii) *The Latin American Free Trade Association*.[3] The Montevideo treaty which established the L.A.F.T.A. was signed on
18 February 1960.[4] The Association, which includes in its
membership all the South American Republics plus Mexico,
has as its principal objective the establishment of a free trade
area within a twelve-year transitional period. However, the
success of the treaty in this regard has been minimal.[5] In this
respect, the failure of the Montevideo treaty to free trade within
the area stands in marked contrast to the success of the General
Treaty in Central America.

[1] Ibid. pp. 113–14.,   [2] *BOLSA Review* (July 1968) p. 403.
[3] For a general discussion of the legal features of L.A.F.T.A., see F. E. Nattier,
'The Latin American Free Trade Association (LAFTA)', 21 *Business Lawyer*
(1965–6) pp. 515–36. See also F. Orrego-Vicuna, 'Developments in the Latin
American Free Trade Association', *Proceedings of the American Society of International
Law* (1967) pp. 174–81. More generally, see M. S. Wionczek (ed.), *Latin American
Economic Integration* (1966) pp. 67–260; 'The Latin American Free Trade Association', *BOLSA Quarterly Review* (July 1960) pp. 1–7; 'Lafta Achievements and
Prospects', *BOLSA Review* (Feb. 1967) pp. 60–70.
[4] For text of this Agreement plus several resolutions on the functions and
organization of the L.A.F.T.A., see *Instruments Relating to the Economic Integration
of Latin America*, pp. 207–337.
[5] *BOLSA Review* (July 1969) pp. 425–9.

As in the case of the General Treaty, the provisions in the treaty of Montevideo relating to inter-Community monetary relations are few. No mention is made of exchange rates. Rather like the Central American Republics, all L.A.F.T.A. countries are members of the Fund, and most have at least formally (however, often the rates at which exchange transactions take place are not based on the agreed par value) established a par value for their currencies with the Fund.[1] Inflation in most L.A.F.T.A. countries is rampant, and resort to both multiple and fluctuating rates is not uncommon. Indeed, it has repeatedly been asserted that unless and until 'the problem of inflation in Latin America is solved, it will be difficult to advance rapidly toward an expansion of intra-zonal trade, even if all trade restrictions are removed.'[2]

As regards exchange restrictions, however, the treaty is not completely silent. Article 3 obliges all member States to eliminate gradually during the twelve-year transitional period all duties, charges, and restrictions (the term 'duties and charges' is defined to mean customs duties and any other charges having equivalent effect—whether of a fiscal, monetary, or exchange nature) on substantially all their reciprocal trade. Although financial restrictions within the area remain, examples of preferential treatment are nevertheless abundant. Argentina requires an advance import deposit of forty per cent on most imports from all sources. Goods imported from L.A.F.T.A. countries, however, are exempt if the goods are included in Argentina's concession lists.[3] Chile, Colombia, Paraguay, and Uruguay, which also operate advance deposit schemes, have likewise excluded from this requirement any L.A.F.T.A. imports which are included in their respective concession lists.[4] Similarly, Paraguay, which imposes an import surcharge on certain imported commodities, excludes L.A.F.T.A. imports from the surcharge.[5] Moreover, to facilitate the settlement of regional payments and thereby encourage still further the removal of restrictions, the central banks of L.A.F.T.A.

---

[1] *I.M.F. Nineteenth Annual Report on Exchange Restrictions* (1968) pp. 24, 41, 43, 85, 97, 132, 291, 337, 340, 470, 473.

[2] W. J. Sedwitz, 'Economic Aspects of Latin American Integration', *Proceedings of the American Society of International Law* (1967) p. 183.

[3] *I.M.F. Nineteenth Annual Report of Exchange Restrictions* (1968) pp. 24–35.

[4] Ibid. pp. 86, 98, 337, 470.   [5] Ibid. p. 337.

countries on 22 September 1965 signed an agreement for a multilateral clearing system.[1] Under the terms of this agreement, the central banks may provide each other with reciprocal lines of credit under mutual guarantee of convertibility and transferability. Bilateral balances are to be settled twice a month and cleared through an agent (Central Bank of Peru).

Finally, any L.A.F.T.A. country whose balance of payments is adversely affected by concessions granted under the Montevideo treaty can seek relief under various escape clauses. First, in accordance with the principle of reciprocity, if a partner State suffers 'significant and persistent disadvantages', it can request other member States to liberalize their restrictions more quickly.[2] However, should such measures prove to be insufficient in correcting the adverse balance of payments situation, the affected participant may—with the prior authorization of the other partner States—impose temporary, non-discriminatory restrictions on imports of commodities listed in the National or Common Schedules.[3] Finally, in cases of emergency, that is, where the seriousness of the situation is such that it requires immediate action, the affected member State need not wait for specific authorization from the other member States, but may act unilaterally. However, any measures taken unilaterally must be immediately notified to the Committee, which may, if it deems it necessary, convene a special session of the L.A.F.T.A. Conference (the principal decision-making body of the Association) to consider the situation.[4] Should any restrictions adopted under these saving clauses be prolonged for more than one year, negotiations with a view to their elimination must be initiated forthwith.[5]

(iv) *C.A.R.I.F.T.A.* The agreement establishing the Caribbean Free Trade Association entered into force on 1 May 1968.[6] It provides for the gradual removal of import duties (where

---

[1] Agreement between the Central Banks of the Member Countries of LAFTA and Regulations for the System of Multilateral Clearance of Balances between the Central Banks of the Countries of LAFTA are both reproduced in English in *Instruments Relating to the Economic Integration of Latin America*, pp. 322–7. See also 'The Clearing Mechanism of the Latin American Free Trade Association', 51 *Federal Reserve Bank of New York Monthly Review* (Oct. 1969) pp. 216–21.

[2] Art. 11.   [3] Art. 24.   [4] Art. 25.   [5] Art. 26.

[6] I.L.M. (1968) pp. 935–77. Its membership was composed of Antigua, Barbados, Guyana, Trinidad and Tobago, Dominica, Grenada, St. Kitts–Nevis–Anguilla, St. Lucia, St. Vincent, Jamaica, and Montserrat.

'import duties' means any tax or surtax of customs and any other charges of equivalent effect—whether fiscal, monetary, or exchange)[1] and quantitative import restrictions (where 'quantitative restrictions' are defined to mean any prohibitions or restrictions on imports whether made effective through quotas, import licences, or other measures with equivalent effect)[2] on the flow of goods between member countries. In addition to the prohibition of exchange restrictions on current visible transactions, Article 25 of the treaty provides that 'The Council shall as soon as practicable, having due regard to international obligations, decide the treatment to be given to invisible transactions and transfers amongst Member Territories with a view to promoting the objectives of this Agreement.' However, the treaty makes no reference to capital movements, and accordingly it would appear that the member States are free to control by means of exchange restrictions the free flow of capital within the area. In case any member State suffers from a balance of payments disequilibrium, it may introduce quantitative import restrictions.[3] The conditions under which such restriction may be introduced and also the provisions for their removal are identical to those provided for in the E.F.T.A. and Anglo-Irish Free Trade Agreement already discussed.[4] No reference is made in the treaty to exchange rates. However, Guyana, Trinidad and Tobago, and Jamaica have all established a par value with the Fund,[5] while the East Caribbean dollar (4·80 East Caribbean dollars to £1 sterling as of March 1971) circulated in Antigua, Dominica, St. Kitts–Nevis– Anguilla, St. Lucia, St. Vincent, and Montserrat.[6]

Art. 4.   [2] Art. 13.   [3] Art. 21.
    [4] See above, p. 271.
    [5] *I.M.F. Nineteenth Annual Report on Exchange Restrictions* (1968) pp. 181, 234, 418.
    [6] The East Caribbean dollar was issued on 6 Oct. 1965 by the East Caribbean Currency Authority, pursuant to the East Caribbean Currency Agreement of 1965, to replace the West Indian dollar at par (the West Indian dollar, which was issued by the British Caribbean Currency Board in Barbados, Guyana, Leeward Islands, Windward Islands, and Trinidad and Tobago, had a fixed relationship to sterling of $WI4·80 = £1). There are no restrictions on the movements of local currency notes between parties to the East Caribbean Currency Agreement.

XI

BILATERAL MONETARY
ARRANGEMENTS

1. *Introduction*

IN addition to being the object of international legal regulation at both the global and the regional levels, international liquidity, exchange rates, and exchange restrictions are also frequently dealt with by States on a bilateral level. Often such bilateral arrangements do no more than reiterate already existing obligations between the two States concerned: that is to say, they repeat such obligations—for example, the duty not to introduce direct financial and commercial controls that have already been imposed on the two States through their participation in either the Fund Agreement, the G.A.T.T., or some other regional treaty arrangement. Or in the case of international liquidity, the swap arrangements to be considered in this chapter do no more than make additional liquidity available to the parties on a reciprocal stand-by basis, in much the same way as the International Monetary Fund makes its resources available to member States on a stand-by basis. Nevertheless, these bilateral arrangements merit some consideration: (1) in spite of the general similarity, they possess certain attributes (this is particularly so of the swap arrangements) that are not to be found in the other forms of international monetary co-operation already discussed; (2) they serve to illustrate, yet again, how far States have moved away from the pre-Second World War notion that exchange rates, exchange restrictions, and international liquidity are matters primarily of national concern; (3) they exist as part of contemporary international monetary law and simply from the viewpoint of 'exhaustion of the subject-matter' require mention in this study. Accordingly in this chapter will be examined first the nature and function of the so-called 'swap' credit arrangements, and secondly the nature and function of the monetary provisions found mainly in treaties of friendship, commerce, and navigation. For reasons of convenience, only United States practice will be examined in depth. Reference will be made to the practice of other States only when it is advantageous for reasons either of clarification or of contrast to do so.

2. 'Swap' Arrangements

(i) *Historical functional analysis.* 'Swap' arrangements have been defined as

des accords aux termes desquels deux banques centrales se cèdent réciproquement des montants équivalents de leurs monnaies, pour une durée fixe, qui, en général, varie de trois à six mois. Du point de vue juridique, l'opération paraît s'analyser en un achat au comptant et une revente à terme de la monnaie du cocontractant. Comme le cours de revente est fixé dès l'origine, l'opération comporte, par sa nature même, une garantie de change.[1]

As suggested by the above definition, the purpose of a swap arrangement is to make available to the two partner States, on a stand-by basis, an agreed amount of currency which can be drawn should either State require additional reserve assets to meet balance of payments requirements.

Although swap arrangements have a history that dates back to the mid nineteenth century,[2] the first contemporary agreement of this type was negotiated in March 1961 when credits in excess of $900m. were made available to the Bank of England by several European central banks to enable the former to counter a speculative outflow of funds which resulted from the revaluation of the Deutsche mark and the Dutch guilder.[3] Since then, the scope of swap arrangements has been greatly expanded. For example, in the case of the United States, the amount of reserves available under central bank swap arrangements has risen from about $700m. in 1962 to over $10,000m. in September 1969.[4] The credit facilities

---

[1] L. Focsaneanu, 'Les aspects juridiques du système monétaire international', 95 *Journal du droit international* (1968) p. 268.
[2] Hirsch, op. cit. pp. 236 ff.
[3] 48 *Federal Reserve Bulletin* (Sept. 1962) p. 1140.
[4] 51 *Federal Reserve Bank of New York Monthly Review* (Sept. 1969) p. 179.

range from $2,000m. with the Bank of England to $100m. with each of the following central banks: the Austrian National Bank, the National Bank of Denmark, and the Bank of Norway.[1] Since the inception of the swap network in March 1962, total drawings up to September 1969 on the lines of credit by the Federal Reserve and its partner foreign central banks have been in excess of $19,500m.[1] As mentioned, central banks will draw on these lines to replenish their reserves in times of payments difficulties, and will reverse the transaction when the situation improves—normally in three to six months. For example, during the speculative rush into Deutsche marks in the spring of 1969, the National Bank of Denmark activated its credit line with the Federal Reserve drawing $50m. (in April) to replenish reserves lost through exchange market pressures. It subsequently drew another $50m. (in May), thus exhausting its swap facility. During June, an inflow of funds to Denmark enabled the National Bank to repay the $100m. to the Federal Reserve, returning the Federal Reserve credit line to a fully available stand-by basis.[1]

(ii) *Legal analysis.* In attempting to ascertain the legal nature of swap arrangements, the lawyer is somewhat hampered by the lack of available documentation. Indeed, official claims would suggest that by and large no formal agreements in the traditional international legal sense—that is, treaties, exchange of notes, etc.—are made, but rather that such arrangements as do exist do so on the basis of gentlemen's agreements.[2] Nevertheless, in so far as the United States swap arrangements are concerned, the following five general principles have been summarized as running throughout all the arrangements:

1. A swap constitutes a reciprocal credit facility under which a central bank agrees to exchange on request its own currency for the currency of the other party up to a maximum amount over a limited period of time, such as 3 months or 6 months.

2. If such a standby swap between the Federal Reserve and the Bank of England, for example, were to be drawn upon by the Federal Reserve, the Federal Reserve would credit the dollar account of the Bank of England with $50 million at a rate of, say $2·80 to the pound while obtaining in exchange a credit on the books of the

[1] Ibid.
[2] Hirsch, op. cit. pp. 242–3.

Bank of England of about £18 million. Both parties would agree to reverse the transaction on a specified date, say, within 3 months, at the same rate of exchange, thus providing each with forward cover against the remote risk of a devaluation of either currency.

3. The foreign currency obtained by each party as a result of such cross credits to each other's accounts would, unless disbursed in exchange operations, be invested in a time deposit or other investment instrument, earning an identical rate of interest of, say, 2 per cent and subject to call on 2 days notice.

4. After consultation with the other, each party would be free to draw upon the foreign currency acquired under the swap to conduct spot transactions or meet forward exchange obligations.

5. Each swap arrangement is renewable upon agreement of both parties.[1]

These five basic principles, as pointed out by Fawcett,[2] show the swap arrangements to be similar to the International Monetary Fund's stand-by facilities—for example, both are short-term in duration, both are initially only credit facilities which must be drawn and subsequently repaid, and both contain exchange rate guarantees. On the basis of (i) these similarities, plus the following additional two submissions: (ii) that central banks can act as agents for and on behalf of States and in that capacity can enter into agreements governed by international law, and (iii) that in the case of the swap arrangements now under discussion, it was the parties' intention when entering into these arrangements to create legally binding agreements, Fawcett concludes 'that "swap" agreements may also be regarded as international agreements, being concluded by central banks exercising State functions, governed in part by the law of the place of performance and in part by provisions of the Fund Agreement . . .'[3] Whether swap arrangements can be regarded as international agreements turns upon the following question: did the two parties intend to create legally binding obligations in international law? The question, then, is essentially one of *opinio juris sive necessitatis*,[4] or in the words of Starke, 'a general acknowledge-

---

[1] 48 *Federal Reserve Bulletin* (Sept. 1962) pp. 1147–8.
[2] Fawcett, 'Trade and Finance in International Law', 123 R.C. (1968–I) pp. 232–7.
[3] Ibid. pp. 236–7.
[4] For a discussion of this concept see Starke, op. cit. pp. 36–7.

ment by States that the conduct or the abstention therefrom is a matter both of legal right and of legal obligation . . .'[1] In the absence of more complete information and documentation on the specific nature of these arrangements, one cannot give an authoritative answer to the question.

3. *Exchange Restrictions and Rates*

Although the monetary provisions of the several post-Second World War bilateral treaties of friendship, commerce, and navigation concluded by the United States of America differ in detail, in substance they are essentially the same. Accordingly, in this section only the monetary provisions of the Treaty of Friendship, Commerce, and Navigation concluded between the United States of America and Japan on 2 April 1953[2] will be examined in detail. However, where provisions in any of the other treaties of Friendship, Commerce, and Navigation concluded by the United States[3] depart significantly from the established norm, they too will be noted. Finally, as already mentioned, bilateral commercial treaties concluded by nations other than the United States will be referred to only for the sake of clarification or comparison.

In Article XII, paragraph 5 of the U.S.A.–Japanese treaty, exchange restrictions are defined in the broadest sense. First, they are deemed to encompass not only those measures which in fact prohibit the making of payments and transfers, but also those measures which in fact only 'delay' or 'interfere with' the making of payments and transfers. In this sense, therefore, it is probably more correct to refer to these provisions not as provisions pertaining to exchange restrictions, but rather as provisions pertaining to exchange controls, it being remembered

---

[1] Ibid. pp. 37, 340.

[2] 206 U.N.T.S. 143.

[3] The following treaties have been concluded by the United States of America since the Second World War with: China, 25 U.N.T.S. 69; Italy, 79 U.N.T.S. 171; Ireland, 206 U.N.T.S. 269; Ethiopia, 206 U.N.T.S. 41; Greece, 224 U.N.T.S. 279; Israel, 219 U.N.T.S. 237; Denmark, 421 U.N.T.S. 105; Japan, 206 U.N.T.S. 143; Germany, 273 U.N.T.S. 3; Iran, 284 U.N.T.S. 93; Nicaragua, 367 U.N.T.S. 3; Netherlands, 285 U.N.T.S. 231; Korea, 302 U.N.T.S. 281; Muscat and Oman, 380 U.N.T.S. 181; Pakistan, 404 U.N.T.S. 259; France, 401 U.N.T.S. 75; Belgium, 480 U.N.T.S. 149; Vietnam, 424 U.N.T.S. 137; Luxembourg, 474 U.N.T.S. 3. For a complete list of commercial treaties concluded by the United States in the period 1778–1960, see R. R. Wilson, *United States Commercial Treaties and International Law* (1960) pp. 331–4.

that for the purposes of this study, exchange controls have been so defined as to include all forms of interference with the consummation of foreign exchange transactions, while exchange restrictions have been so defined as to include only those measures which actually prohibit the making of international payments. For example, the requirement that all foreign exchange transactions be notified to the official monetary authority for statistical purposes is a form of exchange control, but is not an exchange restriction. This requirement may interfere with the making of an international payment and to that extent has a nuisance value, but it does not prevent the payment from actually taking place. Secondly, the provision applies to payments in respect of both current and capital transactions. In contrast, it should be remembered that the Fund's exchange restriction provisions are in the main concerned only with current transactions.

Having defined exchange restrictions controls in this comprehensive manner, the two contracting parties agree in the following sweeping language that they shall not 'impose exchange restrictions as defined in paragraph 5 of the present article . . .'[1] This general prohibition, however, is partially mitigated by a number of permitted exceptions. Either party may introduce exchange restrictions (i) to the extent necessary to prevent its monetary reserves from falling to a very low level, or (ii) to effect a moderate increase in very low monetary reserves.[1] Both these exceptions are essentially identical to the two exceptions enumerated in Article XII, paragraph 2 (a) of the G.A.T.T., which states that any contracting party may introduce quantitative import restrictions in order (i) to forestall the imminent threat of, or to stop, a serious decline in its monetary reserves, or (ii) in the case of a contracting party with very low monetary reserves, to achieve a reasonable rate of increase in its reserves.

However, the introduction and administration of exchange restrictions on the basis of the two permitted exceptions in the U.S.A.–Japanese treaty is subject to the following two general and two particular conditions.

(a) Particular conditions. First, the introduction of exchange restrictions must not be contrary to either party's obligations

[1] Art. XII, para. 2.

under the Fund Agreement[1] which prohibits the utilization of all exchange restrictions in respect of current international transactions. A number of exceptions to this general prohibition are permitted by the Fund Agreement and these have been discussed. They do not, however, include the two exceptions mentioned in the U.S.A.–Japanese treaty. Accordingly, should either Japan or the United States (both being Fund members) seek to introduce exchange restrictions either to prevent their monetary reserves from falling to a very low level or to effect a moderate increase in their reserves, they would need to acquire Fund approval to do so. On the other hand, paragraph 2 of Article XII goes on to state that 'the provisions of the present article do not . . . preclude imposition of particular restrictions whenever the Fund specifically authorizes or requests a Party to impose such particular restrictions'. Under the terms of this provision, should either Japan or the United States seek to introduce exchange restrictions for reasons other than those enumerated in Article XII, paragraph 2, they would be at liberty to do so provided only that they had received prior Fund approval. In short, it would appear that in so far as payments in respect of current international transactions are concerned, paragraph 2 of Article XII neither adds to nor detracts from either party's already existent obligations under the Fund Agreement.[2] Restrictions on capital transactions, however, can be introduced by either party only for reasons which comply with the two enumerated exceptions.[3]

Secondly, paragraph 3 of Article XII provides that when exchange restrictions are in fact introduced under the auspices of Article XII, paragraph 2—just described—they must be administered in such a way as to permit the other party to withdraw in its own currency (a) any compensation arising from the nationalization by one contracting party of any assets

---

[1] The last sentence of Art. XII, para. 2 reads in part: 'It is understood that the provisions of the present article do not alter the obligations either Party may have to the International Monetary Fund . . .'

[2] Cf. Metzger, 'Exchange Controls and International Law', *University of Illinois Law Forum* (1959) p. 323.

[3] In addition, most of the treaties contain a provision which allows either contracting party to introduce restrictions on the inflow of capital. Para. 6 of the Protocol attached to the U.S.A.–Japanese treaty, for example, provides: 'Either Party may impose restrictions on the introduction of foreign capital as may be necessary to protect its monetary reserves as provided in article XII, paragraph 2.'

belonging to nationals of the other contracting party, (*b*) earnings, whether in the form of salaries, interest, dividends, commissions, royalties, payments for technical services, or otherwise, and (*c*) amounts for amortization of loans, depreciation of direct investments, and capital transfers. The nature of these 'privileged withdrawals' clearly implies that they were singled out for special treatment in order to protect the commercial interests which either State may have in the territory of the co-contracting State. The importance of such a provision to the United States, which has a large stake in private foreign investment, is manifest. On the other hand, and as *quid pro quo*, the amount of foreign exchange which may be so withdrawn must be reasonable—reasonableness would, of course, vary with developments in the restricting partner's balance of payments and reserve position. Moreover, such withdrawals will be permitted only if sufficient reserve assets are available after payments have been made by the restricting partner for imports of essential goods and services.

(*b*) General conditions. First, nationals and companies of either party are to be accorded by the other party both national and most-favoured-nation treatment with respect to the administration of exchange restrictions. As discussed in Chapter V, both national and most-favoured-nation treatment do little to offset the discriminatory effects of exchange control. In the case of the former, that is, national treatment:

A system of exchange control applies to everybody residing in the borders of the imposing state, whether these residents are its nationals or not. That means, as Nussbaum points out, that exchange control in fact strikes even more heavily against the nationals of the imposing state than against foreigners. This should be enough to show the inaptness of the standard of national treatment as a valuable means of opposing the discriminatory effects of exchange control.[1]

In the case of the latter—that is, most-favoured-nation treatment—this standard simply requires that the nationality of the person or corporation shall, in the allocation of scarce foreign exchange, be considered an irrelevant factor. Since most exchange control regimes discriminate on the basis of currency

---

[1] W. A. Kewenig, 'Exchange Control, the Principle of Nondiscrimination and International Law', 16 *Buffalo Law Review* (1966–7) pp. 390–1.

and not on the basis of the nationality of the recipient of that currency, most-favoured-nation treatment is likewise of little effect in alleviating discrimination. Indeed, several of the treaties contain provisions which specifically exclude the applicability of most-favoured-nation treatment to discrimination which is practised on a currency basis. So paragraph 13 of the Protocol attached to the Convention of Establishment between the United States of America and France of 25 November 1959[1] provides: 'The provisions of Article X, paragraph 1, shall not preclude differing treatment from being applied to different currencies, as may be required by the state of the balance of payments of either High Contracting Party'; and paragraph 8 of the Protocol attached to the Treaty of Friendship and Commerce between the United States of America and Pakistan of 12 November 1959[2] provides:

The treatment provided in Article XII, paragraph 1, as clarified by reference to Article XXI, paragraphs 1 and 2, has only in view to preclude discrimination on the ground of nationality of persons and companies and does not, for instance, preclude special arrangements providing more favourable treatment for transactions in certain currencies than for transactions in other currencies for balance-of-payments reasons, or the application of residence requirements.

Even in the three commercial treaties concluded by the United States with Italy,[3] Ireland,[4] and Israel,[5] which provide that 'Financial transactions between the territories of the two Parties shall be accorded by each Party treatment no less favourable than that accorded to like transactions between the territories of that Party and the territories of any third currency' and thereby outlaw discrimination based on territory, not nationality,[6] the contracting States have mitigated the severity

---

[1] 401 U.N.T.S. 75.

[2] 404 U.N.T.S. 259. See similarly para. 13 of the Protocol attached to the Treaty of Friendship, Commerce and Navigation between the Kingdom of the Netherlands and the United States of America, 27 Mar. 1956, 285 U.N.T.S. 231, and para. 8 of the Protocol attached to the Treaty of Friendship, Establishment and Navigation between the United States of America and the Grand Duchy of Luxembourg, 23 Feb. 1962, 474 U.N.T.S. 3.

[3] 79 U.N.T.S. 171; 404 U.N.T.S. 326.

[4] 206 U.N.T.S. 269.   [5] 219 U.N.T.S. 237.

[6] Mann, 'Money in Public International Law', 96 R.C. (1959–I) p. 73: 'The distinctive feature of this clause lies in its reference to non-discrimination on a

of these obligations by further providing that 'Either party, in adopting such measures of exchange control as may be necessary from time to time to deal with a stringency of foreign exchange, may depart from the provisions of paragraphs 2 and 6 of Article XII . . .'[1]

In practice, therefore, both national treatment and most-favoured-nation treatment clauses do little in affording protection against the discriminatory allocation of scarce foreign exchange. In this respect, the second general condition which provides that 'Exchange restrictions shall not be imposed by either Party in a manner unnecessarily detrimental or arbitrarily discriminatory to the claims, investments, transport, trade, and other interests of the nationals and companies of the other Party, nor to the competitive position thereof'[2] is more effective. However, even here, the use of the phrases 'unnecessarily detrimental' and 'arbitrarily discriminatory' would suggest that the requisite monetary authority still retains a wide measure of discretion with respect to the discriminatory administration of the exchange control mechanism.[3]

Finally, little mention is made of exchange rates in the U.S.A.–Japanese treaty. Paragraph 3 of Article XII, which deals with privileged withdrawals, simply provides in the last sentence: 'If more than one rate of exchange is in force, the rate applicable to such withdrawals shall be a rate which is specifically approved by the International Monetary Fund for such transactions or, in the absence of a rate so approved, an effective rate which, inclusive of any taxes or surcharges on exchange transfers, is just and reasonable.'

territorial basis. A State subscribing to this clause would seem to have accepted the heavy burden of refraining from any discrimination between "soft" and "hard" currencies.'

[1] Para. 6 of the Protocol attached to the treaty with Israel. See similarly para. 8 of the Protocol attached to the treaty with Ireland, and Article IV of Agreement of 26 Sept. 1951 between Italy and U.S.A. supplementing the Agreement of 2 Feb. 1948, 404 U.N.T.S. 326 at p. 328.

[2] Art. XII, para. 4 of the U.S.A.–Japanese treaty.

[3] The United Kingdom practice in this respect, as illustrated by Arts. 13, 15, and 16 of the Treaty of Commerce, Establishment and Navigation concluded between the United Kingdom and Japan on 14 Nov. 1962, Cmnd. 2085, is similar to the United States practice. See also Art. IX of the Treaty of Friendship, Commerce and Navigation between Japan and the Argentine Republic, 12 *Japanese Annual of International Law* (1968) pp. 172–80.

XII

CONCLUSIONS

'From a condition where there were no rules of law, which was the situation before the late war, we have moved to a point where there has now been established, through institutions and agreements designed to deal with some of the causes of disequilibrium in international balances of payments, a system of limited financial cooperation . . .

s. d. metzger, 'Exchange Controls and International Law', *University of Illinois Law Forum* (1959) pp. 326–7.

THE object of this concluding chapter is to put in perspective, and to make certain general observations on, the present nature of international monetary law. This involves a comparison of the contemporary law with the law, such as it was, in the pre-1945 period, as well as a prognosis of its future development.

Contemporary international monetary law has, through a network of multilateral (both global and regional) and bilateral treaties, subjected to a relatively rigorous legal regime two of the three principal corrective devices which States resort to when confronted with a deteriorating payments situation— namely exchange rate alteration and direct commercial and financial controls. A similar, albeit less pronounced and more recent, development has been taking place with respect to the third corrective device—that is, adjustments in domestic economic policies. Likewise, international liquidity—that is, its quantum, its conditions of use, etc.—is now (but, here again, only to a limited extent) the subject of international legal regulation. When one considers the near non-existence not only of any regulating devices of a legal nature, but of any other form of international monetary co-operation during the inter-war period following the breakdown of the gold standard, the extent and rapidity of the introduction of the rule of law into this area of international relations is particularly striking. Indeed, if the trend continues, it may well be the case, at least in so far as the first two corrective devices are concerned, that certain rules of conduct now provided for in treaties may, through their wide usage, evolve into rules of customary international law. However, it is not intended to pursue here the more general issue of the creation of customary international law by way of treaty. Although clearly not free from controversy, it will suffice to note that in the context of international monetary relations such a process of transition may well be taking place.

What is not open to controversy, however, is the clearly-defined trend towards a greater reliance on, and utilization of, the international legal mechanism as a device for regulating inter-State monetary affairs. The recent establishment of the special drawing rights facility, the placing on a more formal legal basis of certain aspects of the sterling reserve system, and the projected establishment on an institutional basis of a European monetary union are just a few cases in point.

Finally, it must be borne in mind that the international monetary system and accordingly international monetary law are in a rapid and continuing state of evolution. It would be wrong, therefore, to consider the present stage of development of monetary law as being in any sense definitive. All that can be said with certainty is that this evolutionary process will continue and that international monetary law will continue to develop in response to prevailing economic, political, and social conditions. In future, to prevent the established fabric of monetary co-operation from being weakened, new areas of international economic relations, such as non-tariff distortions to trade, will need to be subjected to international legal regulation. Additionally, in the light of practical experience, the nature and form of the regulation of certain economic mechanisms already subject to legal control may have to be reconsidered—for instance, the current provisions on exchange rates which require an essentially fixed rate with alterations being permitted only infrequently may prove to be too rigid and may need to be replaced by a more flexible system.

These and other changes which are bound to occur, however, will only be changes of detail. They will neither alter nor diminish the more general and ever-continuing post-war movement towards the establishment of a more rational, legally-orientated, international monetary system.

TABLE OF CASES

TABLE OF TREATIES

June 1966	Union douanière des États de l'Afrique occidentale; M. S. Wionczek (ed.), *Economic Cooperation in Latin America, Africa, and Asia. A Handbook of Documents* (1969) pp. 279–83.
4 May 1967	Articles of Association for the Establishment of an Economic Community of West Africa; 6 *International Legal Materials* (1967) pp. 776–81.
6 June 1967	Treaty for East African Co-operation; 6 *International Legal Materials* (1967) pp. 932–1057; 7 *Journal of Common Market Studies* (1968) pp. 129–91.
11 December 1967	European Convention on Foreign Money Liabilities; 60 *European Treaty Series*.
7 February 1968	Agreement Establishing the Andean Development Corporation; 8 *International Legal Materials* (1969) pp. 940–58.
2 April 1968	Charter of the Union of Central African States; 7 *International Legal Materials* (1968) pp. 725–34.
30 April 1968	Agreement Establishing the Caribbean Free Trade Association; 7 *International Legal Materials* (1968) pp. 935–77.

TABLE OF OFFICIAL DOCUMENTS AND REPORTS

1. EUROPEAN ECONOMIC COMMUNITY (E.E.C.)

Bulletin of the European Economic Community, Secretariat of the Commission of the European Economic Community, Feb. 1959–Dec. 1967.

Bulletin of the European Communities, Secretariat of the Commission, Jan. 1968–.

Development of a European Capital Market (The), Report of a Group of Experts appointed by the E.E.C. Commission (Brussels, 1966).

General Report on the Activities of the Community, E.E.C. Commission, 1958–.

Journal officiel des Communautés européennes, 1958–.

2. EUROPEAN FREE TRADE ASSOCIATION (E.F.T.A.)

Annual Report of the European Free Trade Association, 1961–.

Stockholm Convention Examined (The), Secretariat of the E.F.T.A. (2nd ed., Geneva, 1963).

3. FRANCE

Journal officiel de la République française, Lois et décrets, juillet 1960, novembre 1960, août 1961, février 1962.

La Zone franc, rapport publié par le Secrétariat général du Comité monétaire de la Zone franc, 1958–.

4. GENERAL AGREEMENT ON TARIFFS AND TRADE (G.A.T.T.)

Activities of GATT (The) 1959/60–.

Agreement on Implementation of Article VI (Anti-dumping Code) (Geneva, 1969).

Basic Instruments and Selected Documents, First Supplement, 1953–.

Basic Instruments and Selected Documents, vols. I, I (revised), II, III, IV.

Use of Quantitative Restrictions for Protective and Other Commercial Purposes (The) (Geneva, 1950).

5. INTERNATIONAL MONETARY FUND (I.M.F.)

Annual Report of the Executive Directors, 1947–.

Annual Report on Exchange Restrictions, 1950–.

Balance of Payments Manual (3rd ed., 1961).

By-Laws Rules and Regulations (26th issue, 1966).

Central Banking Legislation, 2 vols. (1961).

First Ten Years of the International Monetary Fund (The) (1956).

International Financial Statistics, 1948–.

Proposed Amendment of Articles of Agreement, a Report by the Executive Directors to the Board of Governors (1968).

Schedule of Par Values, 1947–.

Selected Decisions of the Executive Directors and Selected Documents (3rd issue, 1965).

Selected Speeches of Per Jacobsson, International Monetary Problems 1957–1963 (1964).

Summary Proceedings of the Annual Meeting of the Board of Governors, 1946–.

6. LEAGUE OF NATIONS

Enquiry into Clearing Agreements, II. Economic and Financial (1935.II.B.6).

'International Financial Conference: Report of the Conference', 1 *Official Journal* (1920) pp. 414–40.

Monetary and Economic Conference, Draft Annotated Agenda Submitted by the Preparatory Commission of Experts, II. Economic and Financial (1933.II.Spec. I).

Monetary and Economic Conference, Reports Approved by the Conference on July 27, 1933 and Resolutions Adopted by the Executive Bureau and the Executive Committee, II. Economic and Financial (1933.II.Spec.4).

Report on Exchange Control Submitted by a Committee composed of Members of the Economic and the Financial Committees, II. Economic and Financial (1938. II.A.10).

7. ORGANIZATION FOR ECONOMIC COOPERATION AND DEVELOPMENT (O.E.C.D.); ORGANIZATION FOR EUROPEAN ECONOMIC COOPERATION (O.E.E.C.)

Agreement for the Establishment of a European Payments Union of 19th September, 1950 (Paris, Dec. 1958).

Code of Liberalisation (July 1960).

Code of Liberalisation of Capital Movements (Jan. 1969).

Code of Liberalisation of Current Invisible Operations (Nov. 1967).

Directives for the Application of the European Monetary Agreement (Mar. 1966).

European Monetary Agreement of 5th August, 1955 (Mar. 1966).

European Monetary Agreement, Annual Report of the Board of Management, 1959–.

European Payments Union, Annual Report of the Managing Board, 1951–8.

Liberalisation of Current Invisibles and Capital Movements, C/60/98, Mar. 1961.

Special Annotated Bibliography, Regional Integration, vol. 1 (INF/BIB(69)II).

8. UNITED KINGDOM

Arrangements for Borrowing by the International Monetary Fund, Mar. 1962, Cmnd. 1656.

Basle Facility and the Sterling Area (The), Oct. 1968, Cmnd. 3787.

Correspondence respecting Position of British Holders of French Rentes issued in the United Kingdom in 1915–1918; Cmd. 3779; 33 *State Papers* (1930–1) pp. 375–86.

Exchange Control, the Act and the Instruments as in Operation on November 1st, 1968 (H.M.S.O., 1968).

Exchange of Notes and Letters concerning the Guarantee by the United Kingdom and the Maintenance of the Minimum Sterling Proportion by Certain Overseas Sterling Area Governments, Nov. 1968, Cmnd. 3834, 3835.

Proposal for an International Clearing Union, Cmd. 6437.

Proposals for Increasing the Resources of the International Monetary Fund, June 1965, Cmnd. 2675.

Special Drawing Rights in the International Monetary Fund, June 1968, Cmnd. 3662.

Statement by Ministers of the Group of Ten and Annex prepared by their Deputies (H.M.S.O., 1964).

9. UNITED NATIONS; UNITED NATIONS CONFERENCE ON TRADE AND DEVELOPMENT

Conference on Trade and Employment, Economic and Social Council (E/Conf. 2/78).

International Monetary Reform and Co-operation for Development, Report of the Expert Group on International Monetary Issues, 13 Oct. 1969 (TD/B/285).

International Monetary System—Issues Relating to Development Finance and Trade of Developing Countries, 23 Oct. 1968 (TD/B/198).

10. UNITED STATES OF AMERICA

American Mexican Claims Commission, Report to the Secretary of State (Department of State Publication 2859, Washington, 1948) Arbitration Series 9.

'Efforts by the United States of America on behalf of American Holders of Portuguese Tobacco Monopoly Bonds', *Papers Relating to the Foreign Relations of the United States* (Washington, 1926) pp. 880 ff.

'Interest of the United States in Clearing and Compensation Agreements and the Gold Bloc', 1 *Foreign Relations of the United States* (1934) pp. 594–614.

Letter of 7 Mar. 1968 from the Secretary of the U.S. Treasury to the Canadian Minister of Finance, 7 *International Legal Materials* (1968) pp. 455–7.

22 *Federal Reserve Bulletin* (Oct. 1936).

48 *Federal Reserve Bulletin* (Sept. 1962).

51 *Federal Reserve Bank of New York Monthly Review* (Sept. 1969).

Proceedings and Documents of the United Nations Monetary and Financial Conference, 2 vols. (United States Government Printing Office, Washington, 1948).

Semi-Annual Reports of the United States Foreign Claims Settlement Commission to the United States Congress, 1949–.

'Tripartite Financial Stabilization Agreement by the United States, France, and the United Kingdom set forth in Simultaneous Statements, September 25, 1936', 1 *Foreign Relations of the United States* (1936) pp. 535–65.

BIBLIOGRAPHY

BOOKS

ALEXANDROWICZ, C. H., *World Economic Agencies: Law and Practice* (London, 1962).

AUFRICHT, H., *Comparative Survey of Central Bank Law* (London, 1965).

—— *The International Monetary Fund: Legal Bases, Structure, Functions* (London, 1964).

BLACKSTONE, W., *Commentaries on the Laws of England*, vol. 1 (16th ed. by J. T. Coleridge, London, 1825).

BODIN, J., *Les Six Livres de la République* (Paris, 1576).

—— *Six Books of the Commonwealth* (abridged and trans. by M. J. Tooley, Oxford, 1967).

BORCHARD, E., *State Insolvency and Foreign Bondholders, Volume I, General Principles* (New Haven, 1951).

BROWN, W. A., *The United States and the Restoration of World Trade* (Washington, 1950).

BROWNLIE, I., *Principles of Public International Law* (Oxford, 1966).

BURNS, A. R., *Money and Monetary Policy in Early Times* (London, 1927).

CALMANN, J. (ed.), *Western Europe: a Handbook* (London, 1967).

CAMPBELL, A., *Common Market Law*, 2 vols. (New York, 1969).

CHENG, B., *General Principles of Law as Applied by International Courts and Tribunals* (London, 1953).

COHEN, B. J., *Balance-of-Payments Policy* (London, 1969).

CROWTHER, G., *An Outline of Money* (rev. ed., London, 1948).

CURZON, G., *Multilateral Commercial Diplomacy* (London, 1965).

DELAUME, G. R., *Legal Aspects of International Lending and Economic Development Financing* (New York, 1967).

DUNN, F. S., *The Protection of Nationals* (Baltimore, 1932).

EINZIG, P., *A Textbook on Foreign Exchange* (2nd ed., London, 1969).

ELLIS, H. S., *Exchange Control in Central Europe* (Cambridge, Mass., 1941).

FATOURUS, A. A., *Government Guarantees to Foreign Investors* (New York, 1962).

FAWCETT, J. E. S., *The British Commonwealth in International Law* (London, 1963).

FEAVEARYEAR, A. E., *The Pound Sterling: a History of English Money* (London, 1931).

FRIEDMANN, W. G. (co-ed.), *Legal Aspects of Foreign Investment* (London, 1959).

—— *The Changing Structure of International Law* (London, 1964).

GANTENBEIN, J. W., *Financial Questions in United States Foreign Policy* (New York, 1939).

GARDNER, R. N., *Sterling–Dollar Diplomacy* (Oxford, 1956).

GOLD, J., *The Fund Agreement in the Courts* (Washington, 1962).

GREENWALD, D., *The McGraw-Hill Dictionary of Modern Economics* (New York, 1965).

GRUBEL, H. G., *The International Monetary System: Efficiency and Practical Alternatives* (London, 1969).

HACKWORTH, G. H., *Digest of International Law*, vol. I (Washington, 1940).

—— *Digest of International Law*, vol. II (Washington, 1941).

—— *Digest of International Law*, vol. V (Washington, 1943).

HALM, G. N., *International Monetary Cooperation* (New York, 1945).

HANSON, J. L., *A Dictionary of Economics and Commerce* (London, 1965).

HAWTREY, R. G., *The Gold Standard in Theory and Practice* (London, 1927).

HIGGINS, R., *Conflict of Interests: International Law in a Divided World* (London, 1965).

HILL, M., *The Economic and Financial Organization of the League of Nations* (Washington, 1946).

HIRSCH, F., *Money International* (London, 1967).

HOLLAND, R. H. (co-ed.), *Law, Justice and Equity: Essays in Tribute to G. W. Keeton* (London, 1967).

HORIE, S., *The International Monetary Fund: Retrospect and Prospect* (London, 1964).

HUDSON, M. O., *International Legislation*, vol. VI (Washington, 1937).

HYDE, C. C., *International Law Chiefly as Interpreted and Applied by the United States*, vols. I, II (2nd rev. ed., Boston, 1947.)

Inter-American Institute of International Legal Studies, *Instruments Relating to the Economic Integration of Latin America* (Dobbs Ferry, N.Y., 1968).

JESSUP, P. C., *A Modern Law of Nations* (Archon Books, 1968).

JUNCKERSTORFF, H. K. (ed.), *International Manual on the European Economic Community* (St. Louis, 1963).

Keesing's Contemporary Archives (1965–6); (1967–8).

KIRSCHEN, ÉTIENNE-SADI, *Financial Integration in Western Europe* (New York, 1969).

KISS, A., *L'Abus de droit en droit international* (Paris, 1952).

LAMBRINIDIS, J. S., *The Structure, Function, and Law of a Free Trade Area* (London, 1965).

LAUTERPACHT, H., *The Function of Law in the International Community* (Oxford, 1933).

MACHLUP, F., *Remaking the International Monetary System: the Rio Agreement and Beyond* (Baltimore, 1968).

McNAIR, Lord, *International Law Opinions*, vol. I (Cambridge, 1956).

MANN, F. A., *The Legal Aspect of Money* (2nd ed., Oxford, 1953).

METZGER, S. D., *International Law, Trade and Finance: Realities and Prospects* (New York, 1962).

MOORE, J. B., *A Digest of International Law*, vol. VI (Washington, 1906).

—— *International Arbitrations Digest*, vol. 3 (Washington, 1898).

MUELLER, M. G. (ed.), *Readings in Macroeconomics* (New York, 1966).

NIELSEN, F. K., *American–Turkish Claims Settlement* (Washington, 1937).

NUSSBAUM, A., *Money in the Law* (Chicago, 1939).

—— *Money in the Law National and International* (rev. ed., Brooklyn, 1950).

O'CONNELL, D. P., *International Law*, 2 vols. (London, 1965).

OFFICER, L. H. (co-ed.), *The International Monetary System: Problems and Proposals* (London, 1969).

OPPENHEIM, L., *International Law*, vol. I (8th. ed., by H. Lauterpacht, London, 1955).

—— *International Law*, vol. II (7th ed., by H. Lauterpacht, London, 1952).

PARDESSUS, J. M., *Cours de droit commercial*, vol. V (5th ed., Paris, 1841).

PEASLEE, A. J., *International Governmental Organizations: Constitutional Documents*, 2 vols. (rev. 2nd ed., The Hague, 1961).

Political and Economic Planning (PEP), *Non-Tariff Distortions of Trade*, vol. XXXV, Broadsheet 514 (Sept. 1969).

ROBERTSON, A. H., *European Institutes* (2nd ed., London, 1966).

ROBSON, P., *Economic Integration in Africa* (London, 1968).

RUSSELL, H. B., *International Monetary Conferences* (1898).

SCAMMELL, W. M., *International Monetary Policy* (2nd ed., London, 1961).

SCHWARZENBERGER, G., *A Manual of International Law* (5th ed., London, 1967).

—— *Foreign Investments and International Law* (London, 1969).

—— *International Law as Applied by International Courts and Tribunals* (3rd ed., London, 1957).

—— (co-ed.), *Law, Justice and Equity: Essays in Tribute to G. W. Keeton* (London, 1967).

SHANNON, I., *International Liquidity: a Study in the Economic Functions of Gold* (Chicago, 1966).

STARKE, J. G., *An Introduction to International Law* (6th ed., London, 1967).

SYNDER, R. C., *The Most-Favored-Nation Clause* (New York, 1948).

TAYLOR, P. A. S., *A New Dictionary of Economics* (London, 1966).

TEW, B., *International Monetary Co-operation 1945–65* (8th ed., London, 1965).

TINBERGEN, J., *International Economic Integration* (2nd rev. ed., Amsterdam, 1965).

TRIFFEN, R., *Our International Monetary System: Yesterday Today, and Tomorrow* (New York, 1968).

VAN MEERHAEGHE, M. A. G., *International Economic Institutions* (London, 1966).

VATTEL, E., *The Law of Nations or the Principles of Natural Law* (trans. of the ed. of 1758 by C. G. Fenwick, Washington, 1916).

WHARTON, F., *A Treatise on the Conflict of Laws or Private International Law* (3rd ed. by G. H. Parmele, Rochester, 1905).

WHEELER-BENNETT, J. W., *Documents on International Affairs, 1933* (London, 1934).

—— *Documents on International Affairs, 1936* (London, 1937).

WHITEMAN, M. M., *Digest of International Law*, vol. VIII (Washington, 1967).

WILCOX, C., *A Charter for World Trade* (New York, 1949).

WILLETT, T. (co-ed.), *The International Monetary System: Problems and Proposals* (London, 1969).

WILLIAMS, J. FISCHER, *Chapters on Current International Law and the League of Nations* (London, 1929).

WILSON, R. R., *United States Commercial Treaties and International Law* (New Orleans, 1960).

WIONCZEK, M. S. (ed.), *Economic Cooperation in Latin America, Africa, and Asia: a Handbook of Documents* (Cambridge, Mass., 1969).

—— (ed.), *Latin American Economic Integration: Experiences and Prospects* (New York, 1966).

WORTLEY, B. A., *Expropriation in Public International Law* (Cambridge, 1959).

ARTICLES

AHOOJA-PATEL, K., 'Economic Co-operation in Africa: the Institutional Framework', 3 J.W.T.L. (1969) pp. 251–71.

ALTMAN, O. L., 'Quotas in the International Monetary Fund', 5 *I.M.F. Staff Papers* (1956–7) pp. 129–50.

—— 'The Management of International Liquidity', 11 *I.M.F. Staff Papers* (1964) pp. 216–47.

AUDRETSCH, H. A. H., 'The E.E.C. and E.F.T.A. Two Solutions regarding Balance of Payments Difficulties', 4 *Common Market Law Review* (1966–7) pp. 419–39.

AUFRICHT, H., 'The Fund Agreement and the Legal Theory of Money', 10 *Österreichische Zeitschrift für öffentliches Recht* (1959–60) pp. 26–77.

—— 'Exchange Restrictions under the Fund Agreement', 2 J.W.T.L. (1968) pp. 297–323.

—— 'The Fund Agreement: Living Law and Emerging Practice', 23 *Princeton Studies in International Finance* (1969).

BAXTER, R. R., 'Responsibility of States for Injuries to the Economic Interests of Aliens', 55 A.J.I.L. (1961) pp. 545–84.

BENTIL, J. K., 'The Legal Framework and the Economic Aspects of the East African Common Market', 4 *The Journal of Law and Economic Development* (1969) pp. 27–47.

BICLET, Y., 'L'Union européenne des paiements', II *European Yearbook* (1956) pp. 151–82.

BINDSCHEDLER, R. L., 'La protection de la propriété privée en droit international public', 90 *Recueil des Cours* (1956–II) pp. 173–306.

BIRNBAUM, E. A., 'Advance Deposit Requirements for Imports', 8 *I.M.F. Staff Papers* (1960–1) pp. 115–25.

—— 'Changing the United States Commitment to Gold', 63 *Princeton Essays in International Finance* (1967).

—— 'Gold and the International Monetary System: an Orderly Reform', 66 *Princeton Essays in International Finance* (1968).

Board of Editors, 'The Measures Taken by the Indonesian Government against Netherlands Enterprises', 5 *Nederlands tijdschrift voor internationaal recht* (1958) pp. 227–47.

BRONZ, G., 'An International Trade Organization: the Second Attempt', 69 *Harvard Law Review* (1955–6) pp. 440–82.

—— 'Conversion of Foreign Currency in Customs Administration', 34 *Texas Law Review* (1955–6) pp. 78–102.

BUSSCHAU, W. J., 'The Role of Gold in World Monetary Arrangements', 2 J.W.T.L. (1968) pp. 363–74.

CARMOY, G. DE, 'Monetary Problems of the EEC', 120 *The Banker* (1970) pp. 21–5.

CARREAU, D. G., 'The Interest Equalization Tax: a U.S. Fiscal Measure to Control Capital Movements', 2 J.W.T.L. (1968) pp. 47–88.

—— 'The U.S. Balance of Payments Programs: New Developments in the American Regulations of Capital Movements', 2 J.W.T.L. (1968) pp. 601–55.

CIPOLLA, C. M., 'Currency Depreciation in Medieval Europe', 15 *The Economic History Review* (1963) pp. 413–22.

CLARK, J. R., 'Foreign Bondholdings in the United States', 32 A.J.I.L. (1938) pp. 439–46.

COHEN, B. J., 'The Reform of Sterling', 77 *Princeton Essays in International Finance* (1969).

COOPER, R. N., 'National Economic Policy in an Interdependent World Economy', 76 *The Yale Law Journal* (1967) pp. 1273–98.

CORBET, H., 'Beachheads of Goodwill Behind Barriers', *The Times* (20 May 1968) p. 1.

CROW, J. W., 'Economic Integration in Central America', 3 *Finance and Development* (Mar. 1966) pp. 58–66.

DACH, J., 'Legal Nature of the Euro-dollar', 13 *The American Journal of Comparative Law* (1964) pp. 30–43.

DARWIN, H. G., 'The European Free Trade Association', 36 B.Y.I.L. (1960) pp. 354–9.

DE LACHARRIÈRE, R., 'L'évolution de la Communauté franco-africaine', *Annuaire français de droit international* (1960) pp. 9–40.

DE LA GIRODAY, J. B., 'The Effects of the European Economic Community on the Banking Business within it', 18 *Business Lawyer* (1962–3) pp. 1025–34.

DE LAUBADÈRE, A., 'Le Statut international du Maroc et l'arrêt de la Cour internationale de justice du 27 août 1952', 6 *Revue juridique et politique de l'Union française* (1952), pp. 429–73.

DEMING, F. L., 'Special Drawing Rights, the Urgent Need for a New Global Monetary Reserve', 3 *The Journal of Law and Economic Development* (1968) pp. 1–7.

DE SAINT-LEGIER, R., 'La Zone franc. Mécanismes. Problèmes internationaux', *Annuaire français de droit international* (1956) pp. 260–78.

DIAB, M., 'The Arab Common Market', 4 *Journal of Common Market Studies* (1965–6) pp. 238–50.

DIEBOLD, W., 'The End of the I.T.O.', 16 *Princeton Essays in International Finance* (1952).

ELKIN, A., 'The Organization for European Economic Co-operation: its Structure and Powers', IV *European Yearbook* (1958) pp. 96–149.

—— 'The European Monetary Agreement: its Structure and Working', VI *European Yearbook* (1960) pp. 148–74.

ELLIS, H. S., 'Exchange Control and Discrimination', 37 *American Economic Review* (1947) pp. 877–88.

EVANS, J. G., 'Current and Capital Transactions: How the Fund Defines them', 5 *Finance and Development* (1968–3) pp. 30–5.

FAWCETT, J. E. S., 'The Place of Law in an International Organization', 36 B.Y.I.L. (1960) pp. 321–42.

—— 'The International Monetary Fund and International Law', 40 B.Y.I.L. (1964) pp. 32–76.

—— 'Trade and Finance in International Law', 123 *Recueil des Cours* (1968–I) pp. 215–310.

FIGGURES, F. E., 'Legal Aspects of the European Free Trade Association', 14 I.C.L.Q. (1965) pp. 1079–88.

FLEMING, J. M., 'The Fund and International Liquidity', 11 *I.M.F. Staff Papers* (1964) pp. 177–215.

FOCSANEANU, L., 'Les aspects juridiques du systèmé monétaire international', 95 *Journal du droit international* (1968) pp. 239–81.

FRIED, E. R., 'International Liquidity and Foreign Aid', 48 *Foreign Affairs* (1969) pp. 139–49.

FRIEDMAN, I. S., 'The International Monetary System. Part I: Mechanism and Operation', 10 *I.M.F. Staff Papers* (1963) pp. 219–45.

—— 'The Fund Agreement as a Code of Conduct', 1 *Finance and Development* (Sept. 1964) pp. 97–103.

GARCIA AMADOR, F. V., 'State Responsibility: Some New Problems', 94 *Recueil des Cours* (1958–II) pp. 365–491.

GIULIANO, M., 'Quelques aspects juridiques de la coopération inter-gouvernementale en matière d'échanges et de paiements internationaux', 124 *Recueil des Cours* (1968–II) pp. 549–687.

GOLD, J., 'The Law and Practice of the International Monetary Fund with Respect to "Stand-by Arrangements" ', 12 I.C.L.Q. (1963) pp. 1–30.

—— 'Maintenance of the Gold Value of the Fund's Assets', *I.M.F. Pamphlet Series* (1965).

—— 'The International Monetary Fund and Private Business Transactions', *I.M.F. Pamphlet Series* (Washington, 1965).

—— 'The International Monetary Fund and International Law: an Introduction', *I.M.F. Pamphlet Series* (1965).

—— 'The Fund and Non-Member States: Some Legal Effects', *I.M.F. Pamphlet Series* (1966).

—— 'Interpretation by the International Monetary Fund of its Articles of Agreement—II', 16 I.C.L.Q. (1967) pp. 289–329.

—— 'The Next Stage in the Development of International Monetary Law: the Deliberate Control of Liquidity', 62 A.J.I.L. (1968) pp. 365–402.

GONZALES DEL VALLE, J., 'Monetary Integration in Central America: Achievements and Expectations', 5 *Journal of Common Market Studies* (1966–7) pp. 13–25.

GROEBEN, Dr. I. C. HANS VON DER, *European Monetary Policy: Towards the Gradual Establishment of a European Monetary System* (Commission of the European Communities, 1968).

HABERLER, G., 'Money in the International Economy', 31 *Hobart Papers* (2nd ed., London, 1969).

HAZLEWOOD, A., 'The Treaty for East African Co-operation', *Standard Bank Review* (Sept. 1967) pp. 2–11.

—— 'The Kampala Treaty and the Accession of New Members to the East African Community', 4 *The East African Economic Review* (1968) pp. 49–63.

HEILPERIN, M. A., 'International Monetary Order: the Missing Link', 119 *The Banker* (1969) pp. 865–9.

HEXNER, E., 'The General Agreement on Tariffs and Trade and the Monetary Fund', 1 *I.M.F. Staff Papers* (1950–1) pp. 432–64.

—— 'Worldwide International Economic Institutions: a Factual Review', 61 *Columbia Law Review* (1961) pp. 354–83.

HORSEFIELD, J. K., 'International Liquidity', 1 *Finance and Development* (Dec. 1964) pp. 170–7.

—— 'The Fund's Compensatory Financing', 6 *Finance and Development* (1969–4) pp. 34–7.

HØST-MADSEN, P., 'What Does it Really Mean?—Balance of Payments', 3 *Finance and Development* (Mar. 1966) pp. 31–40.

—— 'What Does it Really Mean?—a Deficit in the Balance of Payments', 3 *Finance and Development* (Sept. 1966) pp. 171–8.

HUG, W., 'The Law of International Payments', 79 *Recueil des Cours* (1951–II) pp. 511–712.

HYNNING, C. J., 'Balance-of-Payments Controls by the United States', 2 *The International Lawyer* (1967–8) pp. 400–36.

JACKSON, J. H., 'The Puzzle of GATT: Legal Aspects of a Surprising Institution', 1 J.W.T.L. (1967) pp. 131–61.

JASINSKI, P., 'The Control of Capital Movements in France', 3 J.W.T.L. (1969) pp. 209–18.

JASPAR, E. J. E. M. H., 'Réalisations dans le domaine de la coopération Benelux', II *European Yearbook* (1956) pp. 34–59.

JENNINGS, R. Y., 'State Contracts in International Law', *Selected Readings on Protection by Law of Private Foreign Investments* (1964) pp. 175–214.

JESSUP, P. C., 'Responsibility of States for Injuries to Individuals', 46 *Columbia Law Review* (1946) pp. 903–28.

JOHNSON, D. H. N., 'The Case Concerning Rights of Nationals of the United States of America in Morocco', 29 B.Y.I.L. (1952) pp. 401–23.

JOHNSON, H. G., 'The Future of Gold and the Dollar', 3 J.W.T.L. (1969) pp. 117–29.

KANAZAWA, Y., 'Accession of Japan to the Organization for Economic Cooperation and Development (OECD) and the Liberalization of Capital Movements', 11 *The Japanese Annual of International Law* (1967) pp. 24–36.

KATZ, I. S., 'Two Approaches to the Exchange Rate Problem: the United Kingdom and Canada', 26 *Princeton Essays in International Finance* (1956).

KEWENIG, W. A., 'Exchange Control, the Principle of Nondiscrimination and International Trade', 16 *Buffalo Law Review* (1966–7) pp. 377–413.

KINGSON, C. I., 'Investment in Western Europe under the Foreign Direct Investment Regulations: Repatriation, Taxes and Borrowings', 69 *Columbia Law Review* (1969) pp. 1–48.

KRISTENSEN, T., 'Five Years of O.E.C.D.', XIII *European Yearbook* (1965) pp. 100–13.

KROC, R., 'The Financial Structure of the Fund. Part 1: Quotas and Charges', 2 *Finance and Development* (1965) pp. 40–8.

—— 'The Financial Structure of the Fund', *I.M.F. Pamphlet Series* (1967).

KRUTZ, J. W., 'The East African Currency Board', 13 *I.M.F. Staff Papers* (1966) pp. 229–55.

LACHMAN, P. R., 'The Articles of Agreement of the International Monetary Fund and the Unenforceability of Certain Exchange Contracts', 2 *Nederlands tijdschrift voor internationaal recht* (1955) pp. 148–66.

LALIVE, J.-F., 'Unilateral Alteration or Abrogation by Either Party to a Contract between a State and a Foreign National', *Symposium: Rights and Duties of Private Investors Abroad* (1965) pp. 265–79.

LANG, J. T., 'The Right of Establishment of Companies and Free Movement of Capital in the European Economic Community', *University of Illinois Law Forum* (1965) pp. 684–714.

—— 'An Anglo-Irish Free Trade Area', 1 J.W.T.L. (1967) pp. 216–23.

LANYI, A., 'The Case for Floating Exchange Rates Reconsidered', 72 *Princeton Essays in International Finance* (1969).

LAUTERPACHT, E., 'The Contemporary Practice of the United Kingdom in the Field of International Law—Survey and Comment', 5 I.C.L.Q. (1956) pp. 405–46.

LAUTERPACHT, H., 'The International Protection of Human Rights', 70 *Recueil des Cours* (1947–I) pp. 5–108.

LIEFTINCK, P., 'Recent Trends in International Monetary Policies', 39 *Princeton Essays in International Finance* (1962).

LIPSTEIN, K., 'The Place of the Calvo Clause in International Law', 22 B.Y.I.L. (1945) pp. 130–45.

LOOPER, R. B., 'The Significance of Regional Market Arrangements', *University of Illinois Law Forum* (1939) pp. 364–86.

MADAN, B. K., 'Echoes of Bretton Woods', 6 *Finance and Development* (1969–2) pp. 30–8.

MAKDISI, S., 'Restrictions on the Movement of Funds within Latin America', 10 *I.M.F. Staff Papers* (1963) pp. 186–217.

MALLETT, D., 'The History and Structure of O.E.E.C.', 1 *European Yearbook* (1955) pp. 62–70.

MANN, F. A., 'The Private International Law of Exchange Control under the International Monetary Fund Agreement', 2 I.C.L.Q. (1953) pp. 97–107.

—— 'International Delinquencies before Municipal Courts', 70 *Law Quarterly Review* (1954) pp. 181–202.

—— 'Money in Public International Law', 96 *Recueil des Cours* (1959–I) pp. 1–128.

—— 'State Contracts and State Responsibility', 54 A.J.I.L. (1960) pp. 572–91.

MARJOLIN, R., 'L'O. E. C. E. et le développement de la coopération économique européenne', 1 *European Yearbook* (1955) pp. 58–61.

MARSHALL, J., 'Advance Deposits on Imports', 6 *I.M.F. Staff Papers* (1957–8) pp. 239–57.

MENDELSOHN, S., 'Gold Double or Quits', 8 *The Economist Brief Booklets* (1968).

MERWIN, C. L., 'The Road to Bretton Woods', 1 *Finance and Development* (1964) pp. 59–64.

METZGER, S. D., 'Exchange Controls and International Law', *University of Illinois Law Forum* (1959) pp. 311–27.

—— 'Property in International Law', 50 *Virginia Law Review* (1964) pp. 594–627.

—— 'American Foreign Policy and American Foreign Trade', 47 *Texas Law Review* (1969) pp. 1075–84.

MEYER, B. S., 'Recognition of Exchange Controls after the International Monetary Fund Agreement', 62 *Yale Law Journal* (1952–3) pp. 867–910.

MLÁDEK, J. V., 'Evolution of African Currencies. Part I: The Franc Area', 1 *Finance and Development* (1964) pp. 81–8.

MOOKERJEE, S., 'Policies on the Use of Fund Resources', 13 *I.M.F. Staff Papers* (1966) pp. 421–42.

MUNDELL, R. A., 'The International Monetary Fund', 3 J.W.T.L. (1969) pp. 455–97.

NATTIER, F. E., 'The Latin American Free Trade Association (LAFTA)', 21 *Business Lawyer* (1965–6) pp. 515–36.

NICOLETOPOULOS, G., 'Stand-by Arrangements', 1 *Finance and Development* (1964) pp. 192–7.

NIELSON, A., 'Monetary Unions', 10 *Encyclopedia of the Social Sciences* (London) pp. 595–601.

NUSSBAUM, A., 'The Law of the Dollar', 37 *Columbia Law Review* (1937) pp. 1057–91.

—— 'International Monetary Agreements', 38 A.J.I.L. (1944) pp. 242–57.

—— 'Exchange Control and the International Monetary Fund', 59 *Yale Law Journal* (1949–50) pp. 421–30.

OHARA, Y., 'Legal Aspects of Japan's Foreign Trade', 1 J.W.T.L. (1967) pp. 1–32.

ORLOFF, N., 'Economic Integration in East Africa: the Treaty for East-African Co-operation', 7 *The Columbia Journal of Transnational Law* (1968) pp. 302–32.

ORREGO-VICUNA, F., 'Developments in the Latin American Free Trade Association', *Proceedings of the American Society of International Law* (1967) pp. 174–81.

PARKER, E. B., 'Tripartite Claims Commission (United States, Austria, and Hungary): Administrative Decision No. 1', 21 A.J.I.L. (1927) pp. 599–627.

PICKER, S. I., 'Pacific Partnership: the New Zealand–Australia Free Trade Agreement', 7 *Melbourne University Law Review* (1969) pp. 67–96.

POLAK, J. J., 'International Coordination of Economic Policy', 9 *I.M.F. Staff Papers* (1962) pp. 149–81.

—— 'The Outline of a New Facility in the Fund', 4 *Finance and Development* (1967) pp. 275–80.

POLITIS, N., 'Le problème des limitations de la souveraineté et la théorie de l'abus des droits dans les rapports internationaux', 6 *Recueil des Cours* (1925–I) pp. 5–121.

QURESHI, M. A., 'Advance Deposit Requirements for Imports', 8 *I.M.F. Staff Papers* (1960–1) pp. 115–25.

RASHBA, B. S., 'Debts in Collapsed Foreign Currencies', 54 *Yale Law Journal* (1944–5) pp. 1–35.

RE, B. D., 'The Foreign Claims Settlement Commission: Completed Claims Programs', 3 *Virginia Journal of International Law* (1963) pp. 101–20.

—— 'The Foreign Claims Settlement Commission and the Cuban Claims Program', 1 *International Lawyer* (1966) pp. 81–95.

RODE, Z. R., 'The 1968 Amendments to the International Claims Settlement Act of 1949', 63 A.J.I.L. (1969) pp. 296–304.

RÖPKE, W., 'Economic Order and International Law', 86 *Recueil des Cours* (1954–II) pp. 203–73.

RUEFF, J., 'Yet Another Expedient: Special Drawing Rights', 119 *The Banker* (1969) pp. 854–63.

RYDER, F. R., 'The Sterling Area', 1 J.W.T.L. (1967) pp. 179–90.

SCHEIN, E., 'Settlement of World War II Claims', I *International Lawyer* (1967) pp. 444–56.

SCHWARZENBERGER, G., 'The Fundamental Principles of International Law', 87 *Recueil des Cours* (1955–I) pp. 191–385.

SCHWEITZER, P. P., 'International Liquidity and the Fund', 3 *Finance and Development* (1966) pp. 99–106.

SCROGGS, W. D., 'Foreign Treatment of American Creditors', XIV *Foreign Affairs* (1935–6) pp. 345–7.

SEDWITZ, W. J., 'Economic Aspects of Latin American Integration', 61 *Proceedings of the American Society of International Law* (1967) pp. 181–5.

SEGRÉ, C., 'Capital Movements in the European Economic Community', 15 *Banca Nazionale del Lavoro Quarterly Review* (1962) pp. 78–102.

SILARD, S. A., 'The Impact of the International Monetary Fund on International Trade', 2 J.W.T.L. (1968) pp. 121–61.

SIMMONDS, K. R., 'The Central American Common Market', 16 I.C.L.Q. (1967) pp. 911–45.

SOHN, L. B., 'Responsibility of States for Injuries to the Economic Interests of Aliens', 55 A.J.I.L. (1961) pp. 545–84.

SOUTHARD, F. A., 'International Financial Policy, 1920–44', 2 *Finance and Development* (Sept. 1965) pp. 135–43.

STREETIN, P., 'Linking Currency and Development', 46 *International Affairs* (1970) pp. 23–9.

STRONG, A. M., 'Minimizing Monetary Risks in Foreign Trade', *University of Illinois Law Forum* (1959) pp. 355–63.

STRUPP, K., 'L'intervention en matière financière', 8 *Recueil des Cours* (1925–III) pp. 1–24.

SWIDROWSKI, J., 'Bilateralism in Payments and Trade', 5 *Finance and Development* (1968–3) pp. 18–23.

—— 'Exchange Restrictions in 1969', 6 *Finance and Development* (1969–4) pp. 27–33.

SYMONS, E. L., 'The Kennedy Round GATT Anti-dumping Code', 29 *University of Pittsburgh Law Review* (1967–8) pp. 482–516.

TRICKEY, F. D., 'The Extraterritorial Effect of Foreign Exchange Control Laws', 62 *Michigan Law Review* (1964) pp. 1232–41.

VAN DER MENSBRUGGHE, J., 'Consultations with the Fund', 2 *Finance and Development* (June 1965) pp. 90–6.

VAN LYNDEN, C. D. A., 'Benelux', VII *European Yearbook* (1961) pp. 132–51.

VELLES, P., 'Development of the Franc Area and of Franco-African Monetary Co-operation', 2 J.W.T.L. (1968) pp. 89–96.

VON BODO BÖRNER, 'Rechtsfragen des Zahlungs- und Kapitalverkehrs in der EWG', *Europarecht* (1966) pp. 97–128.

DE VRIES, M. G., 'Fund Members' Adherence to the Par Value Regime: Empirical Evidence', 13 *I.M.F. Staff Papers* (1966) pp. 504–32.

—— 'The Decline of Multiple Exchange Rates, 1947–67', 4 *Finance and Development* (1967) pp. 297–303.

—— 'The Magnitudes of Exchange Devaluation', 5 *Finance and Development* (1968–2) pp. 8–12.

—— 'Fluctuating Exchange Rates: the Fund's Approach', 6 *Finance and Development* (1969–2) pp. 44–8.

—— 'Exchange Restrictions: Progress towards Liberalization', 6 *Finance and Development* (1969–3) pp. 40–4.

WADMOND, L. C., 'The Sanctity of Contract between a Sovereign and a Foreign National', *Selected Readings on Protection by Law of Private Foreign Investments* (1964) pp. 139–74.

WAELBROECK, M., 'Free Movement of Goods in the EEC: Decisions of the National Courts', 2 J.W.T.L. (1968) pp. 566–80.

WEEKS, J. K., 'The Cross of Gold: United States Trade and Travel Restrictions and Monetary Crisis', 19 *Syracuse Law Review* (1967–8) pp. 871–89.

WHITE, E. W., *The First Ten Years of the GATT* (Geneva, 1958).

WOODLEY, W. J. R., 'Multiple Currency Practices', 3 *Finance and Development* (1966) pp. 113–19.

YOUNG, J. P., 'United States Gold Policy: the Case for Change', 56 *Princeton Essays in International Finance* (1966).

INDEX